In Nez Perce Country:
Accounts of the Bitterroots and
the Clearwater After
Lewis and Clark

Compiled and edited by
Lynn and Dennis Baird

Moscow
University of Idaho Library

Northwest Historical Manuscript Series

Cover art

The Old Nez Perce Trail by John F. Clymer
©The Clymer Museum and Doris Clymer
Reproduced here with the permission of the Clymer Museum and
Doris Clymer

Cataloging data

In Nez Perce country : accounts of the Bitterroots and the Clearwater after Lewis
        and Clark / compiled and edited by Lynn and Dennis Baird. Moscow :
        University of Idaho Library ; distributed by the University of Idaho Press,
        2003.

    1 v. : ill., maps ; 22 cm. (Northwest historical manuscript series)

    Includes bibliographical references.

    ISBN: 0893015032

1. Nez Percé Indians—History. 2. Bird-Truax Trail (Idaho and Mont.)—History. 3.
Clearwater National Forest (Idaho)—History. 4. Northern Pacific Railroad Com-
pany—History. I. Baird, Lynn N. II. Baird, Dennis W. IV. Series.
OCLC: 51671273   F752.B64I5 2003

Printed in Canada on acid free paper. Designed by Barbara Ham

©2003 by the University of Idaho Library.

Contents

Illustrations and maps

1. Map of the heartland of the Nez Perce people. From *Nez Perce Nation Divided.* Courtesy University of Idaho Press. ©2002.

2. Detail from John Leiberg's 1900 map of the Bitterroot Forest Reserve. U.S. Geological Survey *20th Annual Report, Part 5e.*

3. At the edge of the Weippe Prairie: Crane Meadow, Pheasant Camp, and Lolo Creek in 1933, not much changed from when Lewis and Clark arrived. Washington National Guard Photo, 1933.

4. John Work. UI Library.

5. Benjamin Bonneville. UI Library.

6. Henry Spalding's climate data for Lapwai. Charles Wilkes, *Narrative of the United States Exploring Expedition, Vol. 4.*

7. Common camas plant. U.S. Department of Agriculture. *Range Plant Handbook* (Washington: Government Printing Office, 1937), W 160.

8. DeLacy's 1870 map of Nez Perce Pass and vicinity. NP RR Engineering Department, Chief Engineer's "old vault" files. Minnesota Historical Society.

9. John Mullan's map of the Bitterroots and the Lolo Trail. *Reports of Explorations and Surveys, Vol. 1* (Washington: Beverley Tucker, 1855).

10. Soldier-artist Gustave Sohon's drawing of Lolo Hot Springs. Same source as illustration 9.

11. Rocky Ridge Lookout on the Lolo Trail, about 1920. Clearwater National Forest photo P 725.

12. Sheep were a major ecological force along the Lolo Trail. Sheep grazing near Hemlock Butte about 1930. Photo by K.D. Swan. National Agricultural Library (NAL) photo 199131.

13. A white pine forest near Musselshell Meadows. Photo by K.D. Swan, 1925. NAL photo 199210.

14. Detail from an 1863 Indian Agency map of Nez Perce country showing village locations and stream names. National Archives, College Park. RG 75, Map CA 426.

15. Trixie and the diving elk show at the Fair. *Sights and Scenes at the Lewis and Clark Centennial Exposition* (Portland: Robert Reia, 1905).

16. The Idaho Building at the Centennial Fair. Same as illustration 15.

17. Nez Perce Indians at the Fair. *The Oregon Journal Souvenir Viewbook of the Late Lewis and Clark Centennial Exposition* (Portland: Oregon Journal, 1905).

Foreword and acknowledgements

This publication has, as its geographic scope, the Bitterroot Mountain range in Idaho and the valley of the Clearwater River. In time, it covers events beginning about 1811 and continues into the first half of the twentieth century.

Within those two constraints, the editors have attempted to locate most of the major primary sources dealing with this region in the years after the visit of Lewis and Clark. Many are published here for the first time. Some appear in their entirety, and others are excerpted. The bulk of the accounts published here are from European-American sources, including a few from missionaries and the Indian Agency

The dominant Native American culture of this region is that of the Nez Perce people, as indeed it has been for several thousand years. European invaders in the form of smallpox and other diseases preceded Lewis and Clark, arriving about 1781. As a result, the Nez Perce population that faced later fur traders, missionaries, miners, and settlers was already greatly reduced. Despite the generosity of the Nez Perce people toward these new arrivals, events of the nineteenth century did not treat Native Americans well in the Clearwater country.

The accounts in this volume document a period of rapid change. Within just sixty years of the departure of the Corps of Discovery from the region, the area had several small towns and villages, newspapers, and regular steamboat connections with the Pacific coast. Many of the ancient trails in the region had become roads, and the Nez Perce people had become a minority in their own land.

Much of what is published here deals with the historic trail system in what is now the Clearwater and Nez Perce National Forests, but other accounts deal with the great cultural and economic changes that swiftly transformed the area. The editors have attempted to provide readers with a broad selection of first-hand accounts.

In all cases, the editors have tried to place these documents in their historical context, to provide accurate citations about the location of the originals, and to offer readers of this book some additional sources of information and further reading. This book would not have been possible without the generous help of our many colleagues at the University of Idaho, and of our fellow librarians at Washington State University, Yale University, Harvard University, the Oregon Historical Society, the Minnesota Historical Society, the Hudson's Bay Company Archives, the Nez Perce National Historical Park, the Huntington Library, the U.S. Geological Survey's Denver Library, Northwestern University and the Provincial Archives of Ontario and British Columbia. Donna Smith, Donna Hanson, Rosemary Huskey, Terry Abraham, Stacey Karn, Bill Kerr, Bill Swagerty, Diane Mallickan, Gene and Mollie Eastman, Nakiah Williamson, and Keith Petersen have all been especially generous in their help. We would also like to thank Robbin Johnston, Jeff Fee, and Diane Brower—all of the Clearwater National Forest—for their advice and aid over a long time period. Invaluable botanical help was provided by Karen Gray and Curtis Bjork.

Publication of this book was made possible thanks to a generous grant from the Hon. John Calhoun Smith Fund, which also aided the research effort. The Interlibrary

Loan Department of the University of Idaho Library was, as always, fast and efficient in its help to this project. The authors wish to thank Jennifer O'Laughlin, Hannah Etherton, Carl Westberg, and Marian Murta Bell for service beyond the call of duty.

A volume as rich in names as this would be worthless without an index. Cher Paul has provided a superb index for this volume as a gift to historical understanding and to the University of Idaho.

We have chosen to retain original spellings in this volume and have changed punctuation only to improve clarity. We have avoided the use of the word *sic*. Brackets, and occasionally, footnotes, have been used to provided editorial comments. All accounts that are excerpted have that notation in the introduction for each document.

Finally, the editors would like to acknowledge the generous help provided for the publication of this book by the Library Associates of the University of Idaho.

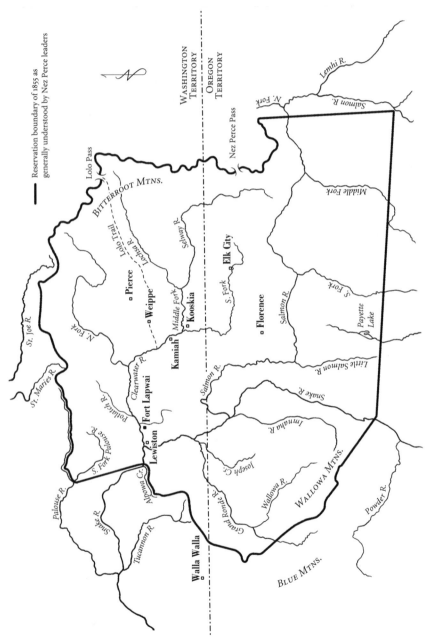

Reservation boundary of 1855 as generally understood by Nez Perce leaders

WASHINGTON TERRITORY

OREGON TERRITORY

Nez Perce Pass

Lemhi R.

N. Fork

Salmon R.

Middle Fork

Lolo Pass

BITTERROOT MTNS.

Lolo Trail

Lochsa R.

Selway R.

St. Joe R.

N. Fork

Pierce

Weippe

Middle Fork

Kooskia

Kamiah

S. Fork

Elk City

Florence

Salmon R.

S. Fork

Payette Lake

Clearwater R.

Potlatch R.

Fort Lapwai

St. Maries R.

Salmon R.

Little Salmon R.

Lewiston

S. Fork Palouse R.

Apowa Cr.

Palouse R.

Snake R.

Tucannon R.

Grand Ronde R.

Joseph Cr.

Imnaha R.

Snake R.

Wallowa R.

WALLOWA MTNS.

Powder R.

Walla Walla

BLUE MTNS.

Figure 1. Map of the heartland of the Nez Perce people.

Introduction

President Thomas Jefferson was one of history's great armchair travelers, a man of immense curiosity about other cultures and places. Even though his home faced to the west, he never traveled more than a hundred miles in that direction from Charlottesville. The publication of two books in 1801, however, caused him to think more deeply than ever about the West as a gateway to the Orient.

The first of these was by the great Canadian explorer Alexander Mackenzie, in which he described his arrival at the Pacific Ocean (in 1793) via the Fraser River. Mackenzie, who had improved his surveying and cartographic skills since an earlier expedition, included a great many important maps in his book—maps that hinted at clear routes to the wealth that lay beyond the great western sea. His fellow countryman, geographer and trader David Thompson, would soon clearly define these routes in practical ways (see Chapter 4). Jefferson found the publication of George Vancouver's *Voyage of Discovery to the North Pacific Ocean*, later that same year, to be even more ominous because of its claims of discovery and title to the Columbia River country. For a President with both commercial and intellectual interests in the Pacific, time and events seemed to be rushing by all too quickly.

So when Lewis and Clark's Corps of Discovery of the Northwest left St. Charles in May of 1804, theirs was an expedition guided by new geographic knowledge and governed by a real sense of urgency. The two Captains and many of their men came from the Army and theirs was, by necessity, a military venture. But the true driving force of their long trek was seeking a water route for commerce. Two rich historical themes of American exploration guided them. First, they were to follow the Missouri River as a possible passage to the Pacific and trade with the Far East. Secondly, they, like their generation and their President, viewed the West as a source of hope and wealth, a true garden abundant with unknown fruits. A leading scholar of nineteenth century American exploration has aptly described Lewis and Clark's westward travels as a "passage through the garden."[1]

---

[1]John Logan Allen, *Passage Through the Garden: Lewis and Clark and the Image of the American Northwest*. (Urbana: University of Illinois Press, 1975), xxvi.

The West of Lewis and Clark was a region little changed by humans. Despite thousands of years of fire and wildlife management by American Indians, it remained a place where nature was the dominating force.[2] The Missouri and Columbia Rivers, which together cover over half of their route, were free of dams and barges. The Army Corps of Engineers, which would later resculpt many of America's rivers, had not yet been conceived. The routes that the Corps of Discovery took over Lemhi, Lost Trail, and Lolo Passes were merely narrow trails leading Native American horsemen into the buffalo country to the east. In beauty, if not necessarily in wealth, the route of the explorers indeed followed the garden path of the Northwest.

Two hundred years later, residents along the route of the Corps of Discovery are preparing for the commemoration of the bicentennial of the Lewis and Clark explorations. Statewide committees in all four Pacific Northwest states, city and local community groups, and some Native American groups are working on the promotion of this anniversary. Anticipation, avarice, and dread, probably in equal parts, motivate the citizens of the region to create programs bringing the wonder of the exploration to a new audience. This book is the University of Idaho Library's contribution to this bicentennial. The book's goal is neither celebration nor condemnation. Instead, its editors hope to let those who came after Lewis and Clark speak in their own words.

Visitors seeking both history and nature along the Missouri River portion of the Lewis and Clark route will have a tough time finding places still resembling those described in the explorers' journals. Six major, main-stem dams and twenty-two others on its tributaries have turned much of this river into a series of lakes.[3] To benefit a now-declining barge industry, the lower Missouri has been "confined by rock or log walls to a narrow, swift-flowing barge canal," eliminating, among other things, "most of the wildlife…that once occupied the environment."[4] In central Montana, only the Missouri River Breaks region, now set aside as a National Monument, has somehow managed to retain its remarkable natural and historic values. Despite some degradation, the river corridor above and below Fort Benton offers those following Lewis and Clark a wild and authentic experience.

West of the Rocky Mountains, most of the route of the Corps of Discovery follows the Snake and Columbia Rivers. Here the scale of transformation makes the

---

[2]There is, however, a growing debate about the impact of American Indian populations on wildlife in the Snake and Clearwater. See Paul S. Martin and Christine R. Szuter, "Megafauna of the Columbia Basin, 1800-1840: Lewis and Clark in a Game Sink," in *Northwest Lands, Northwest Peoples*, ed. Dale D. Goble and Paul W. Hirt (Seattle: University of Washington Press, 1999), 188-204; "War Zones and Game Sinks in Lewis and Clark's West," *Conservation Biology* 13, no. 1 (1999): 36-45; "Game Parks Before and After Lewis and Clark: Reply to Lyman and Wolverton," *Conservation Biology* 16, no. 1 (2002): 244-47; and R. Lee Lyman and Steve Wolverton, "The Late Prehistoric—Early Historic Game Sink in the Northwestern United States," *Conservation Biology* 16, no. 1 (2002): 73-85. The debate over the impact of American Indians of the Plateau on the fire regime is also unresolved.

[3]John E. Thorson, *River of Promise, River of Peril: the Politics of Managing the Missouri River* (Lawrence: University Press of Kansas, 1994), 14-17.

[4]Ed Marston, *Western Water Made Simple* (Covelo, CA: Island Press, 1987), 112-114.

changes along the Missouri look like the work of amateurs. Four major dams along the Columbia River below the mouth of the Snake River have converted the river into lakes, inundating cultural sites, and harming anadromous fish runs. Four other dams on the lower Snake River were built more recently in an effort to transform Lewiston, Idaho into a port.[5] Roads and railroad tracks closely line both banks of the river. Only below Bonneville Dam would modern-day travelers on the path of the explorers find the historical river of Lewis and Clark's time. Elsewhere, they would find in the Columbia "as proud and complex and irreversible a piece of human environmental transformation as can be imagined...."[6]

The terrestrial portion of Lewis and Clark's route to the sea has not fared much better. Much of their route in Montana has been covered by highways. In Idaho, Lemhi Pass still retains its great natural charm, but Lost Trail Pass has been dramatically transformed by a recent large-scale road widening project. Careful followers of Lewis and Clark will discover that just one great historical remnant remains, not perfectly wild and untrammeled, but mostly unchanged due to accidents of both history and nature. This is the Lolo Trail corridor, the subject of much of this book.

The editors have tried to accurately assemble, in proper historical and cultural context, most of the primary sources describing the corridor written after the passage of Lewis and Clark. Deliberately omitted is much reference to Lewis and Clark, the rich missionary history of the Clearwater Valley, the work of the Indian Agency, or the 1877 Nez Perce War. Any one of these topics would occupy a publication ten times longer than this. For these subjects, we will try to provide useful guides to further reading. Those seeking further primary sources on this region would also be wise to turn to the many works compiled by Clifford Drury, as well as the several books of documents published by the University of Idaho Library and the University of Idaho Press.

This book also seeks to provide descriptions of the Lolo Trail corridor as well as of early trail and cultural connections at either end, in Lewiston, Idaho, and at Lolo, Montana. This will be a challenge, since even the name of the region, Lolo, is a problem. A complex and sometimes amusing controversy surrounds the origin of the name of this ancient route, sometimes also called Lu Lu, or Lou Lou. In a masterful summary, Alvin Josephy offered a thorough account of possible origins of Lolo, and concluded that use of the name may date to as early as 1831.[7] But no matter how uncertain the naming conventions may be, the Lolo Trail portion of Lewis and Clark's route remains both the least changed and least understood portion of their whole

[5]National Research Council, *Upstream: Salmon and Society in the Pacific Northwest* (Washington: National Academy Press, 1996), 60-74 and Keith C. Petersen, *River of Life, Channel of Death* (Lewiston, ID: Confluence Press, 1995),127-148.

[6] William Dietrich, *Northwest Passage: the Great Columbia River* (New York: Simon and Schuster, 1995), 398.

[7]Alvin M. Josephy Jr., *The Nez Perce Indians and the Opening of the Northwest* (Boston: Houghton, Mifflin Company, 1997), 665-666.

journey. To understand the import of this route in the nineteenth century, one must look further back into history. The Lolo Trail can also be understood best in the context of broader historical trading and transportation questions. For that reason, this books also examines, to a lesser extent, the Southern Nez Perce Trail.

Finally, the editors have worked to include some information on the Lewis and Clark Centennial celebrations, and on the serious efforts made afterwards to rediscover, preserve, and reinterpret the path of the Corps of Discovery in Idaho.

Readers of this book will find strange spellings and unusual grammar, all of which has been retained from the original sources. They will also find language that today seems crude, insensitive, and sometimes racist. That, too, has been retained and may serve as a useful warning to our readers that the authors of the accounts appearing in this book all carry a full set of nineteenth century cultural baggage. Many scholars of the fur trade and of Plateau life have also warned of the risks in assuming that these early written accounts represent the full truth. Our readers would also be well advised to heed that warning.

2

Trails to the Buffalo Country

The Lolo Trail corridor that Lewis and Clark reached in 1805 was already an ancient and established route of trade and culture. It was situated at one edge of an amazingly complex and sophisticated trading system that covered the Plateau and the Columbia River valley.[1] Even before the arrival of the horse in the Plateau region (about 1730), small bands of American Indians traveled this route in both directions, although the extent and intensity of this pre-equestrian travel is poorly understood.[2] For the Nez Perce people in particular, who had only a minimal tradition of blanket weaving, the Lolo and related trails were important routes to the Great Plains and to the chief source of the buffalo robes they used in winter.[3] This geography plays a large role in Nez Perce narratives.[4] Allen Slickpoo Sr., writing in 1973, noted that the Nez Perce had names for places as far to the east as the Tongue River and what are now the towns of Deer Lodge, Helena, Missoula, and Livingston. Even before the advent of the horse, he added, "hunting expeditions were made by foot to popular and well-known parts of the country [of Montana]."[5] Many prominent Nez Perce leaders also had their birthplace in the buffalo country, including Mark Arthur, a pastor at Lapwai ca. 1900, who was born near Butte. The great scholar of Nez Perce culture, Archie Phinney, working at Lapwai in 1929-30, also documented two traditional texts on life in the eastern buffalo country, "East Country Boy" (k'usa nya ha tswal) and

---

[1]Theodore Stern, "Columbia River Trade Network," in *Handbook of North American Indians, Vol. 12: Plateau* (Washington: Government Printing Office, 1998), 641-45.

[2]C. Milo McLeod, *Lolo Trail Study* (Missoula: Lolo National Forest, 1982), 6 and "The Lolo Trail: A Significant Travel Route Across the Bitterroots," *Archaeology in Montana* 21, no. 3 (1980):118.

[3]The Nez Perce also utilized the fur of other animals for their winter dress. At one time, bison also lived in small numbers among the Nez Perce people, both on the Palouse Prairie and even far up the Lochsa. They were no longer present in Nez Perce country during the time period covered here.

[4]Haruo Aoki, "Nez Perce Oral Narratives," *University of California Publications in Linguistics* 104 (1988): 6.

[5]Allen P. Slickpoo Sr., *Noon Nee-me-poo (We, the Nez Perces)* (Lapwai: Nez Perce Tribe of Idaho, 1973), 29 and 35.

"Coyote the Expeditioner" (itsaya ya k'usaynahawya't).[6] In this latter account, Coyote himself interrupts his work on a fish ladder to go to the buffalo country after learning that "all the people have gone on the big expedition into the east Country."

Other tribal groups, especially the Flatheads, also used these trading routes, often going far down the Columbia River to the great center of exchange at The Dalles. These were long trips in the years before the arrival of the horse. Slickpoo, for instance, believes that small groups of Nez Perce stayed in the buffalo country for periods as long as two years. Records of the Hudson's Bay Company now kept at the Provincial Archives of Manitoba tend to confirm this. For example, Alexander Ross reported in the Flathead Post Journal for the winter of 1824-1825 that twelve Nez Perce lodges were camped near the post, comprising 28 "men & lads," 20 girls, 15 women, 23 children, and 170 horses.[7]

At its Bitterroot Valley terminus, the well-established Lolo Trail that Lewis and Clark encountered was chiefly the result of the passage of many horses. The arrival of the horse among the Indians of the Plains and Plateau proved to be a major transforming force.[8] For no group was this to be more true than of the Nez Perce people. While the Lolo Trail corridor lies on the frontier of their traditional cultural and linguistic boundaries with Salish speakers to the east, the Lolo Trail is chiefly a Nez Perce construct.[9] As a result, the cultural and economic importance of the trail can perhaps best be understood within the context of Nez Perce life, and by the impact of the horse in particular.

While the horse proved important to all the tribal groups of the Northern Plains and the Plateau, probably more than any other tribal group, the Nez Perce took to the horse with zest and energy. They became "the most renowned horsemen of the Plateau and used their horses in most activities."[10] At the time of Lewis and Clark's arrival, the Nez Perce were considered to be the most influential Plateau tribal group, and parties of up to 1,000 individuals traveled widely, their language becoming the trade language for much of the region.[11] Superb horsemanship and husbandry were key components of this leadership.

Many scholars view the arrival of the horse on the Plateau as something of a mixed blessing. The mobility afforded by the horse hastened the spread of disease. The tragic smallpox pandemic of 1781-82 would hardly have been possible without

[6]Archie Phinney, *Nez Perce Texts,* Columbia University Contributions to Anthropology, no. 25 (New York: Columbia University Press, 1934), 70-88.

[7]Flathead Post Journal, HBCA B.69/a/1d.

[8]Frances Haines, "The Northward Spread of Horses Among the Plains Indians," *American Anthropologist* 40 (1934): 436-37 and Theodore Binnema, *Common and Contested Ground: A Human and Environmental History of the Northern Plains* (Norman: University of Oklahoma Press, 2001), 86-106.

[9]Stuart A. Chalfant, *Aboriginal Territory of the Nez Perce Indians* (New York: Garland, 1974), 117-33.

[10]Deward E. Walker Jr., "Nez Perce," in *Handbook of North American Indians, Vol. 12: Plateau* (Washington: Government Printing Office, 1998), 427.

[11]Ibid, 425.

the speed with which horses carried human disease bearers north from New Mexico. Scars from this event were still visible to the pioneer missionary, Asa Bowen Smith, in Kamiah in 1840. The presence of the horse also offered "an increased incentive to engage in warfare," making areas on the periphery of the Plateau, and especially the Northern Plains, "a scene of perpetual equestrian conflict."[12] Yet the horse clearly helped enrich the Nez Perce and other Plateau groups, making the trading and hunting trips to Montana much more of a regular part of the seasonal cycle, simultaneously increasing the importance of the trails across the Bitterroots.[13] This became the time of the "long hunt" in Nez Perce culture.

The horse also proved to be an agent for other kinds of cultural modification. Many Plateau groups may owe part of their notions of "tribe" to the changes caused by the horse, the animal and its mobility proving to be a major contributor both to tribal cohesion and to notions of leadership.[14] At the same time, the role and importance of the village probably declined.

It's also worthwhile to consider something that the Lolo Trail corridor was *not,* and that was a path for migration. There is no cultural or archaeological record of the Nez Perce having arrived from elsewhere. In fact, "neither historical linguistics nor archaeological research…has produced evidence that the Sahaptians [the somewhat broader cultural group with which the Nez Perce people are considered to be associated] have ever resided outside the Columbia Basin. Existing research shows only that they are ancient dwellers of the Columbia Basin…."[15] Instead, it is *creation* that is a more important concept. Nez Perce culture is as rich as any in creation stories, but they are all centered on well-known places easily located to this day. Most lie in Idaho, and some are included in the modern Nez Perce National Historical Park.

Information on the various roles played by the Lolo Trail comes from several sources, many of them outside traditional Nez Perce culture. Among them are the accounts of travelers like Major John Owen (see Chapter Fourteen), who was not only an early settler in the Bitterroot Valley but also an experienced traveler. He never could be considered a "mountain man," and his accounts of his several trips across the Lolo Trail to Walla Walla frequently describe him as being lost. These (and other) accounts help illustrate what is the other important cultural construct surrounding the trail corridor: its immense complexity. A leading Forest Service scholar of the Lolo region, noting that *several* routes traverse the mountains in the

---

[12]Deward E. Walker Jr., "History Until 1846," in *Handbook of North American Indians, Vol. 12: Plateau* (Washington: Government Printing Office, 1998), 139.

[13]Herbert Joseph Spinden, "The Nez Perce Indians," *Memoirs of the American Anthropological Association* 2, no. 3 (1908): 223-23.

[14]Angelo Anastasio, "The Southern Plateau: An Ecological Analysis of Intergroup Relations," *Northwest Anthropological Research Notes* 6, no. 2 (1972): 112 and 129.

[15]Walker, "Nez Perce," 420. For a useful discussion of creation among Sahaptian speakers see Clifford E. Trafzer, *Grandmother, Grandfather and Old Wolf* (East Lansing: MSU Press, 1998), 3 and 22-23.

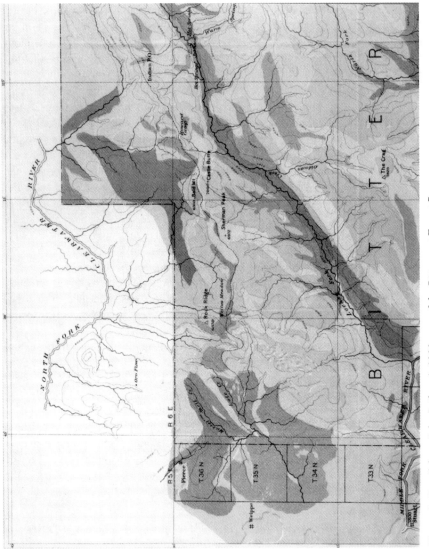

Figure 2. Detail from John Leiberg's 1900 map of the Bitterroot Forest Reserve.

same area, has used the phrase "braided trail system" to describe what can currently be found in the corridor along Forest Road 500.[16] This view of the trail only begins to describe the general complexity of human routes across the Bitterroots. It is also a view of the trail and its use that has been challenged by other scholars, as readers of this book will discover. In any case, research by early geographers laid the groundwork for these ideas of complexity.

J.B. Leiberg, a pioneering ecologist and one of the first government scientists to travel in the Bitterroots, reported on his explorations and research in 1899 and in 1900. He noted that "from time immemorial the Indians had three trails from west to east across the region," the Lolo Trail to the north, the Nez Perce Trail to the south[17], and a central "hunting trail" that appeared to have been heavily managed and manipulated by Native Americans.[18] Describing this hunting trail, Leiberg noted that "its course was along the crest of the Lochsa-Selway divide, and as it ran through the heart of the game region in the Clearwater basins must have been very largely traveled. Most of the fires that can be traced to Indian occupancy appear to have originated along the lines of these trails."

A second scientist in the employ of the Geological Survey, Waldemar Lindgren, spent much of 1899 exploring the Bitterroots south of the Lochsa River Valley, building on earlier field work and photography done by J.B. Lippincott in 1897. The cartography published with Lindgren's study reveals an extensive historic trail system in the Selway River valley, both around Moose Creek as well as to the south, in Bear Creek.[19] All of this early work by geologists and cartographers lends support to a rich body of anthropological information describing settlement and transportation in the Bitterroots.

Working with a vast range of archival and published sources supplemented by informant interviews, Stephen Shawley in 1977 compiled *Nez Perce Trails.*[20] Based on U.S. Geological Survey topographic quadrangle maps, this remarkable atlas of early American transportation clearly demonstrates the great complexity of trade and travel routes near low altitude village sites, as well as in the mountains to the east.

More recently, anthropologist Robert Lee Sappington and others have published the 1891 Billy Williams account that may prove to be the key primary source on the

---

[16]Sandra Broncheau-McFarland, "Tsoop-Nit-Pa-Lu and a Corridor of Change: Evolution of an Ancient Travel Route, Nee-me-poo Trail" (Master's thesis, University of Idaho, 1992), 8.

[17]See Ernst Peterson, "Retracing the Southern Nez Perce Trail with Rev. Samuel Parker," *Montana: The Magazine of Western History* 16, no. 4 (1966): 12-27, for a fine discussion of this southern route.

[18]John B. Leiberg, "The Bitterroot Forest Reserve, Part 2," in *U.S. Geological Survey, 20th Annual Report, Part 5 e* (Washington: Government Printing Office, 1900), 385-388.

[19]Waldemar Lindgren, *A Geological Reconnaissance Across the Bitterroot Range and Clearwater Mountains*, U.S. Geological Survey Professional Paper, no. 27 (Washington: Government Printing Office, 1904), 34 and plate II.

[20]Stephen D. Shawley, *Nez Perce Trails*, University of Idaho Anthropological Research Manuscript Series, no. 44 (Moscow: University of Idaho Laboratory of Anthropology, 1984).

settlement and transportation patterns of the Nez Perce people in the eighteenth and nineteenth centuries. It is a document essential to any study of the Lolo and associated trails.[21]

Between 1889 and 1892, anthropologist Alice Fletcher worked on the Nez Perce Reservation as a special agent in charge of the allotment program mandated by the Dawes Act of 1887. She was also the first of several anthropologists to spend time among the Nez Perce people. In June of 1891, she extensively interviewed Kew-kew'-lu-yah (also known as Billy Williams), a highly respected and knowledgeable elder who had been born about 1815. He produced for her a manuscript map showing village and trail names and locations, a map that other Nez Perce informants found to be highly reliable. Although Fletcher hoped to publish both the map and its information, she never did so in any comprehensive manner, and the information eventually ended up in the National Anthropological Archives of the Smithsonian Institution (Ms. 4558). This is the source of Professor Sappington's important study, mentioned above.

The published version of Fletcher's document is extensively annotated. In two maps, it overlays the Williams' information with modern place name data, confirming the fundamental accuracy and import of Williams' knowledge. In addition to being a major source for the Lolo Trail system (termed "Nah-wal" by Williams), this publication is at least suggestive of the importance of a village site (and route) far up the Selway River. It also offers us some clues about the broad patterns of historic trails across the central Bitterroot Mountains.

Few of the authors of the accounts that follow in this book were aware of the ancient and complicated nature of the route they were traversing. Many were oblivious to this rich history, and still others were too blinded by their vision for the region's future to be encumbered with its past. A small number of these early visitors sought to understand and explain the region, helping to leave us a record of nature and of people still not fully understood.

---

[21]Robert Lee Sappington and others, "Alice Cunningham Fletcher's 'The Nez Perce Country'," *Northwest Anthropological Research Notes* 29, no. 2 (1995):177-220.

3

Reading about Lewis and Clark's Journey Through Nez Perce Country

On their westward journey, Lewis and Clark left the place they called Travelers' Rest (just west of what is now the town of Lolo, Montana) on September 11, 1805. Following the "road" to Lolo Hot Springs, and then traveling over Lolo Pass, they eventually reached the headwaters of the Lochsa River. From there, their route to the Snake River and the Columbia took them high along the divide between the Lochsa River and the North Fork of the Clearwater River. They encountered Nez Perce Indians on the Weippe Prairie north of the Clearwater. Descending into the canyon of that river, and traveling downstream, they eventually left what later became Idaho on October 11, 1805. They followed the Snake River and then the Columbia to their winter quarters near the sea.

The explorers returned to Idaho on May 5, 1806, arriving at the mouth of the Clearwater, a village site known to the Nez Perce people as Shiminekem. Two long delays to await the melting of winter snow preceded a fairly quick trip across the Lolo Trail: just six days versus eleven on the westward stage. They arrived at Travelers' Rest on June 30.

The *Journals* of Lewis and Clark, as well as those of Whitehouse, Gass, and Ordway variously describe their route as being a "road" or sometimes a "path". Gass tells us of the need to cross the lower Clearwater "to get to a better road." Lewis, on the return trip near Lolo Pass, noted that heavy horse traffic from the Bitterroot Valley had changed the trail: "the road was now much plainer and more beaten." Clark has left us some lovely manuscript maps of the trail in his Elskin-bound Journal, now located at the Missouri Historical Society.

All of these accounts are but a small part of a vast (and growing) literature on the Corps of Discovery, too large to even be summarized here. Luckily, most of the primary accounts of Lewis and Clark have benefited from modern scholarship, and those relevant to the Lolo Trail and the period of time the explorers spent in Nez Perce country are listed here:

Gary E. Moulton, ed., *The Journals of the Lewis and Clark Expedition* (Lincoln:

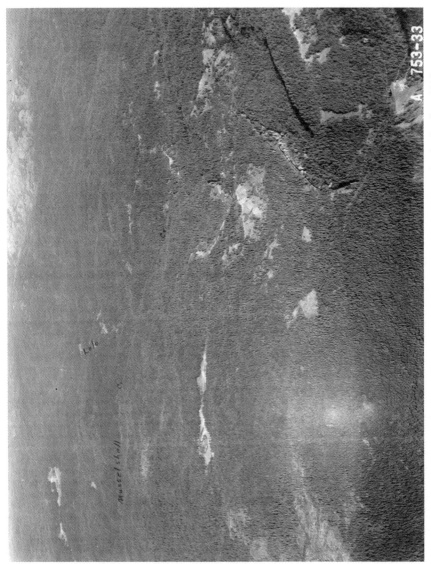

Figure 3. At the edge of the Weippe Prairie: Crane Meadow, Pheasant Camp, and Lolo Creek in 1933.

University of Nebraska Press, 1983-2001). 13 vols.

> *Volume 5: July 28—November 1, 1805.* 198-260
>
> *Volume 7: March 23—June 9, 1806.* 209-350
>
> *Volume 8: June 10—September 26, 1806.* 7-73
>
> *Volume 9: The Journals of John Ordway, May 14, 1804—September 23, 1806 & Charles Floyd, May 14—August 18, 1804.* 222-236 and 305-329
>
> *Volume 10: The Journal of Patrick Gass, May 14, 1804—September 23, 1806.* 140-152 and 222-246
>
> *Volume 11: The Journals of Joseph Whitehouse, May 14, 1804—April 2, 1806.* Pp. 312-347

Volume 1 of this series is called *Atlas of the Lewis and Clark Expedition.* Maps 70-72 and 125 all pertain to the Lolo Trail corridor and to the lower Clearwater River. A great body of primary source correspondence surrounds the expedition, and it has been gathered by Donald Jackson:

Donald Jackson, *Letters of the Lewis and Clark Expedition.* 2nd edition. 2 vols. (Urbana: University of Illinois Press, 1978).

Much of the documentation relating to the life and work of George Drouillard, the expedition's interpreter, has also been collected in one volume:

M.O. Skarsten, *George Drouillard, Hunter and Interpreter for Lewis and Clark, and Fur Trader, 1807-1810* (Glendale, California: Arthur H. Clark Co., 1964).

David Thompson, 1812

On the 26th of February, 1812, Canadian geographer, explorer, and trader David Thompson climbed Mount Jumbo, near what is now Missoula, Montana. Looking south up the valley of the Bitterroot River, he described for his *Journal* the lovely view along the whole of the Bitterroot Range. He was especially attentive to the mouth of Lolo Creek, which he recognized as being the route taken just seven years earlier by Lewis and Clark. Students of Thompson's work have debated, but not resolved, the source of Thompson's great knowledge of this route. He may have read the account of the expedition written by Patrick Gass, which was published in Pittsburgh in 1807.

Thompson was the first European visitor to this valley to leave a written record since the Corps of Discovery passed by in September of 1805 (and May of 1806). He was born in poverty in England in 1770, and was apprenticed to the Hudson's Bay Company (HBC). He arrived at Fort Churchill at the west edge of Hudson's Bay in 1784. By 1790, he had transformed himself into a first-rate surveyor and explorer, working for the HBC in the prairie provinces. In 1797, he went to work for the rival North West Company. For this firm, he roamed further and further west, eventually reaching the Rocky Mountains in 1800. His visit to the Bitterroot Valley came near the end of years of sustained travel and mapping in the Canadian and American West. He was the first European to explore the upper Columbia and the first man to build trading posts in Idaho and western Montana. His explorations were the source of the first genuinely reliable maps of the West, and he played a major role in the political and trading battles over the lower Columbia and the status of Oregon.

Concern over the political implications of Lewis and Clark's trip led the North West Company (in 1806) to send Thompson into the upper Columbia, where he appears to have first met the Nez Perce people in September of 1809. While subject to great historical debate, the work of John Jacob Astor's two western parties appears to have provoked Thompson's explorations in the rest of the Columbia country after 1810. He reached Fort Astoria near the mouth of the Columbia in July of 1811. On this trip (on July 9, at the mouth of the Snake River) he encountered Yellepit, who was still wearing a medal given him by Lewis and Clark. Thompson called him "the Principal Chief of all the tribes of the Shawpatin Indians." While wrong in his assessment of tribal politics, Thompson was correct in his understanding of language patterns along the lower Snake River.

Thompson devoted his later years to writing his *Narrative*, trying to sell his maps, and some work on the U.S-Canada boundary delineation. He died, blind and destitute, in Montreal in 1857, his immense contribution to our knowledge of the West essentially forgotten. He was not "discovered" by scholars until the 1920s.

More information about David Thompson:

Barbara Belyea, "The 'Columbian Enterprise' and A.S. Morton," *BC Studies* 86 (Summer 1990): 3-27.

Barbara Belyea, ed., *Columbia Journals, David Thompson* (Montreal: McGill Queen's University Press, 1994).

This fine book is the best place to read Thompson's 1811 Snake River account.

T.C. Elliott, "David Thompson's Journeys in Idaho," *Washington Historical Quarterly* 11 (1920): 97-103.

T.C. Elliott, "The Fur Trade in the Columbia River Basin Prior to 1811," *Oregon Historical Quarterly* 15, no. 4 (December 1914): 241-51.

Richard Glover, ed., *David Thompson's Narrative, 1784-1812* (Toronto: Champlain Society, 1962).

James J. Holmberg, "Getting out the Word: Patrick Gass's Role in Publicizing the Expedition's Return," *We Proceeded On* 27, no. 3 (August 2001): 12-17.

Alvin M. Josephy Jr., "A Man to Match the Mountains," *American Heritage* 11, no. 6 (October 1960): 60-63, 81-85.

Arthur S. Morton, "The North West Company's Columbia Enterprise and David Thompson," *Canadian Historical Review* 17, no.3 (Sept. 1936): 266-88.

John Nicks "David Thompson," in *Dictionary of Canadian Biography, Vol. 8* (Toronto: University of Toronto Press, 1985), 878-883.

M. Catherine White, ed., *David Thompson's Journals Relating to Montana and Adjacent Regions, 1808-1812* (Missoula: Montana State University, 1950).

Account 4.1: Thompson's View of the Bitterroot Valley. Source: Ontario Provincial Archives, David Thompson Fonds, F443-1, Journal 28. Published with the permission of the Ontario Provincial Archives.

Febry 26th [1812][1] Wednesday — A rainy Night, fine Morng — at 5 1/3 AM set off / came into fine Plains & Hills — went up a high Knowl [Mount Jumbo, just east of Missoula], from whence I / had a fine Prospect of the Country, here I made the following remarks / - the bad weather gathering prevented me from going farther & the Country / is rapidly thawing, the Horses sink deep every step & fatigue much / from the Forks of Courter's Branch with the Southern Branch [from the junction of the Clark Fork and Bitterroot Rivers], by which / Captain Lewis came — join before me bearing So 4 M — from abt 6 M [11 actual miles] beyond / there is a Defile by a bold Brook [Lolo Creek], up which Capt Lewis went to / the first of the Shawpatin Waters [via Glade Creek at Lolo Pass] — the entrance bears S 12 E 10 M - / from where he went abt W by S to a height of Land [Lolo Pass], then descending / the this a day he came to where there are Salmon [near the Powell Ranger Station] — the road is fine / the Salmon westd good for a piece say $^3/_4$ of a day, the Brook [Lochsa River] is / the bounded by High Craigs, which obliged them to cross over / high snowy Mountains for 6 days to where he built his Canoes / on Lewis's Fork [the Clearwater River near Orofino, Idaho] — all these days are for a Person on foot — / Captn Lewis himself & a small Party returned by the Courter's Branch [June 30, 1806] / the main Party took the Route of the Southern Branch [up the Bitterroot and then to Ross's Hole].

---

[1]In this and in the subsequent first hand accounts appearing in this book, words in brackets reflect clarifications by the editors of this book. Words in parenthesis come from the original cited source.

Donald Mackenzie and the Astorians, 1811-1813

Historian Bernard DeVoto had it partially right when he said that "Astoria followed from the expedition of Lewis and Clark as the flight of an arrow follows the release of the bow string."[1] This reaction was no accident, because Meriwether Lewis, immediately upon his return to the east, began to agitate both about the commercial and political import of the Columbia, as well as for government help for new ventures in the region. What DeVoto underestimated was the boldness of John Jacob Astor, a man whom scholar James Ronda has described as "relentless in pursuit of wealth, he embodied all that was calculating and pragmatic in American capitalism."[2]

Astor, a wealthy New York businessman with close ties both to Canadian and Scottish fur traders in Montreal as well as to influential American bankers and politicians, first conceived his Pacific Fur Company plan for the Columbia River late in 1807. Astor was famous for careful planning, and it took some time to assemble both the right people as well as a sound plan for what became the Astorian trading venture to Oregon. He eventually arranged for part of his party to reach the Columbia by ship, and hired a St. Louis merchant, Wilson Price Hunt, to lead an overland group via the Missouri River and the Snake River on to the Columbia. Astor's connections in Montreal produced a cadre of Scots-born traders and mountain men for this party, among them Donald Mackenzie, who in 1810 became a full partner in the venture. Their goal was to establish on the Columbia River an American-led trading operation sufficient in size to provide both economic and political domination over the region. As James Ronda has aptly put it, "fur and flag would join forces to plant American sovereignty along the Great River of the West." The "calculus of national power" was to be a key component of the Astorian venture.

The naval portion of Astor's venture sailed for the Columbia in September of 1810, and had troubles enough of its own facing bad weather and tricky sand bars.

---

[1] Bernard DeVoto, *The Course of Empire* (Boston: Houghton, 1952), 539.

[2] James P. Ronda, *Astoria and Empire* (Lincoln: University of Nebraska Press, 1989), 2.

The Hunt party struggled out of St. Louis on October 21 of that same year, with the more-experienced Mackenzie already at odds with Hunt. While this group did find time to converse, separately, with both Daniel Boone and John Colter (of the Lewis and Clark party) along the way, by November 2, 1811, a whole year later, it had only managed to reach the Snake River valley in southern Idaho. There the party essentially disbanded. Mackenzie and four men were rather vaguely sent north, partner Robert McClellan was dispatched to follow the Snake River east, and the remainder of the party continued on westward along the river.

By the end of November, Hunt's main river party was operating near starvation. They blundered northeast up what is now the Weiser River. Returning to the Snake, they encountered the other party that had been sent west along the river. The cold days up to December 21 were spent in Hells Canyon, when the river parties under Hunt's command finally turned northwest along what would eventually be the route of the Oregon Trail. They reached the site of modern-day Pendleton, Oregon on January 8, 1812, and Astoria on February 15. There they encountered not only the Astorians who had reached the Columbia by sea (including Alexander Ross, Ross Cox, and Gabriel Franchere, who have left us good written accounts), but also Mackenzie and McClellan, who had beaten them by nearly a month.

Neither McClellan nor Mackenzie have left us direct accounts of their wanderings in western Idaho. Mackenzie's family destroyed his papers after his death, and even Washington Irving, who later visited with Mackenzie in New York, "came up with discrepancies."[3] Luckily for history, they described their trip to Astorian clerks Alexander Ross, Gabriel Franchere, Robert Stuart, and in part, to Washington Irving. When Mackenzie returned to Idaho in August of 1812, he took with him the newly-arrived Alfred Seton, who has left us good accounts of the Clearwater country. Clerk Ross Cox, on a trip to Spokane House, wrote a fine description of life among the Palouse Indians.

These accounts, in part based on hearsay, must be supplemented by the remarkable map attributed to a Nez Perce principal chief, Hohastillpelp (Xáxaac Ilpilp, also known as Red Grizzly Bear). He shared with Lewis and Clark a vast and accurate knowledge of the Snake River while the explorers awaited warmer weather near Kamiah, Idaho, in May of 1806. This is map 100 in the University of Nebraska's *Atlas of the Lewis and Clark Expedition* (1983) and clearly portrays the Snake's main tributary, the Salmon River (Tomanmah on the map), the Little Salmon River (Mul pah), what are probably the Payette Lakes, as well as the relationship of these places to the headwaters of the Weiser River. The meadow system (near New Meadows, Idaho) separating the Weiser and Little Salmon was well-known to the Nez Perce people, and some of these place names were used by Astorian Robert Stuart in his account of his trip home in 1812. This map and the few existing published accounts in combination give good reason to assume that when Mackenzie opened his post on the lower Clearwater in the summer of 1812, he was *returning* to that spot.

---

[3]David Lavender, *The Fist in the Wilderness.*(Garden City: Doubleday, 1964), 167 n.5.

More information about Mackenzie and the Astorians:

F.D. Haines, "Mackenzie's Winter Camp," *Oregon Historical Quarterly,* 37, no. 4 (December 1936): 329-333.

David Lavender, *The Fist in the Wilderness* (Garden City: Doubleday, 1964).

Jean C. Nielsen, "Donald McKenzie in the Snake Country Fur Trade, 1816-1821," *Pacific Northwest Quarterly* 31 (1940): 161-179.

James P. Ronda, *Astoria and Empire* (Lincoln: University of Nebraska Press, 1989).

Theodore Stern, *Chiefs and Chief Traders: Indian Relations at Fort Nez Perces, 1818-1855* (Corvallis: Oregon State University Press, 1993).

A.W. Thompson, "New Light on Donald Mackenzie's Post on the Clearwater, 1812-13," *Idaho Yesterdays* 18, no. 3 (Fall 1974): 24-32.

Sylvia Van Kirk, "Donald McKenzie," in *Dictionary of Canadian Biography, Vol. 8* (Toronto: University of Toronto Press, 1985), 557-58.

Account 5.1: 12 August 1812, along the Snake River in western Idaho. Robert Stuart, returning east, remembers how this region was described by Mackenzie. Source: Kenneth A. Spalding, ed., *On the Oregon Trail: Robert Stuart's Journey of Discovery* (Norman: University of Oklahoma Press, 1953), 75.

From the accounts of Messrs. McKenzie & McClellan, this kind of country [i.e., the rugged, mountainous landscape of the Snake River] continues for about 300 miles, by the meanders of the river, which is very crooked: their tract last fall [late November and December of 1811] was as near the bank as possible, but were often compelled to leave it by the intervention of impervious masses of rocks.— they were in all 12 persons, took 21 days constant travelling to the Mulpat river [the Little Salmon, but possibly the main Salmon River], and subsisted during that time on an allowance by no means proportionate to the bodily labor they daily underwent.—being no more than two Ibex and 5 Beaver, the skins of which they preserved, and subsisted on for the last 5 days; the best, and indeed only method of dressing those skins, is, first to singe them well, after which they must be boiled for several hours, then cut into small pieces...

Account 5.2: Washington Irving's 1836 description of Mackenzie and McClellan on the Snake River in late December, 1811. Source: Washington Irving, *Astoria, or Anecdotes of an Enterprise Beyond the Rocky Mountains.* (New York: Belford, Clarke & Co., 1880), 249-50.

Though constantly near to the borders of the [Snake] river, and for a great part of the time within sight of its current, one of their greatest sufferings was thirst. The river had worn its way in a deep channel [Hells Canyon] through rocky mountains, destitute of brooks or springs...At length, after twenty-one days of toil and suffering, they got through these mountains, and arrived at a tributary stream of that branch of the Columbia called Lewis River, of which the Snake River forms the southern fork [Irving is confused here, since the Snake and Lewis are the same river]. In this neighborhood [probably on the lower Clearwater River] they met with wild horses, the first they had seen west of the Rocky Mountains. From hence they made their way to Lewis River, where they fell in with a friendly tribe of Indians [the Nez Perce], who freely administered to their necessities. On this river [the Snake?] they procured two canoes, in which they dropped down the stream to its confluence with the Columbia, and then down that river to Astoria, where they arrived haggard and emaciated, and perfectly in rags.

Account 5.3: Clerk Gabriel Franchere's story of what he learned from Donald Mackenzie and Robert McClellan after they finally reached Astoria. Source: Gabriel Franchere, *Journal of a Voyage on the North West Coast of North America during the Years 1811, 1812, 1813, and 1814* (New York: Redfield, 1854), 144-50.

On the 18th [of January, 1812], in the evening, two canoes full of white men arrived at the establishment [Astoria]…and I recognized Mr. Donald M'Kenzie…He was accompanied by Mr. Robert M'Lellan, a partner, Mr. John Reed, a clerk, and eight *voyageurs*, or boatmen.

Mr. M'Kenzie having overtaken Mr. M'Lellan, their two companies pursued the journey together…In a short time those upon the north bank [i.e., the right bank] came to a more considerable stream, which they followed down. They also met, very opportunely, some Indians who sold them a number of horses. They also encountered, in these parts, a young American, who was deranged, but who sometimes revived his reason. This young man told them, in one of his lucid intervals, that he was from Connecticut, and was named Archibald Pelton[4]; that he had come up the Missouri with Mr. [Andrew] Henry; that all the people at the post established by that trader were massacred by the Blackfeet; that he alone had escaped and had been wandering, for these years since, with the *Snake* Indians. Our people took this young man with them. Arriving at the confluence with the Columbia, of the river whose banks they were following, they perceived that it was the same which had been called *Lewis river*, by the American captain of that name, in 1805 [i.e., they met the Snake River at or near the mouth of the Clearwater, and followed the Snake down to the Columbia]. Here, then, they exchanged their remaining horses for canoes, and arrived at the establishment, safe and sound, it is true, but in a pitiable condition to see; their clothes being nothing but fluttering rags.

Account 5.4: On his way to Spokane, Clerk Ross Cox visits among the Palouse Indians along the Snake River, 31 July-15 August 1812. Source: Ross Cox, *The Columbia River, Or Scenes and Adventures During a Residence of Six Years on the Western Side of the Rocky Mountains Among Various*

---

[4]For more about this man, see J.N. Berry, "Archibald Pelton, the First Follower of Lewis and Clark," *Washington Historical Quarterly* 19 (1928): 199-201.

Tribes of Indians Hitherto Unknown (London: Henry Colburn and Richard Bentley, 1831), 146-54.

The Walla Wallah is a bold, rapid stream, about fifty-five yards wide, and upwards of six feet deep; the water is clear, and rolls over a bed of sand and gravel. On the 31st we moved up to the north side of the mouth of Lewis' River [the Snake River], which is about fourteen miles above the Wallah Wallah; its course is nearly due west, and at its junction with the Columbia it is upwards of six hundred yards wide. The current is very rapid; its waters deep, whitish, and slightly tepid, in which respect it forms a marked contrast to the Columbia, the waters of which are quite clear and cool. The latter river at this place is upwards of one thousand yards wide, and the current descends at an even rate of about four miles an hour. A little below the junction, however, it widens from a mile to a mile and a half, and has several islands, two of which are low and sandy, and are nearly three miles in length. Below these islands, a range of high hills are seen on each side of the river, running nearly from S.W. to N.E., and uncovered by any timber; but at an immense distance, in a southerly direction, a chain of high craggy mountains is visible, from which it is supposed the Wallah Wallah takes its rise. From their colour the Canadians call this chain *Les Montagnes Bleus* [the Blue Mountains]. The banks of both rivers at their junction are low with a gentle rise on each side. The plains are covered with immense quantities of prickly pear, which was a source of great annoyance.

Above Lewis' River the Columbia runs in a northerly direction, below it in a westerly. We remained here three days purchasing horses for the journey inland. Mr. David Stuart and party proceeded in their canoes up the Columbia to the trading establishment which he had formed at Oakinagan River, which falls into the Columbia, from the northward, about two hundred and eighty miles above this place. Mr. Donald Mackenzie and his party proceeded up Lewis' River in order to establish a trading post on the upper parts of it, or in the country of the Snake Indians, his choice to be regulated according to the appearance of beaver in either place. The natives of this district are called the Pierced-nose Indians; but as French is the language in general use among traders in this country, owing to most part of their working men being Canadians, we commonly called them *Les Nez Percés*. They do not differ much from the Walla Wallahs in their dress or language [both are Sahaptian speakers], but are not so friendly, and demand higher prices for their horses. Their habitations are covered with large mats, fixed on poles; some are square, others oblong, and some conical; they are of various sizes, from twenty to seventy feet long, and from ten to fifteen broad. There are no interior divisions, and an opening in the top serves the double purpose of a window and chimney. These dwellings are pretty free from vermin, and are easily changed when occasion arises. The women wear leathern robes, which cover the shoulders, parts of the arms, the breast, and reach down to their legs. The men have robes nearly similar, but not so long, with leggings which reach up half the thigh, and are fastened to a belt round the waist by leathern thongs. They are clean, active, and smart-looking, good hunters, and excellent horsemen. They enjoy good health, and with the exception of a few sore eyes, did not appear to have any disorder. They are fond of their children, and attentive to the wants of their old people. Their saddles are made of dressed dear-skin stuffed with hair; the stirrups are wooden, with the bottom broad and flat, and covered over with raw skin, which when dry becomes hard, and lasts a long time. The bridles are merely ropes made out of the hair of the horses' tails, and are tied round their under jaw. The women ride like men: their saddles are high in front and rear, and formed something likes the humps on a camel's back; and they must bring their horses to a rock or old tree to enable them to mount. The men are hard and unfeeling riders: the rope bridles cut the corners of the poor horses' mouths; and the saddles generally leave their backs quite raw; yet in this state they ride them for several days successively without the least pity for the tortured animals. We got plenty of salmon while we remained here, and some lamprey eels, the latter of which were oily and very strong. Having purchased twenty-five horses, we took our departure on the 3rd of August, and proceeded up Lewis' River, some on land with the horses, but the greater part still in the canoes. The water was very high, and rapid, and in many places the banks steep and shelving, which made the progress of dragging up the canoes very difficult. Poling was quite impossible; for on the off, or outer side, the men could not find bottom with their poles. I remained on shore part of the time with the horses. In some places the path wound along the almost perpendicular declivities of high hills on the banks of the river, and was barely wide enough for one horse at a time. Yet along these dangerous roads the Indians galloped with the utmost composure; while one false step would have hurled them down a precipice of three hundred feet into the torrent below. Even walking along these dangerous declivities, leading my horse, I experienced an indescribable sensation of dread on looking down the frightful abyss.

On the 7th we reached a small stream which falls into Lewis' River from the north [the Palouse River, also called the Pavilion or Drewyer's River]; the mouth is wide, and forms a kind of semicircular bay, but suddenly narrows to about ten or twelve yards. A village of about forty mat-covered tents was situated at its junction with the main river. The inhabitants were busily employed in catching and drying salmon for their winter and spring stock; and as it was here we intended to leave the canoes and proceed to our destination by land, we encamped on the west side of the little bay, and immediately commenced a trade with the natives for horses. This place is not more than fifty miles from the Columbia; but owing to the rapidity of the current, and the many rapids with which it was interrupted, our progress was slow. The business of collecting and catching the horses, which generally occupied until eleven or twelve o'clock each day, also contributed to cause this delay. With the exception of small willow and cotton wood, there are no trees from the Columbia upwards. The ground is covered with loose grass, and abounds in great quantities of prickly pear, the thorns of which are remarkably sharp, and strong enough to penetrate the leather of the thickest moccasins…

The inhabitants of this fishing village were part of the Pierced-nose Indians. We remained here seven days, endeavouring to complete our number of horses, which we at length effected. The natives were hard to deal with, and we had to raise our prices. Several trifling articles were stolen from us, which the chief promised to recover; but he either made no attempt, or the means he used were ineffectual. He apologised for his want of success by saying that the thieves belonged to another tribe higher up the river, and that they had departed with the stolen property. In their dress, language, and dwellings these people differed little from those at the mouth of Lewis' River. On the evening of the 14th we laid up our *bateaux* and canoes in a snug spot covered with willow and loose shrubs, and recommended them to the care of the chief, who promised that they should be carefully preserved until our return the following spring. We made him a present of a fathom of blue cloth, an axe, and a knife; to his wife we gave a few strings of white and blue beads, and three dozen of hawk-bells for her *chemise de cuir* [leather dress]; and among the remainder we distributed a few heads of leaf-tobacco.

We purchased altogether fifty horses to carry the goods and baggage; and from the difficulty we experienced in procuring that number, we were not able to obtain enough for our own use. M'Lennan and I, however, succeeded in purchasing one for our joint use; and Farnham and Pillet got another. The men also obtained a few which occasionally served to relieve them in the progress of their journey. Our destination was fixed for the Spokan tribe of Indians, whose lands lay about 150 miles from Lewis' River in a north-east direction, and among whom we were given to understand the North-West Company had already established a trading post from the east side of the Rocky Mountains. We also engaged an Indian guide to conduct us to the Spokan lands.

Account 5.5: Mackenzie's return to the Clearwater Valley in the summer of 1812 as reported by clerk Alexander Ross. Source: Alexander Ross, *Adventures of the First Settlers on the Oregon, or Columbia River* (Cleveland: Arthur H. Clark, 1904), 218-19.

At the May 1812 meeting of the Astorian partners, it was determined that Donald Mackenzie would return to the Snake River to recover a cache left there and to report on the state of the country. In August of 1812, Mackenzie reached the mouth of the Clearwater after he had traveled "up the same [Snake] river till he reached the very center of the great Shahaptain or Nez Perce nation." Camped on the lower Clearwater:

M'Kenzie now began to learn the true character of the Indians about him. Their occupations were war and buffalo-hunting. Their country did not abound in furs, nor would men accustomed to an indolent and roving life submit to the drudgery of killing beavers. They spurned the idea of crawling about in search of furs; "Such a life," they sad, "was only fit for women and slaves." They were, moreover, insolent and independent. I say independent, because their horses procured them guns and ammunition; the buffalos provided them with food and clothing; and war gave them renown. Such men held but poor prospects to the fur-trader; so that M'Kenzie soon got sick of them, and weary of the place. He then equipped the seven Snake wanderers [French-speaking Canadians who had earlier joined the Hunt party along the upper Snake], and sent them out to trap beaver; but they had to go to the mountains [upriver into the Bitterroots?], and on their way thither the Indians annoyed them, stole their traps, and frightened them back to the post. M'Kenzie then resolved to abandon that post and proceed further up the river; but before taking this step, he went over to Spokane to visit Mr. [John] Clarke [where he learned of the start of the War of 1812, after which he promptly returned to Astoria, arriving there on January 15, 1813, leaving his trade goods in a cache along the Clearwater River].

Account 5.6: Mackenzie's return to the Clearwater in February of 1813, as reported by Alexander Ross. Source: *Alexander Ross, Adventures of the First Settlers on the Oregon or Columbia River* (Cleveland: Arthur H. Clark, 1904), 221-225.

On the twenty-second day after leaving Astoria [about February 24, 1813], Mr. M'Kenzie arrived at his [abandoned] post on the Shahaptain River [the Clearwater near the site of modern day Lewiston]; but was mortified to find his cache robbed.

The Indians indicated their guilt by their shyness, for scarcely one of them came to visit the trader. M'Kenzie therefore summoned the chiefs, and they appeared, expecting no doubt to receive something. When they were all seated, he opened the business of the cache, and demanded the goods; adding, that if they were given up, friendship would again be restored. But they all, with one accord, denied having any knowledge of, or hand in, the pillage or robbery. They admitted the fact of the robbery, but denied that they were in any way accessory to it. They regretted the misconduct of their young men; but the goods were now gone, and they could do nothing; and so the conference ended. Seeing that the chiefs would not assist to recover the stolen property, and that every hour's delay lessened the chance of regaining it, M'Kenzie at once resolved on a bold and hazardous step; namely, to dash into the heart of the Indian camp, and recover what he could. Accordingly next morning, after depositing in a safe place the few articles he had brought with him, he and his little band, armed *cap-à-pie* [head to foot], set out on foot for the camp [located a short distance up the Clearwater River]. On their approach, the Indians, suspecting something, turned out in groups here and there, also armed. But M'Kenzie, without a moment's hesitation, or giving them time to reflect, ordered Mr. Seaton [clerk Alfred Seton, whose own account follows], who commanded the men, to surround the first wigwam or lodge reached with charged bayonets, while he himself and Mr. Reed [John Reed, a clerk who had also been with Mackenzie on the lower Clearwater in late 1811] entered the lodge, ransacked it, turning everything topsy-turvy, and with their drawn daggers cutting and ripping open everything that might be supposed to conceal the stolen property. In this manner they went from one lodge to another till they had searched five or six with various success, when the chiefs demanded a parley, and gave M'Kenzie to understand that if he desisted they would do the business themselves, and more effectually. M'Kenzie, after some feigned reluctance, at last agreed to the chief's proposition. They then asked him to withdraw; but this he peremptorily refused, knowing from experience that they were least exposed in the camp; for Indians are always averse to hostilities taking place in their camp, in the midst of their women and children. Had the Indians foreseen or been aware of the intention of the whites, they would never have allowed them within their camp.[5] But they were taken by surprise, and that circumstance saved the whites. However, as soon as the chiefs undertook the business, M'Kenzie and his men stood still and looked on. The chiefs went from house to house, and after about three hours they returned, bringing with them a large portion of the property, and

---

[5]This is a reference to the traditional Nez Perce law that once strangers or enemies were admitted within the confines of a camp, then peace was to be observed.

delivered it to M'Kenzie, when he and his men left the camp and returned home, bearing off in triumph the fruits of their valour; and well pleased with their hairbreadth adventure; an adventure not to be repeated. And under all circumstances, it was at the time considered the boldest step ever taken by the whites on Columbian ground.

This dispute with the [Nez Perce] Indians led to others; and if the whites got the upper hand in the late affair, the Indians were determined to be even with them in another way—for not a single horse would they sell, and on horse-flesh M'Kenzie and his men had to depend. On this head various conferences took place between the parties, and higher prices than usual were tendered; but the chiefs were inexorable. They had resolved either to drive the whites off their country altogether, or make them pay the most extravagant prices. The object in delaying their departure was to procure horses, which would be absolutely required in the event of Messrs. Stuart and Clark acceding to the views of M'Dougall and M'Kenzie [to abandon the Astorian venture]; but the Indians, free and independent as the air they breathed or the wind that blew, could not brook the restraint which the whites were always affecting to exercise over them. After some little time, all intercourse between the parties was at an end; not an Indian was to be seen about M'Kenzie's camp, except by stealth in the night, to beg, curry favour, or carry reports, yet five of these secret spies were always kept in pay by M'Kenzie to watch the motions of the Indians, and through them he knew every move in the hostile camp.

At this time one of the spies reported that the Indians had plotted together to starve M'Kenzie into terms, or drive him off altogether. M'Kenzie, on his part, had recourse to a stratagem to bring them to terms. Both were on the alert. When the whites had nothing to eat, the articles usually paid for a horse were tied up in a bundle; that done, M'Kenzie, with ten or twelve of his men, would sally forth with their rifles to the grazing grounds of the horses, shoot the fattest they could find, and carry off the flesh to their camp; leaving the price stuck upon a pole alongside the head of the dead horse.

This manoeuvre succeeded several times, and annoyed the Indians very much; some of them lost their best horses by it [Mackenzie was oblivious to the work of the Nez Perce people in horse breeding]. Then it was that they combined to attack the whites in their camp. This news was brought M'Kenzie by one of his hired spies, and was confirmed by the fact of an Indian offering to sell a horse for powder and ball only. From various other suspicious circumstances, there remained but little doubt in the minds of the whites that there was some dark design in agitation. In this critical conjuncture, M'Kenzie again eluded their grasp by ensconcing himself and his party in an island in the middle of the [Clearwater] river. There they remained, in a manner blockaded by the Indians; but not so closely watched but that they appeared every now and then with their long rifles among the Shahaptain horses; so that the Indians grew tired of their predatory excursions, and therefore sent a messenger to M'Kenzie. A parley ensued between the main land and the island; the result of which was, that the Indians agreed to sell horses to the whites at the usual price—the whites, on their part, to give up their marauding practices.

Not withstanding this formal treaty, the whites did not put implicit faith in their Indian allies, nor deem it prudent to leave the island; but the trade in horses went on briskly, and without interruption, M'Kenzie getting all his wants supplied. He bought besides an extra reserve of eighty horses for contingencies, which he sent off to Spokane [to facilitate the abandonment of Astoria]; and on the return of his men he left the island, apparently on good terms with the Indians, and reached the Walla Walla, to join his associates [at the site of Fort Nez Perces, which Mackenzie would later establish], on the 1st of June [1813].

Account 5.7: Clerk Alfred Seton's account of his 1812 trip with Mackenzie to the lower Clearwater River valley. Source: Alfred Seton, *Astorian Adventure: The Journal of Alfred Seton, 1811-1815.* Edited by Robert F. Jones. (New York: Fordham University Press, 1993), 102-10. Reprinted here with the permission of Fordham University Press.

We went on for 15 or 16 days [in August of 1812] until we came to the Forks [the mouth of the Clearwater] of the Fork we were on. We there traded Horses & Mr. McKenzie dispatched Mr. Reed [John Reed] & 4 men to look for the cachés the grand party [the Hunt party] were obliged to make on their voyage across the continent. We kept up the left Hand fork, or the river that Lewis & Clark descended & in three or four days came to the Head of navigable water on this side of the Mountains & the place where L & C had built their c(an)oes [Canoe Camp, located near the present site of Orofino, Idaho]. We encamped in their encampment [Lewis and Clark camped here from 26 September to 7 October 1805]. Here Mr. McK with 4 men went up the river two days march to determine if it had more the appearance of a beaver country above, leaving me with…charge of the goods, &c. It…to reach this from the sea…be made with light canoes in half the time, by our rude calculation we make it Six hundred miles, the current very strong & the last three hundred miles interspersed with frequent rapids.

The face of the Country from the Sea to the Falls of the Columbia is thick woods of Hemlock, Spruce, Pine &c. From there to the spot where we are (about 400 miles) the country is plain, not a tree to be seen, a barren sandy desert producing a little wormwood [sagebrush], & in some places a few miserable tufts of grass—scarcely affording sustenance to the numerous herds of Horses that are every where to be seen, not the least appearance of (crossed out: a) beaver.

The Indians all along the river numerous & powerful & very independent. From the falls to the Sea they are more stationary than above. They live in large lodges on the banks of the river & depending upon its produce for their support. Above the falls they also fish the salmon but do not always procure sufficient for their winter store. The deficiency they make up with H(unting gibi)er [game].

When Mr. McKenzie returned [to Canoe Camp]…it necessary to remove further down…quarters, on account of provisions.

The country he had been through afforded no (crossed out: more) sign of Beaver, to which all our enquiries were directed, & as it was now found that we must lay aside hopes of getting beaver from this quarter, he thought it best to remove down to the Forks which is in the center of a numerous nation of Indians [actually, still in Nez Perce country], from whom by chance we might now and then get a skin, & who abound in Horses which we now perceive must be our only Food.

Accordingly, we removed down and chose upon a spot about 5 miles above the Forks [on the north bank of the Clearwater, near the mouth of Hatwai Creek], on a Prairie where in the beginning of Septr. we commenced building with drift wood, as there was not a tree to be seen. In three weeks we had finished our buildings, which consisted of a store, a house for the men & one for Mr. McK & myself. The method of building was as follows. Logs were piled up about six feet high, fitted to each other in the ends. A ridge pole (was raised) about 4 feet above the square & the…these planks forming the (roof)…(spa)ces filled up with mud—the chimneys in the center of the house built of mud.

Although this building might appear uncouth in the eyes of a man accustomed to view the works of mechanics, yet it fully answered our purpose and served as a shelter from winds and weather.

The river that we are built upon is called by the Natives Shahaptin—from the nation who live at the heads of it, at the scite of whose village Mr. McK was [probably Kamiah]. The river in which this empties itself is called Kamoenum, this latter name [Sgt. Patrick] Gass in his journal gives correct [Ki-mo-ee-nem], he also calls it Lewis River from Captn. Lewis [it is now called the Snake River]. The nation that inhabit the Shahaptin river, are at present gone to war against the Blackfeet & hunt the Buffaloe & will not return before the next spring.

The other nation that live upon the Kamoenum are called Tushep(ais). This is a very powerful & warlike nation divided into many tribes under different chiefs, possessing almost innumerable Horses.[6] With this latter tribe it was that we wintered, and we found them…troublesome set, little valuing or respec(ting)…every opportunity in their power to steal & to give us trouble.

Of their manners & customs I will not pretend to say much, leaving it to a more willing and able pen then mine, a few of the most striking of them I will only observe. Contrary to the custom of most Indians, Female chastity is here regarded in a very particular manner & the woman who breaks through its bounds is regarded in as disgraceful a light, as they are in most civilized countries. The dress of the Women is here, a leather petticoat from the neck to the ankles, which as completely veils their charms as the closest dress in our own country, & when handsomely ornamented with beads, shells, &c. is far from being an ungraceful habit. The common dress of the men is leggins of (d)ressed Deer skin & Buffaloe robes. In the beginning of the summer they are generally employed in war or hunting the Deer. They go to war against the Tuelicums or Snakes who inhabit fur(ther)…(the r)iver & are seperated from the (m)…ridge of mountains. Their arms before white men (crossed out: were) introduced into the country, guns were bow & arrows, the arrows pointed with a sharp flint stone in the shape of a diamond ♦. Most of their bows were of a Hard kind of wood and covered with a rattle snake skin (which abound in this country). There are some of them made of Horn which are much valued among them. Among this nation a few of the (crossed out: Indians) Chiefs are only supplied with guns, but with the Shahaptins who war against the Blackfeet, they are common.

The chiefs appear to possess their power from the number of Horses they have, & only exercise it in time of War. Like the Indians on the other side of the mountains they take the scalp of their enemy killed in battle, & according to the

---

[6]These most likely were Nez Perce. See A.W.Thompson , "New Light on Donald Mackenzie's Post on the Clearwater," *Idaho Yesterdays* 18, no. 3 (Summer 1974): 29-32.

number of scalps in possession, so much is the Possessor respected.

When a chief dies they bury him with his principal articles of dress, arms, &c. & commonly stick a pole over his grave on the top of which is placed the most valuable article in their possession, there to remain untill it rots. They likewise…a number of horses to the manes of the the decea(sed)…(Of t)heir (re)ligion & objects of their worship I never could learn much, as they appear very shy of communicating any thing on that subject.

When we first went among these Indians a Horse could be procured for 40 to 50 loads of ammunition, the price in a few months rose to blankets axes &c.

About the middle of October [1812] Mr. Reed arrived from his voyage to the Caches [those left by the Hunt party along the upper Snake River]. He was accompanied by 4 Frenchmen whom Mr. Crooks left in the mountains last year & who had made their way to the Snake nation, with whom they had passed the winter. Most of the caches had been found & destroyed by the Indians.

As the Indians had been telling us for some time past that white men were building houses two days journey off [at the Astorian post at the junction of the Spokane and Little Spokane Rivers], Mr. McK sent me with four men in the latter end of this month to ascertain who they were. Accordingly we started each one on Horseback with his blanket under him & two meals of dried salmon attached to his saddle, with an Indian for our guide. After (ridin)g hard all day, at night when I aske(d the gui)de what time the next day we…he informed me that I would have to ride three days in the same manner before I could reach the spot [they would have been on the heavily-used Nez Perce and Coeur d'Alene Indian trail, somewhere near the site of Moscow, Idaho, when this question was posed]. As we had only one meal of provision more, this was rather discouraging news.

We did not arrive at Mr. Clarke's who was the person alluded to by the Indians until the third day from this, during which time we had nothing to eat, riding excessively hard all day, & at night when we camped rolling ourselves up in our blanket as close to the fire as we dared to approach—it was rather unpleasant travelling.

Mr. C received me very kindly & treated me to the best his house afforded, which was but Horse. The NW Co. has had an establishmt. for trade here some years [Spokane House], & did not much like the idea of our opposing them. They get their goods from the opposite side of the mountains, (crossed out: where) at the bottom of which they have a post, & they commonly reach this about the middle of November. It is much better Beaver country than where we are, Mr. C having already 14 or 15 packs.

I reached Home [the post on the Clearwater neat Hatwai Creek] again in the beginning of Novem(ber)…(Mr.) Reed had started off with 4 men to live…As affairs looked gloomy in our quarter—no Beaver, nor any to be expected, Horses rising so fast that we are in doubt whether our goods will hold out to spring—Mr. McK thought it best to go and consult Mr. Clarke himself. Accordingly he started, leaving me at the House in charge. During his absence several of our men whom we had sent in pursuit of their living [trapping] returned after having suffered extremely from the cold & hunger. Fearing that this might be the case with all, I dispatched an express immediately to Mr. McK that he might make his arrangements accordingly. He returned a few days after 25th Novr. 1812. While at Mr. Clarkes the NW goods & traders had come in under the charge of Mr. [John

George] McTavish. This gentleman had been as far down as Lake Winnipeg where an express had been sent him from the grand Portage [Fort William, at the west end of Lake Superior] containing a declaration of War between the United States and G Britain [this meant that the two little posts at Spokane were technically at war]. He showed James Maddisons proclomation dated June 19th 1812 to that effect. At thi(s news) must (crossed out: have) regulate in some mann(er the rel)ations of this Company it...(Mr. Mc)K. & Mr. Clarke that it should reach the Sea as soon as possible, also as the N Westers had mentioned (crossed out: a report) that a ship [the Isaac Todd of the North West Company, which was armed] would be at the mouth of the [Columbia] river in the Spring for them. It was concluded upon, that Mr. McKenzie should proceed to the sea with his party after he had sent his goods to Mr. Clarke. I was accordingly dispatched a second time with three men & thirteen horses loaded with merchandise (the beginning of December) but was not destined to reach that place [Spokane]. I fortunately took provision for ten days. At the first days march from the House it began to snow, we pushed on, untill it fell so thick that it compelled us to stop [probably near the site of Moscow]. At this encampment, on the top of a mountain we were unable to stir backwards or forwards for thirteen days. It may easily be conceived in how unpleasant a situation we were. I was the (crossed out: the) only person of the party that had two blankets, with which we made a lodge to prevent the snow from coming in upon us, and all stowed together inside as close as we were able. On the 12th day it rained, when Mr. McK sent off to see if we had passed the mountain, which finding the impractibility at this season of the year, we loaded our (goods) & endeavoured to go back but found the Horses so wea(k from lack) of (past)ure that we were unable to proceed (on horseback)...and on a nipping morning set off to walk thirty miles in two feet snow. We reached the house [back on the Clearwater] an hour before sun set & dispatched fresh horses the next morning for the goods, which all reached the house in tolerable good order.

Seeing the impractibility of getting the property to Mr. Clarkes without detaining us too long time, we concluded to send our Horses there light & to cacher our goods. The Horses were accordingly sent by Mr. Clarkes men, who happened to be with us at the time. The 1st January [January 1, 1813] was the time fixed upon for starting to the sea. An express was sent off to Mr. Reed enjoining him to be at the house the 25th December. Some hunters whom we had in the mountains, hunting beaver, came in. The lakes & rivers had taken with ice & they had been obliged to kill and eat their Horses. One of their party remained about 5 days march off with traps and a gun belonging to the (crossed out: party) Company and his companions said not much inclined to a voyage to the sea. As this was a free man, I was sent to persuade him to accompany us. If he...not to take away his gun and traps...on horseback with two...with his squaw with a strong band of Indians. After some little persuasion, I prevailed upon him to accompany us. The Indians that he was with, were a band of the Tushepas [Nez Perce] who in every respect ressembled their neighbors of the same nation.[7] The same rascally worthless behaviour, endeavouring to take our horses away from

---

[7]Here Seton is unknowingly making the distinction between what many scholars have come to describe as the Upper and Lower Nez Perce people. There are some cultural and linguistic differences between the two.

us, which when they found we would not put up with, they tried how far they could provoke us, which they so completely did that we knocked down one or two in the midst of the village. This made some talk among them, which observing, I went to the chief and told him the consequence if his men behaved again in a similar manner. He immediately got up & addressed them in our favour, when they became more quiet. I gave him then some tobacco & took my leave.

For three last days of this trip [into the mountains looking for his men] I had only one beaver tail for my share of the provisions & walking two thirds of the time as we passed over mountains & precipices where I did not choose to risk my neck on horseback.

I reached the house [on the Clearwater] 25th December and found all our party together. We must(ere)d counting every body 20 men 1 boy & 1 squaw. From (that) time till 1st Jany. [1813] we were employed baling sep(erate)…putting them in caché, and in the night of the last of December we dug holes inside of our houses under the floor & there put the goods, covered them up, and floored it the same as before. We remained here the next day & passed our New Year as jollily as was in our power. We had a famous horse pye & a couple of quarts of real Boston particular with which we regaled ourselves pas mal [not bad] as the Frenchmen say. In the evening we removed our blankets about two hundred yards off, & after letting the dirt from the roof of the house fall upon the Floor, we set fire to the buildings in the hopes by these means the Indians would not discover our goods.

Early next morning [2 January 1813] which was cold & raw we embarked on board our canoes, on our voyage to the sea, the water being low the current was excessively strong and the rapids very dangerous[the party reached Astoria on 15 January 1813].

Account 5.8: Anticipating the end of the Astorian venture, Mackenzie and Seton return to the Clearwater in April of 1813, hoping to recover their hidden trade goods and to purchase large numbers of horses. This is Seton's first hand account. Source: Alfred Seton, *Astorian Adventure: The Journal of Alfred Seton, 1811-1815.* Edited by Robert F. Jones. (New York: Fordham University Press, 1993), 113-14. Reprinted here with the permission of Fordham University Press.

On the 21st April we reached our wintering grounds [on the Clearwater River near Hatwai Creek] & had there the extreme mortification of finding that our caches had been lifted by the Indians & all our property stolen. Mr. Reed with one man was immediately dispatched to Mr. Clark [at Spokane] with the letters from Mr. McDougall & also the account of our loss.

The remainder of us 18 in number, were continually employed from this time untill the 1st June in endeavouring to get back our goods from the natives, in which service we were several times in dangerous and trying situations. Once we arrived at a large village of the Tushepas [the name Seton gave to the Nez Perce people living in the lower Clearwater River valley] in which we understood was a considerable quantity of goods. As we put ashore we observed the men placed on the bank, with their guns in their hands & bullets in their mouths, & one of our (crossed out: the) men observing a sign among themselves as if they intended to shoot Mr. Mc.K, who with myself was advancing towards them (crossed out: selves), he instantly ordered the men to jump on shore with their g(uns) which they immediately did & going up to the Indians, demanded of them our property, of which they denied the p(ossession)…(McKenzie) tol(d th)em that if they wished to fight, we were prepared for them, and that we would not stir from their village untill he got his property. Leaving me to watch the Indians he went into every lodge himself, taking our property wherever it could be found, after which embarking it on board our canoes, we fired 4 or 5 guns to show in their own manner that we were not afraid & encamped about 2 miles off [this village site was probably located near Cherry Lane].

Another time a great war chief whom we distinguish by the name of <u>Le Grand Coquin</u> [the big rascal], came to our camp under the pretence of being a great friend to us, & to better cover his bad intentions, he brought us considerable some trifling articles, promising to return next day with a greater quantity. Next day he did return, accompanied by his band of 60 men all armed with guns. He fortunately found us with a band of Scietogas,[8] whom he addressed in our very camp to join with him against us, & among other arguments, he made use of (which I understood perfectly myself) that we were 18 men, that our (crossed out: camps) guns w(ere few), that we were situated in…without any cover and that they could soon rush upon & destroy us. The old chief that was there answered in our favour, & positively denied having any thing to do with it. Le grand Coquin & his band went off with out taking any notice of us. He was no sooner gone than we fixed our bayonets on our guns & loading them with buckshot, explained to the Indians, that we were coming among them to trade, not to fight, that they had at first stole our property, and that now we would recover by any means, where we could see it. They allowed the justness of this & after smoking with us, took their leave. As circumstances looked rather suspicious we removed our camp about 20 miles down the river on the opposite side [to the site of Lewiston, or perhaps even onto the banks of the Snake River] where we remained untill the 1st June, continually upon our guard night and day. As the Indians would not trade their Horses with us we were under the necessity of killing them, for provision. This displeased the Indians very much for we sometimes killed a favorite animal, but necessity has no law.

We started on 1st June [1813] on our way again to the Fort….

Account 5.9: Seton, in the fur business in New York City in 1835, and associated with Washington Irving and Captain Bonneville, writes a more literary version of his experiences along the Clearwater. Source: "Life on the Oregon, No. 2," *American Monthly Magazine* 5, no. 5 (July 1835): 369-74.

Our *cache*, which I told you in my former communication had been made on hearing the news of the war [of 1812], was on the banks of the Shahaptin [Clearwater] River, a few miles above its junction with the Camoenum [Snake]. We

---

[8] A.W. Thompson, *op. cit.*, concludes that these were Cayuse Indians who happened to be passing through the lower Clearwater River valley. Scietogas was also the term used by Hunt in 1811 to describe his encounter with Cayuse Indians.

had, early in the fall of 1812, ascended the former as far as it was practicable to drag the canoes, with a view of establishing a trading post, which might unite the requisites of procuring furs, and the *de quoi manger* [provisions]. The sterile country through which the Shahaptin poured, promised little for our first object, and the other, which was equally necessary, our bourgeois [Mackenzie] thought could be best attained by building our winter quarters near the confluence of the Shahaptin and Camoenum rivers, and among the Shahaptin nation [the Nez Perce], quiet and peaceable folks, who devoted themselves to the rearing of numerous herds of horse, with which they supplied their more turbulent and warlike neighbors, the Tashepas [Seton's name for the Nez Perce bands living on the lower Clearwater River] of the Camoenum on the one side of their grounds, and the Courtenois [Kootenais] and Flatheads on the other. These nations were in the annual practice of crossing the mountains to hunt the buffalo, and to make war with the Blackfeet Indians. Our huts were built in the beginning of September, and of the drift-wood of the river. When it was decided in the end of December, to carry the news of the war to the coast, deep holes were dug under the floor of one of the huts, there cannily and carefully our wares and merchandise were deposited, the clay with which the interstices of the roof were stopped was let in, and the buildings were burnt. We trusted that, like Cesar's wife, not only intacta, but unsuspected. This was our *cache*. I gave you an account of our return voyage (after having been to the seacoast) as far as the falls of the Columbia, in pursuit of these goods.

Previously to arriving at our destination [in April 1813], rumors met our ears that the restless and villainous Tashepas, whose roving disposition had made them somewhat conversant with the proceedings of white men, had been poking about our premises for weeks; until at length our moveables, which we thought so warily concealed, had been uncovered to their eager eyes; and that the 'bowels of their mother earth' had been rifled of treasures which might have been better hid. Our arrival here [back on the lower Clearwater] found the rumors true—not a 'remnant of packthread, or a shred with which a beggar might patch a garment, but was scattered about.' The avaricious and covetous Tashepas had pillaged the whole. Lengthy and rueful phizes [faces] abounded, when confirmation of our misfortune, as strong as holy writ, was forced upon us. We were naked of effects to trade the *de quoi* [literally, of what?] with the natives. It was useless to say to them, "Uncharitably with us have you dealt; therefore now give us your fat horses, to make a *plat cote* for our *roti* [Seton is unclear. *Plat*=flat, *cote*=side, and *roti*=roasted]" Our only resource, like Snowdon's knight at Coilantogle ford, was in our arms, and like him we constrained to use them.

Mr. Reed, with two men, was sent to Mr. Clarke's establishment, on the Spokan River, to give him notice of the loss, and to carry him dispatches from Astoria [telling him of the end of the Astorian effort]. The remainder of our party, seventeen in number, were employed in endeavoring to get back our goods from the plunderers. In this we were more or less successful. Several villages of the Shahaptins were searched, but few of our wares were found. These people united in saying that a band of the Tashepas, whose dwellings were on the banks of the Camoenum, in a small savannah hedged in by rocks and precipices, and where fearful rapids above and below forbade the approach of canoes, were the robbers [there are several spots along the Snake River, both above and below its confluence with the Clearwater, that meet this description]. The chief of this band might number seven or eight lustres [35-40 years of age]; he had all the characteristics of a prairie Indian, tall, straight, lean, high cheek bones, sharp features, and piercing black eyes....

During our sojourn of the previous fall in his vicinity, the above-mentioned chief had been in the habit of visiting us more frequently than any other of the Indians, sometimes alone, and sometimes with half a dozen or more of his band. He was, in the commencement, a favorite with the Canadians, who had given him the sobriquet of Le Grand Bobillard [big liar], a better acquaintance, however, had, previously to our going to the sea, caused them to change it, to the more appropriate one of Le Grand Coquin [big rascal]. Circumstances had made a kind of familiarity between him and myself. In his visits, at the commencement of our residence in his neighborhood, we would often take our guns—for he and most of his band had them—retire a short distance from our Comptoir, and there exercise ourselves shooting at a mark. The ammunition on these occasions hung at my side, and in loading his gun, I generally managed, although he watched the progress minutely, with my thumb on the spring of the powder-horn, to let in at least a double charge, sometimes much more; and as my rifle bullets rolled down his wide and smooth-bored north-west Indian fusil without much friction, we used to wind them with grass to make a tight fit. One thing was sure, in his firing, which he always did with great deliberation and steadiness, viz., that if the mark was not marked, of which the probability was small, his shoulder would be, and that not lightly. The unvarying certainty with which my bullet went straight *au blanc* [into the white, or main part of the target], owing to the superiority of my gun, caused him to betray the only emotions I ever saw him exhibit. Sometimes we would mount our horses, and "fetching mad bounds," rush headlong in our utmost contention, to gather up an arrow, stuck in the ground, without checking our speed. The recklessness of youth [Seton was just 20 years old at the time], when not by "cares, or fears, or age oppressed," made me his equal in feats of horsemanship. I knew him, however, from a circumstance which took place in a visit to his village, (about four days march, and to which Mr. M'K had sent me with three men, a short time before we went to the sea), for a treacherous knave.

We ascertained one day that a band of the Tashepas, (not that of the Grand Coquin), who had participated in the plunder of our *cache*, were encamped some fifteen miles above us on the Shahaptin River [the location of this camp lends credence to the argument that the Tashepas and the Shahaptins were one and the same—the Nez Perce]. We embarked to pay them a visit. On approaching their encampment, which was done from the opposite side of the river, about one hundred yards wide here, some twenty-five Indians, with guns in their hand, were discovered on the banks, immediately in front of their lodges. A dozen vigorous strokes of the paddle brought us under them. Our bourgeois rapidly swung on shore, and ordered me to follow with the men. An angular path led up the bank: at the turn, halfway up, there was a small platform; the men were in a moment drawn up there. The Indians were at the other extremity of the path, some twenty feet distant. We could see from the protuberance in their cheeks, that their bullets were in the mouths, ready, in Indian fashion, for a fight. Our bourgeois was among them examining each and every gun, and emptying it of its priming. This done, we told them we had come to the country to supply them with arms and ammunition, and thereby enable them to hunt successflly the buffalo, and be on an equal footing with the enemies the Blackfeet. That we did not wish to fight; but were prepared to do so to get back our goods, which, like the cowardly Shoshonies, they had stolen in the night. That now the young chief would smoke with them, while he examined their lodges. He [Mackenzie] told them to sit down, and ordered me to bring a pipe; each took a whiff or two and then passed it on to his neighbor—and while this was doing, the bourgeois with his aid, (Joe La Pierre), ransacked their lodges. He succeeded in recovering some three or four pactins [packs?], with which we re-embarked, and fired a salute, to show the natives, who were mostly young men, without any prominent chief among them, that we were brimful of fight. We went and encamped four or five hundred yards above, on the same side of the river, and on the banks of a brook which paid its tribute here to the Shahaptin, after winding its short and meandering course through cotton-wood trees and willows, whose green and luxurious foliage induced such cool and pleasant shade, and contrasted so strongly with the naked and arid scenery around, that our voyageurs could not withstand its seductions, notwithstanding our close vicinity to unfriendly neighbors. They, however, broke up at once their transitory encampment, and wended their weary way to their own firesides among the crags and precipices of the tumultuous Camoenum [i.e., they returned to the Snake, probably to a spot upstream from the mouth of the Clearwater given Seton's description]. We remained here three or four days, and were joined by a large band of friendly Scietogas [probably Cayuse Indians, but perhaps another Nez Perce band], on their way to the mountains. A day after this junction, I wandered some distance from the camp, near the head of the little brook we were on, looking for gibier, and unsuccessful, was breasting the opposing hill, building *chateaux en Espagne* [daydreaming], when suddenly, on the brow, Le Grand Coquin, with his band of forty or fifty men made their appearance. They were all mounted and in their war costume—deer skin leggins and moccasins, buffalo robes wrapped around their loins and resting on their saddles in front; their faces and bodies painted in various colors; their heads fantastically adorned with feathers; a round shield made of buffalo bulls hide, and buried in the ground until it had shrunk to a sufficient thickness, hung on their bridle-arm; and immediately in front of it rested their guns. Without the usual greeting, Le Grand Coquin abruptly demanded the place of our encampment. I pointed to the trees at the foot of the hill, and told him I would mount behind him and show the way. Behold me, then, on the crooper of his war horse. No loving arm, however, was around him thrown—bolt upright, with knees firmly fixed—the left hand holding my rifle, as it rested on the charger's back in front of me, and right arm full—I felt I had him to advantage; yet ever and anon, as you might even suppose, I made my heels familiar with the gallant war-horse's ribs. One or two gutteral grunts elicited, as group of trees after group were passed. At length the blue smoke of our fires met his eagle glance. Our bourgeois was reclining under a temporary tent made with canoe sails. The men were in groups of two or three, in the shade of some wide-spreading willow, variously employed, but all chattering and smoking. The guns were stacked against the luggage, which, with the canoes, were arranged in the usual manner, to form a sort of bulwark. The Scietoga camp was about a hundred yards distant; their chief, with a few of his young men, was then sitting on a log and smoking, near to the bourgeois' tent. The trampling of the war-chief's band made no commotion in the camp. The keen and knowing eye of the bourgeois recognized them at once, and divined their purpose. He gave no symptoms of surprise, or even of knowledge of their presence. Like statues, they remained for some time not greeted and unnoticed. At length, the Grand Coquin addressed the Scietoga chief. He urged him, (after first bringing to mind their mutual friendly relations), to join with his band, and extirpate the pale-faced traders; he pointed out our defenceless and unprepared position, the paucity of our numbers, and the ease with which we might be destroyed; he mentioned our guns, kettles, knives, ammunition, &c., which would be the reward for the deed—in a word, adduced many arguments to entice the friendly band to become treacherous guests—happily in vain. After due deliberation, the Scietoga chief replied, that peace and friendship existed between the white men and his people, and therefore they would not mingle themselves in such an affair; that the white men had, many moons since, come to his country hungry and destitute, (alluding to Mr. Hart's party) [Seton means the Hunt party, a portion of which under Mackenzie's leadership, had reached the lower Clearwater, starving, in late 1811; the chief could also have been recalling the arrival of Lewis and Clark who reached the Clearwater in equally dire conditions], that he had given them to eat, and sped them on their journey; that since, many more white men had come, bringing with them such articles as were useful, and that he considered the trading-posts the white men were establishing in the country advantageous, because, in a short time, all his young men would have guns like their enemies, the Blackfeet, who had become armed from white men trading with them; that it was true, the chief present, with his young men, could be destroyed, but that the whites were now numerous, and would no doubt revenge the deed. He repeated again that his heart was warm towards the white men; that he had delayed his journey a day to smoke with them; and that he would not consent, while he and his band were present, that harm should come to them. After the Scietoga chief had finished speaking, the band of Le Grand Coquin remained in their statue-like posture for four or five minutes, then suddenly wheeled and left our camp. It was the last time I saw Le Grand Coquin. John Reed, in the succeeding year, went with a party in his vicinity, and they were all massacred [Bannock Indians were involved in this event, which happened near the mouth of the Boise River in southern Idaho].

In the afternoon, the Scietoga chief, on whom the scene had apparently made no impression, for he did not allude to it, told us, that his young men were to continue their journey, and that we would find a pleasant encampment about twenty miles below, on the opposite side of the river, and among the Shahaptins [back near the mouth of the Clearwater]. We bade the old man a cordial farewell, and took his friendly counsel. We went and encamped on the indicated spot, which was immediately on the river, where the bank was precipitous and lofty. The area of our encampment was enclosed by a semicircular line of earth, of about three and a helf [half] feet high, and appeared as if regularly constructed by men similarly situated to ourselves [they camped near the site of Lewiston, at a spot used by other, unknown, white men; perhaps these were the "many more white men" described by the Scietoga chief].

6

The Hudson's Bay Company in Nez Perce Country, 1821-1831

With the demise of the Astorian venture on the Columbia, the Pacific Fur Company's assets, and many of its employees, were absorbed by the Montreal-based North West Company. No post was maintained on the Clearwater River, so in 1818, Alexander Ross helped Donald Mackenzie to construct Fort Nez Perces. This important fur trade post, sometimes also called Fort Walla Walla, was located on the Columbia River at the mouth of the Walla Walla River. While recognizing that this was "the most hostile spot on the whole line of communication," Mackenzie and Ross also appreciated the strategic and economic virtues of the place.[1] Changed by fire and reconstruction, Fort Nez Perces remained an important trading center until it was sacked by Walla Walla Indians in 1855.

In 1821, a rise in violence and a decline in profits led the British government to force a merger between the North West Company and its older rival, the Hudson's Bay Company. Management of the Bay Company's new trading centers on the Columbia fell into the able hands of Governor George Simpson, and before long, under the control of his Chief Factor, Dr. John McLoughlin, based at Fort Vancouver after 1825.

Under its new management, Fort Nez Perces was to play a large role in the history of Idaho and of the Nez Perce people in particular. The vicinity of the Fort, while at the edge of the traditional homeland of the Nez Perce, had long been an important center of trade among Native Americans, Sahaptian speakers especially. Now it became, in addition, a place of acculturation and religious change, and an important center for the great equestrian culture so vital to Nez Perce life. The Fort also came to have growing import for the Hudson's Bay Company, which relied increasingly on the Snake River fur trade for profits in its Columbia Department. Many important trading expeditions, called "outfits" by the Bay Company, departed from this post. Fort Nez Perces also became the chief source of horses for the Bay

---

[1]Alexander Ross, *The Fur Hunters of the Far West* (Chicago: Lakeside Press, 1924), 164.

Company, both as a food source and increasingly for the use of the trapping parties traveling up the Snake or across the mountains to the east.

Several interesting accounts that survive from the early years of the Hudson's Bay Company on the Columbia are included here. Governor George Simpson's account of his visit contains some useful ethnographic information. Samuel Black's 1829 *Report* is informed by his four years along the Snake River and was a response to one of the very first scientific questionnaires in North American history. John Work spent time at the mouth of the Clearwater (in 1826), roamed throughout what is now southern and central Idaho, and also made a rare crossing of the Lolo Trail. The great trader and explorer Peter Skene Odgen also operated from this post and was still working on the Columbia during the chaos of 1847.

George Simpson was born in Scotland in 1786, and as an illegitimate child skipped formal education and entered the sugar trade in London in 1800. The chaotic fight for trading supremacy in America between the Hudson's Bay Company and its rival, the North West Company, provided Simpson an opening. With the help of influential relatives, he was named Governor of the Hudson Bay Company's operations in 1820. In March of 1821, the two rival trading firms merged, and Simpson was named Governor of the new Northern Department, which stretched all the way to the Pacific.

Simpson himself was keen to improve the company's operations west of the Rocky Mountains, and after 1824 the board of directors in London urged upon him a more aggressive policy toward American traders. These two goals led to his trip to the Columbia in the autumn of 1824. The Hudson Bay Company's work in the Columbia, assisted by the appointment of Dr. John McLoughlin as Chief Factor, became quite profitable, and Simpson was named Governor of all North American operations in 1826. The firm's great financial success in America led to a knighthood for Simpson in 1841. Simpson was still Governor when he died near Montreal in September of 1860.

Samuel Black, who was Chief Trader at Fort Nez Perces from 1825-1829, was also born in Scotland, in 1780. He migrated to Canada in 1802, and joined the North West Company in 1804 as a clerk. Black was an eager participant in the often violent conflict with the Hudson's Bay Company and had to travel all the way back to London in 1822 to beg for a job with the merged company. His trip was a success, and he was appointed to the rank of Chief Trader in 1823. After serving briefly at Peace River, he was transferred to Dr. McLoughlin's Columbia River Department the next year. He was appointed to head Fort Nez Perces in 1825 after a short term at Fort Colville.

In 1830, he was transferred to Thompsons River, where he was murdered in February of 1841. Excerpts from Black's important scientific *Report* appear below. This report is especially valuable because Black was the first writer of European origin to remain for any length of time among the Sahaptian-speaking peoples of the lower Snake River.

John Work (sometimes spelled Wark) was no stranger to the fur trade. Born in Ireland in 1792, he went to work for the Hudson's Bay Company at age twenty two.

By 1823, he was working on the Columbia and was assigned to the upriver trade in 1825, reaching the lower Clearwater valley that same year. He served McLoughlin and the Company at Fort Colville and in the Flathead country to the east. Governor Simpson liked and promoted Work, calling him a "very steady pains taking Man, regular, oeconomical and attentive in business, and bears a fair private character. Has been a useful man for many years and must always be so from his persevering steady and regular habits."[2]

When John Work took charge of the annual Snake River Brigade at Walla Walla in 1830, he was playing his part in a broad and far-reaching Bay Company plan to retain its full power, profits, and influence in the Oregon country. Increasing American presence in Oregon and in the Flathead region led the Company's leaders in London, and then Governor Simpson himself, to desperate trading measures. In July of 1827, Governor Simpson offered McLoughlin the clearest possible explanation of the policy that would guide John Work in his trip across Idaho:

"The greatest and best protection we can have from opposition is keeping the country closely hunted as the first step that the American Government will take towards Colonization is through their Indian Traders and if the country becomes exhausted in Fur bearing animals they can have no inducement to proceed thither...The Snake Expedition we look to as a very prominent branch of our business and we wish by all means that it be kept constantly employed; even under all disadvantages and misfortunes that have befallen it, the profits are most respectable, it moreover does much good in over-running and destroying that extended country south of the Columbia which is the greatest temptation to our opponents."[3]

As the successor to Peter Skene Ogden as leader of the Snake Brigade, Work had two of the same obligations: profitability and the creation of a fur desert to thwart the Americans. Ogden's success at this latter goal played a big role in the course of Work's journey from Fort Nez Perces in 1831. Anticipating Work's wish to cross the Bitterroots (by what was termed "a new road") and trap in the dangerous and highly contested Flathead country of Montana, McLoughlin wrote Governor Simpson in March of that year. He hinted at poor returns to come and raised questions of protection, telling the Governor that "it is certain the Snake country is getting nearly exhausted."[4]

The Arrowstone River region (i.e., the headwaters of the Clark Fork River near the site of Deer Lodge, Montana) was believed by McLoughlin and Work to be one of the few remaining places where beaver trapping might be profitable. This fact had also led to a sizeable American presence in the region, chiefly trappers of the American Fur Company led by Kenneth McKenzie and James Kipp. Work and other

[2]"Simpson's Character Book." In *Hudson's Bay Miscellany, 1670-1870*, ed. Glyndwr Williams (Winnipeg: Hudson's Bay Record Society, 1975), 199.

[3]R. Harvey Fleming, *Minutes of Council, Northern Department of Rupert's Land* (Toronto: The Champlain Society, 1940), lxviii.

[4]John McLoughlin, *The Letters of John McLoughlin from Fort Vancouver to the Governor and Committee, 1825-46,* ed. E.E. Rich (Toronto: The Champlain Society,1941), Vol. 1, 228.

traders were also fully aware of the great dangers posed by the Blackfeet Indians in the same area, but Work still chose to take his daughters along on this rough trip. Several dozen others accompanied him. Simon McGillivray Jr., then in charge of Fort Nez Perces, had good reason to write in the Post Journal on September 11, 1831: "Mr. Work left us about 2PM. May success attend his enterprise—a dangerous one."[5] Work's journey was, in fact, to be the very last of the traditional Snake Brigades, with trading, rather than trapping, afterwards coming to the fore.

More information about Fort Nez Perces and the Hudson's Bay Company:

Richard S. Mackie, *Trading Beyond the Mountains: The British Fur Trade on the Pacific, 1793-1843* (Vancouver: University of British Columbia Press, 1996).

> An important synthesis, with special coverage of economics and coastal trading issues. Explains how the Hudson's Bay Company won the commercial battle for the Oregon country, only to lose the political fight.

E.E. Rich, *The History of the Hudson's Bay Company, 1670-1870. Vol. II: 1763-1870* (London: Hudson's Bay Record Society, 1959).

> A balanced and thorough history of the Bay Company. The standard source. Pages 576-600 are of special value for the Snake River country.

Theodore Stern, *Chiefs and Chief Traders: Indian Relations at Fort Nez Perces, 1818-1855.* 2 vols. (Corvallis: Oregon State University Press, 1993-1996).

> The definitive history of trading and cultural change along the Snake River, and a remarkable intellectual achievement. Based on a complete mastery of the sources.

More information about Samuel Black:

Samuel Black, *Journey of a Voyage from Rocky Mountain Portage in Peace River to the Sources of Finlay's Branch and Northwest Ward in Summer 1824* (London: Hudson's Bay Record Society, 1955).

R.M. Patterson has a fine introduction to Black's life in this book.

> Robert Watson, "Chief Factor Samuel Black," *Beaver* Outfit 259, no. 1 (June 1928): 10-12.

George Woodcock , "Samuel Black," In *Dictionary of Canadian Biography, Volume 7* (Toronto: University of Toronto Press, 1988), 78-79.

More information about John Work:

Henry Drummond Dee, "An Irishman in the fur trade: the Life and Journals of John Work," *British Columbia Historical Quarterly* 7, no. 4 (1943): 229-70.

> An important history of Work's life and travels, and a guide to his many journals

---

[5]Hudson's Bay Company. *Fort Nez Perces Post Journal* 1831. Hudson's Bay Company Archives, Provincial Archives of Manitoba, Winnipeg, hereafter cited as HBCA B/146/a/1.

that survive in the British Columbia Provincial Archives.

T.C. Elliott, ed., "Journal of John Work, June-October, 1825," *Washington Historical Quarterly* 5, no. 2 (April 1914): 83-115.

Work's journal of his horse trading at the mouth of the Clearwater River, 15-18 July 1825.

T.C. Elliott, ed., "The Journal of John Work: July 5-September 15, 1826," *Washington Historical Quarterly* 6, no. 1 (January 1915): 26-29.

Contains Work's account of his days spent trading at the mouth of the Clearwater River (27 July-31 July 1826).

E.E. Rich, "John Work," in *The Letters of John McLoughlin, First Series, 1825-38* (Toronto: The Champlain Society, 1941), 356-58.

A concise summary of Work's life by a leading scholar of Hudson's Bay history.

William R. Sampson, "John Work," in *Dictionary of Canadian Biography, Vol. 9* (Toronto: University of Toronto Press, 1976), 850-54.

A good, modern biography with many useful citations to obscure sources.

More information about Sir George Simpson:

John S. Galbraith, "Sir George Simpson," in *Dictionary of Canadian Biography, Vol. 8* (Toronto: University of Toronto Press, 1985), 812-818.

A thorough and insightful biography.

John S. Galbraith, *The Little Emperor: Governor Simpson of the Hudson's Bay Company* (Toronto: Macmillan, 1976).

Concise, scholarly, and unflattering.

Arthur S. Morton, *Sir George Simpson, Overseas Governor of the Hudson's Bay Company* (Portland: Binfords-Mort, 1944).

A friendly and well-researched biography, but written before many key records became available to scholars.

Account 6.1: Governor Simpson's views on the Nez Perce people, written at Fort Nez Perces in November of 1824 (excerpts). Source: Frederick Merk, *Fur Trade and Empire: George Simpson's Journal* (Cambridge: Harvard University Press, 1931), 53-57.

This post has been progressively improving for these last three years but the profit it yields is still very moderate....Its returns this season are estimated at 2000 Beaver got principally from a branch of the Nez Percés tribe called the Caiuses and it does not appear to me that there is a prospect of any considerable increase unless trappers are introduced as the Indians cannot be prevailed on to exert themselves in hunting; they are very independent of us requiring but few of our supplies and it is not until absolutely in need of an essential article or an article of finery such as Guns & Beads that they will take the trouble of hunting....

The Nez Percés tribe is by far the most powerful and Warlike in the Columbia and may be said to hold the Key of the River as they possess and are Masters of the country from the Okenagan down to the Chutes a distance little short of 300 miles by the course of the River. Their lands to the South border on the Snake Country and with the Snakes they are almost continually at War.... If we were in self defence to kill any of the Nez Percés not only would we have thereafter to pass through an Enemy's Country on our way back with the returns & for fresh supplies but all communication between the interior and the Coast might be cut off which would be certain ruin and destruction to the whole [Columbia] Department. I therefore consider it an object of the first importance to keep on terms of friendship with the Nez Percés and not even venture the chance of rupture with them which would involve such serious consequences....

The Nez Percés Tribe when Chief Factor McKenzie first visited them were much more bold saucy and independent than they are now and hostily inclined towards the Whites but he by extraordinary good management obtained much influence over them he however kept a Watchful Eye upon them and never allowed them to enter the Gates of his Fort except for the purposes of Trade....

Account 6.2: Excerpts from Samuel Black's 1829 Fort Nez Perces Report. Source: "Faithful to their Tribe and friends:" Samuel Black's 1829 Fort Nez Perces Report. Ed. Dennis W. Baird. (Moscow: University of Idaho Library, 2000), 27-28.

There is little Government amongst the Indians except on particular Occasions when the Chiefs take the lead form Councils &c. The Chiefs are generally Men of property which when joined w[ith] Talent give considerable influence, if any Talent The Son will Succeed the father but often some Shining Character of Talent Strength & energy will come in.

The General Character of the Indians amongst themselves in Mild & forebearing, except when agitated in a quarrel (which is not frequent) when they tear one another by the Hair strike w[t] stones &c or their Hands & w[t] fists they seldom Kill, there are some more manly & a risque of Death in a quarrel perhaps from Old Feuds; of their Virtues they are mild forebearing & politic Kind to their families faithful to their Tribe & friends never harbouring strong sentiments of Revenge but with a good Cause when they can never forget it. Industrious on a hunting excursion & Fishing Season, other times indolent, they are in general Cheerfull rather Calm but subject to lowness of Spirits by some occurrence Wounding their feelings which amongst themselves appears tender because they seldom speak ill of one another....

Indians in general are very acute & far from being dull of Comprehension very inquisitive fond of Stories from far & other places & old times very sympathetic & only Barbarians or swallow ridiculous stories because they have not been taught. They are seeking for light siting in darkness.

Account 6.3: Leading the "Interior brigade" on a trip through eastern Washington and into Montana, John Work and a large party stop at the site of Lewiston in July of 1825. Excerpts. Source: "Journal of John Work, June-October, 1825," Ed. T.C. Elliott. *Washington Historical Quarterly* 5, no. 2 (April 1914): 83-115.

Sunday 3 [July 1825]
Clear excessive warm weather though there was a little breeze of wind from the N.W. the heat was oppressive.

Continued our journey at 3 clock and encamped at the Flag River [the Palouse River] at 2. There are a few lodges of Indians here who have some horses two of which were purchased from them at 15 skins each. these are the first horses we have seen in this river.

The general appearance of the river the same as yesterday, the shores high and clearer. The general course of the [Snake] river above its entrance it takes a considerable turn to the Eastward and thus bends back to the Westward a little below the Flag River.—From this place to Spokane [House] is about 1½ days march on horseback. [Fort] Nez Perces is about the same distance.

Monday 4
Clear very warm weather, the heat was suffocating.

Expecting that the Indians would bring some more horses to trade we delayed embarking till 8 oclock when we proceeded up the river a short distance where we put ashore at an Indian lodge and bought a horse, which detained us a considerable time.—Two men rode the horses along shore—made but a short days march. The heat and plenty of musquitos which were very troublesome, allowed us to have but little sleep last night. Encamped past 6 oclock.

The current still very strong, the general course of the river from a little above Flag River a little more to the Eastward. Not many Indians on the river and but few horses to be seen.

Tuesday 5
Clear a good breeze of wind up the river which made the heat more supportable than these days past.—The current very strong, course of the river nearly E. the shores high with some times a low point, all parched up with the excessive heat, here there some bushes that are green are to be seen along the shores and in the little valleys or creeks.

Embarked at 3 oclock and encamped a little below the La Monte [i.e., Almota, the same place where Lewis and Clark camped on 11 October 1805]. Made a very short days march as we delayed a good deal along the river at Indian lodges, bought 3 young horses at 18 skins each.

The Indians inform us that a large party went off to Spokane yesterday, and that the Flat Heads and (Pendius) [the Pend d'Oreille Indians] have been with the Indians above and bought a number of horses from them.

Wed.y. 6
Stormy in the night and blowing fresh all day, Wind N.W.

In order to get some salmon from the Indians, delayed embarking till 8 oclock when we proceeded up the river, to La Monte, where we encamped at 10—This is a place of rendezvouse for the Indians but only one lodge is here at present, the others are all off in the plains digging camass. Some Indians were sent off with Tobacco for the Natives to smoke & to apprise them that we were here & would remain a few days to purchase horses from them, and that we would then proceed to the Forks [the confluence of the Snake and Clearwater Rivers] so that such of the Indians as are in that neighborhood may be there to meet us.

Thursday 7
Cloudy blowing fresh from the N.W.—pleasant cool weather.
Several Indians of different tribes arrived at our camp from whom ten horses were traded, 15 to 18 skins each. The most of these horses are young not more than 3 years old and some of them very small. It would have been desirable to get ones of larger size, but the great number required renders it necessary to take such as can be got and not be too choice.

Friday 8
Weather as yesterday.
Trade going on very slowly. A few Indians visited the camp, but only 6 horses were traded one of which was a wild one and was immediately killed for the people. The Natives seem not eager to part with their horses.—Generally young small ones are offered for sale, yet some of those purchased today are good stout horses.—The articles generally paid for a horse are a blanket, 3 pt, 6 Skins, 4 or 5 skins, 1 yd. each of green beads, a few skins of ammunition, a skin of Tobacco, a knife, and sometimes, Buttons and Rings, a skin or two.

Satd.y. 9
Cloudy Warm weather. Wind variable, not blowing so much as these days past.
A few more Indians visited us but only 4 horses were traded & two of those are young ones not broke in. We learns from the Ind.s. that the natives above are collecting on the River to meet us.
The Indians at our camp occupy the most of their time gambling. The River is falling very fast, the water is lowered four to 5 feet perpendicular since it has been at its height this season.

Sunday 10 [July 1825]
Though a fresh breeze from the Eastward the weather was very warm and sultry.
In expectation that the Indians would trade some more horses we delayed embarking till one oclock when we proceeded up the River, seeing that nothing further was to be done. Stopped at the Indian lodges as we passed and bought two unbroken in young horses one of which a beautiful animal, lept so when we was haltered & the man not managing him properly that he tumbled on his head & broke his neck.
The current continues very strong the course of the River from E. to S.E. The appearance of the country continues much the same, the bank very high & mostly rocky, the smooth summits & sides of the hills clothed with dry grass, burnt up with the heat, here and there along the water edge and in some of the deep valleys or coves tufts of willow and poplars, and a few bushes of other kinds. Though the hills and valleys, except on the faces of the steep rocks are well clothed with

vegetation nearly dried up, the country has altogether a barren appearance.

The Indians live (in) sort of houses or lodges constructed of drift wood split & set on end, they are generally high and very large and inhabited by a great many Indians. I counted upwards of fifty at one house the dimensions of which were 40 yards long and 10 wide. These houses are generally high and flat roofed, the one side is occupied by the inhabitants who sit and sleep on the ground, and the other side is appropriated for drying fish which are hung up generally in two tiers the one above the other the lower ones so near the ground that one has to stoop to get under them.—The air has a free circulation through these habitations from the openness of their walls, which makes them cool & comfortable when there is the least air of wind, but in case of rain, from the openness of the roof, very little would be excluded. However, this is an article that seldom troubles them.

The Natives along the River now are generally employed curing salmon and collecting camass.

Monday 11
Cloudy but occasionally very warm. Wind Easterly.

Waiting till the Indians would bring us some horses to trade deterred us from embarking till 8 clock when seeing that only one horses could be traded, we proceeded up the river and as usual stopped to smoke at most of the lodges which we passed which made our progress very slow, however only one horse was purchased till we encamped in the evening when four more were traded, making in all six today.

The appearance of the River and country much the same as yesterday. The course from E. to S. E. The hills along shore appear less elevated towards evening. The Indians near whom we are encamped offered a sturgeon for sale, which shows that these fish ascend this high.

Tuesday 12 [July 1825]
Cloudy blowing fresh from the Westward.

The Indians traded two more Horses which detained us till after breakfast when we proceeded up the River till 11 oclock when we encamped a little below the Forks at the lodge of an Ind. Called Charly where a good many Indians are expected to assemble [they are at Red Wolf Crossing, on the Snake River]. About 70 men collected to smoke in the course of the afternoon. Two horses were traded from them which makes 4 today.

Charly is considered to have a good deal of influence among the natives. A present was therefore made to him and he afterward harangued the Indians from which good effects are expected tomorrow.

Wed.y. 13
Though cloudy part of the day, the weather was very warm and sultry.

A brisk trade of horses commenced in the morning and 15 were purchased during the day, the greater part of which were bought before breakfast. They are much finer horses and the prices rather lower than those procured below.—Horses are more numerous and much better here than in the lower part of the river.— There were not so many Indians with us today as yesterday, but they had more horses. The Indians who visit us today are of four different tribes, Chapoples or Nezperces, Pelooshis [Palouse], Carooris [Cayuse] and Wallawallas. They are very peaceable but a good deal of Tobacco is required to keep them smoking.—

They amuse themselves gambling in the evening they had a horse race.

In the course of the day a message was received from some Indians further up the river, requesting us to go to their place, and more horses would be procured. It seems a kind of jealousy exists among the natives and the one party does not wish to sell their horses at the camp of the other, or that they wish to have the honour of being visited at their own camp.

Thursd.y. 14

Very little Wind, excessively warm, where we are encamped on the stony sandy beach we are literally next to be roasted.

The trade did not go on so briskly as yesterday, only 8 horses were bought, one of which was an unbroken in lame mare to kill, as she was fit for nothing else.

Friday 15

Sometimes a little breeze of wind from the S.E. yet is was clear and so sultry that the heat was oppresive.

Embarked at half past 5 oclock proceeded up the river and in 2 hours arrived at the Forks [at the confluence of the Clearwater and Snake Rivers] and encamped on the E. side of the North branch where a few Indians are encamped shortly after we arrived about 40 of them with the old chief Cut Nose at their head visited us in form, smoked, and were presented with about 3 inches of tobacco each. A trade of horses was immediately commenced and 8 very good ones were soon bought from them, though these people have plenty of horses yet they say they have none, they mean probably that they can spare. This is not Cut Nose's camp, it is further up this branch [i.e., further up the Clearwater].

In the afternoon a party of upwards of 100 men and a good many women on horseback with the son of broken or cut arm, as chief at their head, arrived down the S. branch. the Chief immediately on his arrival presented a horse to Mr. [J.W.] Dease, and received a gun, 6 yds. Of Beads & Tobacco and ammunition 27 skins as a present in return. After smoaking and getting about 3 Inches of Tobacco for each of his people, a trade for horses was opened and 5 very good ones were soon bought which with the one presented and the eight bought in the forenoon make 14 that have been procured to day. These are the best horses we have got yet, they are 18 to 20 skins each.

There is little short of 200 Indians about our camp now, several of those from below accompany us as we advance up, and those encamped here with the band that arrived from the S. branch make about the above number. they are very quiet and peaceable so far.

The country about the Forks is flatter and the hills not so abrupt as farther down. The South branch [i.e., the main Snake River upstream from the site of Lewiston] falls in from the Southward, and the North one from the S.W. the waters of these latter are quite clear, while those of the other are white and muddy the North branch seems not so large as the other, nor does not discharge such a body of water. It may be about 250 to 300 yards wide.

Charlie the chief who accompanied us from our last encampment crossed the river with a horse, and in swimming back either was seized or pretended to be seized with a cramp & called out for assistance. Some of the Indians brought him ashore, where he became very ill and got little better, though at his own request he got 2 or 3 drams, untill evening when he thought he would be the better of an airing and got the men to paddle him in a boat up and down the river and sing at the same time, which must considerably contribute, no doubt, to the recovery of his health.—This man may have some influence among the Indians at least to do injury, but he is undoubtedly an artful knave.

Saturday 16
Cloudy, a storm of thunder with squalls of wind from the Westward and a little rain in the afternoon, last night there was a violent storm of thunder & a great deal of lightening, with squalls of wind and some rain.

A Brisk trade commenced in the morning and 19 horses were bought during the day, they are generally good ones and cost mostly 20 skins each.

At noon Tawerishewa[6] arrived at the head of a troup of 64 men and several women with plenty of horses from up the North branch. After smoking and each of his people being presented a piece of Tobacco he presented fine horses to Mr. Dease and received a present of different articles to the amount of 32 skins in return.—The other chief now here seems not to be fond of this man on account of his being a doctor or medicine chief.

On account of our articles of trade falling short we will not be able to answer these people's expectations in the way of Trade.

Sunday 17 [July 1825]
Cloudy, gusts of wind from the Westward. A heavy thunder storm with strong wind and some rain in the afternoon.

Commenced trading after breakfast & bought horses during the day, four horses were presented during the day by principal men of (Tawerishewa's) band, but they were dearer than if they had been traded on account of the quantity of articles that had to be presented in return. The most of the horses purchased today are very fine ones and cost mostly 20 skins each.

Our articles of trade got short or we would have got more horses. Green Beads, Tobacco and blankets are entirely gone, several blankets were borrowed from the men. The last band of Indians that arrived were considerably disappointed by these articles being nearly gone when they came.

There are about our camp near 250 or 300 Indians. they are very quiet and give us very little trouble, they occasionally get a little tobacco to smoak. They pass the greater part of their time gambling, horseracing & foot racing.

We have traded 112 horses, 5 of which have been killed [to eat]. A fine young white one was drowned crossing the river today.

Monday 18
Cloudy pleasant weather not too warm. Wind Westerly.

Our trade being finished and everything ready, we took leave of our friendly Indians and I and six men and an Indian Charlie as a guide, set out with 106 horses across land to Spokane at ½ past 8 o'clock. two of the horses which were traded had got lame and were not able to start.—We were detained two hours waiting for Charlie who delayed after us to make some arrangements with his family. On account of this delay and not being able to drive quick as one of the

---

[6]This name carries many associations with the location of Orofino: Tewéepuu (Orofino people), Téewe (village site at the mouth of Orofino Creek). It is also similar to the idea of people who wear animal horns (Tewiísnim táaqmaat).

finest horses in the band (Mr. Dease's) being lame which I did not perceive till after we were off, we made but a short days' march.

We passed through a fine country the course from N. to N.W. On leaving the river ranges of high hills had to be ascended [Lewiston Hill and the rolling Palouse region beyond], the country then was not level but a continual succession of little rising hills or hummocks and valleys destitute of trees or bushes except along the margins of little brooks, but pretty well clothed with grass and other plants though rather dried and parched, in some of the valleys along little rivers there are a few trees and bushes besides different plants of an uncommonly luxuriant growth....

Account 6.4: John Work visits the Clearwater in the summer of 1826, accompanied by a very large party which included botanist David Douglas. Source: "The Journal of John Work, July 5—September 15, 1826," Ed. T.C. Elliott, *Washington Historical Quarterly* 6, no. 1 (January 1915): 26-49.

Friday 14 [July 1826]
Embarked early and arrived at Ft. Nezperces about 1 o'clock. Sail wind part of the day. The weather very warm. The cargoes are separated, and that of Nezperces delivered.

Satd.y. 15
The weather very warm, though stormy.

It was expected that a number of horses that are required could be procured from the Indians at Nezperces, but after different councils, and consultations and speeches on both sides it turned out that a promise had been made to the Nezperces Indians to go and trade on their lands which if not fulfilled would disoblige them and make them less inclined to trade.

Sunday 16
Stormy but warm weather.

The forepart of the day occupied with more councils and making presents to the Indians as return for some horses which they had presented before. 7 or 8 horses were afterwards traded.—It appeared however that the number required could not be got in time, and the trading trip up Nezperces River [the lower Snake River] was determined on.

(Learned) that the F.[lat] Head trade would not suffer but little as possible by the late arrival of boats at Colville, Mr. [William] Kittson with the Colville and Mountain boats is to proceed at once to Colville while I am to accompany the trading party and after completing the trade to accompany the party across land and proceed to Colville where I expect to arrive as soon as the boats. By this method no time will be lost whereas had all the Colville men gone to the horse trade the Flat Head summer trade would have been lost as it is it will be too late but it cannot be helped.

Monday 17
Stormy in the night and blowing fresh during the day but nevertheless warm.

The outfit for the horse trade was packed up in the morning and about 3 o'clock in the afternoon the party consisting of Mr. A[rchibald] McDonald, J[ames] Douglas, F. Annance and myself, an interpreter [Jean Toupin, who along with Pierre Dorion, had come west with the overland expedition of the Pacific Fur

Company to Astoria] and 28 men and the Indian chief Charlie embarked in two boats and proceeded till a short way up the Nezperces [Snake] River where we encamped for the night. Bought two or three pieces of salmon from the Indians.—I am directed if possible to purchase at least 60-70 horses, more if possible, 20 of them are for Ft. Colville, the others to go to Okanogan. Mr. D. Douglas accompanies us to make collections of plants [See chapter seven].

Tuesday 18
Weather warm but fine breezes.
Continued our journey before sunrise, and had a good sail wind all day. Camped at night a considerable distance below Flag [Palouse] River. The current very strong and the water high, although it has fallen about 8 feet since its greatest height this season. Several Indian lodges along the river bought a few pieces of fish and half dry salmon. Salmon are very dear here. The Indians have few to spare.

Wedy 19th
Very warm sultry weather no wind.
Embarked early, passed the Flag River about 3 o'clock and encamped late in the evening a good way above it.—Got very few salmon though we saw a good many Indians, Salmon is very scarce. Traded a small sturgeon.—were detained some time by the Indians offering horses for sale but they would not accept the prices offered. A party of them accompany us on horse back along shore.

Thursday 20 [July 1826]
Clear very warm weather very little wind.
Proceeded on our journey early in the morning and encamped early in the evening at a camp of the Pelushes, Colatouche chief, in expectation of buying some horses, two were offered for sale, but the prices asked were far too high indeed the Indians appear not to be very fond of parting with them.—Salmon are also very (dear) we got a few pieces of dry and half dry. Since we left the Fort we have not got in one day sufficiency for a day's rations for the people. however what little we do get still saves a little corn.

Friday 21
Very warm sultry weather. At noon the thermometer in the shade was 94°, and 95° shortly afterwards.
We were detained waiting for the Indians who were seeking some horses to trade, but when they arrived with them, only one small paltry thing was offered and the price demanded could not be given, so after losing all our morning we continued our route not in the best humor, Passed several lodges and purchased a sufficiency of fresh salmon for nearly a days (living) for the people, besides some dry ones to serve the party going overland with the horses.—Encamped in the evening a little above Le Monte [Almota], (which we passed about 4 oclock,) at an Indian camp where some horses (we) expected will be got, but we will probably be detained part of the day tomorrow.—Numbers of the Indians some of whom refused the prices offered them below are accompanying us along shore with their horses.—

Satd.y. 22
Light clouds, very warm, though a little breeze of wind.

Did not move camp today, They were off in the forepart of the day collecting their horses, but they would not trade till the afternoon, when 8 horses were purchased from them at from 14 to 19 skins each. They were all young horses two of them just * but not well broke in. They are to trade three more horses tomorrow morning. Traded 13 fresh salmon which made * a days rations for the people.— The tardiness of the Indians trading their horses is really vexing, they are not keen about trading.

Sunday 23
Oppressively warm weather. Thermometer 100° in the shade at noon.

We were detained till near evening for the Indians who were off seeking their horses, when they returned they were traded, and we struck our tents and proceeded up the river, and stopped at anoth[er] lodge for a considerable time and traded a good a good horse, another was offered but he was too small and we would not take him. We then continued up the river and encamped at another lodge where the Indians promise to sell us some horses tomorrow.—The Indians seem very indifferent about trading their horses, it is really provoking to be detained so long with them.—especially when so little time is to spare.—We have now 12 horses 8 yesterday and 4 today, 11 of which we traded from the Dartry band.

Monday 24 [July 1826]
Sultry warm weather.

Did not move untill afternoon as we waited till the Indians collected their horses when we bought four one of which a small unbroke in one was killed.—In the evening proceeded up the river to another Indian camp and stopped for the night as some horses are expected in the morning.—

Tuesday 25
A breeze of wind the weather cooler than these days past. Bought two horses from the Indians in the morning and started after breakfast and stopped at different lodges as we passed and bought four more horses, making 6 today, all pretty good at 18 to 19 skins each. The Indians have a good many horses but they are not eager to part with them.—Salmon very scarce, we hardly get what fresh ones serve the mess.

Wedy 26
Weather pleasant.

Continued our rout after breakfast, and arrived at Charlie's lodge [Red Wolf Crossing] a little before the forks in the evening. Traded two horses during the day.—

Thursday 27
A little breeze of wind pleasant weather.—

Traded 8 horses at Charlies lodge and in the evening came to the Forks [the confluence of the Clearwater and Snake Rivers] where we found upwards of 200 Indians (men), and two principal chiefs Alunn and Towishpal, Gave the chiefs and some of the principal men a dram of mixed liquor and a smok in the hut the others got a smok and a little tobacco out of doors, Towishpal and another principal man cut noses both presented two horses immediately on our arrival.—We are under the necessity of accepting their presents in order to please the chiefs though we have to give a present in return which makes the horses much dearer in general than were we to trade them—The Indians have been assembled for some days and are now rather short of provisions.

Friday 28
Warm weather, a little wind afterward.

No trade was made untill after breakfast, when the Indians began to come with horses and some chiefs presented more horses which were paid for at a dearer rate than usual in order to encourage the others, a brisk trade was commenced about 10 oclock and continued untill 4 oclock. 37 horses were traded one of which was killed. The price was generally 19 or 20 skins few exceeding 20. They were mostly fine horses. Our blankets and beads are getting short, which was the cause of the trade getting slack towards evening. Blue cloth does not take well with them.

Saturday 29
Pretty cool pleasant weather a shower in the night.

Not having the proper articles blankets and beads in plenty the trade went on but slowly, only six horses were traded, the Indians are doubtless debarred from trading a little by a dance which is stirred up by a Schulas [Cayuse?] chief who arrived yesterday with [illegible]. However we are promised a few horses tomorrow, when we shall complete our trade and be ready to start the day following.—

Sunday 30
Warm weather rather sultry.

Early this morning a quarrel took place between the Interpreter [Jean Toupin] and the Indian chief Charlie. It appears that an Indian woman who passed for a medical character, had been looking at one of the mens hands which was sore and although she exercised none of her skill either in the application or otherwise yet she came to demand payment and applied to the Interpreter who refused her. Charlie interfered when some words took place and the Interpreter was called a dog, he applied the same epithet to Charlie who took up his gun and gave the other a blow, a scuffle ensued, and the noise was the first intelligence I had of the affray, when I ran out and found them wrestling in the other tent and the Indian getting the better, they were separated and the Indian again flew to his gun which was taken from him several Indians had collected by this time, Charlie was now asked was this conduct a return for all the kindness and attention that had been shown him, he replied that he had been called a dog, and that he could not bear the insult, he remained sulky and took up another gun which was also taken from him, an Indian then took him away, Shortly a message came for a yard of tobacco for the Indians to smok and that their hearts would be good. Shortly after another message came for 2 fathoms more and 20 balls and powder, this was refused and word sent to the chief that we wished to have an interview with them Toupe [Toupin] came, but Charlie came accompanied by the whole of the Indians several of them armed and took his station a short distance from the tent where they formed a circle round us. He was black with rage. We immediately went up to him and asked what he meant, and was he not ashamed to begin a quarrel in such a manner about an old woman. After some time sulky silence he replied that his heart was bad towards nobody but Toupie, and that he blamed him for not getting a better price for their horses, he was immediately informed that the accusation was false, that Toupe did nothing but what we desired him, they were also made to understand that, it was to trade horses and not to fight that we came there, but that if no better would do we would fight also and that as Toupe was under our protection and in fact one of ourselves any insult offered him would be offered to us and would be resented.—A demand was again made for tobacco and that then all would be well and that the horse trade would immediately commence. As we were situated, with very little ammunition, ourselves on one side of the river and the horses with part of the men on the opposite side, two of the horses astray among those of the Indians, and two others already paid for not received, and also the great risk we ran of having the others stolen, it was considered advisable to comply with their request except the ammunition, rather than get into a quarrel as we had much to lose and little to gain. The tobacco was accordingly delivered the whole of the Indians smoked and then dispersed.—Charlie is certainly a notorious scoundrel and I consider the original of this quarrel as only a pretext. He sold a horse yesterday and was paid the price agreed upon, but he afterwards asked a blanket more which was refused, this I conceive was in a great measure the cause of the dispute, and the poor Interpreter was the only one he would venture to begin with. He has however been very useful to us since the trade commenced haranguing the Indians to trade their horses, and ever since the dispute he has been again telling them to trade more.—The other chiefs and principal men except (Touispel) evidently wished to make the most of the affair and get as much as they could by it, Old Alumie and his men are particular. however they were disappointed as they only got 3 yds. tobacco and a few small pieces more besides the yard first sent them, and even this was given with reluctance, but we could not well do otherwise. Traded five more horses which finished our goods, found the two that were astray and received the two we had paid the Indians for and crossed the river to where the horses are in the afternoon—Our whole trade amounts to 79 horses, two of which have been killed.

The Indian chiefs crossed to pay us a visit in the evening, and smoked. They seem to regret what has taken place, Charlie himself is ashamed that he should have quarreled about such a trifle. During the dispute, the Indians were all threatening to take back the horses.—

A few young men arrived in the evening from the buffalo [from hunting buffalo in Montana], from them it was heard that the F Heads are now on their way to meet us to trade. Peace is again made between them and the Peegans [Piegans].

Monday 31st.
Pleasant cool weather.
Having everything in readiness, the horses that are for different places pointed out, after an early breakfast Messrs F McDonald, J. Douglas and myself accompanied by six men set out overland [for Spokane] with the horses 79 in number including 2 bought a few days ago from W. Walla by Mr F. McDonald, we encamped in the evening a short distance 15 or 20 miles from flag River [near what is now Uniontown?]. Mr. D. Douglas accompanied us on his botanical pursuits.—Mr A. McDonald took his departure for W. Walla with the two boats and the rest of the men at the same time we came of—The Indians and us were good friends when we parted.

Account 6.5: John Work and the Snake Brigade cross the Bitterroots in 1831. Source: British Columbia Archives, John Work Journals, A/B/40/W89.10A. Published here with the permission of the British Columbia Archives.

Friday, September 16. Moved five or six miles up the river, and crossed it a little below the fork of the Snake River and Salmon River [probably the junction of the Snake and Clearwater Rivers]. We got two canoes from the Inds, yet it was near night when the baggage was all across. Some Indians encamped with us. Some horses were bought from them, but the people are such fools that they outbid each other and gave double the price they ought for a horse.

Saturday, September 17. Marched two and one-half hours, eight miles, up the [Clearwater] river to above the forks where we encamped to allow our horses to feed a little as they have had very little these last two nights. Several Indians joined us in the evening.

Sunday, September 18. There being excellent grazing here for the horses we did not move camp in order to allow them to feed. Some more Indians joined us. They had a religious dance. Some horses were traded from them, and others exchanged. One of them made a present of one, and received a present to the value in return.

Monday, September 19. Marched four hours. twelve miles E.N.E. up the river, the road in places stony, but otherwise good.

Tuesday, September 20. Continued our route up the river three hours, ten miles E.N.E. The road the same as yesterday, some stony spots. We encamped in the evening near the chief Sowites [this word is unclear; may also be "Towshen"] lodge. Some rain in the evening.

Wednesday, September 21. Heavy rain in the nights and forepart of the day, fine weather afternoon.

The unfavorable weather deterred us from moving camp in the morning. Afterwards we did not start on account of the illness of one of Satrouxs [Soteaux'] little daughters, who is dieng. The chief Towishen [illegible] made us a present of a Moose for the people to eat.

Thursday, September 22. Fine weather. Continued our route three hours, E.N. up the river. A good deal of the road very stony, and bad for the horses feet. We were recommended by some of the Indians to take the road on the opposite side of the river as there were less stones. They advised us to keep to the N. side as it was shorter and leveller. There is all along good grazing for the horses.

Friday, September 23. Stormy, raw, cold weather in the morning, fine afterwards.

Proceeded three and three-fourths hours, eleven miles E.N.E. up the river. The country here becomes more hilly, and the hills approaching close to the river on both sides [they are approaching the site of Orofino]. Our road the most of the day along the brow of the hill, and was good except a short piece which was stony in the morning.

Saturday, September 24. Cold in the morning, but fine weather afterwards.

Continued our journey one and one-half hours, five miles up the river to a fork [the mouth of the Clearwater River's North Fork] which falls in from the northward, where we encamped with some Indians as it would have been too long to go on to another encampment [if on the south bank, they would have spent the night at

Figure 4. John Work

Lewis and Clark's Canoe Camp]. There is plenty of grass for the horses.

Sunday, September 25. Continued our journey up the river to where the road leaves the river [probably at Jim Ford Creek; Lewis and Clark came down this creek on their way to Canoe Camp] to strike into the country to Camass Plain [the Weippe Prairie]. The country hilly and partially wooded.

Monday, September 26. Fine weather, but cooler in the morning.

Quitted the river and proceeded across the country five hours, twenty miles E.N.E. to Camass Plains. The road [i.e. the trail along Jim Ford Creek leading to near modern day Weippe] through a woody country, very hilly in the morning but pretty level afterwards. Found some Indians here. It is a great place for collecting camass.

Tuesday, September 27. Sharp frost in the night, and cooler in the morning, fine weather during the day.

Did not raise camp in order to allow the horses to feed before taking the summits [of the Bitterroot Range, now clearly visible to the east]. Some horses were traded from the Indians, and some exchanged. It is very difficult to effect any bargains with them.

Wednesday, September 28. Sharp frost in the night, fine weather afterwards [the party is now at an elevation of about 3000 feet].

Proceeded on our journey five and one-half hours, eighteen miles N.N.E. to a little plain [near or at Musselshell Meadow], the greater part of the way through very thick woods and difficult road though well frequented.

Thursday, September 29. Frost in the morning, fine weather afterwards. Did not raise camp owing to one of Soteaux' children, a little girl, who has been some time ailing dieng this morning.

Friday, September 30. Fog and frost in the morning, fine weather afterwards. Proceeded on our journey eight hours, twenty-four miles N.N.E. through continual thick woods and up several steep hills, and encamped in a valley, where there is very little grass for the horses, and very little water [Work appears to have strayed somewhat to the north of the traditional route of the Lolo Trail].

Friday, September 30 [date duplicated in the original]. Began to rain a little before daylight, and rained all day. In the evening a great deal of thunder with very heavy rain and hail.

Raised camp and moved one and one-half hours, four miles N.N.E. to a little valley where there is a little grass for the horses. The country here has been burnt and is pretty bare of wood.

Saturday, October 1. Began to snow in the night, and snowed all day. The bad weather deterred us from raising camp. M. Plant lost a colt yesterday.

Sunday, October 2. Some snow in the morning. Cold weather, the snow thawing. Continued our journey eight and one-half hours, twenty-four miles N.N.E. over very steep hills and through thick wood, and encamped later in the evening in a deep valley with little or no grass and & nothing but branches and leaves for our horses to feed upon [possibly in upper Cayuse Creek]. We let them loose in the night and expect we will be able to find them in the morning as they can be traced in the Snow. Our Indian guides returned for us this morning, we have now fallen on the great road [the Lolo Trail, which lay a short distance to the south]. There is a better place for encamping on the hill behind us, but we did not know it. Two horses gave up on the way. [several unclear words follow]. The snow on the hills is about nine inches deep. Both people & horses much fatigued, and completely drenched on arrival at the camp. The soft melting snow falling off the trees wet everything.

Monday, October 3. Fair weather till towards evening when it began to snow.

Continued our journey four and one-half hours, N.N.E., seventeen miles over steep hills, through thick woods, and encamped later in the evening on a hill the side of which was clear of woods, and where we had the satisfaction to find a good deal of grass for our horses, though it is covered with snow [probably Bald Mountain near Castle Butte]. By daylight all hands were on the move seeking the horses, the most of them were found sooner than expected (some) of them could not be found during the day though the people went in search of them till late, but the one trusted to the other, and I think did not seek effectually for them.

Tuesday, October 4. Snowed thick nearly all day [elevation here is about 6500 feet], the snow melting a little.

Did not raise camp on account of the bad weather, and to allow people to seek the stray horses, they were off in quest of them all day, three of them were found. There are still missing 7. viz 1 belonging to C. Plante[7], 1 to Louis Boisvert, 1 A. Letendre, 1 A. Finlay, 1 J. Rocquebin, 1 R. Coo & a mule of the Coy's

Wednesday, October 5. Snowed most part of the day, the snow melting as it falls.

Continued our route five hours 15 miles N.N.E. through thick woods and over some hills, one very steep:- and encamped later in a small swamp with scarcely any grass, and that little covered with snow, so that the poor, starving horses could not get at it. Owing to the snow falling and the bad weather the people & horses much fatigued. A dismal encampment.

Thursday, October 6. Snowed the most of the day.

It was late before the horses were found, & some of them not till the evening. We nevertheless raised camp and marched four and one-half hours, twelve miles N.N.E. over a hilly country thickly wooded, and encamped in the evening on the side of a hill clear of woods, and very little snow with a little grass, and herbage scattered thickly over it. Our poor horses will be able to find a little. A few lodges of the people remained behind to seek the stray horses and some of them who had found their horses thought the weather too bad to march . A horse, belonging to G. Paus [unclear; perhaps "Paris"], died at the encampment. Some more horses gave up on the way.

Friday, October 7. Snowed thick, and cold weather the most of the day.

Proceeded on our journey five and one-half hours, fifteen miles, and encamped where there is a little feeding for the horses on the declivity of a hill where there is a little snow and pretty clear of wood . The people who remained behind came up with the camp. They found all the horses that were astray yesterday, but two cannot be found today one of J. Desland & 1 of T. Tewatcon. Two of the men, J. Louis and J. Rocquebin who went back to our station of the 1st in quest of stray horses, but saw nothing of them. The snow on the mountains there is nearly 2 feet deep, it was with difficulty they could keep the track. We have not yet had a snow a foot deep. The road today lay over hills, one of them very

---

[7]A brother of Antoine Plante, who, in 1852, settled in the Spokane River Valley and operated an important ferry in what is now the town of Opportunity. Both Plantes were with Work in 1831.

steep, and the road embarrassed with fallen wood.

Saturday, October 8. Fair weather.

Continued our journey five and one-half hours, fifteen miles over a succession of hills and down a very steep bank to the river [the Crooked Fork, somewhere above the Powell Ranger Station], which we left on the (25) September. Here we stopped for the night though we are among the woods, and scarcely any grass for the horses, but we apprehend several of the horses would not be able to get to a little station ahead, but we do not know how far. Here we have no snow. Two horses one of Plant & 1 of Gilbert were lost [blank] gave up by the way. Two lodges Soteaux & C. Groslin pushed on ahead.

Sunday, October 9. Rained in the night and forepart of the day.

Raised camp, and marched two and one-half hours, eight miles up a steep, long hill to a small creek, with some swampy clear ground on its banks where there is a good deal of good grass for the horses, of which they are in much need [the location of this camp is very unclear, but they may be in upper Pack Creek, at or near Lolo Pass]. Some of the people remained behind to allow the horses to feed and repose. They said they found a little grass among the hills.

Monday, October 10. Rained and a little snow fell in the night and forepart of the day.

The bad weather deterred us from raising camp, moreover, our horses are in much need of feeding and this is a good place. Some of the people who were behind came up, some remain behind still.

Tuesday, October 11. Very heavy rain all day.

On account of the bad weather we did not raise camp. Though the horses have a good feeding this continual rain is much against them, & a great many of them are very lean.

Wednesday, October 12. Continual rain and sleet in the night and all day.

Did not raise camp. The rest of the people who remained behind came up, they are completely drenched.

Thursday, October 13. Overcast, fair weather forepart of the day, rain in the evening.

Raised camp and proceeded three and one-half hours, eleven miles N. to a small plain at hot spring on Loloo's River [Lolo Hot Springs, which is located about eight miles north of Lolo Pass along Lolo Creek]. The road today not hilly but very much embarrassed with fallen wood and fatiguing on the horses. Three gave up by the way, and three were lost at the encampment and could not be found, and one lost on the road. The people who are ahead killed fourteen beaver.

Friday, October 14. Light rain in the morning, it then faired a little, but the rain soon came on again and continued all day.

Raised camp and marched five and one-half hours, fifteen miles N. [i.e. east] to a little fork which falls in from the westward [probably Grave Creek]. The road very hilly and slippery and miry, and exceedingly fatiguing both on the horses and people. Some of the horses gave up on the way owing to the bad road and bad weather. This was a most harrassing day both on the men & horses. Some of the people were out hunting but without success. There are a few chivereau [deer] about this plain. Pichette killed a bear.

Saturday, October 15. Overcast, showry weather.

Did not raise camp in order to allow the horses to repose a little and feed after the hard days work yesterday, they are much fatigued. Those that were left behind yesterday were brought up to the camp this morning. Several of the people out hunting. Soteaux killed 2 deer, Gardipie, 1 deer, T. Smith 2 and C. Groslin 1 sheep.

Sunday, October 16. Clear fine sunny weather.

Did not raise camp in order to allow the horses to feed as there [is] pretty good grass here, and as we must soon begin night guard. It was, moreover generally necessary to dry our things, they were nearly rotten. Some of the horses which were left behind were brought up. A part of the people raised camp and moved a short encampment farther on. Some of the people were out hunting.

Monday, October 17. Cloudy, showery weather.

Raised camp and proceeded three hours, nine miles E.N.E. [down Lolo Creek] to a nice plain where there is a good feeding for the horses. The men ahead killed [blank] beaver & 1 elk & 2 bear.

Tuesday, October 18. Cloudy, showery in the afternoon.

Continued our journey six hours, E.N.E. twelve miles down the river to Bitter root River [to Traveler's Rest, where Lewis and Clark began their trip across Bitterroots], the road good. Here we commenced night guarding on our horses. Some of the people out hunting, but with little success [From here Work's party turned north toward the site of Missoula, and then east up the Clark Fork toward Deer Lodge].

Editors' note:

It turned out that Work and his employers had good reasons to be worried about this trip to the Deer Lodge country. From various causes, eight of his men were killed, and Work himself was wounded in an attack by Blackfeet Indians. By the time he and his party reached Fort Nez Perces in July of 1832, 41 of his horses had been lost in the Bitterroots and another 107 stolen, lost, or eaten elsewhere. While 309 buffalo were killed on the trip, the profits, as expected, were very small.

Back at Fort Vancouver in August, he told his old friend Edward Ermatinger: "This last [trip] my friend has been a severe duty on me, all my perseverance and fortitude were scarcely sufficient to bear up against the danger, misery, and consequent anxiety to which I was exposed." Work felt that he was "blessed with the possession of my scalp which is rather more than I had reason to expect."[8]

---

[8]As quoted in Lois H. McDonald, ed., *Fur Trade Letters of Francis Ermatinger Written to his Brother Edward* (Glendale, CA: Arthur H. Clark, 1980), 151 and 156. The original correspondence is chiefly in the British Columbia Provincial Archives.

New scholarship has provided some valuable insights into the goals of the Hudson's Bay Company in the Columbia. See Jennifer Ott, "Ruining the Rivers in the Snake Country: The Hudson's Bay Company's Fur Desert Policy," *Oregon Historical Quarterly* 104, no. 2 (Summer 2003): 166-195.

7

Botanist David Douglas visits the Clearwater in 1826

The young Scottish botanist, David Douglas, arrived by sea at the mouth of the Columbia in April of 1825, to begin what proved to be two years of extensive botanical research in the Columbia Valley. He had been sent into the commercial domain of the Hudson's Bay Company, uninvited and unexpected, by the Royal Horticultural Society. Operating on minimal funds and often with the generous help of John Work and Dr. John McLoughlin of the Bay Company, Douglas was able to travel over the next two years into the Blue Mountains of eastern Oregon, along much of the lower Clearwater, and probably south to the vicinity of what came to be called Craig Mountain. His work, which a leading scholar has described as being in the broad tradition of "imperial botany," can be best understood today as an element of a long tradition of efforts by various royal institutions to learn more of the world.[1]

During much of 1825 Douglas inventoried plants and traveled the region around Fort Vancouver, but managed also to reach Celilo Falls on the Columbia and to see much of the Willamette River valley. After a tough winter at Fort Vancouver, he spent most of the Spring of 1826 at Walla Walla (Fort Nez Perces), and along the Spokane and Okanogan Rivers, meeting many important Hudson's Bay Company traders in the process. In June, he made two long trips into the Blue Mountains south of Walla Walla. In mid-July he was back at Fort Nez Perces, where he joined John Work on his trip to trade horses on the lower Clearwater (see previous chapter).

Douglas returned to the Columbia River after a short trip back to England and also did some botanizing in California. After a brief visit to the Blue Mountains, he journeyed to Hawaii. In July of 1834 he apparently fell into a pit used to trap animals, and was killed. He was ultimately buried on Oahu.

Douglas has left us two differing accounts of his trip to the Clearwater. The most complete account appears here, a version not published until 1914.

---

[1] John Gascoigne, *Science in the Service of Empire* (Cambridge: Cambridge University Press, 1998), 162.

More information about David Douglas:

George Barnston, "Abridged Sketch of the Life of Mr. David Douglas," *Canadian Naturalist and Geologist* 5 (1860): 120-32, 200-08, and 329-49.

An important account written by a friend and contemporary.

John Davies, *Douglas of the Forests* (Seattle: University of Washington Press, 1980).

A "severely" edited version of the Journals written by Douglas.

Peter Fish, "Western Wanderings: Our Man on the Trail of David Douglas," *Sunset* 201, no. 5 (November 1998): 14-16.

An interesting account of Douglas sites and monuments in Hawaii.

Athelstan George Harvey, *Douglas of the Fir* (Cambridge: Harvard University Press, 1947).

A scholarly, reliable, and well-written biography. Fully documented.

Susan Delano McKelvey, "Douglas Makes His First Visit to the Northwest Coast of America and Then Spends Two Years in England," in *Botanical Exploration of The Trans-Mississippi West, 1790-1850* (Jamaica Plain, Mass.: Arnold Arboretum of Harvard University, 1955), 299-341.

A very scholarly and thorough guide to the botanical discoveries made by Douglas in 1825-26.

William Morwood, *Traveler in a Vanished Landscape: The Life and Times of David Douglas* (New York: Clarkson Potter, 1973).

An imaginative and novelistic account of Douglas' life.

F.G. Young, ed., "Literary Remains of David Douglas, Botanist of the Oregon Country," *Oregon Historical Quarterly* 5 (1904): 215-71 and 325-69.

A reprint of the original prepared by Dr. William Hooker and published in *Companion to the Botanical Magazine* 2 (1836).

Account 7.1: Excerpts from the account Douglas wrote of his visit to the upper Columbia in 1826. Source: David Douglas, *Journal Kept by David Douglas During His Travels in North America, 1823-1827* (London: Wesley & Son, 1914), 200-202.

Douglas is writing on 24 July 1826 while camped on the Snake River, just below the mouth of the Clearwater.

Salmon are caught in the river and in some of its branches near the Rocky Mountains, but by no means so plentiful as in the Columbia nor of such good quality. We obtained occasionally a few of them from the Indians, but their extreme indolence prevents them from catching barely what serves themselves. Our general fare was horse-flesh cooked by boiling, and sometimes roasted on the point of a spike before the fire. I learn that the wants of the natives are simple and they require but little to support life in original simplicity. From the oppressive heat I found great relief by bathing morning and evening, and although it causes weakness in some degree, I have some doubt if I had not I should not have been able to continue my trip. On Monday arrived at the branches of the river at dusk [at the site of Lewiston, Idaho], where was a camp of three different nations, upwards of five hundred men able to bear arms. One called Pelusbpa, one the Pierced nose (Chawhaptan), and Chamuiemuch. The chiefs or principal men came and stayed with us till bed-time and presented some favourite horses.

Tuesday 25th till Monday 31st July. As I understood from my companions [John Work and others] that their stay would be for a few days, I was desirous of making a trip to the mountains, distant about sixty miles, the same ridge I visited last month further to the south-east [he had previously visited the Blue Mountains, which are south-west of Lewiston]; but as they had not yet made any arrangement with the natives, it was not thought prudent to go from the camp, so I was guided by their advice. On Wednesday a conference was held and ended favourably and with great splendour by dancing, singing, haranguing, and smoking. All were dressed in their best garments, and on the whole presented a fine spectacle and certainly a new one to me. On Thursday at daylight—Mr. McDonald having been so kind as to send one of his men (Cock de Lard) [one of the many Bay Company employees of French or Quebec ancestry] with me, more as a companion than guide, for he was as much a stranger as myself—we set out in a south-easterly direction, the country undulating and very barren [they are headed toward Craig Mountain]. In the course of the day passed only two springs, and as I was uncertain if more were near and the day far spent, I camped at four o'clock in the afternoon. Found only one species of *Pentstemon* and a few seeds. Very warm. On Friday reached the mountains at nine o'clock and took my breakfast (dry salmon and water) among some very large trees of *Thuya occidentalis* [*Thuja plicata*, western red cedar], the spot pointed out to me by the Indians where Lewis and Clarke built their canoes, on their way to the ocean, twenty-one years ago [Canoe Camp, generally believed to be the spot where the canoes were built, is located about thirty miles east of this spot]. I left my man to take care of the horses at the foot of the mountain, while I ascended to see if it afforded anything different from what I had seen before. Reached the highest peak of the first range at 2 P.M., on the top of which is a very remarkable spring, a circle 11 feet in diameter, the water rising from 9 inches to 3 $^1/_2$ feet above the surface, lowering and rising at intervals, in sudden gushes; the stream that flows from it is 15 feet broad and 2 $^1/_2$ deep, of course running with great force as its fall is 1 $^1/_2$ foot in 10 and it disappears at the foot of the hill in a small marsh [U.S. Geological Survey *Water Supply Paper No. 53* (1901), 79-81, describes a spring very much like this one, located in the Craig Mountains near Lake Waha]. I could find no bottom to the spring at a depth of 60 feet. Surrounding the spring there is a thicket of a species of *Ribes* belonging to section *Grossulariae* [gooseberries], 12 to 15 feet high, with fine delicate fruit of a very superior flavour and large, nearly as large as a musket-ball. This fine species I have not seen before; should it prove new, I hope it may be called *R. Munroi* [probably *Ribes niveum*], as I have called the spring Munro's Fountain [after Donald Munro, a gardener at the Royal Horticultural Society]; at the same time how delighted he would feel to see such in the garden. Found in seed, nearly ripe, *Ribe viscosissimum,* and, lest I should not meet with it in a better state, gathered a quantity of it. Found a few seeds of *Paeonia,* but not so ripe as I should have wished, with a small species of *Vaccinium* [huckleberries] and a few seeds of *Xylosteum* [either honeysuckle or snowberry] which I saw in blossom on the mountain near Spokane in May.

I joined the man and horses at six o'clock and set out for my encampment of last night. On arriving and looking for something to eat, I found that only salmon for one day had been put in by the man in mistake, and both having a good appetite we mutually agreed to make for the camp. Set out at dusk (Cock de Lard undertaking to be guide) before the moon rose, at least before it became visible; he took us out of the way about ten miles. Arrived at camp at sunrise, when I threw myself down in one of the tents to sleep. I had not been asleep more than two hours when I was hurriedly aroused to take on myself the profession of a soldier, a misunderstanding having taken place between the interpreter [Jean Toupin] and one of the chiefs; the latter accusing the former of not translating faithfully, words became high till at last the poor man of language had a handful of his long jet hair torn out by the roots. On the Indian being reproved, he went off in a fit of rage and summoned his followers, amounting to seventy-three men. All arrived and came to our camp with their guns cocked and every bow strung. As every one of our party had done all in his power that it should be mutually and amicably adjusted and been refused, every one seemed more careless for the result than another. We (thirty-one of us) stood to our arms and demanded if war was wanted; it was answered 'No, we want only the interpreter killed, and as he was no chief there could be but little ill done.' They were told that whatever person we had in our party, whether chief or not, or only if it was an Indian under our protection, should they attempt to kill or disturb him in the least, certainly they would know we had been already in war. The coolness that seemed to be the prominent feature in our countenance had the desired effect of cooling their desire for war and made them glad to ask for peace, which in our part was as willingly granted them. Many speeches were made on the occasion, and, if it may be allowed to judge from gesture and the language of nature, many of them possess qualifications that would be no disgrace to a modern orator. Although there is much repetition in their harangues, delivered with much vehemence and intense feeling, they are uniformly natural and certainly calculated either to tie the knot of affection and sympathy, or rouse the mind to discord and war. I have observed speakers and hearers so overcome that they sobbed and cried aloud, and the proceedings delayed until they recovered. This affair was concluded in the usual way—exchange of presents. Although friendship had again been restored, it would have been imprudent to have gone from the camp; therefore I employed myself putting in order those collected and airing some seeds. On Sunday at midday we rose camp and pitched on the northern shore of the north branch [at the foot of Lewiston Hill].

Monday, July 31st to Friday, August 4th. Early in the morning I had the plants and seeds which were collected carefully secured in one of the saddle-bags. Parted with Mr. McDonald, who descended the river; and Mr. Work with two men and myself took our departure overland in a north-easterly course to Kettle Falls on the Columbia [headed for Spokane, Douglas passed through the Palouse country near or just west of Moscow, a place that he found hot and "destitute of timber."].

8

Captain Benjamin Bonneville among the Nez Perce, 1832-1834

Captain Benjamin L.E. Bonneville, on leave from his duties as an officer in the small American Army, spent three years on a trading and information gathering mission in the West. Many scholars believe that he was also on a spying mission. He spent nearly two months in the autumn of 1832 camped among Nez Perce and Flathead Indians along the upper Salmon River, in what is now Lemhi County, Idaho, returning to them the following summer. In the early months of 1834, on a trip designed to challenge the Hudson's Bay Company, he spent several days among what would come to be called the Joseph Band of the Nez Perce people along the Grande Ronde River. On this same mission, headed for Fort Nez Perces, he visited among the Nez Perce at Asotin and Red Wolf Crossing. He returned briefly to Fort Nez Perces and the Grande Ronde Valley in the summer of 1834 and within a year was back in St. Louis, where his adventures had commenced.

Bonneville was born in Paris in April of 1796, and was raised in a household there that counted the revolutionary writer Thomas Paine as a resident. The chaos of the French Revolution drove most of Bonneville's family to New York in 1803, where the child grew up in the Paine household. In 1813, Bonneville was appointed to the United States Military Academy, from which he graduated as a brevet Second Lieutenant at the end of 1815. By 1820, he had the full rank of First Lieutenant and was ready to begin a long career as an infantry officer on the western frontier, serving in Arkansas, Texas, and elsewhere. After 1830, as a Captain, he served at Fort Gibson in Osage country, where he met the frontiersman and explorer Joseph R. Walker. Shortly after this meeting, Bonneville began to formulate plans to obtain a long leave from active duty, and to spend several years in what would become Wyoming, Idaho, Oregon, and Washington.

Our knowledge of what Bonneville did, and why, is clouded by several facts. While some firsthand Bonneville letters are in the National Archives and have been published (see citations that follow), not many survived. For various reasons, most of Bonneville's journals and maps fell into the hands of Washington Irving, who

Figure 5. Benjamin Bonneville

was, even in 1836, a famous and popular writer. As a consequence, most of what we know of Bonneville's time among the Nez Perce people comes to us through Irving, who purchased the notes, some maps, and other sources that Bonneville had been using to prepare his own account. None of these primary sources have been located by modern scholars; we must rely upon Irving's *The Adventures of Captain Bonneville* and the few surviving National Archives records to tell the story.

The orders that accompanied Bonneville's leave from the Army suggest that intelligence gathering was to be part of the Captain's work. We also know that the commercial side of Bonneville's venture was financed in large part by Alfred Seton, whose account of the Clearwater appears earlier in this book. Much of the background to Bonneville's western adventure remains a mystery.

Published here are excerpts from Bonneville's account of his time along the upper Salmon River, and also the story of his visit to the Snake River in the early spring of 1834. On this latter trip, he reached the Hudson Bay Company's Fort Nez Perces on March 4, 1834, where Chief Trader Pierre Pambrun greeted him with civility. It was part of what a leading scholar of the fur trade has termed a "courageous but naïve challenge" to the Bay Company, and one that "ended ignominiously."[1]

While this first foray against the power of the Hudson's Bay Company ended in a failure, Bonneville still had the last laugh. After fighting in Mexico and surviving a court martial, Bonneville was named commander at the new U.S. Army post of Fort Vancouver in 1852, serving there until May of 1855. Fort Vancouver had been the seat of power of the same company that drove Bonneville out of the Columbia in 1834.

Bonneville retired to Fort Smith, Arkansas, after minor service in the Civil War, and died there in 1878 at the age of 82, the oldest retired officer in the Army.

Further reading about Benjamin Bonneville:

J. Nelson Barry, "General B.L.E. Bonneville, U.S.A.," *Annals of Wyoming* 8 (April 1932): 610-620.

Contains the text of Bonneville's July 1833 report from Wind River.

"Benjamin Louis Eulalie de Bonneville," In *American National Biography, Vol. 3* (New York: Oxford University Press, 1999), 182-83.

"Benjamin Louis Eulalie de Bonneville," In *Dictionary of American Biography, Vol. 2* (New York: Charles Scribner's Sons, 1929), 438.

"Benjamin Louis Eulalie Bonneville," In *Encyclopedia of Frontier Biography, Vol. 1* (Glendale: Arthur H. Clark, 1988), 136.

"Documents, General B.L.E. Bonneville," Anne H. Abel-Henderson, ed., *Washington Historical Quarterly* 18, no. 3 (July 1927): 207-30.

---

[1]David J.Wishart,. *The Fur Trade of the American West* (Lincoln: University of Nebraska Press, 1979), 156.

Elgin V. Kuykendall, *Historic Glimpses of Asotin County, Washington* (Clarkston: Press of the Clarkston Herald, 1954), 4-13.

An extremely well-informed explanation of Bonneville's 1834 visit.

John Francis McDermott, "Washington Irving and the Journal of Captain Bonneville," *Mississippi Valley Historical Review* 43, no. 3 (December 1956): 459-467.

An important summary of the status of original records regarding Bonneville.

Edgeley W. Todd, "Benjamin L.E. Bonneville," In LeRoy R. Hafen, ed. *The Mountain Men and the Fur Trade of the Far West, Vol. 5* (Glendale: Arthur H. Clark, 1968), 45-63.

The most important account of Bonneville's life and western exploration.

Account 8.1: Bonneville describes the people that he met while on the upper Salmon in the autumn of 1832. Source: Excerpts from Bonneville, camped on the Wind River, to General Alexander Macomb, General in Chief of the U.S. Army, 29 July 1833, In Anne H. Abel-Henderson, "Documents: General B.L.E. Bonneville," *Washington Historical Quarterly* 18, No. 3 (July 1927): 210-219.

> General,
> This country I find is much more extensive than I could have expected, as yet, I may say I have actually visited, only, the heart of the Rocky Mountains, or in other words, the head waters of the Yellow Stone, the Platte, the Colorado of the West, and the Columbia. I have therefore remained...I have constantly kept a journal, making daily observations of course, country, Indians &c....
> The Flatheads 100 warriors with out 150 Nez Percez warriors detached from the lower Columbia, range upon the heads of the Salmon River, the Recize Amere, and towards the three forks of the Missouri, the Flatheads are said to be the only Indians here, who have never killed a white man, they and the Nez Perces are extremely brave in defense, but never go to war, are the most honest and religious people I ever saw, observing every festival of the Roman Church, avoiding changing their camp on Sundays tho, in distress for provisions. Polygamy so usual among all Indians, is strictly forbidden by them. I do not believe three nights pass in the whole year without religious meetings. They defend themselves from the Black Foo[t]. Descend the Columbia waters. The great body of the Nez Percez and the large bands of the Pend 'Oreilles. Here horses may be said to abound [Bonneville has not yet been to the Columbia, and is apparently relying here on what he was told by the Nez Perce he met along the Salmon River], some individuals having from 2 to 3,000 head, upon which they live, together with roots....

Account 8.2: Washington Irving's version of the story of Captain Bonneville's visit on the Imnaha, Grand Ronde, and Snake Rivers in early 1834. Source: Washington Irving, *The Adventures of Captain Bonneville, U.S.A., in the Rocky*

Mountains and the Far West. Author's Revised Edition (New York: G.P. Putnam, 1849) 269-99.

With a small, starved party, Bonneville has climbed out of Hells Canyon on the Oregon side, a few miles upstream from the mouth of the Salmon River. The geographic notations provided here generally follow those suggested by Judge Elgin Kuykendall in his 1954 book, *Historic Glimpses of Asotin County*, cited above.

Their provisions were now exhausted, and they and their horses almost ready to give out with fatigue and hunger; when one afternoon, just as the sun was sinking behind a blue line of distant mountain, they came to the brow of a height from which they beheld the smooth valley of the Immahah [Imnaha River] stretched out in smiling verdure below them.

The sight inspired almost a frenzy of delight. Roused to a new ardor, they forgot, for a time, their fatigues, and hurried down the mountain, dragging their jaded horses after them, and sometimes compelling them to slide a distance of thirty or forty feet at a time. At length they reached the banks of the Immahah. The young grass was just beginning to sprout, and the whole valley wore an aspect of softness, verdure, and repose, heightened by the contest to the frightful region from which they had just descended. To add to their joy, they observed Indian trails along the margin of the stream, and other signs, which gave them reason to believe that there was an encampment of the Lower Nez Percés in the neighborhood, as it was within the accustomed range of that pacific and hospitable tribe.

The prospect of a supply of food stimulated them to new exertion, and they continued on as fast as the enfeebled state of themselves and their steeds would permit. At length, one of the men, more exhausted than the rest, threw himself upon the grass, and declared he could go no further. It was in vain to attempt to rouse him; his spirit had given out, and his replies only showed the dogged apathy of despair. His companions, therefore, encamped on the spot, kindled a blazing fire, and searched about for roots with which to strengthen and revive him. They all then made a starveling repast; but gathering round the fire, talked over past dangers and troubles, soothed themselves with persuasion that all were now at an end, and went to sleep with the comforting hope that the morrow would bring them into plentiful quarters.

Chapter 31

A tranquil night's rest had sufficiently restored the broken-down traveler, to enable him to resume his wayfaring; and all hands set forward on the Indian trail. With all their eagerness to arrive within reach of succor, such was their feeble and emaciated condition, that they advanced but slowly. Nor is it a matter of surprise that they should almost have lost heart, as well as strength. It was now (the 16th of February [1834]), fifty-three days that they had been travelling in the midst of winter; exposed to all kinds of privations and hardships: and for the last twenty days, they had been entangled in the wild and desolate labyrinths of the snowy mountains; climbing and descending icy precipices; and nearly starved with cold and hunger.

All the morning they continued following the Indian trail, without seeing a human being; and were beginning to be discouraged, when, about noon, they discovered a horseman at a distance. He was coming directly towards them; but on discovering them, suddenly reined up his steed, came to a halt, and, after reconnoitring them for a time with, seemed about to make a cautious retreat. They eagerly made signs of peace, and endeavored, with the utmost anxiety. To induce him to approach. He remained for some time in doubt; but at length, having satisfied himself that they were not enemies, came galloping up to them. He was a fine, haughty looking savage, fancifully decorated, and mounted on a high-mettled steed with gaudy trappings and equipments. It was evident that he was a warrior of some consequence among his tribe. His whole deportment had something in it of barbaric dignity: he felt, perhaps, his temporary superiority in personal array, and in the spirit of his steed, to the poor, ragged travel-worn trappers, and their half-starved horses. Approaching them with an air of protection, he gave them his hand, and, in the Nez Percé language, invited them to his camp, which was only a few miles distant; where he had plenty to eat, and plenty of horses; and would cheerfully share his good things with them.

His hospitable invitation was joyfully accepted: he lingered but a moment, to give directions by which they might find his camp; and then, wheeling round, and giving the reins to his mettlesome steed, was soon out of sight. The travellers followed, with gladdened hearts... [but fatigue set in and they failed to reach the camp that day.]

The next morning, Captain Bonneville awakened from his long and heavy sleep, much refreshed; and they all resumed their creeping progress. They had not been long on the march, when eight or ten of the Nez Percé tribe came galloping to meet them, leading fresh horses to bear them to their camp. Thus gallantly mounted, they felt new life infused into their languid frames, and dashing forward, were soon at the lodges of the Nez Percés. Here they found about twelve families living together, under the patriarchal sway of an ancient and venerable chief. He received them with the hospitality of the golden age; and with something of the same kind of fare: for, while he opened his arms to make them welcome, the only repast he set before them consisted of roots. They could have wished for something more hearty and substantial; but, for want of better, made a voracious meal on these humble viands. The repast being over, the best pipe was lighted and sent around: and this was a most welcome luxury, having lost their smoking apparatus twelve days before, among the mountains.

While they were thus enjoying themselves, their poor horses were led to the best pastures in the neighborhood; where they were turned loose to revel on the fresh sprouting grass: so that they had better fare than their masters.

Captain Bonneville soon felt himself quite at home, among these quiet, inoffensive people. His long residence among their cousins, the Upper Nez Percés [see the previous account], had made him conversant with their language, modes of expression, and all their habitudes. He soon found, too, that he was well known among them, by report at least, from the constant interchange of visits and messages between the two branches of the tribe. They at first addressed him by his name; giving him his titles of captain, with a French accent: but they soon gave him a title of their own; which, as usual with Indian titles, had a peculiar signification. In the case of the captain, it had somewhat of a whimsical origin.

As he sat chatting and smoking in the midst of them, he would occasionally take off his cap. Whenever he did so, there was a sensation in the surrounding circle. The Indian would half rise from their recumbent posture, and gaze upon his uncovered head, with their usual exclamation of astonishment. The worthy captain was completely bald; a phenomenon very surprising in their eyes. They were at a loss to know whether he had been scalped in battle, or enjoyed a natural immunity from that belligerant infliction. In a little while, he became known among them by an Indian name, signifying "the bald chief." "A soubriquet," observes the captain, "for which I can find no parallel in history, since the days of 'Charles the Bald.'"

Although the travellers had banqueted on roots, and been regaled with tobacco smoke, yet, their stomachs craved more generous fare. In approaching the lodges of the Nez Percés, they had indulged in fond anticipations of venison and dried salmon: and dreams of the kind still haunted their imaginations, and could not be conjured down. The keen appetites of mountain trappers, quickened by a fortnight's fasting, at length got the better of all scruples of pride, and they fairly begged some fish or flesh from the hospitable savages. The latter, however, were slow to break in upon their winter store, which was very limited: but they were ready to furnish roots in abundance, which they pronounced excellent food. At length, Captain Bonneville thought of a means of attaining the much-coveted gratification.

He had about him, he says, a trusty plaid [jacket]; an old and valued travelling companion and comforter; upon which the rains had descended, and the snows and winds beaten, without further effect than somewhat to tarnish its primitive lustre. This coat of many colors had excited the admiration, and inflamed the covetousness of both warriors and squaws, to an extravagant degree. An idea now occurred to Captain Bonneville, to convert this rainbow garment into the savory viands so much desired. There was a momentary struggle in his mind, between old associations and projected indulgence; and his decision in favor of the latter was made, he says, with a greater promptness, perhaps, than true taste and sentiment might have required. In a few moments, his plaid cloak was cut into numerous strips. "Of these," continues he, "with the newly developed talent of a man-milliner, I speedily constructed turbans *à la Turque*, and fanciful head-gears of divers conformations. These, judiciously distributed among such of the womenkind as seemed of most consequence and interest in the eyes of the *patres conscripti*, brought us, in a little while, abundance of dried salmon and deers' hearts; on which we made a sumptuous supper. Another, and a more satisfactory smoke, succeeded this repast; and sweet slumbers answering the peaceful invocation of our pipes, wrapped us in that delicious rest, which is only won by toil and travail."

As to Captain Bonneville, he slept in the lodge of the venerable patriarch, who had evidently conceived a most disinterested affection for him; as was shown on the following morning. The travellers, invigorated by a good supper, and "fresh from the bath of repose," were about to resume their journey, when this affectionate old chief took the captain aside, to let him know how much he loved him. As proof of his regard, he had determined to give him a fine horse; which would go further than words, and put his good-will beyond all question. So saying, he made a signal, and forthwith a beautiful young horse, of a brown color, was led, prancing and snorting, to the place. Captain Bonneville was suitably affected by this mark of friendship; but his experience in what is proverbially called "Indian giving," made him aware that a parting pledge was necessary on his own part, to prove that this friendship was reciprocated. He accordingly placed a handsome rifle in the hands of the venerable chief; whose benevolent heart was evidently touched by this outward and visible sign of amity.

Having now, as he thought, balanced this little account of friendship, the captain was about to shift his saddle to this noble gift-horse, when the affectionate patriarch plucked him by the sleeve, and introduced him to a whimpering, whining, leathern-skinned old squaw, that might have passed for an Egyptian mummy, without drying. "This," he said, "is my wife; she is a good wife—I love her very much.—She loves the horse—she loves him a great deal—she will cry very much at losing him.—I do not know how I shall comfort her—and that makes my heart very sore."

What could the worthy captain do, to console the tender-hearted old squaw; and, peradventure, to save the venerable patriarch from a curtain lecture? He bethought himself of a pair of earbobs: it was true, the patriarch's better-half was of an age and appearance that seemed to put personal vanity out of the question: but when is personal vanity extinct? The moment he produced the glittering earbobs, the whimpering and whining of the sempiternal beldame was at an end. She eagerly paced the precious baubles in her ears, and, though as ugly as the Witch of Endor, went off with a sideling gait, and coquettish air, as though she had been a perfect Semiramis.

The captain now saddled his newly acquired steed, and his foot was in the stirrup, when the affectionate patriarch again stepped forward, and presented to him a young Pierced-nose, who had a peculiarly sulky look. "This," said the venerable chief, "is my son: he is very good; a great horseman—he always took care of this very fine horse—he brought him up from a colt, and made him what he is.—He is very fond of this fine horse—he loved him like a brother—his heart will be very heavy when this fine horse leaves the camp."

What could the captain do, to reward the youthful hope of this venerable pair, and comfort him for the loss of his fosterbrother, the horse? He bethought him of a hatchet, which might be spared from his slender stores. No sooner did he place the implement in the hands of the young hopeful, than his countenance brightened up, and he went off rejoicing in his hatchet, to the full as much as did his respectable mother in her earbobs.

The captain was now in the saddle, and about to start, when the affectionate old patriarch stepped forward, for the third time, and, while he laid one hand gently on the mane of the horse, held up the rifle in the other. "This rifle," said he, "shall be my great medicine. I will hug it to my heart—I will always love it, for the sake of my good friend, the bald-headed chief.—But a rifle, by itself, is dumb—I cannot make it speak. If I had a little powder and ball, I would take it out with me, and would now and then shoot a deer: and when I brought the meat home to my hungry family, I would say—this was killed by the rifle of my friend, the bald-headed chief, to whom I gave that very fine horse."

There was no resisting this appeal: the captain, forthwith, furnished the coveted supply of powder and ball; but at the same time, put spurs to his very fine gift-horse, and the first trial of his speed was to get out of all further manifestation of friendship, on the part of the affectionate old patriarch and his insinuating family.

Chapter 32

Following the course of the Immahah, Captain Bonneville and his three companions soon reached the vicinity of the Snake River. Their route [north] now lay over a succession of steep and isolated hills, with profound valleys.[2] On the second day, after taking leave of the affectionate old patriarch, as they were descending into one of those deep and abrupt intervals, they descried a smoke, and shortly afterwards came in sight of a small encampment of Nez Percés.

The Indians, when they ascertained that it was a party of white men approaching, greeted them with a salute of fire-arms, and invited them to encamp. This band was likewise under the sway of a venerable chief named Yo-mus-ro-y-e-cut; a name which we shall be careful not to inflict oftener than is necessary upon the reader. This ancient and hard-named chieftain, welcomed Captain Bonneville to his camp with the same hospitality and loving kindness that he had experienced from his predecessor. He told the captain that he had often heard of the Americans and their generous deeds, and that his Buffalo brethren (the Upper Nez Percés,) had always spoken of them as the Big-hearted whites of the East, the very good friends of the Nez Percés.

Captain Bonneville felt somewhat uneasy under the responsibility of this magnanimous but costly appellation; and began to fear he might be involved in a second interchange of pledges of friendship. He hastened, therefore, to let the old chief know his poverty-stricken state, and how little there was to be expected from him.

He informed him that he and his comrades had long resided among the Upper Nez Percés, and loved them so much, that they had thrown their arms around them, and now held them close to their hearts. That he had received such good accounts from the Upper Nez Percés of their cousins, the Lower Nez Percés, that he had become desirous of knowing them as friends and brothers. That he and his companions had accordingly loaded a mule with presents and set off for the country of the Lower Nez Percés; but, unfortunately, had been entrapped for many days among the snowy mountains; and that the mule with all the presents had fallen into Snake River, and been swept away by the rapid current. That instead, therefore, of arriving among their friends, the Nez Percés, with light hearts and full hands, they came naked, hungry, and broken down; and instead of making them presents, must depend upon them even for food. "But," concluded he, "we are going to the white men's fort on the Wallah-Wallah [to the Hudson Bay Company's Fort Nez Perces, located at the mouth of the Walla Walla River], and will soon return; and then we will meet our Nez Percé friends like true Big Hearts of the East."

Whether the hint thrown out in the latter part of the speech had any effect, or whether the old chief acted from the hospitable feelings which, according to the captain, are really inherent in the Nez Percé tribe, he certainly showed no disposition to relax his friendship on learning the destitute circumstances of his guests. On the contrary, he urged the captain to remain with them until the following day, when he would accompany them on his journey, and make them acquainted with all his people. In the meantime, he would have a colt killed, and cut up for travelling provisions. This, he carefully explained, was intended not as an article of traffic, but as a gift; for he saw that his guests were hungry and in need of food.

---

[2]Eureka Creek, Knight Creek, and north of the mouth of the Salmon River, Cook Creek. This area is difficult to traverse even today.

Captain Bonneville gladly assented to this hospitable arrangement. The carcass of the colt was forthcoming in due season, but the captain insisted that one half of it should be set apart for the use of the chieftain's family.

At an early hour of the following morning, the little party resumed their journey, accompanied by the old chief and an Indian guide. Their route was over a rugged and broken country; where the hills were slippery with ice and snow. Their horses, too, were so weak and jaded, that they could scarcely climb the steep ascents, or maintain their foothold on the frozen declivities. Throughout the whole of the journey, the old chief and the guide were unremitting in their good offices, and continually on the alert to select the best roads, and assist them through all difficulties. Indeed, the captain and his comrades had to be dependant on their Indian friends for almost every thing, for they had lost their tobacco and pipes, those great comforts of the trapper, and had but a few charges of powder left, which it was necessary to husband for the purpose of lighting their fires.

In the course of the day the old chief had several private consultations with the guide, and showed evident signs of being occupied with some mysterious matter of mighty import. What is was, Captain Bonneville could not fathom, nor did he make much effort to do so. From some casual sentences that he overheard, he perceived that it was something from which the old man promised himself much satisfaction, and to which he attached a little vainglory, but which he wished to keep secret; so he suffered him to spin out his petty plans unmolested.

In the evening when they encamped [Judge Kuykendall concluded that this was February 22, 1834, and that they were just inside what is now Asotin County], the old chief and his privy counselor, the guide, had another mysterious colloquy, after which the guide mounted his horse and departed on some secret mission, while the chief resumed his seat at the fire, and sat humming to himself in a pleasing but mystic reverie.

The next morning, the travellers descended into the valley of the Way-lee-way, a considerable tributary of Snake River.[3] Here they met the guide returning from his secret errand. Nother private conference was held between him and the old managing chief, who now seemed more inflated than ever with mystery and self-importance. Numerous fresh trails, and various other signs, persuaded Captain Bonneville that there must be a considerable village of Nez Percés in the neighborhood; but as his worthy companion, the old chief, said nothing on the subject, and as it appeared to be in some way connected with his secret operations, he asked no questions, but patiently awaited the development of his mystery.

As they journeyed on, they came to where two or three Indians were bathing in a small stream. The good old chief immediately came to a halt, and had a long conversation with them, in the course of which he repeated to them the whole history which Captain Bonneville had related to him. In fact, he seems to have been a very sociable, communicative old man; by no means afflicted with the taciturnity generally charged upon the Indians. On the contrary, he was fond of long talks and long smokings, and evidently was proud of his new friend, the bald-headed chief, and took a pleasure in sounding his praises, and setting forth the

---

[3]They were entering the lower valley of the Grande Ronde River, probably going down Joseph Creek. This is *Weliiwe*, in Nez Perce, referring to the bright color of the water in this river.

power and glory of the Big Hearts of the East.

Having disburdened himself of every thing he had to relate to his bathing friends, he left them to their aquatic disports, and proceeded onward with the captain and his companions. As they approached the Way-lee-way, however, the communicative old chief met with another and a very different occasion to exert his colloquial powers. In the banks of the river stood an isolated mound covered with grass. He pointed to it with come emotions. "The big heart and the strong arm," said he, "lie buried beneath that sod."

It was, in fact, the grave of one of his friends; a chosen warrior of the tribe; who had been slain on this spot when in pursuit of a war party of Shoshokoes, who has stolen the horses of the village The enemy bore off his scalp as a trophy; but his friends found his body in this lonely place, and committed it to the earth with ceremonials characteristic of their pious and reverential feelings. They gathered round the grave and mourned; the warriors were silent in their grief; but the women and children bewailed their loss with loud lamentations. "For three days," said the old man, "we performed the solemn dances for the dead, and prayed the Great Spirit that our brother might be happy in the land of brave warriors and hunters. Then we killed at his grave fifteen of our best and strongest horses, to serve him when he should arrive at the happy hunting grounds; and having done all this, we returned sorrowfully to our homes."

While the chief was still talking, an Indian scout came galloping up, and, presenting him with a powder-horn, wheeled around, and was speedily out of sight. The eyes of the old chief now brightened; and all his self-importance returned. His petty mystery was about to explode. Turning to Captain Bonneville, he pointed to a hill hard by, and informed him, that behind it was a village governed by a little chief, whom he had notified of the approach of the bald-headed chief, and a party of the Big Hearts of the East, and that he was prepared to receive them in becoming style. As, among other ceremonials, he intended to salute them with a discharge of fire-arms, he had sent the horn of gunpowder that they might return the salute in a manner correspondent to his dignity.

They now proceeded on until they doubled the point of the hill, when the whole population of the village broke upon their view, drawn out in the most imposing style, and arrayed in all their finery.[4] The effect of the whole was wild and fantastic, yet singularly striking. In the front rank were the chiefs and principal warriors, glaringly painted and decorated; behind them were arranged the rest of the people, men, women, and children.

Captain Bonneville and his party advanced slowly, exchanging salutes of fire-arms. When arrived within a respectful distance, they dismounted. The chiefs then came forward successively, according to their respective characters and consequence, to offer the hand of good-fellowship; each filing off when he had shaken hands, to make way for his successor. Those in the next rank followed in the same order, and so on, until all had given the pledge of friendship. During all this time, the chief, according to custom, took his stand beside the guests. If any of his people advanced whom he judged unworthy of the friendship or confidence of the white men, he motioned them off by a wave of the hand, and they would

---

[4]They were probably at a site near the mouth of Joseph Creek called *Inaan 'Yeewewee* or *Ineeneniyiwewi*, which may refer to the sunny side of a hill; this is close to the spot often called "Joseph's Place."

submissively walk away. When Captain Bonneville turned upon him an enquiring look, he would observe, "he is a bad man," or something quite as concise, and there was an end of the matter.

Mats, poles, and other materials were now brought, and a comfortable lodge was soon erected for the strangers, where they were kept constantly supplied with wood and water, and other necessities; and all their effects were placed in safe keeping. Their horses, too, were unsaddled and turned loose to graze, and a guard set to keep watch upon them.

All this being adjusted, they were conducted to the main building or council house of the village, where an ample repast, or rather banquet, was spread, which seemed to realize all the gastronomical dreams that had tantalized them during their long starvation; for here they beheld not merely fish and roots in abundance, but the flesh of deer and elk, and the choicest pieces of buffalo meat. It is needless to say how vigorously they acquitted themselves on this occasion, and how unnecessary it was for their hosts to practise the usual cramming principle of Indian hospitality.

When the repast was over, a long talk ensued. The chief showed the same curiosity evinced by his tribe generally, to obtain information concerning the United States, of which they knew little but what they derived through their cousins, the Upper Nez Percés; as their traffic is almost exclusively with the British traders of the Hudson's Bay Company. Captain Bonneville did his best to set forth the merits of his nation, and the importance of their friendship to the red men, in which he was ably seconded by his worthy friend, the old chief with the hard name, who did all that he could to glorify the Big Hearts of the East.

The chief, and all present, listened with profound attention, and evidently with great interest; nor were the important facts thus set forth, confined to the audience in the lodge; for sentence after sentence was loudly repeated by a crier for the benefit of the whole village.

This custom of promulgating every thing by criers, is not confined to the Nez Percés, but prevails among many other tribes. It has its advantage where there are no gazettes to publish the news of the day, or to report the proceedings of important meetings. And in fact, reports of this kind, viva voce, made in the hearing of all parties, and liable to be contradicted or corrected on the spot, are more likely to convey accurate information to the public mind, than those circulated through the press. The office of crier is generally filled by some old man, who is good for little else. A village has generally several of these walking newspapers, as they are termed by the whites, who go about proclaiming the news of the day, giving notice of public councils; expeditions, dances, feasts, and other ceremonials, and advertising any thing lost. While Captain Bonneville remained among the Nez Percés, if a glove, handkerchief, or any thing of similar value, was lost or mislaid, it was carried by the finder to the lodge of the chief, and proclamation was made by one of the criers, for the owner to come and claim his property.

How difficult it is to get at the true character of these wandering tribes of the wilderness! In a recent work, we have had to speak of this tribe of Indians from the experience of other traders [in the employ of Astor] who had casually been among them, and who represented them as selfish, inhospitable, exorbitant in their dealing, and much addicted to thieving [as reported by Irving in his book, *Astoria*].

Captain Bonneville, on the contrary, who resided much among them, and had repeated opportunities of ascertaining their real character, invariably speaks of them as kind and hospitable, scrupulously honest, and remarkable, above all other Indians that he had met with, for a strong feeling of religion. In fact, so enthusiastic is he in their praise, that he pronounces them, all ignorant and barbarous as they are by their condition, one of the purest-hearted people on the face of the earth.

Some cures which Captain Bonneville had effected in simple cases, among the Upper Nez Percés, had reached the ears of their cousins here, and gained for him the reputation of a great medicine man. He had not been long in the village, therefore, before his lodge began to be the resort of the sick and the infirm. The captain felt the value of the reputation thus accidentally and cheaply acquired, and endeavored to sustain it. As he had arrived at that age when every man is, experimentally, something of a physician, he was enabled to turn to advantage the little knowledge in the healing art which he had casually picked up; and was sufficiently successful in two or three cases, to convince the simple Indians that report had not exaggerated his medical talents. The only patient that effectually baffled his skill, or rather discouraged any attempt at relief, was an antiquated squaw with a churchyard cough, and one leg in the grave; it being shrunk and rendered useless by a rheumatic affection. This was a case beyond his mark; however, he comforted the old woman with a promise that he would endeavor to procure something to relieve her, at the fort on the Wallah-Wallah, and would bring it on his return; with which assurance her husband was so well satisfied, that he presented the captain with a colt, to be killed as provisions for the journey: a medical fee which was thankfully accepted.

While among these Indians, Captain Bonneville unexpectedly found an owner for the horse which he had purchased from a Root Digger at the Big Wyer. The Indian satisfactorily proved that the horse had been stolen from him some time previous, by some unknown thief. "However," said the considerate savage, "you got him in fair trade—you are more in want of horses than I am: keep him, he is yours—he is a good horse; use him well."

Thus, in the continual experience of acts of kindness and generosity, which his destitute condition did not allow him to reciprocate, Captain Bonneville passed some short time among these good people, more and more impressed with the general excellence of their character.

Chapter 33

In resuming his journey, Captain Bonneville was conducted by the same Nez Percé guide, whose knowledge of the country was important in choosing the routes and resting places. He also continued to be accompanied by the worthy old chief with the hard name, who seemed bent upon doing the honors of the country, and introducing him to every branch of his tribe. The Way-lee-way, down the banks of which, Captain Bonneville and his companions were now travelling, is a considerable stream winding through a succession of bold and beautiful scenes. Sometimes the landscape towered into bold and mountainous heights that partook of sublimity; at other times, it stretched along the water side in fresh smiling meadows, and graceful undulating valleys

Frequently in their route they encountered small parties of the Nez Percés, with whom they invariably stopped to shake hands; and who, generally, evinced great curiosity concerning them and their adventures; a curiosity which never failed to be thoroughly satisfied by the replies of the worthy Yo-mus-ro-y-e-cut, who kindly took upon himself to be spokesman of the party.

The incessant smoking of pipes incident to the long talks of this excellent, but somewhat garrulous old chief, at length exhausted all his stock of tobacco, so that he had no longer a whiff with which to regale his white companions. In this emergency, he cut up the stem of his pipe into fine shavings, which he mixed with certain herbs, and thus manufactured a temporary succedaneum, to enable him to accompany his long colloquies and harangues with the customary fragrant cloud.

If the scenery of the Way-lee-way had charmed the travellers with its mingled amenity and grandeur, that which broke upon them on once more reaching the Snake River, filled them with admiration and astonishment. At times, the river was overhung by dark and stupendous rocks, rising like gigantic walls and battlements; these would be rent by wide and yawning chasms, that seemed to speak of past convulsions of nature. Sometimes the river was of glassy smoothness and placidity; at other times it roared along in impetuous rapids and foaming cascades. Here, the rocks were piled in the most fantastic crags and precipices; and in another place, they were succeeded by delightful valleys carpeted with green sward. The whole of this wild and varied scenery was dominated by immense mountains rearing their distant peaks into the clouds. "The grandeur and originality of the views, presented on every side, " says Captain Bonneville, "beggar both the pencil and the pen. Nothing we had ever gazed upon in any other region could for a moment compare in wild majesty and impressive sternness, with the series of scenes which here at every turn astonished our sense, and filled us with awe and delight."

Indeed, from all that we can gather from the journal before us, and the accounts of other travellers, who passed through these regions in the memorable enterprise of Astoria, we are inclined to think that Snake River must be one of the most remarkable for varied and striking scenery of all the rivers of this continent. From its head waters in the Rocky Mountains, to its junction with the Columbia, its windings are upwards of six hundred miles through every variety of landscape. Rising in a volcanic region, amidst extinguished craters, and mountains awful with the traces of ancient fires, it makes its way through great plains of lava and sandy deserts, penetrates vast sierras or mountainous chains, broken into romantic and often frightful precipices, and crowned with eternal snows; and at other times, careers through green and smiling meadows, and wide landscapes of Italian grace and beauty. Wildness and sublimity, however, appear to be its prevailing characteristics.

Captain Bonneville and his companions had pursued their journey a considerable distance down the course of Snake River, when the old chief halted on the bank, and dismounting, recommended that they should turn their horses loose to graze, while he summoned a cousin of his from a group of lodges on the opposite side of the stream.[5] His summons was quickly answered. An Indian of an active, elastic form, leaped into a light canoe of cotton-wood, and vigorously plying the paddle, soon shot across the river. Bounding on shore, he advanced with a

---

[5]Judge Kuykendall believed they were across the Snake from the mouth of Captain John Creek, *Heteewisinme*, or *Taawissin'me*, referring to a black tailed buck or its antlers.

buoyant air and frank demeanor, and gave his right hand to each of the party in turn. The old chief, whose hard name we forbear to repeat, now presented Captain Bonneville, in form, to his cousin, whose name, we regret to say, was no less hard, being nothing less than Hay-she-in-cow-cow. The latter evinced the usual curiosity to know all about the strangers, whence they came, whither they were going, the object of their journey, and the adventures they had experienced. All these, of course, were amply and eloquently set forth by the communicative old chief. To all his grandiloquent account of the bald-headed chief and his countrymen, the Big Hearts of the East, his cousin listened with great attention, and replied in the customary style of Indian welcome. He then desired the party to await his return, and, springing into his canoe, darted across the river. In a little while he returned, bringing a most welcome supply of tobacco, and a small stock of provisions for the road, declaring his intention of accompanying the party. Having no horse, he mounted behind one of the men, observing that he should procure a steed for himself on the following day.

They all now jogged on very sociably and cheerily together. Not many miles beyond, they met others of the tribe, among whom was one, whom Captain Bonneville and his comrade had known during their residence among the Upper Nez Percés, and who welcomed them with open arms. In this neighborhood was the home of their guide, who took leave of them with a profusion of good wishes for their safety and happiness. That night they put up in the hut of a Nez Percé, where they were visited by several warriors from the other side of the river, friends of the old chief and his cousin, who came to have a talk and a smoke with the white men. The heart of the good old chief was overflowing with good-will at thus being surrounded by his new and old friends, and he talked with more spirit and vivacity than ever. The evening passed away in perfect harmony and good-humor, and it was not until a late hour that the visiters took their leave and recrossed the river.

After this constant picture of worth and virtue on the part of the Nez Percé tribe, we grieve to have to record a circumstance calculated to throw a temporary shade upon the name. In the course of the social and harmonious evening just mentioned, one of the captain's men, who happened to be something of a virtuoso in his way, and fond of collecting curiosities, produced a small skin, a great rarity in the eyes of men conversant in peltries. It attracted much attention among the visiters from beyond the river, who passed it from one to the other, examined it with looks of lively admiration, and pronounced it a great medicine.

In the morning, when the captain and his party were about to set off, the precious skin was missing. Search was made for it in the hut, but it was nowhere to be found; and it was strongly suspected that it had been purloined by some of the connoisseurs from the other side of the river.

The old chief and his cousin were indignant at the supposed delinquency of their friends across the water, and called out for them to come over and answer for their shameful conduct. The others answered to the call with all the promptitude of perfect innocence, and spurned at the idea of their being capable of such outrage upon any of the Big-hearted nation. All were at a loss on whom to fix the crime of abstracting the invaluable skin, when by chance the eyes of the worthies from beyond the water, fell upon an unhappy cur, belonging to the owner of the hut. He was a gallows-looking dog, but not more so than most Indian dogs, who, take them in mass, are little better than a generation of vipers. Be that as it may, he was instantly accused of having devoured the skin in question. A dog accused is generally a dog condemned; and a dog condemned is generally a dog executed. So it was in the present instance. The unfortunate cur was arraigned; his thievish looks substantiated his guilt, and he was condemned by his judges from across the river to be hanged. In vain the Indians of the hut, with whom he was a great favorite, interceded in his behalf. In vain Captain Bonneville and his comrades petitioned that his life might be spared. His judges were inexorable. He was doubly guilty: first, in having robbed their good friends, the Big Hearts of the East; secondly, in having brought a doubt on the honor of the Nez Percé tribe. He was, accordingly, swung aloft, and pelted with stones to make his death more certain. The sentence of the judges being thus thoroughly executed, a post mortem examination of the body of the dog was held, to establish his delinquency beyond all doubt, and to leave the Nez Percés without a shadow of suspicion. Great interest, of course, was manifested by all present during this operation. The body of the dog was opened, the intestines rigorously scrutinized, but, to the horror of all concerned, not a particle of the skin was to be found—the dog had been unjustly executed!

A great clamor now ensued, but the most clamorous was the party from across the river, whose jealousy of their good name now prompted them to the most vociferous vindications of the innocence. It was with the utmost difficulty that the captain and his comrade could calm their lively sensibilities, by accounting for the disappearance of the skin in a dozen different ways, until all idea of its having been stolen was entirely out of the question.

The meeting now broke up. The warriors returned across the river, the captain and his comrades proceeded on their journey; but the spirits of the communicative old chief, Yo-mus-ro-y-e-cut, were for a time completely dampened, and he evinced great mortification at what had just occurred. He rode on in silence, except, that now and then he would give way to a burst of indignation, and exclaim, with a shake of the head and a toss of the hand toward the opposite shore—"bad men, very bad men across the river;" to each of which brief exclamations, his worthy cousin, Hay-she-in-cow-cow, would respond by a deep guttural sound of acquiescence, equivalent to an amen.

After some time, the countenance of the old chief again cleared up, and he fell into repeated conferences in an under tone, with his cousin, which ended in the departure of the latter, who, applying the lash to his horse, dashed forward and was soon out of sight. In fact, they were drawing near to the village of another chief, likewise distinguished by an appellation of some longitude, O-push-y-e-cut; but commonly known as the great chief. The cousin had been sent ahead to give notice of their approach; a herald appeared as before, bearing a powderhorn, to enable them to respond to the intended salute. A scene ensued, on their approach to the village, similar to that which had occurred at the village of the little chief.[6] The whole population appeared in the field, drawn up in lines, arrayed with the

---

[6]Bonneville and his party have arrived at He·sutí·n or Asotin ("place of the eels"). O-push-y-e-cut is Apás Wahéykt ("flint necklace"), sometimes spelled Apash WyaKaikt. He became known to later white visitors as Looking Glass Sr. He was a man of considerable influence among the Nez Perce people, and, arriving late from the Buffalo country, played a major role in the negotiations at Walla Walla over the 1855 Treaty. He died in January of 1863 and was succeeded by a son of the same name.

customary regard to rank and dignity. Then came on the firing of salutes, and the shaking of hands, in which last ceremonial, every individual, man, woman, and child, participated; for the Indians have an idea that it as indispensable an overture of friendship among the whites as smoking of the pipe is among the red men. The travellers were next ushered to the banquet, where all the choicest viands that the village could furnish, were served up in rich profusion. They were afterwards entertained by feats of agility and horseraces; indeed, their visit to the village seemed the signal for complete festivity. In the meantime, a skin lodge had been spread for their accommodation, their horses and baggage were taken care of, and wood and water supplied in abundance. At night, therefore, they retired to their quarters, to enjoy, as they supposed, the repose of which they stood in need. No such thing, however, was in store for them. A crowd of visitors awaited their appearance, all eager for a smoke and a talk. The pipe was immediately lighted, and constantly replenished and kept alive until the night was far advanced. As usual, the utmost eagerness was evinced by the guests to learn every thing within the scope of their comprehension respecting the Americans, for whom they professed the most fraternal regard. The captain, in his replies, made use of familiar illustrations, calculated to strike their minds, and impress them with such an idea of the might of his nation, as would induce them to treat with kindness and respect all stragglers that might fall in their path. To their inquiries as to the numbers of the people of the United States, he assured them that they were as countless as the blades of grass in the prairies, and that, great as Snake River was, if they were all encamped upon its banks, they would drink it dry in a single day. To these and similar statistics, they listened with profound attention, and apparently, implicit belief. It was, indeed, a striking scene: the captain, with his hunter's dress and bald head in the midst, holding forth, and his wild auditors seated around like so many statues, the fire lighting up their painted faces and muscular figures, all fixed and motionless, excepting when the pipe was passed, a question propounded, or a startling fact in statistics received with a movement of surprise and a half suppressed ejaculation of wonder and delight.

The fame of the captain as a healer of diseases, had accompanied him to this village, and the great chief, O-push-y-e-cut, now entreated him to exert his skill on his daughter, who had been for three days racked with pains, for which the Pierced-nose doctors could devise no alleviation. The captain found her extended on a pallet of mats in excruciating pain. Her father manifested the strongest paternal affection for her, and assured the captain that if he would but cure her, he would place the Americans near his heart. The worthy captain needed no such inducement. His kind heart was already touched by the sufferings of the poor girl, and his sympathies quickened by her appearance; for she was but about sixteen years of age, and uncommonly beautiful in form and feature. The only difficulty with the captain was, that he knew nothing of her malady, and that his medical science was of the most haphazard kind. After considering and cogitating for some time, as a man is apt to do when in a maze of vague ideas, he made a desperate dash at a remedy. By his directions, the girl was placed in a sort of rude vapor bath, much used by the Nez Percés, where she was kept until near fainting. He then gave her a dose of gunpowder dissolved in cold water, and ordered her wrapped in buffalo robes and put to sleep under a load of furs and blankets. The remedy succeeded: the next morning she was free from pain, though extremely languid; whereupon, the captain prescribed for her a bowl of colt's head broth, and that she should be kept for a time on simple diet.

The great chief was unbounded in his expressions of gratitude for the recovery of his daughter. He would fain have detained the captain a long time as his guest, but the time for departure had arrived. When the captain's horse was brought for him to mount, the chief declared that the steed was not worthy of him, and sent for one of his best horses, which he presented in its stead; declaring that it made his heart glad to see his friend so well mounted. He then appointed a young Nez Percé to accompany his guests to the next village, and "to carry his talk" concerning them; and the two parties separated with mutual expressions of kindness and feelings of good-will.

The vapor bath of which we have made mention is in frequent use among the Nez Percé tribe, chiefly for cleanliness. Their sweating houses, as they call them, are small and close lodges, and the vapor is produced by water poured slowly upon red hot stones.

On passing the limits of O-push-y-e-cut's domains, the travellers left the elevated table lands, and all the wild and romantic scenery which has just been described. They now traversed a gently undulating country, of such fertility that it excited the rapturous admiration of two of the captain's followers, a Kentuckian and a native of Ohio. They declared that it surpassed any land they had ever seen, and often exclaimed, what a delight it would be just to run a plough through such a rich and teeming soil, and see it open its bountiful promise before the share.[7]

Another halt and sojourn of a night was made at the village of a chief named He-mim-el-pilp, where similar ceremonies were observed and hospitality experienced, as at the preceding villages.[8] They now pursued a west-southwest course through a beautiful and fertile region, better wooded than most of the tracts through which they had passed. In their progress, they met with several bands of Nez Percés, by whom they were invariably treated with the utmost kindness. Within seven days after leaving the domain of He-mim-el-pilp, they struck the Columbia River at Fort Wallah-Wallah, where they arrived on the 4th of March, 1834.

---

[7]Judge Kuykendall stated that Bonneville reached the mouth of Alpowa Creek via a trail over Lewiston Flat and Vineland to Dry Gulch, and then down the Snake River to the Alpowa.

[8]This village was near the mouth of Alpowa Creek. The man that Bonneville met here was Hími·n ?ilpílp ("wolf red"), sometimes spelled Hemene Ilppilp, and known to many white travelers in the region as Red Wolf. This village was also the site of Red Wolf Crossing.

9

Christian missions in the Clearwater region: an annotated bibliography and three accounts

No institution, including the U.S. Government, had a longer period of contact with the Clearwater region in the nineteenth century than the Protestant missionary effort. Its first Idaho missionary, Henry H. Spalding, began his famous work at Lapwai in 1836 and was soon joined by Asa Smith at Kamiah. However, the Whitman killings of November 1847 brought an end to this early proselytizing. Spalding himself returned to Lapwai as a government employee between 1862 and 1865, and again in 1871. Beginning with the American Board of Commissioners for Foreign Missions (ABCFM) and continuing through the era of the McBeth sisters, the missionary arm of the (chiefly) Presbyterian Church, under various forms of organization, maintained a continual presence in the region until 1932. The hiatus after 1847 seemed, in many ways, to make the church more influential. The Indian policy of the Grant administration (Grant's "Peace Policy" of 1869) only served to reinforce this role, since Lapwai Indian Agent John Monteith owed his appointment to the Presbyterian Church.

There is a vast and nearly overwhelming literature surrounding the hundred year history of Protestant missionaries in central Idaho. Much of it deals with missionary activities and squabbles. But Spalding was an able botanist who traveled widely up and down the Clearwater, and may have been the first European to see Wallowa Lake. He also kept detailed climatic data for this region (some of it published in the "Wilkes" chapter of this book) and brought together what became the Allen collection of Nez Perce clothing. From his post at Kamiah, Asa Bowen Smith proved to be a serious student of Nez Perce language and culture, and, although in many ways a narrow and angry man, has given to history some great insights on the seasonal round of life in the Clearwater region. The McBeth sisters have left us a vast correspondence useful in understanding Nez Perce culture during a time when notions of property began to cause disruptions in old patterns of life. These missionaries also hosted many passing visitors, several of whom have left valuable accounts of the Clearwater country.

A surprisingly large portion of the vast correspondence left by these missionaries consists of bickering and back stabbing. The term "Christian charity" seldom comes to mind. Only a small portion is outward looking, and most descriptions of the Nez Perce people are condescending. Nevertheless, many insightful letters do exist. In the text below, the editors of this volume provide excerpts from a long and very informative letter by the Rev. Asa Bowen Smith, who lived at Kamiah from 1839 to 1841. Smith was the best linguist among the Protestant missionaries, having studied Nez Perce with Lawyer, who then lived at Kamiah. Smith is also the author of a long (74 pp.) study of the Nez Perce language, written in 1842 after he left the Clearwater. Even so, Smith missed many things. He was either unaware of, or hostile to, the complexities of traditional Nez Perce religious life. His knowledge of economic life and labor was also quite superficial.

The bibliography that follows describes most of the primary sources for this missionary correspondence. Roman Catholic missionaries, most of them Jesuits, arrived in the region somewhat later. The first of them to encounter the Nez Perce people was Fr. P.J. DeSmet, who met them along the Jefferson River in August of 1840. He reported to Fr. Blanchet, in Oregon, that "The Nez Percés appeared to me tired of their self-styled ministers with wives, and show a great preference in favor of Catholic priests." With a few exceptions, their first hand accounts remain unpublished. Many are at the Oregon Province Archive, at Gonzaga University, and others are in St. Louis.

Further reading about the missionary era:

Early missions:

Clifford M. Drury, ed., *The Diaries and Letters of Henry H. Spalding and Asa Bowen Smith Relating to the Nez Perce Mission, 1838-1842* (Glendale: Arthur H. Clark, 1958).

> An indispensable collection of primary sources. It clearly demonstrates the linguistic and cultural skills of Smith. Accounts of Spalding's "itinerating trips" are also included. Drury was a Presbyterian minister based in Moscow, Idaho, in the 1930s.

Clifford M. Drury, *Henry Harmon Spalding* (Caldwell, Idaho: Caxton Printers, 1936).

> The standard, irreplaceable biography of Spalding. This volume also makes great use of the vast Spalding correspondence, now widely scattered in various collections and still partly unpublished.

Clifford M. Drury, ed., *The Mountains We Have Crossed: Diaries and Letters of the Oregon Mission, 1838* (Lincoln: University of Nebraska Press, 1999).

> An important source of primary accounts, especially those of women members of the various missions. A reprint of the 1966 edition, with a new introduction.

American Indian Correspondence: The Presbyterian Historical Society Collection of Missionaries' Letters, 1833-1893 (Wilmington, Delaware: Scholarly Resources

Microfilms). 35 reels.

A major repository of primary source material including hundreds of letters and other items dealing with central Idaho (Spalding, McBeth, Monteith, Deffenbaugh, etc.).

Papers of the American Board of Commissioners for Foreign Missions (Woodbridge, CT: Research Publications, Inc). Unit One: Letters to Domestic Correspondents. 148 reels. Unit Six: Missions of the American Continent and to the Islands of the Pacific. 138 reels.

A vast collection of missionary correspondence. Unit 6, reels 783 and 791 are especially important.

Other published letters, diaries, and journals:

Archer Butler Hulbert and Dorothy Hulbert, eds., *Marcus Whitman: Crusader.* 3 volumes. (Denver: Stewart Commission of Colorado College and the Denver Public Library, 1936-41).

Contains much missionary correspondence relative to Idaho.

The *Oregon Historical Quarterly* and the *Washington Historical Quarterly* have published over twenty letters and other first hand accounts dealing with the Clearwater, and some also appear in issues of the *Whitman College Quarterly.*

Accounts of visitors:

Cornelius J. Brosnan, *Jason Lee: Prophet of the New Oregon* (New York: Macmillan, 1932).

An important Methodist missionary in Oregon, Jason Lee, spent five days in April of 1838 at the Spalding Mission. Pp. 92-97 of Brosnan's book provide a reliable account of what Lee, a very perceptive visitor, saw.

Jason Lee, "Diary of Reverend Jason Lee—III," *Oregon Historical Quarterly* 17 (1916): 416-21.

Lee's own, somewhat brief diary entries of his visit to the Spalding Mission.

Joel Palmer, *Journal of Travels Over the Oregon Trail in 1845-1846* (Cincinnati: J.A. James, 1847). Reprinted 1993 by the Oregon Historical Society.

Palmer, an early emigrant overland to Oregon, returned to Indiana in March of 1846 to pick up his family. On a cattle-selling mission, he spent over a week with the Spaldings in early April. Palmer's book not only includes his own, lengthy observations (Pp. 231-241), but an appendix provides a Nez Perce vocabulary and a long letter from Spalding himself describing the region's economic prospects. An important account.

Leonard J. Arrington, "A Mormon Apostle Visits the Umatilla and Nez Perce in 1885," *Idaho Yesterdays* 31, no.1-2 (Spring/Summer 1987): 47-54.

An interesting account of a visit by a very perceptive observer, Lorenzo Snow.

Later missions:

Kate McBeth, *The Nez Perces Since Lewis and Clark* (New York: F. Revell, 1908).

An important history of both the Nez Perce people and missionary work among them by a Presbyterian missionary who spent thirty six years in Idaho.

Kate and Sue McBeth: Missionary Teachers to the Nez Perce (WWW site)

A huge repository of primary source documents, maps, and photos relating to these two missionary sisters, but also to the history and culture of the Nez Perce people after contact. Much of this site consists of never-before-published items. The full text of many rare government reports is also included.

URL: www.lib.uidaho.edu/mcbeth (Accessed August 2003)

The Nez Perce point of view:

Allen P. Slickpoo, Sr., "The Nez Perce Attitude Toward the Missionary Experience," *Idaho Yesterdays* 31, no. 1-2 (Spring/Summer 1987): 35-37.

A rare account by a leading figure of the Nez Perce people.

Memorial of the Nez Perce Indians Residing in the State of Idaho to the Congress of the United States. Presented by Mr. Borah. Compiled by Starr J. Maxwell. (Washington: U.S. Government Printing Office, 1911). 62nd Cong., 1st Sess. S. Doc. 97. SS 6108. Reprinted 2000 by the University of Idaho Library, with an introduction by Diane Mallickan.

An important primary source for Nez Perce life at the turn of the last century.

The Roman Catholics:

Robert Ignatius Burns, *The Jesuits and the Indian Wars of the Northwest* (New Haven: Yale University Press, 1966).

Scholarly and well-written. Based on vast research in primary sources.

Robert C. Carriker, *Father Peter John DeSmet: Jesuit in the West* (Norman: University of Oklahoma Press, 1995).

A modern, reliable, and very well-written biography of the most important Roman Catholic missionary in the region.

Hiram M. Chittenden, *Life, Letters and Travels of Father Pierre-Jean De Smet, S.J.* 4 vols. (New York: P.J. Harper, 1905).

A vast and amazing collection of DeSmet letters and reports. While it lacks many DeSmet letters located in recent years, this set is remarkably thorough.

Account 9.1: Excerpts from a letter of Asa Bowen Smith to the Rev. David Greene (Corresponding Secretary of the ABCFM, in Boston), written from

Kamiah and dated Feb. 6ᵗʰ 1840. Source: Records of the American Board of Commissioners for Foreign Missions. Oregon Mission Correspondence. Houghton Library, Harvard University. Printed here with the permission of Wider Church Ministries of the United Church of Christ, the successor to the ABCFM.

Much of this letter is devoted to debunking what Smith felt were the inaccurate and overly optimistic descriptions of the Nez Perce people that had been propagated in various missionary magazines by the Rev. Henry Spalding.

I do not say that there is nothing interesting or encouraging here. We do find that which is interesting. But at the same time we find difficulties & discouragements arising from various sources—difficulties too of such a nature as seriously affect our usefulness among this people. Some of these I will mention as I have already noted them down in my journal.

The first I will mention is the self-righteousness of the people. As a general thing the people consider themselves already good. They have thrown away their old hearts as they say, that is they have left off their old practices of lying, stealing, &c, & are now worshipping God & giving heed to his word. Hence they are indeed Pharisees, resting on their own good works, & how to drive them off from this ground & tear away their sandy foundation, I know not with my present knowledge of their language. Often do they come to me & tell me of their good works & endeavor to convince me that they are good, but when I tell them that they cannot get to heaven by self-righteousness, that such feelings are wrong & it is only those who feel themselves to be sinners & as such apply to Christ for salvation, they immediately take the opposite ground & rest their hopes on the acknowledgment of their sins. Thus they will shift their ground as occasion requires, while their hearts remain the same....

Another discouragement is the scattered condition of the people, & the impossibility of bringing them together in any considerable numbers at any place.

The Nez Perces [about 3,000 people in all, according to the census conducted by Smith] are scattered over a large extent of country, as I have already stated. Their country, including the Kayuses, as they are now considered all one tribe, cannot contain less than 30,000 square miles, & perhaps 40,000—so that there cannot be more than one inhabitant to *ten* square miles. They however live in small bands along the rivers & small streams, at considerable distances from each other on lands belonging to themselves. By common consent or perhaps by fear of each other, each band has control over the land belonging to it, & this is the hunting or fishing ground of that band. It is not common that one infringes on the rights of another. They are usually careful especially at the hunting season, not to hunt on another's ground. Still however there are places where they assemble for particular purposes on the lands of others. This is the case with regard to the *kamosh* ground & other places of roots. Many of the bands have no roots on their own lands. Hence they go to the lands of others where they dig roots, or obtain them in exchange for fish. Consequently the people are extremely scattered, living in little bands varying usually from 10 to 100 or 150. One band numbers 235. Should one band attempt to live constantly on the land of another, it would subject both to serious inconveniences in their present mode of living. Game is already scarce, & it is all the people can do to live in their present scattered condition. The same difficulty occurs in respect to gaining their subsistence from cultivation. Good land is found only in small tracts here & there on the banks of streams, not enough in any one place to collect any considerable number, except in the region where Dr. W[hitman] is. ...Thus it is that we can have but few within our reach, to whom we can give instruction....

They may indeed assemble at the stations at certain seasons in considerable numbers but it is only for a very few weeks, & then they must go to their respective places in search of food.

The greatest number that have been at this station at any time is about 275. It was but a short time however that there were so many. Most of them went away three or four weeks since in search of food & will not return again till the Spring opens.

Another discouragement is the wandering habits of the people [i.e., their seasonal round of life]. The people are not only scattered, but they are wandering from place to place during almost the entire year. The manner in which they live renders it necessary for them to wander. Their food consists of dried buffalo meat, venison, fish, various kinds of roots, & even the moss which grows on the pines, berries, &c. These articles are all obtained in different places, hence they must wander to obtain them. The summer is a very busy time with the people, especially with the women, as they dig all the roots. They commence digging roots in May or the last of April & sometimes without interruption till near the 1st of July when they go for salmon or buffalo. They dig roots however more or less till winter comes. Those who go to buffalo are gone usually from three to four months. Some of them remain a year or more in the buffalo country, & some remain there constantly. Out of 497 people who belong within 15 miles of this place, 249 are now in the buffalo country & only 248 in this vicinity.

In the winter they must go where they can get game. If it is not to be found on the ground where they reside in the summer, they must go some where else.

This draws them away from some of the stations very much during the winter. Most of the Kayuses & many of the lower Nez Perces winter at the Falls of the Columbia River, 100 miles below Walla Walla, where is an abundance of salmon, which they buy of the natives there. We can therefore do but little with the people. There are but a few of them within our reach, & that few usually but a small part of the year.

Another discouragement is the small number of the people & the fact that they are decreasing in numbers & according to present appearances will at no distant day become extinct. The highest estimate that has been made of the Nez Perces is 5000. But we are now satisfied that this estimate is too large. Mr. Rogers [his assistant] & myself have commenced numbering the people. We have obtained the number of each band as far as we have proceeded by means of the principal man or chief of that band. In many cases they have done it themselves & brought us a bundle of [counting] sticks for each individual of the band. We have thus far numbered 1,421, & we think that certainly one half & perhaps more are already numbered. All the large bands are numbered. Two in the region of the Salmon River are numbered, one of 151, & the other 235. (This river is called on the map I have before me, N. Fork or Lewis or Snake River.) All who live on the Koos-koos-kee River [the Clearwater], on which are situated this station & that of Mr.

Spalding's have been numbered amounting to 950. On Snake River we have as yet numbered only 85. The Nez Perces are scattered along the Snake River from the mouth of Salmon River down to the Koos-koos-kee & some distance below. Yet they are all very small bands, much smaller than those which have been numbered. I think that all who live on the Snake River cannot exceed in number those on the Koos-koos-kee. This includes all except the Kayuses & a few Nez Perces who are united with them by marriage &c. Their number is small indeed. Their country stretches along the south side of the Columbia River, not however including the River, but along the southern tributaries of the Columbia, & extends from the country of the Nez Perces down to the range of mountains where are the falls of the Columbia, 100 miles below Walla Walla. This remnant of a tribe has in fact become united with the Nez Perces & there are but few of the old people who now speak the Kayuse or Waiiletpu language. The whole number cannot exceed 3000, including both the Nez Perces & Kayuses. The Nez Perces language, however, is spoken to some extent by the principal man of some of the adjacent tribes, but scarcely at all by the common people.

The number of this people is evidently diminishing & has been for many years. From the accounts of the people, it appears that formerly the number of people was much greater than at present. The excavations in the ground where the people formerly had their lodges indicate that the number of people was much greater than at present.

The causes which have diminished the people are as follows: 1st Disease—It appears from the accounts of the people that epidemics have formerly prevailed among them, carrying off many people in a short time. No epidemic has however prevailed among them very recently. Twice during the remembrance of the most aged among this people has the small pox been among them. The first time it visited them must have been 60 or perhaps 70 years ago [i.e., about 1780]. Some very old people, I should think 70 or 80 years old & perhaps more, relate that when they were children a large number of people both of the Nez Perces & Flatheads wintered in the buffalo country. In the spring as usual the people from this region went to buffalo. Instead of finding their people as they expected they found their lodges standing in order, & the people almost to an individual dead. Only here & there one survived the disease. It seems to have been the most virulent form of the small pox. From thence it followed the people to this region & swept through the whole country, very few surviving the attack of the disease. Some fled & thus avoided the contagion.

The small pox again visited this country soon after Lewis & Clarke were here, perhaps two years after; but it was a milder form, perhaps the varioloid & did not prove so fatal. Many however died. The marks of this disease are now to be seen on the faces of many of the old people....

2. Wars. In past years large numbers of this people have been cut off in wars with the Blackfeet & Snakes. Thus it is that the number of men have been diminished, till at present but few men are left. The number of women is much greater than that of men. I will give the number of men belonging to several bands as an example of the small proportion of men. All the young men who are unmarried are included among the men—in one band of 235, there are 60 men. In one of 143, there are 30 men. One of 125, 27 men—one of 102, 17 men; one of 110, 18 men; one of 84, 23 men; one of 63, 6 men.

3. Polygamy & the consequent degradation of the females—Till recently polygamy has been the constant practice of this people, but now most of the Nez Perces have abandoned this practice & are living with one wife, yet the effects of this sin together with its attendant evils are still felt—The marriage vow is usually not considered at all sacred among this people. Women are taken & put away at pleasure & there is no law to call them to account for it—Adultery is by no means uncommon among this people—Hence there are but few children. In consequence of the degradation of females, they are subjected to every kind of hardship. They dig all the roots, cut all the wood & carry it on their backs, pack all their effects when they travel, while the men live at their ease—Consequently abortions are very frequent among them & many children die almost as soon as they are born—Probably not less than half the children are destroyed in this way, so that in fact births are very infrequent among them. From May last to the close of this year, there were only two births among the people belonging near this stations. During the same time there were seven deaths.* Since the commencement of this year however there have been already three births & but two deaths—Since writing this I have heard of three deaths of those from this place in the buffalo country during the winter....

Another discouragement is the fact that this people have no form of government, & no law among them. The inconvenience & perplexity of living in such a state of society will readily be seen. But this is not the principal difficulty we have met with on this ground. The people have no law and consequently understand not the nature of law. There are indeed those among them who are called chiefs. But these have no power. Their law is mere advice. The people regard them or not as they please.

To be a chief amounts merely to nothing. There are three classes of chiefs among this people distinguished by the manner in which they become chiefs—1st. Those who have been brave in war, leaders, &c. There are but few remaining of this class & soon they will all be gone.

2nd. Next to the war chiefs are the *mush* chiefs, that is, those who have become chiefs by making feasts & feeding the people. Gratifying the people's appetites is the one principal way to gain their influence, & obtain power over them.

3d. The Tobacco chiefs, that is those who have become chiefs by being presented with tobacco at the Forts, & deal it out to the people & this get an influence over them. The two last classes are mere gratifyers of the people's appetites.

The power of the chiefs amounts to very little & the people do that which is right in their own eyes.

They know nothing of the restraints of law, have no idea of penalty, & apparently no idea of justice. Justice with them seems to mean nothing more than expediency or propriety. Every thing of this nature seems foreign to them. Hence it seems impossible to make them understand the nature of divine law, its holiness & justice, the nature of its penalty, &c....

Another difficulty of a similar nature arise from the fact that the people have had no system of religion. Missionaries often complain of the difficulties they meet with from the prevailing religious system of the natives & the difficulty of applying

---

* 3 at this place & 4 in the buffalo country.

the words, which are used in reference to their superstitions, to religious subjects. But I apprehend the difficulty is far greater where there is no religious system, & an entire destitution of terms to apply to religious subjects. How, for instance, can we give this people any idea of the priesthood, of sacrifices, & other kindred subjects. They have nothing like it among themselves, & no terms to use in reference to those subjects. Had we the terms, altho' they might have been associated with all that is impure & debasing, & had we some form of religion with its various institutions, however corrupt by which to illustrate, & convey correct ideas to their minds, I should feel it to be a great acquisition.

In view of these facts, my heart often sinks within me, & I am led to exclaim, How shall the object for which we have been sent hither be accomplished?

Account 9.2: The "census" of the Nez Perce people taken in November of 1839 by Cornelius Rogers and the Rev. Asa Bowen Smith, at Kamiah. Source: Records of the American Board of Commissioners for Foreign Missions, Houghton Library, Harvard University. Published here with the permission of Wider Church Ministries of the United Church of Christ, the successor of the ABCFM.

Smith had a very high opinion of his own worth, and this census was an effort to demonstrate to the American Board in Boston that the number of inhabitants in Nez Perce country was too low to warrant Smith's assignment in the region.

No. of Nez Perces Nov. 12th 1839

Names of chiefs.	Total No. of men		no. of men here!		Whole No.		Whole No. here
Lawyer	30	*Boys*	10	*Girls*	143		53
Takansuatis	5		None		17	*Children*	None
Isaac	27	22	10	17	125	39	47
Pakatash	17	24	11	25	102	49	57
Kentuck							
Husinmalakin	18	28	14	32	110	60	91
Benjamin	28	18		19	84	37	
Silas	10	8		6	38	14	
Solomon	2	2		1	7	3	
Billy					151		111
Ellis	60				235		
Hinpelakin	6				63		
Tahnaiask	6				33		
Jacob	17				85		
James	16				64		
Tialihlikt					19		
Noah					46		
luimashwahaikt*	20				66	*Total* 1988	
Samson					33	1421	

[at the top of the second page of the manuscript]

				W. 16	
		248		P. 12	
Joseph	168			C. 16	497
Apashwahaikt		150	1421	248	
Between the 2 preceding		98	416	249	
		——	——		
		416	1837		
Red Wolf		90	90		
		——			
		1927	*the No of Nez Perces*		

from the Red Wolf's place upward in cluding
all on the Kuskuski, Snake & Salmon Rivers

*This name is unclear in the original manuscript.

Account 9.3: A letter from Benjamin Alvord to John Proctor, a Boston clergyman. Source: same as account one. Also on reel 791, frame 294+ of the ABCFM microfilm collection. Published here with the permission of Wider Church Ministries of the United Church of Christ, the successor to the ABCFM.

An 1854 assessment of the impact of Protestant missionaries on the Nez Perce people. The author is Major Benjamin Alvord, who had commanded Fort Dalles, personally knew most Nez Perce leaders, and was a careful student of their culture. As a brevet General, Alvord commanded volunteer troops in the Columbia during the Civil War and played a major role in negotiating the 1863 Treaty, called the "steal treaty" by Nez Perce historians.

Worcester, Mass
Sept 10 1854

John C. Proctor Esq
Boston

My dear sir

Herewith I enclose to you the statement I promised you concerning the Nez Perces Indians in Oregon and the possibility of the reestablishment of the missions of the American Board of C. for F. Missions in that interesting tribe.

Do what you please with my paper—I prefer its publication without my name— But you may use my name freely to the members of the Board.

If you deem it desirable or important, then my consent even to publication of my name—I would waive my objection, if any good could be attained by the use of it.

With the kindest regards to your family & Mrs Butler I remain very truly yours

Benj^m Alvord
Major U.S.A.

P.S. I was in command at the Dalles of the Columbia up to July 1854. These matters have been dwelt upon a little in my dispatches to the government but they have not been published.[1]

The Nez Percés Indians in Oregon

It may be interesting to the friends of the American Board of Commissioners for Foreign Missions to know that the effects of a mission abandoned in 1847, which the Board has established among the Nez Percés in Oregon are still exhibited in a remarkable manner. This tribe lives near the Rocky Mountains on the waters of the Kooskooskie, a branch of the upper Columbia. When the mission among the Cayuse was broken up—by the massacre of the lamented Whitman and his party in 1847, the mission among the Nez Percés was also abandoned. But the latter tribe never shared in the hostile feeling of the Cayuse, and declined on that occasion to join in a war against the whites, and have since steadily and repeatedly refused to join in any such scheme. The mission however was abandoned. If maintained, the communications of the missionaries with the lower Columbia would have been temporarily cut off by the warlike state of the Cayuse and other tribes.

In the Spring of 1853 a white man who had passed the previous winter in the Nez Perces country came in to the military post at the Dalles of the Columbia and on being questioned as to the manners and customs of the tribe, he said that he had wintered with a band of several hundred in number and that the whole party assembled every morning and evening for prayer, the exercises being conducted by one of the tribe and in their own language. He stated that on Sundays they assembled in like manner for exhortation and worship—The writer of this communication made repeated inquiries, and these accounts have been confirmed by the statements of others who have resided among the Nez Percés.

Thus six years subsequent to the abandonment of the mission, its benign effects are witnessed among that interesting people. It would not be pretended that the whole tribe is religious or that there was a real conversion in many instances. But here is evidence of the establishment of good habits and customs. All concur in representing them to be remarkably moral Indians. Gambling is their chief vice, & existed with them when Lewis & Clarke first visited the tribe in 1805. We are happy to learn that little or no ardent spirits have yet made their way thither.

It is the largest tribe in Oregon, containing about 3000 souls. They possess greater elements of improvement than any Indians west of the Rocky Mountains.

They have lively intellects, are docile, and seem anxious to be instructed. If any tribe on the Pacific coast can attain a condition promising eventual civilization, it must be the Nez Percés. Located near the Rocky Mountains, and fortunately remote from the path of the emigrants and all contact with whites, they remain as yet uncontaminated by the vices which our border population are too sure to

---

[1]One important Alvord report *was* eventually published (in 1858). Dated February 7, 1853, it is: *Report of Brevet Major Benjamin Alvord, captain, 4th infantry, commanding at Dalles of the Columbia, Oregon, concerning the Indians in the Territories of Oregon and Washington, east of the Cascade mountains.* 34th Congress, 3rd Session. *House Executive Document 9.* (Serial Set 906). Reprinted in *Northwest Anthropological Research Notes* 32, no. 1 (Spring 1998): 53-67.

communicate. Thus situated their knowledge of the Americans has been every way favorable, and they have always been decidedly friendly to us from the day that Lewis & Clarke (who treated them very kindly) came among them in 1805. The Whitman massacre occurred in 1847 before our Government had taken possession, organized a Territorial Government, and before any U.S. Troops had reached that country. The Cayuse have dwindled in numbers to one hundred warriors and there can scarcely be a doubt that newly established missions would be secure from like calamities.

It is safe to assert, that there is not within the territory of the United States in the whole Indian race, such another field for benevolent action as in this interesting tribe. The Government through its agents has often promised much, but done little or nothing for this people. This spring some ploughs [two illegible words] have been sent as presents to their Chiefs. They want ploughs, seeds, a blacksmith, schools and missions. They often express regret at the abandonment of the mission. They show the first element of budding improvement by wishing their children to be educated, if they themselves must die in ignorance.

We trust it will be long before the Whites will wish for their lands. Therefore the Government will have no occasion soon to form a treaty with them. Thus it will be years before the Government will establish any schools among them in compliance with treaty stipulations. Still it would be right and proper for Congress to authorize now the establishment of schools, the furnishing of seeds, blacksmiths and ploughs, and the appliances of civilization. The only provision in the acts of the recent session of Congress relating to the Indians in Oregon is an appropriation for the extinguishment of the Indian title. Precedents could be named, when Congress has made appropriations for the benefit of the Indians when no treaty stipulations required them. Such a course would be eminently humane, politic and just towards a tribe which has remained steadfastly attached to our people and Government, at a time when surrounding tribes have shown disaffection. Many of the latter desired to cling to the English during the protracted negotiations when the Oregon Boundary ascertain[ed].

But it is difficult to procure any action of Congress in such matters; and no friend of the Nez Percés would wish to invite any action of the Government which would soon lead to any extinguishments of Indian title and immigration of whites to that region. Therefore it may deserve the serious consideration of the American Board whether a revival of their missions in that tribe will not be judicious. If ever on the Pacific Slope an Indian tribe shall attain a position as promising of final civilization and Christianity as that of the Cherokees and Choctaws, it will be the tribe we have made the topic of this communication. The Cherokee nation is now as civilized as was that of England in the days of Alfred. History has recorded the agency of Christianity in redeeming "the sea-girt isle" from barbarism. Those who founded missions and schools among the Cherokees may flatter themselves that they thus planted seed which may take root and give birth to a great people. Shall an office equally beneficent and fruitful in brilliant results be performed toward the Nez Percés Indians?

10

Naval visitors:
the Wilkes Expedition of 1841

Britain was not the only nation to see the link between scientific exploration and political power. While a hiatus of nearly forty years followed the success of Lewis and Clark's government exploration of the Columbia region, by 1838 the young American republic was ready to join in the growing effort to study the world. The chief vehicle for this effort was the United States Exploring Expedition of 1838-42, better known as the Wilkes Expedition after its commander, Navy officer Charles Wilkes.

The expedition was originally conceived by its backers in Congress and in the scientific community as a commercial and scientific voyage to South America, the islands of the South Pacific, and above all, to Antarctica. In the end, those visits were all completed, but the long delays and general confusion that surrounded the expedition's departure allowed some political concerns to be added. Wilkes' trip came to be linked rather vaguely to the western mapping efforts of John Charles Fremont. To support this effort in the West, Wilkes was also directed to explore and map the Columbia River in the Northwest and to closely examine Mexican holdings in California.

Sailing from Antarctica and Hawaii, Wilkes and his ships arrived off the coast of present-day Washington state in May of 1841. The Commander soon dispatched an exploration party deep into the interior of the region. This group was led by Lieutenant R.E. Johnson, who proved to be a rather poor leader. In volume four of Wilkes' final report, we learn that this small exploring party was to visit Fort Colville, then travel south to Lapwai, and return downstream to Nisqually via Walla Walla and the Yakima River. This exploration intruded into the heart of the trading territory of the Hudson's Bay Company, and came at a time when British claims for lands south of the 49th parallel were under growing American pressure.

Despite the obvious political goals of this exploration, two capable scientists were sent with Johnson. They were Charles Pickering, a well-regarded naturalist and anthropologist, and botanist William D. Brackenridge, who, somewhat mysteriously, is always called J.D. Brackenridge in the various reports published by Wilkes.

In early June, this party carefully examined Hudson's Bay Company posts at Okanagan and Colville, where they were treated with amazing courtesy. They visited with the Walker and Eells missionary families later that month at the Chimikaine (or Tshimakain) Mission west of what is now Spokane. On June 22-23, minus Johnson, the expedition passed through the Palouse country just west of the Palouse Range, probably on the Nez Perce Indian trail that crosses near Tomer Butte, southeast of present day Moscow, Idaho. They reached the Clearwater River just below the mouth of Lapwai Creek on June 25, 1841.

The publishing history of the various volumes of reports from Wilkes and his staff is so convoluted that an entire book has been devoted to just this topic. The whole effort was characterized by fraud and incompetence, and some of the information was never published at all. Wilkes himself did a good job of summarizing the trip to Lapwai, although he remained on the coast. He worked with Lt. Johnson on his account, using the diaries and journals of the other participants. Pickering's report was published but is a rare and obscure document. The notes made by Brackenridge on this trip are contained in a manuscript owned by the Maryland Historical Society and were published in 1931.

Appendix 13 of volume four of Wilkes' official summary report, which was privately published in 1845, also contains three years of climatic data for Lapwai (1837, 1840, and 1841) compiled by Rev. Henry Spalding, the earliest scientific data of any kind published for Idaho. 1840 was especially warm, with highs above 100° in three consecutive months.

The Wilkes Expedition produced many disappointments as well as some substantial achievements. The work inland in the Pacific Northwest was especially valuable from a scientific viewpoint, as the Wilkes party was among the first to recognize the great agricultural potential of the Palouse region.

More information about the Wilkes Expedition:

Harley H. Bartlett, "The Reports of the Wilkes Expedition, and the Work of the Specialists in Science," *Proceedings of the American Philosophical Society* 82, no. 5 (June 1940): 601-19.

This article is an early effort to make sense of the vast Wilkes primary literature.

Barry Alan Joyce, *The Shaping of American Ethnography: the Wilkes Exploring Expedition, 1838-1842* (Lincoln: University of Nebraska Press, 2001).

Chapter five and six are an important summary of Wilkes' work in the west.

Susan Delano McKelvey, "Brackenridge, 'Horticulturist' of the United States Exploring Expedition, Makes Two Trips in the State of Washington, and Travels Overland from the Columbia River to the Bay of San Francisco," In *Botanical Exploration of the Trans-Mississippi West, 1790-1850* (Jamaica Plains, Massachusetts: Arnold Arboretum of Harvard University, 1955), 685-729.

A thorough and reliable account of the botanical achievements of the Wilkes Expedition in the Northwest.

David B. Tyler, *The Wilkes Expedition.* (Philadelphia: American Philosophical Society, 1968).

This book is the definitive history of the expedition and is a reliable guide to the publication history. Chapter 18 covers the trip to Lapwai and the Clearwater.

Charles Wilkes, *The Narrative of the United States Exploring Expedition During the Years 1838, 1839, 1840, 1841, and 1842.* Volume 4 (Philadelphia: Lea and Blanchard, 1845).

Pages 456-67 cover the inland trip along the Clearwater and back to Walla Walla.

Account 10.1: Excerpts from Wilkes' official account. Source: Charles Wilkes, *Narrative of the United States Exploring Expedition. Vol. 4* (Philadelphia: Lea and Blanchard, 1845), 459-66.

On the 22d [of June, 1841], they traveled thirty miles in an east-northeasterly direction, from the Spokane [River]. The country they passed over would be called hilly, with lakes and open glades intervening: the soil was poor, with sand and stones; a few scattered pines were seen on the hills, and around the lakes were cotton-wood and willow bushes....

On the 24th, they passed through a fine rolling prairie country, producing very fine pasture, and being well watered, though destitute of wood. The distance made to-day was thirty miles. The plants seen were Convolvus, Frasera, Habenaria, Calochortus, Baptisia, and Trifolium: this last is a good plant for cattle.[1]

During the day, they met a party of Indians travelling, with abundance of spare horses, and in this case they were carrying even their tent poles, with which one of their horses was loaded: a proof that underwood of the description used is scarce in the country. Within thirty miles of Lapwai, the mission station on the Kooskooskee [the Clearwater], they crossed a small tributary of the Snake river [the Palouse River], thirty feet wide and two deep. It was very winding, and its general course was southwest. About twenty miles distant, in a south-southeast direction, they discovered a high snowy peak, which is situated near the Grande Ronde, and is the highest point of what is termed the Blue Ridge [the Blue Mountains]. On its summit the snow remains all the year round.

Beyond the Snake or Lewis river, was a long even-topped ridge, wooded on its upper parts, and covered with snow. This is the mountain which Mr. Drayton ascended near the Wallawalla. From the northwest, it has the appearance of an extensive and elevated table-land.

On the 25th, about noon, they reached the Kooskooskee, which is two thousand feet below the plain they had been travelling on. It is here eight hundred

---

[1]Convolvus: There is a genus *Convolvulus*, possibly the putative native morning glory, *Calystegia sepium*. Frasera: Its common name is also frasera. Habenaria: bog orchid. Calochortus: mariposa lily or cat's ear. Near Spokane, it could have been either, or both. Baptisia: Probably *Thermopsis*, mountain pea. Trifolium: Clover (probably *T.douglasii*, a tall and quite spectacular plant).

feet wide, and a powerful stream. Lewis and Clarke fell upon this river about forty-five miles above this place, and it is not difficult to imagine how they were induced to suppose that they had reached the great river flowing to the west, so totally different is it from the Ohio and Missouri. The missionaries informed me, in explanation of this, that the Indians have names for all the nooks and points along the rivers, but none for the rivers themselves: they further state, in reference to these travellers, that when they made their appearance, the Indians for some time doubted whether they were really men, so overgrown were they with beards, and of course so different from this beardless race.

Mr. Spalding has built himself a house of two stories, with board floors, as well as a grist and saw mill. For these he procured the timber in the mountains, and rafted it down himself; in doing which he has not neglected to attend to the proper sphere of his duties, for his labors will compare in this respect with those of any of his brethren. His efforts in agriculture are not less exemplary, for he has twenty acres of fine wheat, and a large field in which were potatoes, corn, melons, pumpkins, peas, beans, &c., the whole of which were in fine order.

This part of Oregon [i.e., present-day Oregon, Washington, and Idaho] is admirably adapted to the raising of sheep: the ewes bear twice a year, and often produce twins. One ewe was pointed out to our gentlemen, that had seven lambs within three hundred and sixty-three days. Horned cattle also thrive, but the stock is at present limited. The Indians have a strong desire to procure them. A party was persuaded to accompany a missionary, and take horses over to St. Louis, to exchange for cattle. When they reached the Sioux country, the chiefs being absent at Washington, they were attacked and all murdered, except the white man.

Mr. Spalding, during his residence of five years, has kept a register of the weather...

The greatest heat experienced during his residence was in 1837: on the 23d July, in that year, the thermometer was 108° in the shade....Mr. Spalding remarks, that, since his residence, no two years have been alike....

Among the other duties of Mr. Spalding, he has taught the Indians the art of cultivation, and many of them now have plantations. The idea of planting seeds had never occurred to the Oregon Indians before the arrival of the missionaries. Mr. Spalding kindly lends them his ploughs and other implements of husbandry: and in a difficulty occurring with some of them, he had only to threaten them with the loss of the plough, to bring the refractory person to reason. One of the Indians had entirely abandoned his former mode of life, had built himself a log cabin, and both himself and his wife were neatly dressed in European costume. The women were represented as coming a distance of many miles to learn to spin and knit, and assist Mrs. Spalding in her domestic avocations.

Mr. Spalding gave his assembled flock some account of the Expedition, and a short sketch of the people we had seen, which the Indians listened to with great interest, and appeared to comprehend perfectly, with the aid of a map.

Mr. Spalding stated, that the number of Oregon Indians whom he had ascertained to have visited the United States was surprising. He informed our gentlemen that he had sent letters to Boston in eighty-one days from the Dalles, by means of Indians and the American [fur trade] rendezvous; and, what was remarkable, the slowest part of the route was from St. Louis to Boston. The communication is still carried on by Indians, although it was generally supposed to be by free trappers. He considers that these tribes, both men and women, are an industrious people.

Our thanks were due to Mr. Spalding for his kindness in exchanging horses, which enabled our party to proceed more comfortably, and to carry forward their collections.

On the 26th, they left the mission at Lapwai, accompanied by the missionaries and their ladies, intending to visit some of the rude farms of the natives. These are situated in a fertile valley, running in a southerly direction from the Kooskooskee. The farms are from five to twelve acres each, all fenced in, and on these the Indians cultivate wheat, corn, potatoes, melons, pumpkins, &c. One of them, in the year 1840, raised four hundred bushels of potatoes and forty-five bushels of wheat. With part of the potatoes he bought enough buffalo meat to serve him through the winter. All these lots were kept in good order, and several had good mud houses on them. The great endeavor of Mr. Spalding is to induce the Indians to give up their roving mode of life, and to settle down and cultivate the soil; and in this he is succeeding admirably. He shows admirable tact and skill, together with untiring industry and perseverance in the prosecution of his labours as a missionary; and he appears to be determined to leave nothing undone that one person alone can perform. In the winter, his time and that of his wife is devoted to teaching, at which session their school is much enlarged.

On their way, they fell in with some half-breeds, going to hunt buffalo. Among them were four brothers, all fine-looking young men, and very much alike. Many of the Indians, as has before been remarked, visit the buffalo-grounds. These have been constantly changing, and, within the memory of many of the hunters, their limits have been very much circumscribed. From the accounts we have received, these animals are not now found west of the Portneuf river, and their range has been materially changed since the arrival of the whites. Instead of now migrating to the south during the winter, they are reported as seeking a more northern clime, and are now found as far north as 64°: four degrees farther in that direction than their former range. This abandonment of their feeding-grounds is unknown in any other American animal, and may forebode their extinction at no very distant day.

At 3 p.m., after travelling fifteen miles, they reached the banks of the Snake river, at the forks. On their way down the Kooskooskee, they had met with numerous herds of horses belonging to the Indians; and here they found the owners, consisting of about one hundred and fifty persons. There was but one building, which was of a circular form and a hundred feet in diameter. It was built of rails or rough joists set on end, which supported a roof of the same material, and served the double purpose of sheltering the inhabitants and drying their fish. The different families were arranged around the walls in the interior. These Indians paid no attention to our party while passing, but soon after sent up two canoes, to ferry them and their luggage over the river; which being finished, they went away without demanding any thing for their services, and exhibiting a sort of independence, characteristic of this race when they think themselves well off or rich.

The party crossed the Snake river about a mile above its junction with the Kooskooskee....

There are a number of singular customs prevailing among the Nez Percés, perhaps a greater number than in any other nation of savages. That of overcoming the "Wawish," or spirit of fatigue, if it may be so translated, is the most remarkable; for this is a ceremony to enable them to endure fatigue, that has long been practised among them, and is still kept up. The operation continues for three, five, and seven days, and is often repeated. It is begun on the first day by taking three or four willow sticks, eighteen inches long, and thrusting them down the throat, in order to cleanse the stomach by bringing up bile, blood, and coagulated matter; a hole is then prepared, of a sufficient depth for a man to sit upright, with his head above the ground. This is usually dug near a running brook....

The officers at Wallawalla mentioned, that some of the Indians had remarkable powers of undergoing fatigue, and instanced the case of one who preformed the journey from Dr. Whitman's mission-house to the forks of the Clearwater, a distance of one hundred miles, between morning and sunset. This man is in the habit of performing this treatment on himself annually.

The Indians around Lapwai subsist for the most part upon fish, roots, and berries: the latter they make into cakes; moss is also eaten by them. Half of these Indians usually make a trip to the buffalo country for three months, by which means they are supplied with the flesh of that animal.

The school at the station has in winter about five hundred scholars, but in the summer not one-tenth of that number attend. Our gentlemen heard some of the pupils read. Only two are converts to Christianity, the principal chief and another; eight or ten, however, are reported as showing signs of piety.

The men are industrious, for Indians. The mission have a saw-mill at this place, capable of sawing three thousand feet per day.

The usual game of the Indians, which have been already described, are played here. The wages for the performance of any task are paid for in clothing, blankets, horses, &c.

Their salmon-fishing is conducted with much industry, and lasts from daylight until ten o'clock at night. Supper is their principal meal.

The scalps of enemies are taken in war, and the war-dance is always performed.

Girls are offered as wives to the young men by the parents: the ties of marriage are very loose, and wives are put away at pleasure. This privilege is also allowed to the women, which places the two sexes much more on a par than among the tribes west of the mountains.

The medicine men and women are much in repute here. Before any sorcery or divination is performed, they retire to the mountains for several days, where they fast, and where they pretend to have an interview with the waiakin or wolf. When they return, they relate the conversation they have had with him, and proceed to effect cures, &c. They are looked upon as invulnerable, and it is believed that balls fired at them are flattened against their breasts. If affronted or injured, they predict death to the offender, and the doom is considered inevitable. They use the same means of extricating diseases that have been before described.

Wild animals are now comparatively few, when compared with their former numbers. They consist of wolves, large and small, who prowl around the dwellings; lynxes, bears, of the gray, brown, black, and yellow colours, the former of which were the most numerous. Beavers and otters are now both scarce. Rats, both water and musk, are seen in numbers.

[Table] XIII.

Meteorological observations at Lapwai, or Kooskooskee, Nez Perce Mission, Oregon Territory, Lat. 46° 30' N., Long. 118° 30' W., 468 miles from the mouth of Columbia River; by the Rev. H.H. Spalding.

XIII.

METEOROLOGICAL OBSERVATIONS AT LAPWAI, OR KOOSKOOSKEE, NEZ PERCES MISSION, OREGON TERRITORY, LAT. 46° 30' N., LON. 118° 30' W., 468 MILES FROM THE MOUTH OF COLUMBIA RIVER ; BY THE REV. H. H. SPALDING.

1837.

MONTHS.	Greatest cold.	Day of the month.	Greatest heat.	Day of the month.	Before sunrise.	4 P. M.	9 P. M.	Average monthly mean.	Greatest monthly range.	Greatest daily range.	Fair days.	Cloudy days.	Rainy days.	Snowy days.	RESULTS.
JANUARY.	9°	12	63°	22	25·9°	41·7°	31·9°	36°	39°	10°	9	9	8	4	
FEBRUARY.	11	11	76	20	29·4	54·9	33·1	42·5	58	48	14	9	1	4	
MARCH.	14	11	84	17	35·4	66·6	41·2	49	70	46	18	6	5	2	Mean temp. 56·2°
APRIL.	34	25	86	29	46·8	69·4	53·5	60	52	44	12	14	3	1	Fair days, 159
MAY.	28	13	95	16	53·5	73·1	57·6	61·5	67	49	13	9	9	—	Cloudy days, 77
JUNE.	46	9	94	24	59·7	78·3	67·3	70	48	28	9	8	13	—	Rainy days, 85
JULY.	26	2	108	23	56·8	79	67·8	67	72	58	20	3	8	—	Snowy days, 14
AUGUST.	38	14	101	10	58·5	84·6	71·1	69·5	63	49	21	6	4	—	
SEPTEMBER.	31	14	90	1	56·3	72·6	65·5	60·5	59	45	22	2	6	—	
OCTOBER.	26	28	90	11	35·9	66·9	46·9	58	64	48	15	—	18	—	
NOVEMBER.	18	20	70	5	34·6	48·8	44·2	44	52	31	6	11	10	3	

XIII.—CONTINUED.

1840.

MONTHS.	Greatest cold.	Day of the month.	Greatest heat.	Day of the month.	Before sunrise.	4 P. M.	9 P. M.	Average monthly mean.	Greatest monthly range.	Greatest daily range.	Fair days.	Cloudy days.	Rainy days.	Snowy days.	RESULTS.
JANUARY.	9°	31	52°	18	33°	43°	36·4°	30·5°	43°	21°	12	12	6	1	
FEBRUARY.	19	1	62	26	38·3	47·2	40·4	35·5	43	20	2	12	11	4	Mean temp. 53·6°
MARCH.	9	19	80	31	35·9	53·6	41·4	44·5	71	42	12	10	5	4	Fair days, 172
APRIL.	27	28	80	1	40·8	60·7	46	51·3	53	42	12	10	6	2	Cloudy days, 93
MAY.	30	11	87	22	46	61·9	54·67	53·2	57	43	10	14	7	—	Rainy days, 88
JUNE.	47	1	99	30	59·1	85·7	65·3	73	52	45	22	8	—	—	Snowy days, 12
JULY.	48	10	104	12	60·6	90	68·8	76	56	42	24	4	3	—	
AUGUST.	50	20	107	12	63	88·9	70·3	73·2	57	43	23	7	1	—	
SEPTEMBER.	48	29	100	19	58·9	86·4	41·1	75	52	40	16	5	9	—	
OCTOBER.	27	24	78	3	38·1	59·4	46·6	52·1	51	37	23	5	3	—	
NOVEMBER.	23	29	58	14	35·7	50·3	40·8	40·5	35	22	6	3	21	1	
DECEMBER.	19	31	55	14	36·8	46·8	41	37	36	23	12	3	16	—	

Mean temperature, 1837, 56·2°
Do. do. 1840, 53·6
Aggregate mean, 109·8' = 54·9°.

XIII.—Continued.

1841.

MONTHS.	THERMOMETER.											WEATHER.				RESULTS.	
	Greatest cold.	Day of the month.	Greatest heat.	Day of the month.	Before sunrise.	4 P. M.	9 P. M.	Average monthly mean.	Greatest monthly range.	Greatest daily range.		Fair days.	Cloudy days.	Rainy days.	Snowy days.		
JANUARY.	26°	16	28°	26	20·04°	29·4°	25°	27°	74°	46°		9	10	4	8	Average mean temp.	50·3°
FEBRUARY.	14	10	66	28	22·7	44·4	27·8	35	80	42		17	4	4	3	Fair days,	70
MARCH.	26	10	69	15	—	—	—	47·5	—	34		15	6	10	2		
APRIL.	30	13	76	19	—	—	—	53	—	44		5	9	14	1	Cloudy days,	45
MAY.	38	5	94	26	—	—	—	66	—	39		17	5	8	—	Rainy days,	48
JUNE.	44	5	102	23	—	—	—	73	—	35		7	11	8	—	Snowy days,	14

Mean temperature, 1837, 56·2°
Do. do. 1840, 52·6
Do. do. 1841, 50·3

Aggregate mean, 159·1 = 53°.

Figure 6. Henry Spalding's climate data for Lapwai

Account 10.2: Excerpts from the account of Dr. Charles Pickering, naturalist. Source: Charles Pickering, *The Races of Man and their Geographical Origin* (London: Bell, 1876), 21-31.

On the following day [24 June 1841, after leaving a Spokane Indian encampment] we passed through a similar encampment, but, being desirous of avoiding unnecessary trouble, we did not visit it. Further on [in the modern day Palouse hills], we met a party in motion, with all their horses and other property. Infants on the board were suspended to the flanks of the horses, a practice said to be "derived from the eastern side of the mountains," and the lodge-poles were disposed in such a manner that one end was left trailing on the ground. Several of the horses were spotted black and white, such being favorites with the Oregon natives.

On the 25th we arrived at Lapwai, the missionary establishment of Mr. Spalding, situated on the Kooskoosky River. This was the first stream flowing into the Western Ocean, reached by Lewis and Clarke; and "the tradition of that expedition still remains among the natives; of surprise at the personal appearance of the new-comers, and at the sight of strong beards." Nevertheless, it was said that "no idea of difference of race, such as is recognized by Europeans, ever enters into the heads of the natives." Several of the ladies of the American mission had traveled by land from the United States; and they were, I think, the first White females seen in Oregon.

In the mission-house we had a meeting of natives, to whom some of the principal events of our voyage were narrated; and with the aid of a map, they seemed entirely to comprehend the course. As some shadow of governmental protection might be useful to residents in this remote quarter, the occasion of our visit was stated in these words: "our great father had sent out his ships to look after his children in all parts of the world." In return, they gave us some specimens of native eloquence, which however did not come up to our anticipations; the burden of their story seemed to be, that "they were themselves a poor miserable people." No one can be regarded as altogether safe in the "Indian country," and, from some superstitious idea, a member of the Hudson Bay Company had recently been assassinated.

Mr. Spalding had neat cattle and sheep, which thrive remarkably well; also a mill and plot of ground cultivated by irrigation, a novel idea to the farmer from the United States. A field of wheat looked remarkably well, as also various garden vegetables; and maize succeeds here, and even it is said at Colville, although it had hitherto failed on the coast. Many of the natives had followed Mr. Spalding's example, and he gave them the character generally of being "an exceedingly industrious people." Here was abundant evidence, were any needed, that the North American tribes are in nowise averse to the arts of civilization, or devoid in any respect of the common attributes of humanity.

The plantations of the natives, situated in a small lateral valley, were visited on the following morning. One man had adopted entirely the customs of the Whites, having built himself a comfortable log-house, while his wife, an interesting-looking woman, was neatly attired in European fashion. The little valley seemed, in fact, an earthly paradise, which I could not quit without misgivings as to the future.

Account 10.3: Excerpts from the account of William D. Brackenridge, botanist. Source: O.B. Sperlin, ed., "Our First Horticulturalist—The Brackenridge Journal," *Washington Historical Quarterly* 22, no. 1 (January 1931): 51-54 [Transcribed from the original in the Maryland Historical Society]. Printed here with the permission of the Pacific Northwest Quarterly and the University of Washington.

June 24th [1841]. Our course today lay over a fine rolling prairie country producing as fine pasture as I ever beheld in my life, well watered, though destitute of wood. On our left as we rode along was observed a range of Pine woods tending in an East & West direction [the Palouse Range], distant from us at one time not more than 8 miles.

Courses today S.E. by South, distance gone, 30 miles. Plants observed— Coronilla sp: Frazera, Habenaria, Calochortus, Baptisia, Trifolium sp: a good plant for Cattle.[2]

25th. Made the Kus-Kutskii river about mid-day; had to ride two miles up along its banks before we came opposite Mr. Spaulding's Station, when a boat was immediately sent over for us. We found Mr. S and family living in snug and comfortable House into which we were heartily welcomed. Mr. S. took me out in the afternoon to shew me his farm and Cattle. The former consisted of 20 acres of fine Wheat, a large field in which were Potatoes, Corn, Melons—Musk & Water—

---

[2]The Coronilla was probably *Lathyrus nevadensis*, Nevada sweet pea. It's also worth noting that the Wilkes Expedition frequently got their specimen labels switched, with plants from west of the Cascades identified as coming from east of the mountains, and vice versa.

Pumpkins, Peas, Beans &c &c the whole in fine order. He shewed me a Yew that had 7 Lambs in one year, viz: 2 in the early part of January, 3 in June, and 2 in Decr. Yews breed with him twice every year, he shewed me also 30 sheep the of(f) spring of two Yews in three years. He also has built a Saw and Grist mill, both of which is at the use of the Natives when they apply; to improve the social condition as well as to introduce habits of industry among the Natives Mr. S. is doing much. Mrs. S. has regularly about her a number of young feamales, which she is teaching to Card, Spin, Weaves Blankets & Knit stockings. Mr. S. has made a great many hand Looms, & he shewed me blankets which had been wove(n) by a Native on one of these which was not much inferior to Mackinaws.

He has also given them Cattle, Sheep, Seeds of Wheat, Corn, Potatoes &c and made them Plows & other empliments of Agriculture.

We had a large Meeting of Natives in his House, when we endeavoured to impress on their minds the utility of taking the advice and following the example of Mr. S. in cultivating the Soil & raising Cattle, to which the all agreed—todays ride 15 miles.

26th. This morning, I had again to reduce the bulk of specimens by parting with some of the paper. I afterwards in Co. with Mr. Waldron [T.W. Waldron, who left no account of this trip] cross'd the River in order to exchange some of our broke down Horses for fresh ones, in which Mr. S. was very liberal, giving us Horse for Horse and a spare one. We left the mission at 11 A.M. accompanied by Mr. & Mrs. Spaulding, also Mr. & Mrs. [Asa Bowen] Smith now residing with the former [after hastily abandoning their mission as Kamiah]. On our way we visited the farms of the natives, which lay up a rich valley running in a South direction from the Kus-Kutskii. These farms are all well fenced in. these extend from 4 to 12 acres, in which the(y) cultivate Wheat, Corn, Potatoes, Melons & Pumpkins. One of them raised last year /40—400 bushels of Potatoes, & 45 bushels of Wheat, with part of the Potatoes he bot. dried Buflo. meat sufficient to serve him during the winter, thus enabling him to remain at home, in place of going out all summer on the hunt. The whole of the lots we visited wer(e) kept in good order, and several had good mud Houses built on them. Mr. S.'s object is to have them give up or relinquish their roving habits and to settle down and cultivate the soil, in which he is succeeding admirably, and if industry and perseverance on his part is to effect the object he has in view—that of improoving their social condition & instilling into their minds the principals of religion—also to get them to settle down in his vicinity, he certainly has left nothing undone that one man could perform. And for my own part I wish him all the success that his industry merits. A(t) 3 P.M. came upon the banks of the *Snake River*, where we found at a Salmon station a number of Indians of the Snake tribe [these, too, would have been Nez Perce Indians] to the amount of 70, having about them a flock of fine Horses to the number of 400. On passing the(y) paid no attention to us, but soon after sent up two Canoes to ferry our luggage over. The Native in charge of the Canoes when the(y) had finished went of(f) without demanding anything for their trouble, shewing that the(y) are an independent people, a trait of character which generally follows when they become rich in Horses,—at least such is the fact so far as I have observed among Indian tribes. The Snake River where we crossed was about one mile above its junction with the Kus-Kutskii, its breadth about 250 yards, destitute of bushes or trees on its banks. This river abounds in Salmon, in Kus-Kutskii the water is so clear that the Natives say that the(y) cant spear them....

11

Botanist Charles A. Geyer (Karl Andreas Geyer) visits Spalding, 1844

One of the many seeking their fortune and fame through exploration in the American West was the German botanist Charles A. Geyer (born Karl A. Geyer). Described as a "capital swimmer and an excellent pedestrian,"[1] Geyer had the opportunity to build on these skills as he traversed the inland Northwest, a corner of the country he referred to as "Upper Oregon." Geyer was a botanical collector by profession, adding his findings to the field of descriptive botany by supplying herbaria with his gathered specimens for taxonomists to evaluate and classify. Skilled botanical collectors performed important fieldwork and needed to be able to identify the new and unusual as well as have the skills necessary to package these collections so that the results could be used in the laboratory. Collectors were sponsored in their quests, with the sponsors receiving the collections in return.[2]

Geyer had the necessary botanical knowledge to be a collector, skills that he had gained from an apprenticeship in Zabelitz and as an assistant in Dresden's Royal Botanic Garden. Coupled with this knowledge was a lively intellect, a sense of adventure and ambition, as well as some initial charm that attracted sponsors and potential business partners. There was also an essence of tiresomeness that led many of his original supporters to grow weary of his company. Captain John C. Fremont was among these; after two expeditions with Geyer, he refused to take him on subsequent trips. Missionary wife Mary Walker noted Geyer's arrival at the mission near Spokane Falls, December 25, 1843: "A German botanist arrived and took supper with us".[3] He stayed on and on. She wrote on July 7, 1844: "We are tired on account

---

[1]Grace Lee Nute, "Botanizing Minnesota in 1838-39: It was a perilous undertaking," *Conservation Volunteer* 8, no. 44 (January/February 1945): 5.

[2]For a good explanation of this, see Thomas R. Cox, "Charles A. Geyer, Pioneer Botanist of Upper Oregon," *Idaho Yesterdays* 43, no. 1 (Spring 1999): 12.

[3]Clifford M. Drury, "Botanist in Oregon in 1843-44 for Kew Gardens, London," *Oregon Historical Quarterly* 41 (1940): 182. Drury is quoting from Mrs. Elkanah Walker's diary, a typescript of which is at the Washington State University Library.

of Mr. Geyer but do not know what to do with him; we are determined to be rid of him." Finally, there is the notation of September 16, 1844, "We met Mr. Geyer [on the trail between their home and Fort Colville] of whom we took final leave."[4] Author Susan Delano McKelvey puts forth other damning evidence of Geyer's personality in her masterful work, *Botanical Exploration of the Trans-Mississippi West*. "Since Geyer's letters are often mentioned and quoted in this chapter, I comment upon them briefly. I found them wearisome, cumulatively so, and suspect that the recipients had a similar reaction, for Geyer more than once complains that he has received no reply. They give the impression that Geyer was a self-satisfied individual and inclined to be critical of those in his own station in life."[5]

In spite of his difficulties with interpersonal relationships, Geyer has had thirteen plants named in his honor and secured his place in history. His poetic descriptions of his travels are remarkable when one considers that English was not his native language. His keen observation skills coupled with an analytical mind led him to see ecosystems before there was a discipline that allowed such observations. These same skills helped him to view the role of fire in the propagation of species, and to make conclusions about the nature of the American in his relationship to government and civilization. His writings provide yet another colorful glimpse of the world that was. Geyer reached the Clearwater country in 1844 after a long overland trip which began in St. Louis in May of 1843.

Account 11.1: Geyer's account from June 1844. Source: Charles A. Geyer, "Notes on the Vegetation and general character of the Missouri and Oregon Territories, made during a Botanical journey from the State of Missouri, across the South Pass of the Rocky Mountains, to the Pacific, during the years 1843 and 1844," *London Journal of Botany* 5 (1846): 201-08 and 516-21. Excerpts.

The footnotes marked with an asterisk are Geyer's own, and are inserted in the text in a smaller type size to maintain clarity and continuity.

The plains and plateaux of Upper Oregon present themselves in the form of an amphitheatre, when viewed from north-west, only interrupted by mountain ranges. They appear terraced above each other with irregular ascents and confines, at about 1000 feet difference of altitude.

The rivers of Upper Oregon are all torrents and tributaries of the great Columbia, a river of second-rate magnitude in North America. Those tributaries rush from every point of the compass, except west, hurrying with fearful velocity towards their main channels; forming, one and all, for more than a thousand miles, dangerous rapids and whirlpools in close succession. They are, for the most part, difficult and dangerous, or unfit to navigate, even the united Columbia is only free from obstruction for about 120 miles above its mouth...

---

[4] *Ibid*, 183.

[5] Susan Delano McKelvey, *Botanical Exploration of the Trans-Mississippi West, 1790-1850.* (Jamaica Plains, Mass.: Arnold Arboretum of Harvard University, 1955), 770.

Before we enter on the descriptions of the subregions, we must mention the fact, that Oregon has as many floras as summer months. No spot is too arid to lodge a pretty plant, no rock too burning! It is not uncommon in a period of three weeks to see a plain covered with snow, decked with flowers, and so burnt up again, that you can find nothing to testify of the gaudy blossoms, which have been dried by the sun, and swept away by the wind…

We will now leave the further details of this chapter, and place ourselves again on the Koos-Kooskee [Clearwater], to ascend the westerly côte in order to examine the

III.-Sub-region of the level parts of Upper Oregon, and the high cold plains to the extreme left; elevation about 4,000 feet.

The Saptona, or Nez Percez, Indians, to whom this territory belongs, annually resort to these plains, not only to dig their *Gamass* [camas] and farinaceous roots, known by the name of "Nez Percez bread-root," but to graze their immense herds of horses and cattle. The country has several climates, along the Koos-Kooskee and Lewis [Snake] river it is decidedly temperate; the grass remaining green during winter, and little or no snow lying on the ground. Above, on the highlands, however, frost is felt even in the midst of summer; and during the days (end of June, 1844) which I spent there, we had 2°to 4° Reaum, below freezing point, every night. Nevertheless, vegetation is luxuriant, even the tender flowers of *Cypripedium* [Lady's slipper] stand the frosts well, and the pasture is excellent, as the thriving herds belonging to the Indians sufficiently prove.

These tesselated plains are separated by low, snowy, pine-clad mountain ridges, appearing to be spurs of the Blue Mountains, which finally, according to my informant, form a dividing ridge between the desert plains and the tributaries emptying directly into the Columbia, and those of Lewis [Snake] river. The latter streams traverse the high plains, nearly parallel with the ridges, and are immersed in defiles, then almost perpendicular côtes being walled by rudely-formed pseudo-columnar basalt, and remaining filled with ice for the whole summer months. Following these streams, the banks become steeper, and the basalt more regular, till, at the mouth of the Salmon river,* it assumes the regular columnar form throughout.

*Here, but a few miles from the mouth of Salmon river, the Saptona Indians strike their summer camp, for the purposes of digging Gamass and bread-root, and to get salmon, as well as to graze their herds of horses, numbering twenty-five thousand, and their cattle, of which they already possess considerable numbers. They leave these high, cold regions again at the approach of winter, and retire with their herds to the temperate valleys, somewhat after the manner of the Swiss herdsmen.

The Gamass and bread-root digging is nearly finished when the first salmon is caught, and when the buffalo-hunters of the tribe set out for their distant hunting-grounds, on the waters of the Yellow-stone river, on the uppermost forks of the Missouri. Other parties equip themselves to meet the American emigrants to Oregon, and offer grain, horses, &c., in return for other necessaries, especially American cattle. A feast is generally given before all these parties separate, races and dancing are their chief pastimes, but the vulgar among them resort to ruinous gambling.

The Saptonas, or Nez Percez Indians, unlike their north-eastern neighbours, with whom they come in close connexion, lead generally an active, prudent life, under the surveillance of an American Missionary, belonging to the American Board of Foreign Missions, the Rev. Mr. Spalding, who resides at Lapwai, on the Koos-Kooskee. The Saptonas are the only northerly tribe of Indians, to my knowledge, with whom the missionaries have so far succeeded as to render, in eight years' tuition only, the greater part of the tribe independent of hunting, by cultivating the soil, and rearing cattle and sheep. Scrupulously do they

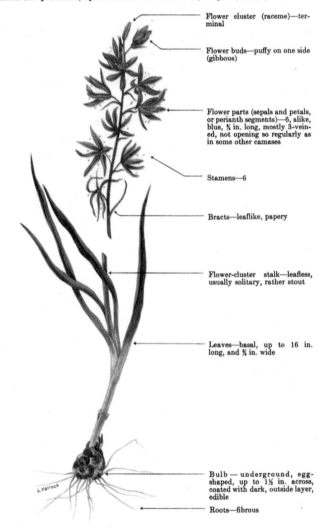

COMMON CAMAS

Quama'sia qua'mash, syns. *Camas'sia esculen'ta, C. qua'mash, Q. esculen'ta* [1]

Flower cluster (raceme)—terminal

Flower buds—puffy on one side (gibbous)

Flower parts (sepals and petals, or perianth segments)—6, alike, blue, ¾ in. long, mostly 3-veined, not opening so regularly as in some other camases

Stamens—6

Bracts—leaflike, papery

Flower-cluster stalk—leafless, usually solitary, rather stout

Leaves—basal, up to 16 in. long, and ¾ in. wide

Bulb — underground, egg-shaped, up to 1½ in. across, coated with dark, outside layer, edible

Roots—fibrous

L. Hallock

[1] *Q. esculen'ta* Raf., not (Ker) Coville.

Lith. A. Hoen & Co.

67401°—36——33

Figure 7. Common camas plant. U.S. Department of Agriculture (the Saptonas) attend to their fields, and one may see them, at two o'clock in the morning, at work that they may be able to go to school in the afternoon. The greater number read and write their own language well, and every one was eager to show me his hymn-book, copied by himself, nicely penned, and very clean. The women of this tribe distinguish themselves from their neighbours by cleanliness and rich dresses. I found several of them engaged in carpet-weaving and dyeing wool, under the superintendance of Mrs. Spaulding. Mr. S. is by far the most successful Indian missionary deputed by the American Board of Foreign Missions. Undaunted by the haughtiness of his pupils, he overcomes all obstacles. He boldly left off the absurd custom of teaching the Indian to pray, before endeavouring to fill his hungry stomach; but persevered in making the poor creature understand that he must acquire property, to become independent of hunting, and that that property must be realized by rearing domestic animals and tilling the land. In the fall of 1844, several Indian families had raised that season two hundred bushels of fine wheat, from two to four hundred bushels of peas, and the same quantity of potatoes. Considering that such families own from one to three or four thousand horses, and twenty to thirty head of cattle, one may imagine that they are very rich, for the value of such property increases considerably by the present influx of emigrants. A grist-mill has been erected by Mr. S., on the mission premises, where the Indians get their corn ground; attached to it is a saw-mill, to cut timber for building houses; some of the chiefs were already at it, eager to exchange the tent for the house. By responding to the efforts of Mr. Spalding, and amassing property, it is unavoidable that the whole nation imbibes a degree of avarice, of which I justly accuse the Saptonas. Far from feeling grateful to the Mission and to their excellent teacher, they demand every thing gratuitously, and torment their instructor by that insolent haughtiness so peculiar to them. Mr. S., however, does not swerve an inch from his original plan, and operates now and then on their ambition, slowly but effectually. The American Board of Foreign Missions has committed an error in not aiding Mr. Spalding, or giving and entrusting to his hands the surveillance of all the Missions of the Board in Oregon. They leave him to struggle alone, and consequently the credit and praise belong solely to him.

The scientific reader will pardon this digression from my subject, for I have longed to do justice to Mr. S., and took advantage of this occasion. Those who have travelled in North America, and visited Indian Missions, will be, as I am, aware of their fruitless efforts to civilized the Indians, and of the immense sums squandered liberally by the American citizens for that laudable object. Here was the only place where I found the result propitious, beyond my expectation, and to make that rare case known to philanthropists, is the sole excuse I can offer for this deviation.

If we ascend the walled terraces of the Koos-Kooskee, we find the rocks covered with *Bartonia parviflora* [blazing star], *Calycadeniæ* [tarweed] , *Lygodesma* [*Lygodesmia*, rush-pink, or more probably, *Stephanomeria*], and *Polygonum* [knotweed] (335), growing round groups of *Peucedanum* [biscuit-root; desert parsley]; *Composita* [daisy family] (361) and *Troximon* [a synonym for both *Agoseris* and *Microseris*] (446); (but one plant in bloom), appearing abundant on the grassy border of the first terrace. On the plains near Peloose [Palouse] river appears another species of the noble *Calochortus* [mariposa or sego lily], of which I could get no specimens, and only saw the large-winged fruit (*C. pterocarpus* of my Journal [probably *Calochortus nitidus*]). Here also, and in fact almost throughout Upper Oregon, on grassy, moist slopes and in shady meadows, grows the *Umbellifera* [parsley family], *Helosciandium* 576,* the tubers of which are one of the dainty dishes of the Saptonas, and truly a delicious root.

*This is probably *Helosciadium Californicum*, Dougl., an inconspicuous *Umbellifera*, perennial, with a black tuberous root. By boiling the tubers like potatoes, they burst open lengthwise, showing a snowy-white, farinaceous substance, which has a sweet, cream-like taste, and somewhat of the aroma of young parsley leaves. This plant, it seems to me, would be an excellent acquisition to our kitchen-gardens; for the purpose of introducing it, I gathered a great quantity of seeds, which are now in possession of Messrs. Lucombe, Pince, and Co., at Exeter, and who may possibly have raised plants. It holds in Oregon exactly that place which the wild carrot does with us; and I feel sure that the tubers would similarly increase in size by cultivation [*Lomatium cous*].

Ascending another height, I found a group of *Penstemon* [beardtongue] bushes, No. 478, 2-3 ft. high, with above a hundred stalks, springing from a ligneous, thick rhizoma, each bearing a raceme of large pink-rose flowers. Still higher up, and almost on the plateau, appears another species of *Espeletia* [*Helianthella uniflora*, little sunflower] (419), very abundant, and in place of *Esp. helianthoides*. The root of this species is less resinous than that of the others, and was formerly dug by the Indians and eaten. Above, on the pine-groved plateau, grow masses of *Galium septentrionale* [bedstraw] and a species of *Asperula* [sweet woodruff], filling the small enclosed prairies. In the grassy pine-groves I found the *Viola* (407), and later again, in open moist prairies, *Œnothera* [evening primrose] (496), *Epilob.* [*Epilobium*, willow-weed] (518), and *Rumex* [dock or sorrel] (488). On the brink of a mountain rivulet, fringed with colossal *Pines, Poplar,* and *Willows,* I gathered *Ribes* [gooseberry or currant family] (507), a shrub about 6 feet high, with erect flowering racemes, smelling like *Prunus Padus* [plum or cherry family]. I never met with it before nor afterwards, but was told by the Indians that it bears a brownish-red berry, of very agreeable taste. Many of the common plants of the Green Mountain defiles grow here, as *Epilobium latifol.* [broad-leaved willowherb] (229), and *E. coloratum, Carices* [sedges], *Mimulus* [monkeyflower], &c.

The lower slope of the snowy pine-clad ridges teems with flowers of every hue; the pretty *Castilleias* [paintbrushes], *Phlox, Pentstemon, Swertia,* and most of those mentioned in the Green Mountain excursion; besides several rare ones, in the collection. Amongst them is the elegant *Cypripedium,* very showy and abundant, growing in tufts, 1-3 flowered, of a delicious fragrance, with a large white lip, streaked with yellow and purple. I found afterwards a single tuft of it, on a grassy mountain, near Spokan river. Other plants growing with it are *Gymnandra* [*Besseya rubra*, red besseya] (421), *Pedicularis* [lousewort] (422), *Lupinus* [lupine] (423), *Peucedanum* (517) Pentst. (418), *Thaspium?*[angelica] (414), *Erigeron* [fleabane] (502), *Fragaria* [wild strawberries] (612). The shady recesses of the woods abound with *Actaea* [baneberry] (520), 5-6 feet high, with white flowers and purple berries, *Pulmonaria* [*Martensia*, bluebells] (458), *Aspidium* [name of any of several ferns], (341), *Pyrola* [wintergreen], *Viola, Linnaea* [twinflower], &c. Following these rivulets to their source in the plains, we come to a vegetation of *Gamass, Veratrum* [false hellebore], *Carices, Polygonum* (405), *Aira* [hairgrass] (342), *Ranunculus* [buttercup], and many other plants mentioned before. The moist plains are often stony, and are the habitat of the *Ferula* [*Lomantium,* biscuitroot] (220*), with *Espeletia* (419), groups of *Senecio* [groundsel] (484), and *Sida* [probably *Sidalcea,* checker mallow] (404), *Iris Missourensis, Alopecurus genuiculatus* [water foxtail], *Beckmannia* [sloughgrass], *Trichodium* [*Agrostis,* bentgrass], and others of common occurrence.

*This plant grows also on the Platte river, in stony moist meadows. It has an irregular tuber, much like celery, but with a many-headed rhizoma. The leaves and umbels, with all their parts, are upright, and appear as if folded up; only during flowering time these parts spread for a short time. For this reason, the Indians assert that two kinds of bread root grow together, which are, in fact, one and the same plant. The roots, when dug, are washed clean, dried, and pounded to flour. To the bread, which they bake or rather smoke over their tent-fires, they give an oblong, rectangular form, about 3 feet long, 1 foot wide, and 3-4 inches in thickness, leaving a round hole in the middle, to fasten it on the pack-saddle. Such bread keeps nearly six months, if well baked. If is insipid, when it has not acquired a mouldy or smoky taste. It gets so hard when old, that it must be soaked in water for several hours before one is able to bite it; yet the Indians, who are accustomed to it from their childhood, like it much.

Leaving the main ridge of the Blue Mountains to our extreme left, we descend again, at the junction of the Koos-Kooskee and Lewis river, to the valley, which, being stony, has a very rugged appearance. It is not so with the valleys of the small rivulets; they are generally spacious, fertile, and appropriated to agriculture by the Indians, mostly by means of drainage, for it is excessively hot in these valleys, their almost perpendicular basaltic côtes averaging 1,500 feet in height. Thickets of *Celtis* [hackberry] and *Crataegus* [hawthorn] are also filled with *Rhus* [sumac], *Ribes, Spiraea,* and *Rose* bushes. The same is the case in the sterile valley of Lewis River, the ground densely covered with *Euphorbia* [spurge], *Erodium* [probably *Geranium*], or *Thlaspi* (655), and the discoid *Cotula* [pineapple weed]. Lower down appear again the scarlet *Sida* (*S.obliqua*, Nutt.), joining the sub-fertile region and sandy desert, as in Missouri territory. Crossing the côte westward, we pass over a region of prairies, deeply furrowed with ravines. On this tract I observed sundry species of *Espeletia*, which I had not seen before; none, however, either in flower or fruit; their vegetation was over, but I could distinctly trace the form of their leaves.*

*The leaves of the different species of *Espeletia* seem to take the form of some other *Compositae*. Those of *E. helianth.* resemble *Doronicum*; those of #. 395, *Silph, terebinthaceum*; of 419, *Scolymus*; of the above, *Lactusa virosa* and others.

At considerable distances I met with a few scattered plants of *Bartonia laevicaulis*, in full splendour. Soon we reach the valley of Upper Walla-Walla river, the territory of the haughty Cayuses, the handsomest Indians in Upper Oregon, nearly related to the Saptonas, whose language they have adopted, and with whom they make common cause in any undertaking.

Further reading:

Frederick V. Coville, "Added botanical notes on Carl A. Geyer," *Oregon Historical Quarterly* 42 (1941): 323-24.

Thomas R. Cox, "Charles A. Geyer, pioneer botanist of upper Oregon," *Idaho Yesterdays* 43, no.1 (Spring 1999): 11-32.

An important and thorough look at Geyer's accomplishments.

Clifford M. Drury, "Botanist in Oregon in 1843-44 for Kew Gardens, London," *Oregon Historical Quarterly* 41 (1940): 182-188.

Charles A. Geyer, "Botanical information. Notes on the Vegetation and general character of the Missouri and Oregon territories, made during a botanical journey from the State of Missouri, across the South Pass of the Rocky Mountains, to the Pacific, during the years 1843, and 1844," *London Journal of Botany* 4 (1845): 479-484.

Geyer's own account of how he came to the Northwest.

Susan Delano McKelvey, *Botanical Exploration of the Trans-Mississippi West, 1790-1850* (Jamaica Plain, Mass., Arnold Arboretum of Harvard University, 1955), 770-791.

Grace Lee Nute, "Botanist at Fort Colville," *Beaver* 277 (September 1946): 28-31.

Grace Lee Nute, "'Botanizing' Minnesota in 1838-39," *Conservation Volunteer* 8, no.44 (January/February 1945): 5-8.

J. Orin Oliphant, "Botanical labors of Henry H. Spalding," *Washington Historical Quarterly* 25 (1934): 93-102.

H.G. Reichenbach, "Charles Andreas Geyer," *Hooker's Journal of Botany and Kew Garden Miscellany* 7 (1855): 181-83.

Sharon Ritter, *Lewis and Clark's Mountain Wilds: A Site Guide to the Plants and Animals They Encountered in the Bitterroots* (Moscow: University of Idaho Press, 2002).

A lovely and reliable guide to the Bitterroots and the Lolo Trail.

12

Early accounts from the Southern Nez Perce Trail, 1835-1870

There is a great and unresolved debate about why "Old Toby," the Shoshone Indian guide who was assisting Lewis and Clark in the summer of 1805, chose to avoid the ancient route to the west over the Southern Nez Perce Trail. Certainly this route was as obvious and well known as the Lolo Pass route eventually chosen. It is also arguably easier of access, and clearly shorter. Beginning just north of what is now Gibbonsville, Idaho, this route follows the high rugged divide between the Salmon River and the upper Selway River, eventually reaching the South Fork of the Clearwater River near Elk City, Idaho. A variant route follows the West Fork of the Bitterroot River. The route traverses National Forest land known now as the Magruder Corridor, and is located between the two great wilderness areas of central Idaho.

This historic trail was used by the Nez Perce people to reach more southern buffalo hunting country, and also as their route to the Tetons and to the trading rendezvous held in the upper Snake River valley. It was also well known to the Shoshone Indians, and probably to the Flatheads. It remained in use as an important trading route at least until 1870, with early miners at Elk City reporting the passage of hundreds of Nez Perce men and women during the time when the Treaty of 1863 was being debated. Miners arriving in the new Idaho gold regions along the South Fork and west toward the Florence Basin also used the trail. Wellington Bird had his wagon road builders explore the route, as did the Northern Pacific Railroad somewhat later.

The first written record of this route is that of the Rev. Samuel Parker, excerpts of which follow. Parker was headed for the Oregon country as an agent of the American Board of Commissioners for Foreign Missions (ABCFM). The Board, which would soon dispatch Marcus Whitman and Henry Spalding to the same region, was using the fifty-five year old Parker to locate possible mission sites. They were responding to a delegation of Nez Perce and Flathead Indians who had arrived in St. Louis in 1831, supposedly seeking information on the religion of the whites.

Parker reached the Salmon River valley in late summer of 1835. He was traveling with a Nez Perce "village" led by a man he called "Charlie." Some twenty years later, in 1856, Chief Lawyer told General Isaac Stevens' staff that he, too, had accompanied Parker across the Bitterroots. Parker was an observant man and a remarkable traveler. In 1836, he investigated a possible return east through Nez Perce country, but took a ship home via Hawaii instead.

In 1853 and 1854, military and civilian surveyors under the command of Isaac Stevens, the Governor of Washington Territory, reached the Bitterroot Valley. They were there to "ascertain the most practicable and economical route for a railroad from the Mississippi River to the Pacific Ocean." Basing themselves at Fort Owen, Lieutenant John Mullan explored the Lolo Trail (1854) and other routes, while a civilian engineer, A.W. Tinkham, crossed the Southern Nez Perce trail. Excerpts of Tinkham's report are published in this chapter. Tinkham's small party entered the valley of the West Fork of the Bitterroot River on November 20, 1853, an amazingly late time of the year for so rugged a trip. He unfortunately was not accompanied by an artist, and so we have no images of this route.

The beginning of the Civil War coincided with the discovery of gold in the Clearwater Valley. Trespass on the Nez Perce reservation of 1855 became widespread, and mining interest soon expanded east toward what became Elk City, and south into the Florence Basin. The 1863 Treaty, which deprived the Nez Perce of most of the reservation previously negotiated with Stevens, was one result of this mining expansion. The other was political pressure on the federal government to provide a better transportation system into what soon became Idaho Territory. In March of 1865, Congress appropriated funds to construct the Virginia City to Lewiston Wagon Road, with an Iowa physician, Dr. Wellington Bird, appointed to head the project. In the summer of 1866, Bird sent his engineer, George B. Nicholson over the Southern Nez Perce Trail to ascertain if that route was more suitable than the Lolo Trail route to the north. Nicholson found the southern route to be more open and full of grass ("accomplished by the Indians firing the woods"), but overall, less suited than the Lolo Trail route. Nicholson's report appears in *With Bird and Truax*, cited below.

But the rush of technological advance soon brushed wagon road construction aside, and the attention of both government and business leaders in the region shifted to plans to complete the Northern Pacific Railroad, which was to run from Minneapolis to Tacoma. Although this company suffered from poor management and financial turmoil during much of its history, the firm's surveyors and engineers were shrewd enough to build on the research of Isaac Stevens and his government expedition. Construction of the route was made possible by one of the largest business subsidy programs in the nation's history, the 47 million acre Northern Pacific Land Grant, approved by Congress in 1864.

The field work of the Stevens survey was conducted by an able corps of military and civilian surveyors (see, for example, John Mullan's Lolo Pass account, which appears elsewhere in this book). The work of these men led Stevens to conclude that the best railroad route through the Bitterroots would follow the Clark Fork River toward Lake Pend Oreille. The leaders of the Northern Pacific soon reached the same conclusion, but under some political pressure, decided to complete short surveys of alternate routes, including Lolo Pass, the Southern Nez Perce Trail, and even the valley of the Salmon River. Documents relating to the survey of the Southern Nez Perce Trail appear as the third account in this chapter. This survey was conducted by W.W. de Lacy in the autumn of 1870, and was part of a broader survey of the Big Hole and Bitterroot Valleys. De Lacy, facing heavy snow, got no further west than the Selway River, but has left us two fine maps of the region. One is reproduced here.

Further reading:

William P. Cunningham, *The Magruder Corridor Controversy: A Case History* (M.S. Thesis, University of Montana, 1968).

A reliable modern history of the area, based on rare primary sources.

Stanley Davidson, "Worker in God's Wilderness," *Montana: The Magazine of Western History* 7, no. 1 (January 1957): 8-17.

A good, well-illustrated summary of Samuel Parker's life, based on secondary sources.

Myron Eells, "Rev. Samuel Parker," *Whitman College Quarterly* 2, no. 3 (October 1898): 3-34.

A good account of the religious life and impact of Parker, using many primary sources.

Ernst Peterson and H.E. Andersen, "Retracing the Southern Nez Perce Trail With Rev. Samuel Parker," *Montana: The Magazine of Western History* 16, no. 4 (October 1966):12-27.

An authoritative and well-illustrated guide to Parker's likely route.

Pearl Russell, "Analysis of the Pacific Railroad Reports," *Washington Historical Quarterly* 10, no.1 (January 1919): 3-16.

The best explanation of the complicated history of this survey.

O. Frank Schumaker and James E. Dewey, *A History of the Salmon River Breaks Primitive Area* (Grangeville: Nez Perce National Forest, 1970).

An anecdotal history of the area by two veteran Forest Service employees.

Eugene B. Smalley, *History of the Northern Pacific Railroad* (New York: G.P. Putnam's Sons, 1883).

The best account of early railroad route planning in the Bitterroots.

George Thomas, *A Survey and Evaluation of Archaeological Resources in the Magruder Corridor* (Pocatello: Idaho State University Museum, 1969).

A fine survey of the rich archaeological resources of the trail region.

With Bird and Truax on the Lolo Trail: Building the Virginia City to Lewiston Wagon Road, 1865-1867. Ed. Dennis W. Baird (Moscow: University of Idaho Library, 1999).

Using the National Archives and other sources, contains the full text of all reports associated with this early civil works project.

Account 12.1: Excerpts from the account of Rev. Samuel Parker's visit in 1835-36. Source: Samuel Parker, *Journal of an Exploring Tour Beyond the Rocky Mountains.* 3rd Edition (Ithaca: Mack, Andrus & Woodruff, 1842), 116-26 and 280-84. Reprinted 1990 by the University of Idaho Press.

September 18th. [On the Idaho-Montana divide, northwest of modern day North Fork, Idaho] We passed over a mountain six thousand feet high, occupying more than half a day to arrive at the summit. These mountains are covered with woods, excepting small portions, which are open and furnish grass for our horses. The woods are composed mainly of fir, spruce, Norway pine, and a new species of pine....

We arose early on the 19th, and commenced our day's labor, and by diligence went more than twice the distance than when we were with the village [he has joined a smaller group of Nez Perce]. We were much annoyed by trees that had fallen across the trail. Encamped upon the south-east side of a high mountain, where there was a large opening, a spring of water, and a good supply of grass for our horses [near Blue Nose Mountain].

Sabbath. 20th. We continued in the same encampment. I expressed my wish to the chief, that the day should be spent religiously, and that he should communicate to his men, as well as he was able, the scripture truths he had learned. This was faithfully done on his part, and he prayed with them with much apparent devotion....

Left our encampment, on the 22nd [at Parker Mountain], at an early hour and continued our mountainous journey. Parts of the way the ascent and descent was at an angle of 45°, and in some places even more steep; sometimes on the verge of dizzy precipices; sometimes down shelves of rock.... The question often arose in my mind, can this section of country ever be inhabited, unless these mountains shall be brought low, and these valleys shall be exalted? But they may be designed to perpetuate a supply of wood for the wide-spread prairies; and they may contain mines of treasures....

Took an early departure, on the 24th [from Horse Heaven Flat, west of Salmon Mountain], from our encampment, and made good progress throughout the day. About the middle of the day, we came where we could look forward without the sight being obstructed by mountains [on Burnt Knob], and it was pleasant to have a prospect opening into the wider world. We continued to descend, until we came into a valley of considerable extent [probably the upper Meadow Creek valley], through which flows a large branch of the Coos-coots-ke....Here was a band of horses, belonging to the Nez Percés, which they left last spring. They were in fine order.

Monday, 28th, my health was improved, and we made a long day's march and emerged from the mountains about two o'clock in the afternoon. Not finding water as we expected, we were obliged to travel on until near night, when we came to another branch of the Coos-coots-ke [probably the South Fork of the Clearwater], at which we found several lodges of Nez Percé Indians. A salute was fired, and then we were welcomed with a ceremonious, but hearty shaking of hands. They feasted us with excellent dried salmon, for which I made them some small presents. I was rejoiced to find myself safely through the Salmon river mountains, and convalescent....

Thursday, October 1st. [Probably along Lapwai Creek] Arose early with substantially better health, for which I cannot be too thankful. After travelling a few miles, we came to several lodges of Nez Percés, who gave us their kind welcome, and seemed, as at the other lodges, much pleased to see their first chief. They manifested the same feelings on learning who I was, and the object of my coming into their country, as their countrymen did whom we met at the [Green River] rendezvous....

We arrived, two o'clock in the afternoon, at the Lewis branch [the Snake River] of the Columbia river, near the confluence of the Coos-coots-ke. Though this is a large river, yet on account of the summer's drouth there is less water flowing down its channel that I anticipated.

This country differs much from what I had expected; for while the soil is generally good, and furnishes a supply for grazing, yet there is such want of summer rains, that some kinds of grain cannot flourish, especially Indian corn. The crops sown in the fall of the year, or very early in the spring, would probably be so far advanced before the severity of the drouth, that they would do well. In general there is great want of wood for building, fencing and fuel; but at the confluence of these rivers a supply may be brought down the Coos-coots-ke. This place combines many advantages for a missionary station.

I began to doubt the correctness of the statements of some travelers, in regard to the great numbers of wild horses, and the immense multitudes of wolves, which they say they saw this side of the Rocky Mountains; for as yet I had seen no wild horses, and only a *very few* wolves.

[May 1836, returning up the Columbia to the Clearwater valley] In company with several Nez Percé Indians who had come down from their own country to escort me, I commenced my journey on the ninth, and pursued the same route by which I came last autumn. Nothing eventful marked our way, and we arrived at the [mouth of the] Snake or Lewis river, the evening of the eleventh, where we found several lodges of the Nez Percés, who gave us a very cordial reception, and a warm-hearted shake of the hand, the common expression of Indian friendship....

We arrived at the Cooscootske early in the afternoon of the third day after leaving [Fort] Walla Walla [also known as Fort Nez Perces], making the distance about 120 miles. The whole country has put on the loveliness of spring, and divested itself of the dreariness of winter, and the grandeur of the mountain scenery appeared to rise before me with new freshness and delight. The Indians are assembling in great numbers from different and distant parts of the country, to enquire about the religion that is to guide them to God and heaven; and which they also think has power to elevate them in the scale of society in this world, and place them on a level with intelligent as well as Christian white men....

Saturday, May 14th. Very many of the natives are coming in for the purpose of keeping the Sabbath with me; but as I have little prospect of the arrival of my interpreter, I shall probably be left to commiserate their anxiety, while it will be out of my power to do them good....

The Nez Perces have been celebrated for their skill and bravery in war. This they have mentioned to me, but say they are now afraid to go to war; for they no longer believe that all who fall in battle go to a happy country. They now believe that the only way to be happy here or hereafter, is by knowing and doing what God requires....

Sabbath, 15th. The interpreter I had been expecting did not arrive, and consequently much of what I wished to say to these hundreds of Indians, could not be communicated for the want of a medium. I felt distressed for them. They desired to celebrate the Sabbath after a Christian manner. When the chiefs came and enquired what they should do, I told them to collect the people into an assembly and spend the hours of this sacred day in prayer and singing, and in conversation on those things about which I formerly instructed them. They did so, and it was truly affecting to see their apparent reverence, order, and devotion, while I could not but know that their knowledge was limited indeed....
[Accompanied by a young Nez Perce chief named Haminilpilt—Red Wolf, Parker then decided to return home via Walla Walla and Colville, having already seen the preferred Nez Perce route to the east, the Southern Trail]

Account 12.2: Excerpts from A.W. Tinkham's accounts of November-December 1853. Source: *Reports of Explorations and Surveys, Vol. 1* (Washington: Beverley Tucker, 1855), 276-81, 374-77, and 625-29. 33rd Congress, 2nd Session. Senate Executive Document No. 78. Serial Set 758.

On November 20th, with a fresh band of animals, and renewed outfit of provision, &c., I was in camp, halting on the Sabbath, some nine or ten miles from Lieutenant Mullan, up the valley of St. Mary's river [i.e., the Bitterroot River]—a mild moist day, raining gently most of the day, with a temperature rising to near 50° above zero. About twenty-six miles from Lieutenant Mullan's winter post, and some sixty miles above Hell Gate [Missoula], the St. Mary's forks to the southeast and southwest. Here we left the fine open valley characterizing the St. Mary's river, and tracing up the western fork, the wooded hills immediately closed in upon the stream; the valley narrowed until it was not over a quarter of a mile wide; patches of snow discovered themselves, and the air grew chilly. A few miles further the snow was several inches deep, the streams were partially or wholly frozen; and when, on November 23d, about 24 miles up the valley from where we entered it, we left the stream near its source, there a brook only twelve feet across, the snow was still deeper; and a mile or two farther on, as we ascended the mountain divide, whose western waters are tributary to the Kooskooskia [Clearwater], the snow was two feet, and soon after two and a half feet deep. The passage of this divide [near modern day Nez Perce Pass] was very laborious; is by the trail some twenty-five miles long, attaining a summit elevation of 7,040 feet, the trail keeping mostly on the open hill-tops, and with its ascent and descent, and the snow, gave us three days of hard labor, during most of which time our animals had nothing to eat…With a precipitous descent of 2,000 feet the trail drops down to the bed of the Kooskooskia [actually, to the Selway River valley, a river which, with the Lochsa, forms the Middle Fork of the Clearwater], which we cross at a level of 3,760 feet above the sea[1], and immediately turn again to the mountain on its opposite side, and wind up their steep projecting spurs and ridges. There was no snow in the valley of the Kooskooskia; the stream was thirty to sixty feet wide and two feet deep at the crossing. All this country is wooded mainly with pines, firs, spruces, and hemlocks. A few miles farther on [near Salmon Mountain] we again entered the snow…finally, on the 17th of December, emerging into the unwooded (save in the bottom) valley of the Clearwater river, a few miles above its junction with the Kooskooskia…All of the route lay over high ground, probably very little if any of it so low as 3,000 feet, and then rising as high as 8,000 feet….

With a single exception—a sharp, exposed and elevated ridge, where the wind had drifted the snow until it was piled to the depth of probably ten feet—I found the snow nowhere deeper than at the camps where commenced the snow-shoeing and packing…the average depth for the whole mountain portion of the trail…would be less than two feet. In this elevated route, with the depth of the snow, there was a very remarkable and unexpected mildness of temperature. The temperature was never quite so low as the extreme endured on the prairies, and the weather was occasionally warm.

A few miles from the mountains I found the Nez Perce Indians—remaining with them nearly a week. Their horses and cattle, with some young calves, were grazing in the river valley and slopes. The short grass of the river bottom was still bright and green. In the small gardens of the Indians, pea-vines, started from the seed of the summer crop, were several inches high, and the whole appearance of the valley was in contrast with the cold and snow of the mountains. A slight fall of snow occurred while I was there.

On the 30th day of December I reached [Fort] Wallah-Wallah. The wooded country ends with the mountains, and then commences the great plain known farther north and west as the great Spokane Plain…The bottom lands of the Clearwater were to some extend cultivated by the Indians, and looked fertile—a dark, gravelly soil. Their corn was of good size and heavy; wheat of good weight. Corn, wheat, peas, potatoes, and melons, are produced by the Indians. The upland plains, where I traversed them, showed a good dark soil, exposing fragments of trap-rock, and were generally clothed with good grass, on which were feeding large bands of Indian horses. Mr. [William] Craig, who lives on the Lapwai among the Nez Perces, about forty-five miles from the mountains, has about eight acres of land under tillage, with opportunity for extending his field as he pleases. Peas, corn, wheat, squashes, onions, potatoes, melons, &c., all thrive well there, and Mr. Craig spoke favorably of the productiveness of the soil. His field was on the river bottom, while the hills bordering on the river afforded excellent pasturage for horses, cattle, and goats. On the high plain between the Clearwater river and

---

[1]Tinkham's party crossed the Selway not far upstream from the ancient Bear Creek archaeological site, probably used by the Nez Perce and their ancestors for the past nine thousand years.

his house I found eight inches of snow, lasting only for a short distance. There is none on the Lapwai, and none thence to Wallah-Wallah....

Our guide, Charleer, a handsome Nez Perces lad, showed himself to be thoroughly acquainted with the particular route we travelled, and was very faithful.

[Tinkham also included a detailed itinerary of his route, not published here. Writing from the Hudson's Bay Company post at Fort Walla Walla on 2 January 1854, Tinkham also sent a letter to Isaac Stevens summarizing the trip. In this letter, Tinkham explained why his 25 horses had to be sent back to the Bitterroot Valley and the trip to the Lapwai completed on foot, "the trail being very hilly and tiresome"].

Account 12.3: Excerpts of survey reports of the Northern Pacific Railroad, November 1870. Source: Records of the Northern Pacific Railway Company. Engineering Department, Chief Engineer's "old vault" files. Published with the permission of the Minnesota Historical Society.

Forks of the Bitterroot River
Nov 12th 1870

E.F. Johnson Esqr
    Chief Engr Northern Pacific R.R.
    120 Broadway   New York
Dear Sir:

After I had written to you from Helena, I started for Ft.Owen arriving there the same day that my party did....

Nov. 16th. Since writing the above I have been up to the head of the West Fork of Bitter Root River and on to the divide separating it from the Clearwater. As it had been storming so much for the last few days I was doubtful whether I could get up there. Within about 7 miles of the summit the trail goes up the mountain to a height greater than that of the divide. Here and on the divide I found about two feet of snow and the depth increasing toward the Clearwater [i.e., toward the Selway River]. This and the fallen timber soon made it impossible to go further and I therefore went with much difficulty to the divide, took an observation and looked over the country & observed what I could. It stormed occasionally while I was there....

The west fork of the Bitter Root as far as the place marked "Forks at foot of mt where trail quits the valley &c" is quite open, and has no rocky canons, and very little rock of any kind near the valley, although there are many points of rock & rocky bluffs above it on both sides. There are large flats on both sides of the stream, and a railroad up to the above point could be laid without difficulty. There are places where the foot hills come down to the river opposite each other & form narrow places but there is always a narrow flat on one or both sides. There would be many curves required but none, I think, too sharp. The last 6 miles to the foot of the divide is very straight and very narrow, but there appears to be a small flat to it all along, and no rocky bluffs or canons. The divide itself is very thin on top, (100 yds), across which there runs an old Indian trail (called a buffalo trail) which runs to the North Fork of the Salmon River. I was in this valley and on that trail twice about 9 years ago and was on the same trail again in my exploration of Salmon

River this summer. I have marked it on my map going to Hughes Gulch. The branch of the Clearwater which heads opposite to and in the divide is in appearance (& in reality) just like the 6 miles just spoken of—is very narrow but has a small bottom and no rocky canons for about 10 miles. Then passes through a canon at the head of which is a small prairie where the Southern Nez Percé trail crosses the Ck (about 100 ft wide) & then there is another canon beyond which I know nothing. In 1861 I went down from the southern Nez Percé trail, into this small valley and remained three days, in order to recruit my horses, and I remained one day on the small prairie above mentioned. I remember the ground perfectly well. The mountain side opposite the prairie is very steep where the trail goes up (This is a little sketch of the ground).

From having viewed the country & seen much of the Clearwater from many points, I am inclined to think that beyond this the country is very rough.

The divide is about a mile long and has a depression in the middle at which the observation was taken [probably Nez Perce Pass]. The surrounding mountains are nearly 8000 ft. high....

I hope that the above information may be satisfactory....

I am with much respect Your Obt Servt
W.W. de Lacy

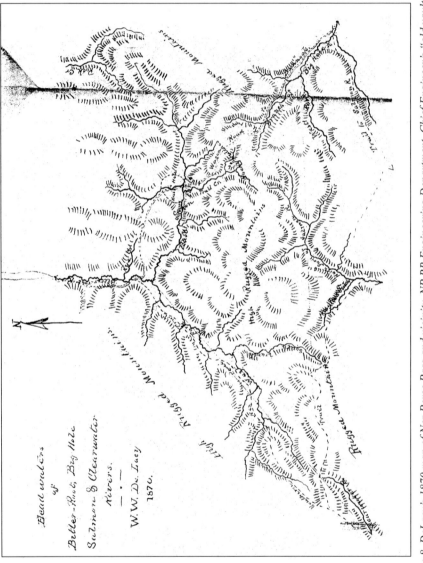

Figure 8. DeLacy's 1870 map of Nez Perce Pass and vicinity: NP RR Engineering Department, Chief Engineer's "old vault" files.

13

The mysterious Dr. John Evans, 1851-1859

The Lolo Trail in the mid-nineteenth century was apparently an almost irresistible attraction for physicians. Before 1870, three of them, all in the employ of the government, had crossed the trail region. The written account of the first of them, that of Dr. John Evans, has never been located, although other Evans letters allude to the Clearwater country. The accounts of the other two, Richard Lansdale and Wellington Bird, appear later in this book.

Of the many visitors to the Clearwater, none has left so confusing and mysterious a story as that of Doctor John Evans, the Chief Geologist for Oregon and Washington, 1851-55. This is chiefly because only a fragmentary written record survives for Evans. The uncertainly about Evans' real accomplishments is compounded by his involvement in the Port Orford, Oregon, meteorite mystery (also called the "meteorite hoax"), which harmed his reputation. Evans proved good at begging for money from the Treasury and poor at actually completing reports. Most were either lost or never actually completed.

Evans was often accompanied by an even more mysterious and little known French portrait and landscape painter, Eugene de Girardin. This artist was born about 1828 into an aristocratic family in the west of France, but became estranged from his family after a short and failed career at the College of Vendome. Like many young Frenchmen before him, he left for North America, arriving in St. Louis sometime in the summer of 1849. There, after briefly working as a "commission merchant, a peddler, and a mule driver," he encountered Dr. Evans and probably Evans' well known employer, U.S. Geologist David Dale Owen. On just two hour's notice, these men hired Girardin as an artist for their geological research trip to the Badlands. This adventure ended in late summer at Fort Union, near the confluence of the Yellowstone and Missouri Rivers.

Dr. Evans himself returned down the Missouri after the geological research ended at Fort Union. Girardin's situation is less clear. A Girardin drawing of Mount Adams, dated July 1852, survives from what might have been a continued association with Evans. Between 1853 and 1855, both Girardin and Evans were employed by Isaac Stevens in work on the Pacific Railroad Surveys. Drawings of the Cascades, the St. Mary's (Bitterroot) Valley, and Fort Colville all survive from this time period. The Evans journal of 1853, now located at the Library of Congress, states that "de Girardin, Artist," was with Evans at Fort Pierre on July 22, 1853.There are no accounts in this journal of any parting of the ways. We can assume that when Evans reached Fort Owen in the Bitterroot Valley in mid-September of 1853, headed for Lolo Pass, Girardin was still with him.

The certain links to Dr. Evans end at this point, but Girardin clearly continued his artistic work in the Northwest. In 1854, he was on the Spokane River and Vancouver Island as well as at Walla Walla. From 1855, we have images of Olympia and the Grand Coulee, plus a large set of portraits from Fort Colville. In 1856 the artist drew many men living near what is now the home of the Grande Ronde Confederated Tribes. In 1857, Girardin painted old Fort Nez Perces in ruins and many Nez Perce men at Walla Walla.[1] Some Palouse River drawings survive from 1859, which was apparently when Girardin left the Northwest, probably for France.

It is very likely that Girardin worked with Dr. Evans during at least some of these years, but there is no known direct evidence of this. Girardin appears to have died about 1888, probably in Panama.

More, but not a lot more, is known about Dr. John Evans.

He was born in Portsmouth, New Hampshire, in February of 1812, the son of a New Hampshire judge. After studying in Andover, Massachusetts, he moved to Washington, D.C., working there as a clerk in the Post Office Department for eight years. In May of 1835, he married Sarah Zane Mills, the daughter of the designer of the Washington Monument. They eventually had three sons and one daughter.

The Evans family moved to St. Louis in 1839, where John Evans earned his M.D. degree at St. Louis University. During this time he became acquainted with Dr. B.F. Shumard, a leader of the St. Louis Academy of Science. In 1847, both men were hired by Dr. David Owen, who was then conducting a government geological survey of Iowa, Wisconsin, and Minnesota. No evidence survives to indicate why physician Evans became geologist Evans.

The General Land Office extended the range of its geological survey westward to the Badlands of Nebraska in 1849. Girardin joined Evans on this expedition, which was completed with the help of the American Fur Company. Evans was the survey's business manager and map maker, and his work was well received. In March of 1851, this reputation proved sufficient for Evans to be named by the General Land Office to conduct a geological survey west of the Cascade Mountains. $3500 was appropriated for this purpose, a figure that proved to be wildly inadequate.

In October of 1851, Evans (and probably Girardin) was at Oregon City, having reached that point overland via Flathead Lake, Lolo Pass, and Clearwater and Snake Rivers. On the 18th of June of this year, Evans helped Father Pierre-Jean De Smet,

---

[1]Girardin's full color painting of one of these men, Jesse the Bear Paw, appears on the book jacket of Dennis Baird, Diane Mallickan, and W.R. Swagerty, eds., *Nez Perce Nation Divided* (Moscow: University of Idaho Press, 2002).

the famous Jesuit missionary and explorer, save the lives of cholera victims on board a Missouri River fur trading boat.[2] Reaching Oregon, Evans immediately wrote to beg the Interior Department for an additional $10,000. Dr. Shumard joined Evans in Oregon on this trip, arriving by sea. The two men remained in the Oregon country into the following summer.

Evans worked with Isaac Stevens in Washington, D.C. in the spring of 1853, sharing his knowledge of the West. Stevens had been named head of one of the western railroad surveys, and was also the new Governor of Washington Territory. Evans was now able to wear two hats. He was still U.S. Geologist, but along with Girardin, was employed by the railroad survey. Evans left St. Louis for the Pacific on May 18, 1853. The party also included Lt. John Mullan. The detailed geologic studies prepared by Evans on this trip were never received in Washington. A long letter explaining what *should* be in such a study has survived. The Library of Congress owns a journal of this trip which ends abruptly with the author at Fort Owen, ready to leave for Lolo Creek. The Smithsonian owns a detailed Evans journal, written near Fort Vancouver and at Spokane, from the summer of 1854. In September of that year, Evans reached the valleys of the Tucannon and Touchet Rivers on his way to Walla Walla.

Other parts of the Evans journal at the Smithsonian describe a trip to Fort Colville in 1855, and a lengthy exploration of the Umpqua and Willamette Valleys in 1856. These journals, not necessarily in Dr. Evans' own handwriting, provide useful botanical and geological information. Their author also took time late in 1856 to induce the Washington Territorial Legislature to memorialize Congress on the work of Dr. Evans, and to demand more money for him.

These travels and the continued quest for more money produced a second appropriation from Congress, for $23,500. By 1857, Evans was back in the nation's capitol, apparently working on his final report to the General Land Office. Some letters survive, suggesting that a report was actually completed, or nearly so. Congress, with the Civil War now fast approaching, never made a third appropriation for publishing the report. No copy of anything resembling a final report by Dr. Evans is known to exist.

In 1860, Evans was named geologist for a government expedition to the Isthmus of Panama, the Chiriqui Expedition. Evans died in Washington in April of 1861, shortly after his return from Panama.

Dr. Evans, probably accompanied by Eugene de Girardin, appears to have crossed the Lolo Trail on two occasions. Even though he routinely kept a detailed journal, none has, to date, been located for either trip. Girardin's paintings survive for places on either side of the Nez Perce heartland, and the artist painted Nez Perce men at Walla Walla. If Girardin painted along the Lolo trail, which seems likely, those images also remain missing.

---

[2]DeSmet to the Father General, In Hiram M. Chittenden and Alfred T. Richardson, Eds., *Life, Letters and Travels of Father Pierre-Jean De Smet, S.J., Vol. 2* (New York: Francis Harper, 1905), 638-43.

More information about Dr. John Evans and Eugene de Girardin:

Richard W. Evans, "Dr. John Evans, U.S. Geologist, 1851-1861," *Washington Historical Quarterly* 26 (1935): 83-89.

Charles T. Jackson, M.D., "Biographical Sketch of the Late John Evans, M.D.," *American Journal of Science* 32 (1861): 311-18.

Erwin F. Lange, "Dr. John Evans, U.S. Geologist to the Oregon and Washington Territories," *Proceedings of the American Philosophical Society*, 103 (1959): 476-84.

Howard Plotkin, "John Evans and the Port Orford Meteorite Hoax," In Roy S. Clarke Jr., Ed., *The Port Orford, Oregon, Meteorite Mystery.* Smithsonian Contributions to the Earth Sciences, No. 31. (Washington: Smithsonian Institution Press, 1993), 1-24.

François Rouget de Gourcez, *Eugène de Girardin: Watercolors ans [sic] drawings of North America, Nebraska, Dakota, Washington, Oregon, Idaho, Utah, Vancouver Island, 1849-1859* (Paris: Privately Published, 2001).

B.F. Shumard, "Dr. John Evans," *Transactions of the Academy of Science of St. Louis,* (1863): 162-64.

David A. White, "David D. Owen and Dr. John Evans, 1852," In *News of the Plains and Rockies, 1803-1865, Vol. 4* (Spokane: Arthur H. Clark, 1998), 415-33.

Primary sources:

John Evans, *Descriptive Catalogue of Geological Specimens Collected in Oregon and Washington Territory, 1857.* Smithsonian Institution Archives. RU 305.

John Evans, *John Evans Papers, 1854-56, and 1860.* Smithsonian Institution, Archives and Manuscripts. Entry SIA 7198, Box. 1.

Also includes his *Diary*, Ft. Vancouver, July 1854-August 1856.

John Evans, *John Evans Diary, July- September 1853.* Library of Congress, Manuscripts Division.

This diary ends with Evans at Travelers Rest near Lolo, Montana.

John Evans, *Letters of John Evans.* Microfilm of manuscript. (Washington: National Archives, 1974).[3]

Mostly letters from General Land Office and Secretaryof the Interior files. The film is owned solely by the University of Houston Library.

---

[3]The letters that were filmed for this project were never returned to their proper locations in the Interior Department records at Archives II in College Park. Other Evans letters, *not* filmed for this project, are also missing. The authors of this book have also never been able to obtain an explanation of just why the University of Houston is the sole owner of this film collection, although they were possibly filmed at the behest of a member of their faculty.

John Evans, "Letter to Lt. G.R. Warren, USA, Office of Explorations and Surveys, War Department, January 30, 1859," In National Archives, College Park. Records of The Secretary of the Interior, RG 48, Entry 726: Reports, Field Notes, and Related Reports, 1855-1863. Box 1, item 13 & Box 3, item 158.

Evans Collection. Special Collections Division, Georgetown University Library.

Contains many family letters and a tiny photo of John Evans.

Eugene de Girardin, "A Trip to the Bad Lands in 1849," *South Dakota Historical Review* 1 (1936): 51-78.

Includes an account published earlier in *The Palimpsest* 8 (March 1927).

Eugene de Girardin, "Voyage dans les Mauvaises Terres du Nebraska," *Le Tour du Monde* 280 (1864): 49-64.

Heavily illustrated version; includes a map by Dr. John Evans.

Grand Ronde Confederated Tribes Web site. www.grandronde.org.

This site includes several Giradin drawings of Champoeg men done in April of 1856. These are among 20 Girardin drawings in the National Archives of Canada, Bushnell Collection. Most are of men at Fort Colville.

Account 13.1: Excerpts from a letter sent by Dr. John Evans on November 21, 1859, to Samuel A. Smith, Commissioner of the General Land Office. Source: NARA RG 49, General Land Office, Miscellaneous Letters Received (Univ. of Houston film).

Washington, Nov. 21st, 1859

Hon. Saml. A. Smith
Commr. Genl. Land Office
Sir:
In compliance with the verbal request alluded to in my letter of the 14th instant, I have the honor to present a few of the results of the geological survey of Oregon and Washington Territories, contained in the report ordered to be printed [but never actually printed] at the last session of Congress...
On a large tributary of the Columbia the Kooskooskie River, is a mountain of iron ore, more lofty than the celebrated iron mountain is Missouri, and fully equal in richness. The analysis of surface specimens by Dr. [D.D.] Owen, which probably for ages have been exposed to atmospheric influences, gives the following result.

Water	0.05		
Silica	1.90		
Peroxide of iron	89.95	Metalic iron	62.99
Alumina	6.90		
Alkalies	0.10		
Loss	1.10		
	100.00		

Some of the soils of the pacific coast and the Nez Perces Country, between the Bitter Root and Cascade mountains, are very remarkable. They are similar in their constituents, and probably equal to the celebrated soil near Olmutz, Morave, which has been cropped for 160 years successively, without either manure, or naked fall over, yielding every season very abundant crops....

The following is an analysis of one of the soils referred to made by Dr. D.D. Owen.

Nez Perces Country

Moisture expelled at 400° F.	6 250
Organic matter	9 550
Insoluble silicates	72 650
Lime	320
Oxide of iron	5 530
Alumina	3 800
Sulphuric acid	090
Potash	280
Magnesia1	080
Phosphoric acid	220
Loss	230
	100 000

14

John Owen on the Lolo & Southern Nez Perce Trails, 1852-63

Few men of any background traveled through more of the Plateau region of the West than did the Bitterroot Valley's John Owen (1818-1889). In his twenty or so years of residence at the fort that bore his name, he journeyed on foot and on horse over 23,000 miles, ranging from the Great Salt Lake to Puget Sound and the lower Columbia River Valley. A series of diaries and journals, most now in the Montana Historical Society (Mss. 44), chronicle his life and travels. On several occasions he passed through the Clearwater country, usually via the Lolo Trail, but at least once via the Southern Nez Perce Trail. For a man with so immense an experience in wild and remote country, he also reported himself to be thoroughly lost on a remarkable number of occasions. The authors of *Montana Genesis* got it right: "He was in no sense a mountain man or frontiersman, or even an able woodsman."[1] Like many of his European contemporaries in the region, his career was a mixture of private trading and exploration coupled with years in the employment of the federal government (as the Flathead Indian Agent, 1856-62).

John Owen purchased the site of his "fort" from the Society of Jesus in 1850, paying $250. The Jesuits, under the leadership of Fathers DeSmet, Point, and Mengarini, had established the St. Mary's Mission near modern day Stevensville in 1841, responding to a request from the Salish people of the Bitterroot Valley (and their Iroquois mentors). For a variety of reasons, the Jesuits decided to close the mission, and sold it to Owen, who was newly arrived in the Bitterroots. A former Army suttler with the courtesy title of "Major," Owen reached the valley early in 1850 with his Shoshone wife, Nancy.

While he roamed widely throughout his life, Owen managed to transform Fort Owen into a center of profit, hospitality, and even civilization. The Stevens' Railroad

---

[1]Stevensville Historical Society, *Montana Genesis; A History of the Stevensville area of the Bitterroot Valley* (Missoula: Mountain Press, 1971), 18.

Survey and Mullan Road projects all proved especially beneficial to the fort's financial success. Most of the travel documented below was commercial in nature. Owen had a fine knowledge of Salish and Nez Perce culture, and his dozens of unpublished letters in the records of the Indian Agency constitute a rare and little used primary source of information. Owen kept the fort active until 1871, when his mind began to fail. He died, apparently insane, in Pennsylvania in 1889.

Often accompanied by family members, and often lost, Owen crossed the Lolo Trail westbound in September and October of 1852, had a harrowing trip across the Southern Nez Perce trail in July and September of 1854, and a trip westbound in August of 1857. A final trip eastward from Lewiston came in July of 1863, taking just thirteen days (on 17 July, Owen reported "further travel to Bald Mtn side Ind Camp"), but leaving only a brief journal account.

Further reading:

Seymour Dunbar, and Paul C. Phillips, *The Journals and Letters of Major John Owen* (New York: Edward Eberstadt, 1927). 2 vols.

> A comprehensive and well-edited collection, with a fine introduction.

Helen Addison Howard, "Major John Owen, Independent Trader of Old Oregon," In *Northwest Trail Blazers* (Caldwell: Caxton, 1963), 111-124.

> A thorough and accurate account, with a fine assessment of Owen's impact on history and the region.

Stevensville Historical Society, *Montana Genesis: A History of the Stevensville Area of The Bitterroot Valley* (Missoula: Mountain Press, 1971).

> A third of this well-written volume deals with the St. Mary's Mission and Fort Owen. Has great illustrations, but, unfortunately, no footnotes.

Dan L. Thrapp, "John Owen," In *Encyclopedia of Frontier Biography, Vol. 2* (Glendale: Arthur C. Clark, 1988), 1097.

> A very brief but reliable account of Owen's life.

George F. Weisel, *Men and Trade on the Northwest Frontier as Shown by the Fort Owen Ledger* (Missoula: Montana State University Press, 1955).

> A well-edited version of the Ledger Book, plus a vast array of biographical data about John Owen and his many customers. Based on years of research.

Account 14.1: Excerpts from the account of the September 1852 trip. Source: Seymour Dunbar and Paul C. Phillips, *The Journals and Letters of Major John Owen, Vol. 1* (New York: E. Eberstadt, 1927), 51-55.

Tuesday Sept 21st /52 Left Fort Owen for the Dalles party Robinson Crusoe Nancy Madam Harris & 2 children & Ind boy Nine pack animals Made a late start the Morning being unfavorable Crost St Marys [the Bitterroot River] close to fort and continued down west bank some 12 Miles & left trail & turned into the left & a few Miles Struck Lo Lo fork & camped packs Wet & heavy....

Friday 24 [having left Lolo Hot Springs] followed up the Small strip of prarie four mile or so & took the Mts Some 6 Miles brought us down on to the Crk again which we Crossed & made a long & sharp ascent in Crossing some Spurs we came over to a Small prariecrost the upper end & over some riges & came out on to another nice prarie & camped Made not over 15 Miles to day [camping somewhere near Lolo Pass] Animals jaded trail very fair for the Mts Kiled 6 Mt grouse

Saturday 25 Made a late start two of the animals Missing Noon before we Moved trail took up the Small steep prarie a Mile or so & then the Mts Some 6 Miles brought us down on to Lo Lo fork again which we Crossd & made a sharp and long ascent Night Caught us in the Mts haltd & tied up No water or grass found Snow Enough for Coffee hard trail to day on the Animals Made not over 10 or 12 Miles to day fine mess Mt Grouse

Sunday 26 Made an Early start without breakfast in order to reach grass & water for the animals No small job to day to drive hungry animals through the timber packs quite troublesome traveld Some ten Miles & found Some grass in the Mts but no water Campd—there is snow on the Mt Sides Grass Moderate trail hard to day passd No Water fine Mess Mt Grouse

Monday 27 After travelling Some 6 Miles we reached a very Small Spring on Side Mt but not sufficient for Stock Some 11 Miles further travel we came down on to a Spring branch which we followed down a short distance & Campd there is some grass this is the first water I have seen Sufficient for Stock in the travel Since crossing the river the 25 Excepting a Spring on Side of Mt Some 2 or 3 Miles this side of Crk the trail has been more open to day but Very hilly some rock & but little fallen timber there is but little grass on the route so far Not adapted for Stock by any Means Coming down one of the back bones to day could see a small Str over to the right with Small Strip of prarie Some 6 or 8 Miles off of the trail

Tuesday 28 Crossed Several Steep & Rocky points trail still Continues open with but little fallen timber traveld Some 6 $^{1}/_{2}$ hours without Meeting with any water and Came to a Small Spring on top of Mt & Campd Not water for the animals here they eat snow off the Sides Mt & during the day they find Small pools standing in the road from the Melting of Snow Madam Harris lost one of her horses Yesterday poor and completely given out We are Moving Slow Say in the 6 $^{1}/_{2}$ hrs travel Some 15 Miles Not More Kill a Grouse & Pheasant latter large

Wednesday 29 After Moving Some 2 Miles brought us down on to a very Nice little Mt Stream which we Crossd & took the Mts again which We continued in Some 3 $^{1}/_{2}$ hrs & came out on to a Small opening with Water a very pretty place for a camp which We followed & crossd one of the highest ridges I think that We have been on the ascent was tedious & Sharp on top of Which We came to a Small opening with water & Campd

Thursday 30 Snow fell about a foot last night would lay by to day but fear losing trail made a late Start and one Sharp ascent with that exception & the Snow the road much better country more open & not so Mountainous traveld but 4 $^{1}/_{2}$ hours to day & that afoot Came to a Small Spring on Mt. Side and Campd We have prospect of a Clear day to Morrow as is has Stopd Snowing & the Sun made its appearce

Friday Oct 1st Made an Early Start with prospect of a fair day but a few hrs out

& it commenced Snowing & contd it all day Crossd two high Mts and Night Caught us on the third I was ahead with the boy & three pack animals We halted unpacked Made a fire and waited for the female portion to come up they had the bedding pack groceries Kettle &c I waited until quite late I had Some dried Meat with Me Made a repast and fixd a bed of peshamoes [buffalo skin saddle blankets] & went to Sleep No water but plenty snow we passed no water during the day trail not so open & some fallen timber traveld to day 9 hrs but slow and disagreeable [they were still on the Lolo Trail, probably somewhere at the head of Weitas Creek]

Saturday Oct 2 Woke up Early this Morning and Sent boy back to see after the Women he was gone about an hour & came up with them they had fell behind & could not see the trail & halted for the Night We got off before 9 o'clock & 2 hrs travel brought us out on to an opening which we followed up & passed through a strip of [illegible words] & came out on to another opening much larger—I crossed & campd Only a short March so that the animals already Jaded might have an opportunity of regailing themselves being the first green grass they have had for some time travld Some 3 hrs to day to Morrow I hope to get out of the Mts as it seems to do nothing else but Snow on them trail Not good to day Some fallen timber & plenty of Snow

Sunday Oct 3 Made an Early start & soon took the Mts Some 3 hrs travel brought us down on to a small spring with water left the Women with 4 pack Animals at Noon Night caught me in the Mts came down on to a Small stream tied up and Campd sent boy back for Women to dark to go far could not find them traveld 9 hrs to day

Oct 4 Started without waiting for the Women & traveld Some5 hrs & came down on to Small prairie which we followed up [probably Musselshell Meadows] passed through strip timber & came out on to a Much larger prairie & campd [probably the Weippe Prairie] Sent Boy back to see after Women Was gone an hour came back Not finding them traveld 6 hrs to day – grass fine to night

Tuesday Oct 5 Sent boy back again this Morning & after an absence of 4 hrs came up with Women Made a late Start followd up Several Strips prarie Crossd a small Mtn & came down on to a [unclear] of prarie that lets us out on to Clear Water Valley Made a 1 horse camp

Wednesday 6 Laid by Went to village [Kamiah]

Thursday 7 Moved to Village

Friday 8 Travld 7 hrs over rolling hills in part campd in Second gulch a ravine

Saturday 8 Move to Craigs [to William Craig's home on Lapwai Creek]

Account 14.2: Excerpts from the account of the westward July 1854 trip and eastward trip in September. Source: John Owen Papers (Mss. 44), Montana Historical Society Archives, Box 1, Folder 6. Published here with the permission of the Montana Historical Society.

29 [July 1854] Saturday [heading for the Dalles] This Morning We found pools of Standing Water Within Some Six Miles of our Camp but Saw No running Water until we reached the Stream Called Clear Water...After reaching Clear Water My Brother Continued on down the Stream & I with a boy crossed & too up a Small

branch [Lapwai Creek] coming to Spauldings Mission Some ten Miles to Mr Craigs Ranch Whom O found at home & well Mr [Henri] Chase & Wife also there Mr Craigs Crop of Wheat oats corn & vegetables looked fine plenty of fresh rich Milk butter & New potatoes Which I relished very much

Sunday 30 Retd this morning by the same trail to Spauldings Mission & crossed Clear Water…

16 Sept 1854 Saturday Made a Short Camp over to Canon River [the Tucannon River] High Wind all day after being camped at Loui Raboins [a French-Canadian fur trader and sometimes resident] Some few hours Mr Torrance came from the Utilla River [the Umatilla River] Came up on his Way to Mr Craigs. Hired a Man Named Jackson

17 Sunday Made a Moderate camp on to a Small Creek Called the Pa ta ha left a Mule and a horse behind probably Mr Chase will bring them up

18 Monday Some three hours travel brought us over to Red Wolf Creek which we followed down to Snake River then taking up Snake to the Mouth of Clear Water at which place I found No Canoes and had to follow the river on up Some Six Miles further over a rocky and very bad trail to a point on the river Known as Lookinglass's place [Asotin] a Nes Perce chief from whom I procured Some Canoes & Men to cross us

19 Tuesday I succeeded in Crossing the river in good time & packed up and was Soon on the Move in the Mean time Mr Chase Came up in Six hours travel Reached Mr Craigs & Campd…

Saturday 23 After a rest of three days feasting all the time on Melons Tomatoes Corn &c Which I found in great abundance at Mr Craigs Which he turned out to Myself and party with a liberal hand I again took up the line of March and Made but a Short Camp Mr Craig & Chase accompanying Me a short distance to have a parting glass. Camped in a deep Cooley in which I found Sufficient Water for the animals with good grass and plenty of wood left at Mr Craigs two Mules and three horses I also left at Raboins on To Canon one Mule. Took from Mr Craig two Govt horses which I found fresh & fat Supposed to have been lost from Lieut Mac Feelys train [part of the Stevens Survey] on Way from Bitter Root Valley to the Dalles in the fall of /53 I however can put them to good use…

26 Tuesday Cleared off about ten o'clock to day after which time we had a beautiful day one horse Minus this Morning Made a Short Camp over on to Lawyers Creek leaving three of My party behind to look up the lost horse I am now going close to the base of the Bitter Root Mountains Which with No bad luck We will reach in two More Camps the stream I am on is a tributary of Clear Water…

Thursday Sept 28" 1854 rather late about raising camp as I expected to Make but a Short March and Wait for the two Men Sent back Yesterday for the lost horse to Come up I have marched about ten Miles & finding Myself lost I thought it best to Camp I again halted on Lawyers Creek Which I have been following up from My last Camp—I should have Crossed it Some five Miles back and taken the hills for the foot of the Mountain My guide being gone & having but little locality Myself accounts for My Missing the Proper trail I Soon became Conscious that all was Not right I did Not remember following up the Stream So far and as good luck would have a Nes Perce Indian Came into Camp a short time after I had halted & gave me to understand I was lost I readily fess'd the Con & got him to Consent to pass the Night With Me and put Me in the proper trail in the Morning.

Friday 29 Made a fair Start with the old Nes Perce Patriarch as guide he Soon gave Me to understand that there were two roads one that followed up the Creek & the other leaving it...I concluded it best to leave the Creek & take [east] across the hills...I Was Six hours in the Mts before I could find a Suitable place to halt for the Night I then found a Small low bare Spot With grass & rushes & Water Sufficient for My Camp One Night It was dusk before all the packs got in and the Animals and Men both appear Much jaded We are Now in the region of Snow....

September 30" 1854 Morning Cloudy [after first losing a pack mule and then finding it in deep brush] When getting down Some distance it halted probably for reflection to get back on the ridge again & find the trail was the trouble. I saw the ridge running around far above where I Supposed the road passed but to get there was No Small difficulty Hoping the train Might yet be in hearing distance I commenced halloing at the top of my voice but could hear Nothing but the Echoes of my Cries reverberated by the Surrounding Mountains I Sat a few Moments ruminating...I Continued on Some three Miles further & Came to a Small Stream running through a very pretty Narrow prarie Some Six miles long [possibly the American River]...

Sunday Oct 1st [spent, with the help of "the old Nes Perce Indian," and the "old Wife," rounding up missing animals]

Monday Oct 2" We followed the Creek down on which we were Encamped Some three Miles & too the Mt. Which I found tedious the road in places bad from fallen timber We were five hrs in Reaching the Summit on which I found Some three or four beautiful Springs the Water of which I am camped on to Night Some five Miles from the Summit brought Me down to a beautiful Strip of Prarie with fine Soil & Magnificent grass I have followed it down Some four miles how Much further it Runs I do Not Know. I see in the Trail Some tracks from the appearance of Which I should think they had passed on Yesterday I hope they are Not Lieut. Mullans & his party as I was anxious to see him before his departure from the Bitter Root Valley [A.W. Tinkham of the Mullan party passed near this spot the previous December, and Mullan himself, on this very day, was camped about ninety miles away, just east of Lapwai] It May however be an Indian trail

Tuesday Oct 3 we followed the Small Stream down Some 3 Miles & took the Mt. Which was not as tedious as the one Yesterday Still there Were Some Very Sharp ascents & descents but Not long trail open & good Except where I found rock Which Was hard on the Animals feet three hrs travel brought Me through the Mt down on a beautiful Prarie with a beautiful Stream of Water Some ten feet Wide gravely bottom I followed the Stream up Some four Miles in its Meandering Course & the prarie gradually grew narrower until the Mts Made down So close on both Sides as to form but a Neck through which the Stream run [possibly upper Meadow Creek] I followed up the Neck on the Mt Side which I find Very low here with timber all dead for two Miles further When another beautiful but smaller prarie presented a Most Enchanting Sight here I Called a halt for the day though Early still My animals Show they are fatigued My packs are to heavy for the road traveled to day five hours I don't think we have Made over 2$^{1}/_{2}$ Miles to the hour My old Nes Perce friend leave Me this Morning I Made Some Small presents by way of Keeping on the fair Side for Some time May need his Services. The grass here is Excellent and it Would Make a fine Summering ground for Stock out of the reach of Blackfeet & I think I shall adopt it in future as My best Course to get together a good band of animals Keep them at the fort until you can Cross the Mt & then drive them over and form a Summer Encampment remain until about this time & Cross back again

Wednesday oct 4" Made Ice last Night in a Cup. Full ½ in. thick On the March in good time been in the Mts all day Crossd Some high ridges but the ascents & descents Were Not Sharp or tedious trail first rate Wide & open No obstructions from fallen timber & but little or no rock timber Much Smaller than on Mts back & Much thinner passed Several beautiful Springs traveld only four hrs to day Which brought Me to a Narrow opening Some ½ Mile wide & 2 long at the upper End of Which I halted I am favoring My animals all I can in fact they require it. My Camp Not over ten Miles to day grass fair A nes Perce Indian driving a horse Came up as We were Camping he is on his way to the Flatheads

Thursday Oct 5 towards Sunrise it had the appearance of breaking away but Soon Clouded over again & Settled down into a Confirmed Storm I Could Not lay by We have two or three hight Mts. to cross & I am fearful of Snow I raised Camp in the rain & a very disagreeable drive We have had of it too. On Some of the highest points it Snowed & blew fiercely our March was Seven hrs long Six of Which brought up to what I think is a fork of Salmon River [probably Sabe Creek] Which I followed up passed one of two Small openings Crossed a ridge & found another opening & Camped the trail to day open & good with Exception of a very little which was obstructed by fallen timber

Friday Oct. 6" Well if one did Not Care about telling the truth he Would Say last Night & to day fair but Not So— About the time We turned into our Blankets it Comcd raining & Continued it until daylight Except the few intervals it filled up by Snowing Day light however Came & the Surrounding hills had a rather White appearance with the Still overhanging clouds which threatened a Continuation of the Storm Which was fully carried out So Much So that I was Not able to raise Camp...to have raised camp to day would have been cruel My apichamons [saddle blankets] & Saddles Say Nothing about the bales from Yesterdays March were completely Saturated with Snow & rain...I have been Much longer than I expected In fact I thought I should have been home in ten days from leaving Mr Craig's Ranch or I should have been better Supplied

Saturday oct 7 A Stormy Night it held up towards Morning & Seemed as though it would break away I raised Camp & Soon Struck the Mt when it Commenced Snowing in good Earnest & Kept it up all day I have traveld seven hrs & I think have crossed the Worst Mt. Of any—Snow Most of the day from ten to fifteen in. trail to day open Some few obstructions I am Campd at the foot of the Mt [probably just west of Salmon Mountain] I cross to Morrow prospects dull in point of Weather but on we Must go further delay is dangerous left one Animal back Some three Mules give Completely out & Could Not reach Camp It is Snowing good & fast at the present speaking been afoot all day and Can Say I am tired Without fear of being doubted

Sunday 8. Gloomy in the Extreme Snowing all Night & Seems disposed to Keep it up today Raised Camp in the Storm Apichamons Saddles Cords & Every thing that was the least damp frose stiff I think the hills have been Worse on our animals to day than previous the ascents & descents Not long but very Sharp

Snow Most of the day until We Commenced getting down when it gradually all disappeared I am Encamped on Clear Water the Same Stream I Campd on the 25 last Month [he is camped on the upper Selway River, which is a tributary of the Clearwater] Sent back for the lost horse this Morning but he was found dead probably chilled to death for We are at a great altitude We have two More Mt. To Cross & that we take at the start from here his head Can be Seen towering far above us

[The next two days were spent, hungry and often afoot, the party divided, floundering across Nez Perce Pass.]

Wednesday 11" Over Jordan's Stormy shores at last—Our trail this Morning took along the Mt. Side a few Miles & Struck the foot of Prarie Knob which we had to ascend which appeared to Me as Much like a fly ascending to the Summit of a Sugar Loaf as any thing I can well Compare it to— Well our trail today was been hilly with Small timber—after reaching the Summit of the ridge overlooking My Camp our descent was More tedious & Sharp than any previous but We are Now done with the Mts. I have been Much deceived in My own Judgement about the road [they have at last reached the headwaters of the West Fork of the Bitterroot River]....

Saturday 14 Moved in good time followed river down Some distance before Coming out into the Bitter Root Valley....

Account 14.3: Lolo Trail accounts of July and August, 1857. Source: John Owen Papers (Mss. 44), Montana Historical Society Archives, Box 1, Folder 7. Published here with the permission of the Montana Historical Society.

16 [July] Thursday....Met an Old Indian who reports Dr Lansdale [see Chapter 16 of this book for more information] close coming up from below by the Lolo fork pass of the Bitter Root Mts concluded this Evening to let things remain as they are for the present & take the interpreter in the Morning & Start to Meet him I hope it May be true [that he was being replaced as Indian Agent] for I am heartily tired of the Agency. I find it destitute of provisions the public fund all Expended & have been for some time. A year pay due some of the hands & Nothing but promises to offset it with. The Superior of the Oregon & Washington Mission from California accompanied by Some two other priests had been up on a Visit to the St Ignatius Mission...

22 Wednesday left in company with Dr Lansdale for Agency After resting an hour at Mr McArthurs We Moved on & reached the Agency about sun set quite tired but soon revived our drooping Spirits with a glass of good old Whiskey which was sent Me by Col Craig from fort Walla Walla May the Snow of Many Winters Set lightly upon his brow...

24 [August] Monday Made a start for Vancouver accompanied by Mr C.E. Irvine [Caleb E. Irvine, a former Army officer, horse trader, and later employee of the Mullan Road project] & My two Indian Voyageurs Antoine & Charles Campd on Lolos fork some Six above where it comes out into Bitter Root Valley

25 Tuesday Road Mountainous with fallen timber travelling bad. Made 5½ hrs travel & campd on Lolos fork again flushed a covy of Blue Grouse got two shots Bagd None—

26 Wednesday road bad for some 8 Miles Mountainous & fallen timber travld 5½ hrs Campd at Warm Springs [Lolo Hot Springs]

27 Thursday off Early in 4 hrs travel we reached quite a good sized prarie on the divide [Packer Meadows] which after leaving we had a long tedious & sharp descent on to Clear Water [the upper Lochsa] Which we crossed & had a sharp & tedious Ascent up on the Mt again our descent after reaching the highest point has been gradual—Most of the Way along the Backbone of the Mt. After a tedious March of Six hrs from the prarie we found what appeared to be an old Campg ground— Mr Irvine soon found a Cold Spring some 150 yds from the trail & We were glad to camp for the night in the saddle 10 hrs

28 Friday Road Rocky & Mountainous Some 4 miles to a Small spring Made a tedious ascent & descent down on to a Small Stream in a densely timbered bottom Came to a small lake [one of the Lost Lakes?] crossed a small stream found we had missed the trail & Campd Early 5½ hrs

29 Saturday We soon found the trail We left last Evening & we have had a hard days March Making some Six sharp & tedious ascents & descents in the Saddle 8 hrs Camps in a Small opening on the Mt ridges Met some Indians to day En Route for Buffaloe

30 Sunday Moved in fair time have had a tedious day in the Saddle 11 hrs. Crossd Several tedious ridges in fact it has been Mt. Ridge after Mt. Ridges Met Some flat head Indians returning home Camps in a small prairie in the Mt

31 Monday travelling bad bushes wet road hilly with plenty of fallen timber a very tedious day in the Saddle 11½ hrs. passed two creeks some 10 Miles back came out on to a good sized prarie [possibly Musselshell Meadows] & Campd all of us quite tired

September

1 Tuesday off in fair time Made a Mistake in the trail soon discovered it 4 hrs travel brought us out to Camash [Weippe] prairie road fair through Small prarie openings & along the Mt Slopes We had one long & tedious ascent & descent [across the deep valley of Lolo Creek] Some 10 Miles after passing Camash prairie campd early on Clear Water Met the Nez Perce Camp their Crops looked Well in the Saddle 8 hrs

2 Wednesday 3½ hrs to first Gulch 1¾ to Second in which we found water & campd Made about 25 miles [they were on the ancient trail between Kamiah and Lapwai]

3 Thursday 6 hrs travel to Craigs old Ranch [William Craig, at this time, was mostly living near Walla Walla] 4 hrs further to Snake river at the Mouth of Clear Water Campd on right bank tired bagd 3 Grouse

4 Friday The Indian ferried us ovr in good time traveled 8 hrs & camps on Pa ta ha low down—

5 Saturday 2 hrs travel to Canon [Tucannon River] 8 hrs further to Col. Craigs ranch Within 1½ Miles of New fort Walla Walla [a reference to the U.S. Army post built near the site of modern day Walla Walla in 1856. The original Fort Walla Walla, also known as Fort Nez Perces, was located thirty miles away, near the mouth of the Walla Walla River]. The Garrison Command by Col. Steptoe a very pleasnt Gent....

15

Railroad and wagon road surveys of the Lolo Trail and Lochsa Region, 1854-1879

Isaac Stevens had three charges in his work in the Pacific Northwest. As Governor of the newly established Washington Territory, he was to organize an entire structure of government for a territory that included all of the modern states of Washington, Idaho, and Montana. In addition, the new territorial government hoped to extirpate Indian titles to land both west and east of the Cascades. Stevens also remained head of the Pacific railway survey's northern route, a project of the War Department. In this latter effort, he relied on a cadre of remarkably capable surveyors and explorers. The best of these was probably Lt. John Mullan, who conducted the surveys in most of the Bitterroot Range.

In the summer of 1854, Mullan turned his work to the major remaining unsurveyed route—the historic trail taken across the Bitterroots by Lewis and Clark leading west up Lolo Creek from its junction with the Bitterroot River. His account is thorough and often insightful, and in one instance almost poetic in its description of nature. Like many other observers, Mullan even found himself to be an admirer of the seasonal round of Nez Perce life.

The two railroad surveys of 1870-71, which are published here for the first time, were part of the normal work of the Northern Pacific as it reached Montana. The Lolo Pass route, after Mullan's research, was never considered seriously. These surveys could best be described as a sort of insurance policy for the company. They do, however, offer some new insight into the origins of the name "Lo Lo."

The 1879 Northern Pacific survey, also published here for the first time, is filled with humor, astute political observations, and a large dose of cynicism. While providing some valuable information about the conditions of the Clearwater country, it is more useful for its look at small town boosterism.

Further reading:

Louis C. Coleman, *Captain John Mullan: His Life* (Montreal: Payette Radio, 1968).

A nicely researched but poorly edited account of Mullan's life.

Philip G. Eastwick, *Report of the Northern Pacific Railroad's Survey of the North Fork of the Clearwater River in 1871* (Moscow: Univ. of Idaho Library, 1999).

Complete account of the North. Fork survey, with maps and photos.

Addison Howard, "Captain John Mullan," *Washington Historical Quarterly* 25 (1934): 185-202.

An excellent early look at the impact of Mullan's work in the West.

Helen Addison Howard, "Captain John Mullan, the Road Builder," In *Northwest Trail Blazers* (Caldwell: Caxton, 1963), 145-171.

Emphasizes road work, but provides useful information on Mullan's life.

Derek Jensen and George Draffan, *Railroads and Clearcuts* (Spokane: Inland Empire Public Lands Council, 1995).

A thorough and well-researched account of what became of NP lands at places like Lolo Pass.

Montana: the Magazine of Western History 33, no. 3 (Summer 1983).

A special issue devoted entirely to Montana railroad history.

Paul C. Phillips, "John Mullan," In *Dictionary of American Biography, Vol. 13.*(New York: Scribners, 1934), 319-20.

A short biography with several suggestions for further reading.

Alan Rolston, "The Yellowstone Expedition of 1873," *Montana: the Magazine of Western History* 20, no. 2 (April 1970): 20-29.

Despite its title, a reliable account of NPRR exploration in Montana.

Eugene B. Smalley, *History of the Northern Pacific Railroad* (New York: G.P. Putnam's Sons, 1883)

A reliable account, by an insider, with good coverage of western route plans.

Dan L. Thrapp, "John Mullan," In *Encyclopedia of Frontier Biography, Vol. 2* (Glendale: Arthur Clark, 1988), 1032.

A short but very useful summary of Mullan's life.

Account 15.1: John Mullan's 1854 Survey of the Lolo Trail. Excerpts. Source: *Reports of Explorations and Surveys to Ascertain the Most Practicable and Economical Route for a Railroad from the Mississippi River to the Pacific Ocean Made Under the Direction of the Secretary of War in 1853-4, Vol. 1* (Washington: Beverley Tucker, 1855) 529-37. 33rd Congress, 2nd Session. Senate Executive Document No. 78. Serial Set 758.

Fort Vancouver, November 12, 1854....
Having, therefore, examined this route [the route via St. Regis Borgia], I did

not deem it inexpedient to follow a different route on my way to Fort Walla-Wallah. The only route left to be examined in the whole range of the Bitter Root mountains, was the pass by what is called the Lo-Lo's fork of the Bitter Root river. The route had been represented to me to be very rugged and difficult, and by others as feasible and practicable. I therefore decided that, as Mr. Doty was to take the route by the Coeur d'Alene country, I would examine the Lo-Lo's Pass, and meet him at Fort Walla-Wallah. Accordingly we left the Bitter Root valley together on the 19th of September, encamping at the crossing of the river, after a march [from Fort Owen] of twenty-miles; but owing to the straying away of one of my animals, we remained in camp on the next day, but resumed our march on the 21st, which commenced clear, bright, and pleasant. We halted a few minutes to [let John Mix Stanley] make a sketch of the entrance to Lo-Lo's Pass, when we crossed the river to the left bank [at Lewis and Clark's Traveler's Rest site].[1] The stream, at the crossing, is well timbered with cotton-wood and poplar, and is fifteen yards wide, with good banks on either side, and channel-water two feet deep. The mountains on each side of its valley, which here is five hundred yards wide, are quite high, and well timbered with pine and cedar. The trail for six miles being on the left bank, through a low prairie bottom, at the end of this distance we crossed to the opposite bank, still finding an excellent road passing through beautiful pine openings. A short distance farther we crossed the stream a third time, when our trail, being up the left bank, passed over a series of side-hills, some of which proved quite steep and fatiguing to our animals. But little fallen timber was, however, found on these mountains. The growth being quite large, was consequently much scattered, thus affording a good road. Up to 3 p.m. we crossed two small streamlets coming in from the north, upon the second of which we halted to rest the animals, having travelled a distance of 20½ miles. A better road could be made by following the valley of Lo-Lo's fork. Of course, many crossings of the stream would be inevitable; but as the water here is very shallow, the crossings would be of minor importance, considering the advantages to be gained by a level road. Resuming our march at 4 p.m., we continued for three miles along the side-hills, through fallen timber, when we crossed and immediately recrossed the Lo-Lo's fork. At this point we reached a very beautiful prairie, about one-third of a mile in length. This place afforded us an excellent camp; though, following the advice of our guide, we travelled a distance of four miles farther. When we encamped. Finding no grass, our animals started on the back trail an hour after reaching camp; but it now being sunset, it was too late to retrace our steps.

September 22. Remained in camp during this day—our animals having strayed back to our camp of last night. Sent two men back in search of them, and in the meanwhile we made a corral. The men arrived at sunset with all but four animals. We put them in the corral, where we kept them all night without grass, and on the morning of the 23d resumed our march at an early hour, our road for seven miles leading up and along the sides of very high and steep mountains, obstructed by much fallen timber, which proved very fatiguing to our animals. Gaining a high point of view, we had a prospect in every direction, where nothing was seen save an immense bed of high, rugged, pine-clad mountains. At the end of seven miles we again struck the Lo-Lo's creek at its forks. Here we found a small prairie, with

---

[1]Published in Volume 12 of *Reports of Explorations and Surveys*, opposite page 180.

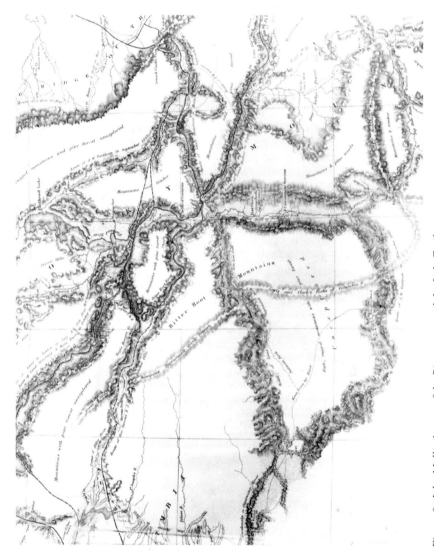

Figure 9. John Mullan's map of the Bitterroots and the Lolo Trail.

very excellent grass, affording a fine camp to a large party. The many signs of elk tracks seen through this prairie, shows that this is a great resort for this animal— the great quantities of willow affording them an abundance of food. The mountains around this prairie are quite low and pine-clad. Our trail lay along the southern fork of the creek, which we crossed several times. The bed is covered with large rocks and boulders of sandstone. Each fork is ten yards wide, with bluff banks on either side. At a distance of two miles from the junction of the forks, we reached a range of hot springs [Lolo Hot Springs, visited by Lewis and Clark on September 13, 1805], flowing from a bed of light, coarse-grained friable sandstone. These springs are highly impregnated with sulphur, and are of the same degree of heat as those I found in the "Big Hole," the temperature of which was 132° Fahrenheit. Here occurs a small prairie, with very good grass, affording an excellent camp. The rock in the vicinity of these springs being easily disintegrated by the weather, presents quite a wild and picturesque appearance, being worn and rounded in every possible conceivable shape. They formed truly a relief to the eye from the monotonous character of the country through which we had been travelling. The accompanying sketch shows the vicinity of these springs, though no good point of view could be selected to sketch the rocks themselves as they appeared in nature. We stopped at these springs, where the men enjoyed a bath, and the animals the excellent grass here found. Leaving these springs, we commenced the ascent of the dividing range of mountains which separate the waters of the Bitter Root river from those of the Salmon fork of the Clearwater. This divide we found lower than the mountains along the Lo-Lo's creek, though covered with pine, and in some places much obstructed by fallen timber. At a distance of seven miles from the hot springs we reached a prairie of two miles in length, where we encamped for the night [Packer Meadows, near Lolo Pass]. Through this prairie flows a small creek to the headwaters of the Clearwater, called by Messrs. Lewis and Clark "Glade creek." Here we found good grass; but is was with the greatest difficulty that we could restrain our animals from taking the back track, and only succeeded by guarding them during the whole night. Having been deprived of grass last night, we could not possibly tie them up or deprive them of grass. The night was clear and pleasant, though with a very heavy frost.

September 24. We resumed our march this morning at an early hour, crossing Glade creek three times, when we commenced the ascent of a high and steep mountain about nine miles across, rendered difficult by stones, rocks, and fallen timber. At the end of this distance we struck the main northern branch of the Kooskooskia river [the Crooked Fork of the Lochsa], which we found to be a stream about ninety yards wide, flowing, with an exceedingly rapid current, over a rocky, stony bed. It is bounded on each side by high, steep, rugged pine-clad mountains. Crossing the Kooskooskia, we began the ascent of another very steep mountain, the road, in addition, being obstructed by fallen timber. For eight miles we continued up and along steep mountains, thickly timbered with spruce and hacmatack. At the end of this distance our course tended for six miles more to the north, leaving the river at a distance of four miles to our left—our road still winding along and up steep, high, and rugged mountains. At a distance of four miles we reached the top of the mountains, where we could see in every direction, and nothing met our view but one immense bed of pine-clad mountains. There was a ridge to our south and east that had a general direction of northeast and

Figure 10. Soldier-artist Gustave Sohon's drawing of Lolo Hot Springs.

southwest, presenting a series of high jagged peaks, all destitute of timber. Having travelled a distance of twenty-five miles, we encamped on the top of a high mountain, where we found a spring of water on the trail [see appendix one for more information on this and other camping spots]. We found no grass for our animals, and were compelled to tie the most of them without grass or water. We found growing along the sides and tops of the mountains to-day a great abundance of the bear-grass, which grows in large, long bunches, and retains its beautiful green color throughout the whole year. It is never eaten by the animals, however hungry they may be. We met to-day for the first time the mountain ash, growing in great abundance on these mountains in a bush form, and bearing a bright red berry. The tree is fifteen feet high. Towards evening our guide became embarrassed as to the route, as we came to a point of the mountains where the road forked. We, however, took the right-hand trail, which proved to be the present one travelled. When Captains Lewis and Clark crossed these mountains, they took the left-hand trail, which proved, by their description, as difficult, if not more so than the one we followed. At sunset, after a long and fatiguing march, we encamped on the summit of a high mountain, where we found a spring of clear pure water. The night was cold and windy, and on the following morning we experienced great difficulty in finding our animals; most of them broke loose during the night, and strayed off many miles into the thick timber, while some took the back track to our camp of last night. We sent two men on the trail, who found ten, and, having searched through the dense forest, we found them all by 11 o'clock. They presented a meager and gaunt appearance, and showed the affects of the want of grass. At 12 m. we resumed our march. When at a distance of two miles we saw a deep hollow, with good grass. Here I sent one of the men to see if there was water. On his finding water, I concluded to encamp, although not midday, rather than travel with the prospect of finding no grass at our night camp. At this place we found an excellent spring of pure water, and an abundance of rich, green buffalo-grass. Towards sunset it began to rain heavily, with wind from the east southeast, and continued with great force throughout the whole night. We had to-day a commanding view of the mountains, and took a sketch of the prominent ridge running northeast and southwest, it forming the great landmark of this region.

September 26. Commences mild and pleasant, having rained heavily throughout the night. The atmosphere this morning was pure and pleasant. We resumed our journey at an early hour, our animals having fared well on the rich grass of last night. Our trail during the earlier part of the day lay up the sides and over steep mountains; but towards noon the road became perceptibly better, the mountains lower, and the trail easier travelled. We still had a commanding view of the mountains during the whole day, some of the higher peaks of which were covered with snow, especially the peaks of the prominent range referred to yesterday. To-day the mountains toward the north appeared very high and rugged, while those to our front and south still retained their rugged features. At a distance of fourteen miles from our camp we reached a spring of clear water on a bare mountain, having a beautiful southern exposure. Here we observed fresh tracks of horses—probably the Indians hunting. Six miles farther we saw a small lake. It was midway of a high, bare, steep mountain, on the southern side. A short distance farther we struck a small creek, running towards the north; and as we had travelled some distance without water, our animals scented it from afar, and were nearly frantic when approaching it. Here we reached a series of springs issuing from the sides of the mountains. Five miles farther we reached a large and beautiful prairies bottom, through which ran a pure mountain streamlet. Here the grass was most excellent and abundant, and formed a pleasant relief from our anxiety, as we fully expected to be compelled to encamp again without grass. The mountains to-day still continued covered with white pine, mountain ash, alder, and balsam fir; though, as a general thing, the timber was more sparse to-day than any day since leaving the Bitter Root valley, the mountains in some places being formed solely of rock, principally free-stone. We passed two creeks to-day, on the second of which we encamped.

September 27. Commences clear, mild and pleasant. Having encamped high on the side of a mountain, we had a grand and pleasing view. The hills at our feet appeared swimming in lakes of mist, while the distant mountain-tops were lit up by the bright rays of a genial sun, and all nature seemed to wear a pleasing and smiling garb. We started at seven o'clock, our road during the whole day being along he sides and up the steep rugged mountains, the trail being obstructed by fallen timber, though not as difficult as yesterday and the preceding days. At fifteen miles from our camp we reached a large and bare mountain [Bald Mountain, described by Lewis and Clark in the same manner], where we found the grass most excellent, with several springs of clear pure water gushing from its side, affording an excellent camping ground. The mountains around still continued to be covered with balsam fir [probably subalpine fir at this elevation], save those only which were formed solely of freestone. We observed to-day large numbers of the mountain grouse, the blue jay, and a species of the large rock squirrel, a specimen of which we preserved. After a march of twenty-five miles we encamped on the northern exposure of a mountain, where we found good grass and water.

September 28. Resuming our march this morning, we continued along the sides of the mountains, rendered difficult by the great quantity of fallen timber along the trail, which at times led over the steep and rugged mountains, which proved truly fatiguing and trying to our animals. We still continued to be surrounded by a labyrinth of mountains, all clad with pine, balsam fir, mountain ash, honeysuckle, cedar and willow, with much underbrush, and some of the higher peaks covered with perpetual snow; numerous springs of pure cold water were seen flowing from mountain sides. At fifteen miles from our camp of 27th we reached a small creek running towards the north; three miles farther we reached a second creek, also flowing towards the north and running through a small but beautiful prairie, with good grass, affording an excellent camping ground. We had made only eighteen miles yet; the road had proved so fatiguing to our animals, that I concluded to encamp. The soil in this prairie we found most excellent, being of a rich dark-colored loam; in fact, with but few exceptions the soil of the route to-day has been most excellent, especially in the narrow gorges and the small intervening valleys of the mountains, the soil in some places being formed solely of the decayed leaves and timber; but in these places the ground is forever shaded by the exceedingly large trees found along the whole route. Immense beds of freestone were to be seen along the sides of the mountains, the presence of which was indicated by the outcroppings in many places. We observed to-day two species of grouse; one with a red segment, and the second with a yellow segment of a circle above the eyes. The latter weighs from two to four pounds. The flesh of these last is very excellent, and when cooked is very white and not unlike the ordinary grouse of the mountains. They are quite tame, and remain sitting on the ground except when frightened, when they betake themselves to the trees; they are of a lead-gray color on the breast, the feathers near the tail being speckled white and black; they make a hooting noise, not unlike that of the owl. We observed also many blue jays, small rock squirrels, rabbits, and mountain weasel, or mink.

September 29. Commences bright and pleasant. We resumed our march at an early hour, our trail still leading over the high and rugged mountains, much obstructed by fallen timber. Gaining a high point of view, we caught a glimpse of the distant prairies [the Weippe Prairie, lying about twenty miles to the west], which was a sight truly refreshing after our rugged toiling through the mountains. The mountains to the north and south still continue to be very high, though, on account of the hazy, smoky atmosphere, we could not see them very distinctly. We noticed on the trail to-day for the first time great quantities of cedar, some of the trees growing to enormous sizes, though none so large as those in the Coeur d'Alene country, the largest that I measured being thirty-six feet in circumference. We noticed also the box [*Pachistima*, mountain boxwood], the white maple, the ground willow, and the cherry [*Prunus emarginata*, bitter cherry], the latter bearing a red bitter fruit, that tastes not unlike the green English cherry. No game save a single grouse was seen during the day. At seven miles from our camp we reached a small prairie with two small lakes, affording excellent grass. Here we observed the long-leafed pine, growing from ten to fifteen feet high. A few miles farther we reached a second prairie, through which flowed a small stream, towards the north. Our road for the remainder of the day led through an immense pine and cedar forest, being much obstructed by underbrush. Seventeen miles from our camp we reached a rapid stream of fifteen yards wide, flowing towards the west. We crossed a fork of this creek from the northeast. At its mouth it flows through high pine-clad mountains over a rocky bed. After travelling a distance of thirty miles we reached a large and beautiful prairie, with grass two feet high, through which flowed a stream two feet deep, towards the southwest, with a rapid current. We had thus descended the last of the rocky range, and had now before is an open and somewhat inviting country. We had thus been in the mountains eleven days, our road being rugged and rough during the whole time. The prairie upon which we to-night encamped extended for five miles in length and one in width, and was surrounded by thick pine forests. We had during the morning a view for the first time of the Blue mountains, about one hundred miles distant.

September 30. We resumed our march at an early hour, following down the creek upon which we had encamped for a distance of two miles through pine openings, affording us an excellent and level road. Here the trail tended more to the north, leading over a series of hills covered with fallen timber. Here we reached a small creek from the east flowing through a low bottom fringed with willow, the sides of the hills or mountains being clad with pine. We followed this creek for six miles through beautiful pine openings with small patches of prairie, affording us an excellent road. In these prairies the soil is very fertile, being a rich dark loam. At the end of six miles we again entered the thick timber, crossing a small divide [Brown's Ridge] separating two creeks that flow into the Clearwater; the timber upon this divide we found to be principally cedar and fir. We soon fell upon the head of a second creek flowing towards the west, and called by the Nez Perces Indians Esh-ske-esh-skil [probably Jim Ford Creek or Haywood Creek, also known as Mis-sah], and two miles farther reached the main Camash prairie [at modern day Weippe]. It is two miles wide and six or eight in length, perfectly level, and enclose on all sides by forests of pine growing from sixty to eighty feet in height. Through the prairie is a small creek or slough, around which they encamp during the camash season. It is a great resort for all the Indians in this vicinity, principally the Nez Perces, Coeur d'Alenes, and sometimes Spokanes, it being a favorite racing ground with all the Indians. Here we struck a large trail which tended to the Nez Perces' camp; this Camash prairie being sixteen miles from our camp of yesterday, and twelve to the Clearwater river. Six miles from the Clearwater [heading for Kamiah] we reached a large creek flowing with a rapid current over a rocky, stony bed, through high, rocky, steep mountains. This creek is called by the Nez Perces Nahwah [Lolo Creek, the word Nahwah also being associated with the Lolo Trail]; it is twenty yards wide, and empties into the Clearwater about twenty miles below the Nez Perce' camp; we crossed this creek and began the ascent of a steep mountain, the last of the Rocky and Bitter Root ranges. This mountain was formed principally of a light friable rock, containing much mica. Gaining the summit of this mountain, we had an excellent view in every direction. In front of us lay the broad ocean of prairie upon which we were about to enter, and behind us the immense bed of rugged and uninviting mountains with which we had been but too familiar. To the south lay distinctly in view some steep spurs of the Snake River chain towering high in the sky [the Seven Devils], while towards the north lay the rugged chain bordering the Coeur d'Alene country on the south. It was after sunset when we reached the Clearwater, which we found to be a stream one hundred and thirty yards in width, channel-water two feet deep, and flowing in some places with a rapid current, over a rocky and pebbly bed. The valley of this stream is about nine miles wide, and bounded on each side by high, steep clay banks, destitute of timber. While descending the steep hill to gain the river we met with large quantities of volcanic rock lying scattered over the ground, presenting a vesicular honey-combed surface. We crossed the Clearwater after dark, and at a mile distant reached a few lodges of Nez Perces Indians encamped on the Komyer creek [Lawyer Creek]. Here is the country of the Nez Perces Indians, where they have large fields enclosed, large herds of cattle, and an abundance of the fruits of nature. The soil here is very fertile, and the winters are represented as being very mild. They raise large quantities of wheat, potatoes, beans, peas, and onions. The Salmon river, which is only two days distant, affords them an abundance of fish. Large quantities of berries are found on the streams flowing into the Clearwater. Their Camash prairie is only twelve miles distant; nature thus affording them every advantage and every means of sustaining life, and causing them to live happily and contented. At present they are provided with no mill, the want of which they feel very much; at present they make use of the wheat by either boiling or pounding it.

The journey across the mountains having proved very fatiguing to our animals, I concluded to rest a day in camp with the Indians, and did not resume our journey until 4 p.m. on the next day, having been delayed in searching for some of our horses that had strayed from camp. We lost them yesterday, and though the men were in search of them all day, they were unable to discover them. I was disposed to believe my Indian friends had cached them; for it was only after offering them a large reward that they started in search of them, when in a few minutes they brought them in. I was at this place forcibly reminded of the national characteristic meanness and avarice of these Indians. I have met them many times in the mountains, and they have to me always displayed those same traits of character. I desired one of them to accompany me on my journey, but he demanded such an enormous reward for his services that I told him I preferred travelling along to being imposed upon by them.

Resuming our march, our course tended over the high bluffs bounding the Clearwater on the south for a distance of three miles, our course being 5° north of west magnetic. At the end of this distance we reached the high, broad, rolling prairie, over which we travelled five miles, to a fork of the river now dry, but when supplied with water, flows through a deep, narrow, rocky gorge or ravine. At six miles farther we reached a second creek, containing water also, flowing through a narrow ravine, the creek being fringed with willow and a few broad-leafed cotton-wood trees; a few scattering pines were also to be seen growing along the slopes of the hills. Having travelled a distance of fourteen miles, we encamped on the right bank of the creek, having travelled until after sunset, in order to reach good grass and water. We found the old grass of the prairie burnt, but the young grass was now springing up. We had an excellent view of the Rocky mountains from the west, as also of the mountains bordering the Snake river [Craig Mountain], all being clad with pine. The day was bright and pleasant, and the night clear and mild.

October 3. Commences clear and bright, though cool. Ice made this morning about daybreak. Resuming our journey at an early hour, our trail lay over the rolling prairie for a distance of six miles, when we reached a creek emptying into the Clearwater, and flowing through a deep, narrow gorge of volcanic rock about one hundred feet deep. From this point, for eight miles, our trail lay over a rolling prairie, when we entered an open pine forest, through which we travelled for a distance of eight miles, when we reached a small stream running towards the west, and called by the Nez Perces Lappahwat, which we followed for a distance of six miles, when we reached the trading establishment of William Craig, where we encamped, having travelled a distance of twenty-eight miles. The Lappahwat valley is five hundred yards wide, bounded on each side by high, bare hills or bluffs, and the soils is quite fertile. Here we found several fields enclosed, and at night the Indians brought us onions, cantaleups, pumpkins, and tomatoes, being the first we had seen for twenty-one months; they proved truly refreshing. The climate here is mild, and all garden vegetables are found to grow well, and in great abundance. The soil in many places is a rich loam, and about two feet deep; in fact, since leaving the mountains we have found the soil very fertile. Through this valley, as also in those already passed, we found large bands of Indian horses, and on arriving at Mr. Craig's we found hogs, goats, and chickens in great abundance.

October 4. Commences bright and pleasant. Having secured a guide at the Nez Perce's camp, we resumed our journey, which lay down the valley of the Lappahwat to its junction with the Clearwater, thence down the left bank of the Clearwater to its junction with the Snake river or Lewis's fork of the Columbia, where we encamped for the night. The valley of the Lappahwat near its mouth we found to be half a mile wide, and contains many Indian farms; the soil here is very fertile, and large fields of corn and potatoes are here grown. At the mouth of this creek, on the right bank, is Spalding's old mission, which was abandoned after the Whitman massacre [in 1847]. This place being well sheltered by the high hills and bluffs of the valley, renders it a very desirable station for a trading post or a large farm, or an Indian agency. The grass along this route, however, we found very sparse, being either burnt, or destroyed by the large bands of horses roaming over it. The rock along these bluffs is volcanic. The valley of the Clearwater we found to be half a mile wide, and the river one hundred and fifty yards wide, with a rapid current. The bluffs on the right bank are high and steep, and perfectly destitute of timber and grass, whole those to the south are quite low, and covered with a rich growth of nutritious grass.

October 5. Commences cold and rainy. It rained moderately during the night, accompanied by a heavy wind from the west; and having encamped on the bare rocks of the beach, our camp this morning proved truly uncomfortable. As soon as the wind lulled, we crossed the Snake river in a canoe that we had secured the day before. We made the crossing without difficulty, and at 12 m. resumed our march along the left bank of the Snake and Clearwater rivers; the water is of a deep sea-green color, and is very deep. The banks are formed of gravel and rounded water-stones, the marks of which show that at the high stage of water the river is from ten to fifteen feet higher than we found it. Our road along the Snake river was much obstructed by rocks and stones for a distance of seven miles, when we reached a great bend of the stream, the river turning towards the north, which here is two hundred yards wide, and flows with a rapid current, with falls and cascades, through high, steep bluffs or hills; those on the right bank being covered with a very sparse growth of grass, while those on the left are formed mostly of columnar rock, fragments of which are continually falling, obstructing the pathway along the whole route. On reaching the bend referred to we left the river, our course being nearly due west. Here we reached a small stream or run flowing from the west, through high, steep bluffs, similar in every respect to those along the Snake river. This creek is called by the Nez Perces the Alpahwah. It is bordered by the willow, long-leaved cotton-wood, birch, sumach, cherry, white haw, honeysuckle, and gooseberry. It is from eight to ten yards wide and fifteen inches deep, and its valley bordered on each side by high, bare bluffs. Having travelled a distance of twelve and a half miles, we encamped on the left bank of the Alpahwah, at its forks, finding very good grass and an abundance of wood. On reaching the Snake river this morning, the guide, who was a Shawnee Indian [probably Ben Kiser, who also served as an interpreter at the October 1855 Blackfoot Council] who had accompanied us from the Bitter Root valley, desired to return. Permission was granted him, when he returned on foot, packing his saddle and bedding to the nearest Indian camp....

Taking a retrospective view of the country passed over from the Bitter Root valley to the Nez Perces' camp, I can arrive at but one conclusion—that the route is thoroughly and utterly impracticable for a railroad route.

From the head of Lo-Lo's fork to the Clearwater the country is one immense bed of rugged, difficult, pine-clad mountains, that can never be converted to any purpose for the use of man.

This is the route followed by Messrs. Lewis and Clark, in 1804 [1805], and by Dr. [John] Evans, the United States geologist for Oregon, in 1850. In a conversation with the latter named gentleman, he told me that it is by far the most difficult and uninviting that he has ever examined in all his tours through the Rocky mountains; and I am compelled to say that, in all my explorations in that region, I have never met with a more uninviting or rugged bed of mountains. The whole country is densely timbered, save at a few points where small patches of prairie occur sufficiently large to afford camping grounds; but beyond this is cannot be converted to any useful purpose....

Account 15.2: Excerpts from Dr. Wellington Bird's 1867 report on the construction of a wagon road across the Bitterroots. Source: Dennis W. Baird, ed., *With Bird and Truax on the Lolo Trail: Building the Virginia City to Lewiston Wagon Road, 1865-1867* (Moscow: University of Idaho Library, 1999), 16-18.

In deciding upon the character of the work it was better for me to do under the circumstances, several considerations were taken into account.

1[st]It was apparent that with labor costing from four to six dollars per day, with the heavy cost of subsisting men it was impossible to grade an available wagon road bed for the whole distance with the means at my command, and an unfinished road or road graded for a part of the way would be of no present utility whatever as the road is really only needed and would be only used for travel over the entire distance and but little for any local business or travel.

2ndA track opened and graded throughout to admit the passage of loaded pack trains over it would be of great and immediate utility in transporting goods from the Columbia river to Montana that being the only present method by which goods can be transported to the territory from the Columbia river by <u>any</u> practicable route, and the opening of this route would make the distance near a hundred miles less than any route traveled from Lewiston to Hells Gate, Helena, Fort Benton or Virginia City.

I believed I could open such an available trail [abandoning the idea of a wagon road] the entire distance with the money in my charge. I therefore decided to commence work to this intent....

The road to Oro Fino was opened as a wagon road the entire distance but the difficulty of crossing the Clearwater hills renders it unavailable as a wagon road and is used only for the transit of pack trains. I availed myself of this Oro Fino road and included it in my survey to a point fifteen miles east of the ferry at the Clearwater, where the road bearing off towards the north. I leave it continuing on across a camas meadow (Oyipe Prairie) three miles and then passing through a succession of narrow belts of timber alternating with meadows; reach Muscle Creek the end of this second division; following this eastwardly course I leave Oro Fino about twelve miles to the north.

Muscle Creek is an inconsiderable stream which I had bridged but which can be easily forded at almost any season when the road can be traveled. At this point begins a third division, and here the ascent commenced which within twelve miles reaches an additional elevation of about three thousand feet or about fifty eight hundred (5800) feet above the level of the sea, making one of the highest points on the route. At this point also begins the dense evergreen forest which continues to Warm Springs [now called Lolo Hot Springs, a site also visited twice by Lewis and Clark] in the upper end of the valley of the Bitter Root Loulou, a distance of ninety two miles....

Account 15.3: North's 1870 Survey for the Northern Pacific Railroad. Source: Northern Pacific Railway Company. Engineering Department. Chief Engineer's "Old Vault" Files. Minnesota Historical Society. Published here with the permission of the Minnesota Historical Society.

20 Dec[r] 1870
Edw[d] P. North
Report to Edw[d] F. Johnson
Chf Eng[r] NPRR
In relation to exploration across the Bitterroot Mts from Missoula M.T. to Lewiston Idaho

Edwin F. Johnson Esq[r]
    Consulting Eng N.P. RR
        Dr. Sir:
            In conformity to your letter of instructions dated New York Apl 30 '70 I procured two of Green's Mountain Barometers, a pocket aneroid & other things necessary for my outfit & left this city May 5th reaching Helena M.T. with Frank Moberly my Ass't on the morning of the 19th.

I there engaged a pack train and proceeded to Missoula. I made a reconnoisance from that place via Lou Lou fork of the Bitter Root the Kooskooskai & Clearwater to Lewiston, Idaho Examining particularly the possibilities of approach to the summit on both sides.

I also examined generally the route by the way of the North Fork of Clearwater, Fish Creek & the Missoula River from Lewiston to Missoula.

I found two passes, one from Fish Creek to the Fish Lake branch of the N Fork of the N. Fork of the Clearwater through which the Moose City trail passes - The elevation of this pass I found to be 5841 ft above the sea. 560 [illegible] above the summit by the Lou Lou and Kooskooskai. The other from the head of Trout Creek to the middle branch of the North Fork of North Fork of Clearwater was $6\frac{1}{2}$ ft lower ($5834\frac{1}{2}$) but the descent from each toward the Missoula was very abrupt and the crookedness of the N. Fork increases the distance form Lewiston to Missoula about 90 miles over that by the Lou Lou.

I also examined the country with regard to the possibilities of a line westward following down either one of the branches of the St Jo. Hangman's Creek or the Peloose. I found the country in that direction so very broken shedding into the N. Fork that considering the unfavorable nature of the ascents of both and Trout Creeks and these [illegible] no practicable pass at the head of Cedar Creek, I abandoned any further exploration of this route.

The summit of the Lou Lou pass I found by computing my observations with the months means at Astoria as given by Col R.S. Williamson in his work on Barometric Hypometry to be 5282 ft above the sea. The distance between Missoula & Lewiston is about 251 miles. This distance however is liable to be either increased or diminished by the route and grades adopted at the summit, and the number of river crossings made on the Kooskooskai.

The ascent from the valley of the Hellgate to the summit will be about 2000 ft and the descent from the summit to Lewiston about 4600 ft unless it is done to make the line more direct between Missoula and the mouth of the Lou-Lou there will be no necessity of undertaking two grades. From Lewiston to the Salmon or Tudor's branches of the Kooskooskai both being practicable the distance is about 197 miles. The grade for this distance will be a gradually ascending one with probably 60 or 70 ft to the mile for the maximum.

The ascent by the Salmon branch from its mouth to the summit is 1308 ft. and by Tudor's Creek 1168 ft. The distance along the valley of either creek is about 8 miles, but abundant support can be obtained for a grade of from 100 to 110 ft to the mile. The summit is a marshy prairie.

The descent to the Hot Springs 1040 ft is possible by two branches of the Lou Lou, the distance by either will vary but little from 8 miles. Mules and support can be gained for almost any grade. But assuming that an auxiliary engine will be used on both these grades I doubt if it will be advisable to increase the distance, by locating a grade on either side of the summit requiring less than double the engine power necessary to draw trains over the [illegible: nuling?] grades on the Kooskooskai and Lou-Lou respectively.

Going down the Low-Low from Hot Springs to the Bitter Root, a distance of 29 miles – 40 or 45 ft to the mile will probably be the maximum grade required.

The Clearwater from Lewiston to its junction with the Kooskooskai [Lochsa], about 105 miles lies in a deep valley for the most part clear from timber with bottoms of generally small width and in some places the rocks come down to the waters edge. The river is crooked, requiring considerable curvature though only at Big & Dead Man's Eddys are any curves very abrupt. It will probably be necessary to bridge the Clearwater twice near Big Eddy.

The two bridges will probably cost $60.000. My estimate for the cost of the road-bed and bridging on this portion of the route, aside from the cost of bridges above mentioned is $45.000 per mile for a single track.

From the junction of the Kooskooskia with the Clearwater to the point where the line will commence to ascend to the summit by the maximum gradient about 90 miles, the country is mostly heavily timbered and the river, though preserving its general direction very well, is more crooked than below, and has 4 quite abrupt turns where we will have either to bridge it or submit to 10° curves. The bridging will reduce the distance and probably aggregate the expense of the line. There are about 20 miles of cañon along a portion of which the road bed (as above) will probably cost $200.000 per mile, but then the work will be well distributed being on narrow points of rock running into the river.

Above the lower Cañon are timbered bottoms, which extend (with interruptions) to the mouth of the Salmon branch

I estimate the cost per mile for the grading and bridging as above for the distance at $83.500.

In crossing the summit from the mouth of Salmon branch or Tudor's Creek to the Hot Springs, I estimate 20 or 24 miles at $100.000 for the road bed as above according to the grade and route adopted. This distance is timbered. (This estimate of distance covers the increase required to bring the grade within proper limits.)

From Hot Springs, the valley of the Low Low is generally well wooded, and narrow, though at and around Hot Springs there are prairies and near its mouth broad bottoms. The general course of the stream is direct with however, frequent curves. I think the best location through the valley would be the most direct line, crossing the stream where necessary, as the Lou-Lou is a narrow shallow stream not subject to much rise and apparently carrying no driftwood in its course. Three of four miles below the mouth of Lou-Lou the line will cross the Bitter Root and from there will pass over a table land to the Hell Gate River opposite Missoula.

I estimate the distance from Hot Springs to Missoula, 40 miles and the cost per mile as above including the bridges over the Bitter Root $22.500. This would make the total distance form Lewiston to Missoula 259 miles, and by adopting in each instance the shortest distance for the descent from the summit, comparable with judicious grades, and bridging the Koooskooskai where it will shorten the line I have no doubt the distance between Lewiston and Missoula could be reduced to 250 miles. The work on this line will be found to be well distributed with an abundance of timber for trestles, temporary bridges and ties. But the country from the summit prairie to the forks of the Kooskooskai, and the Clearwater is nearly destitute of forage and a wagon road from four miles above Kamai to the mouth of the Lou-Lou, will have to be constructed for the use of the contractors. This road 200 miles long at $50.00 per mile will cost $1,000.000 and after the railroad is completed, will be necessary to the settlers on the company's land. The wagon road will have to be proceeded by a trail along the valley of the Kookooskai 95 miles, which will probably cost $90.000. The opening of this trail will be the first work to be done if this route is adopted as it will cheapen the transportation of supplies &c for the locating parties, and will be [illegible] in the construction of the wagon road.

The aggregate of all three estimates amounts to $15,885.000 or say $1,200 per mile and it is confidently believed, this estimate will fully cover the cost of constructing the road from Lewiston to Missoula excepting iron & ties. The several estimates of distance were made principally from the time occupied in walking or riding over the route, and may be erroneous. From an inspection of Government Maps since my return I judge if an error has been committed it is in overestimating distances. While this would not affect the cost per mile it would lower the aggregate.

Snow, Climate &c.

The salubrious climate of the Bitter Root valley is fully set forth in Gov Stevens Report of an Exploration for a Pacific Railroad.

The valley of the Clearwater varying as it does in altitude must of course have different climates. At Lewiston the snow seldom lies over two days. At Reed's Ferry and Kamai, 50 & 65 miles East of Lewiston, respectively, the snow is seldom over a foot & a half to two feet deep, and on the river bottom does not lie long. The temperature of all this country being influenced by a warm wind from the Pacific, which I am told blows almost continuously during winter. Nor can the snow be very deep or lie long on the table lands which at that point are about 1200 ft above the river, as the Nez Perces have large bands of horses some of them being said to own over one thousand head which subsist through the entire [winter] on the grass of the prairie.

From Kamai to the summit I could learn nothing of the winter temperature, or the snowfall. What ever the amount of snow may be, it cannot drift, as the branches of the firs are bent down, showing that the snow lies where it falls. And down the Kooskooskai and Lou-Lou I saw no traces of snow slides so that the expe[illegible] shedding of the Union & Central Pacific lines with its liability to derange the traffic of the road by [illegible] will be [illegible]

From Lewiston to about 15 miles above Kamai, the rock are Basaltic – some columnar excepting near the mouth of the North fork where there is Granite and Gneiss the latter a fine quartz for masonry and easily quarried. From that point – 15 miles above Kamai to the summit there is Gneiss to [illegible] and Gneiss none of the showing any signs of disintegration, the worst of it being very favorably situated for quarrying.

From the summit to the Hot Springs the rock is [illegible] granite, but not of so good quality, the crystals of Feldspar being [illegible] and some of it showing signs of disintegration but no difficulty will be found in [illegible] enough of good quality for masonry.

From a short distance below Hot Springs to the mouth of Lou Lou the rock is mostly [illegible] not suitable for bridge masonry. I was undercautious of a Loop Dyke at the crossing of the Kooskooskai, and in Lapwai about 4 miles from the Clearwater is a bed of variegated marble which makes I am told, excellent lime.

Nez Perce County Idaho of which Lewiston is the County town contains 720 mules and 744 Chinese. The value of property is personal $540.72, Real $192.050. This does not include the property of the Nez Perces the majority of whom live on their reservation (see accompanying map) [not found in the NPRR files] and are said to number over 1000 warriors. They are remarkably ambitious & intelligent, nearly all of them in addition to owning large bands of horses, grow wheat, which they clean very nicely, oats, corn, potatoes, pumpkins, mi[illegible], and garden vegetables generally, irrigating their land where necessary. They are also building houses and do not make their squaws do all the work.

One showed me the work marks on his hand and asserted he was "Just like white man". Nearly all of them can talk English a little and I found them uniformly polite and obliging.

I was at Kamai on the 4th of July where a large portion of the tribe was assembled, and though apparently nearly all drank, there was very little drunkenness: their dance at night was conducted with perfect decorum.

The Nez Perce reservation which commences 10 miles east of Lewiston is about 58 by 30 miles in its extreme dimensions and contains, in round numbers 1140 square miles, lying on both sides of the Clearwater. The country is cut up by the river & its affuents [?], along two rather narrow bottoms of which are farms of great [illegible].

The table lands, which are rolling are covered with bunch grass, and occasional park like groves of yellow pine. The same land on the North side of the Clearwater produced last year I am told, 60 bu of wheat to the acre. At Cold Spring ranch the only farm on this tribal land, 40 bu of oats were raised to the acre.

This table land is however subject to late and early frosts. The warm dry hill sides, presenting as they do any direct exposure to the sun, must eventually become favorite points for vine growers. (The grapes grown at Walla-Walla – 80 miles west are of an excellent flavor and their peaches fully equal the best grown in Delaware.) The fruit trees that have been set out grow rampantly and peaches pears, plums, and apples bear fruit at 3 or 4 years from the graft.

This land does not produce as much under Indian cultivation as it would in the hands of whites, but in a short time they will probably all become producers and white men seem inclined it is said to marry into the tribe. Above the reservation the table lands become more broken, running at length into the Bitter Root mountains and the Yellow pine is gradually displaced on the river bottom and hills near the river by Cedar, very large & fine which will average 3 1/2 ft through. White Pine averaging about 2 ft in diam. & after attaining an altitude of about 3000 ft above the sea Spruce is found that is from 1 1/2 to 4 ft in diam.

The Red, Yellow & White Fir extends from the river, to near the tops of the mountains, and from the junction of the Kooskooskai with the Clearwater to the mouth of Lou-Lou. Black Pine is found from the summit to Hot Springs and on the mountain sides very large and tall Tamaracks. On the hill sides with a Southern Exposure through nearly the whole distance very good yellow pine is found. Mr. Moberly who spent about a week on the LoLo a branch of the Clearwater reports very large Cedar on it and nearly all that basin heavily timbered with the trees above mentioned. The head of the Oro Fino and the country that drains into the North fork is also generally heavily timbered almost to the summit of the Bitter Root mountains.

All of this country will have to ship its lumber by the Railroad and very little of it can be got to market without the aid of a railroad.

This region is I suppose, excepting that immediately around Puget Sound, the best timbered region left in the U.S. There are about 6000 sq miles the waters of which flow into the Kooskooskai and Lou-Lou full sixty percent of which I judge is covered with first class timber, besides that on the Lo-Lo and Clearwater. The water power available on the Kooskooskai and its affluents which are numerous is ample for saw mills and all other purposes for which such power is required. For getting the timber of this exterior region to market I think that a system of narrow gauge railroads may [illegible] could be advantageously adopted, built mostly on trestles which would cost but little more than wagon roads & be more effective.

There will be very little arable land on the Kooskooskai in the valley of the LoLo. Mr. Moberly reports some beautiful prairies and more that will be arable when [illegible]. On the northern Nez Perce trail, north of the reservation, there is a great deal of excellent hay land, that would undoubtedly grow small grain, but I fear it is to frosty for Indian Corn, which matures in the warm valleys of the Clearwater & its tributaries.

This country is remarkably beautiful. The prairies covered with grass often waist high following the course of small streams and surrounded with gently rising pine covered hills. One is continually meeting with ranch sites that with very little labor could be made beautiful villa sites.

Around the Hot Springs of the Lou Lou and on the summit are prairies from 100 to 3 or 4000 acres in extent.

The hot springs 4040 ft above the sea or about the altitude of Salt Lake have a temperature of about 170° F. I regret that I had no thermometer with me that marked over 120°. There are three very strong springs & the Indians have hollowed out pools below them, for baths. It will I think with its bracing mountain air beautiful scenery and the possibility of fine drives, become a place of popular resort. About 18 miles above the mouth of the Lou-Lou is a branch from the North which for 5 miles has wide bottoms. Form 7 miles above the mouth of the Lou-Lou the bottoms are broad and the hill sides are covered with groves of Yellow pine, or with bunch grass. The Bitter root valley is remarkably productive, where irrigated, garden vegetables, and all grains except winter wheat, for which there is not snow enough doing well.

I could not learn the amount of grain grown, but grist mills are in operations, (at Missoula, Ft Owens & Burnt Creek). The climate of the valley is, as far as I could judge from any limited stay there, much like that of Salt Lake City. I think that the fruit trees which the farmers are just commencing to set out will succeed as well as in Salt Lake Valley.

If it is determined to make an instrumental survey of this route, advantages should be taken of low water on the Kooskooskai, as there the line could be run mostly between high and low water marks saving time & expense in cutting out the line. The river commences rising toward the last of May, and is not down to low water mark until the last of July.

The river can be reached with wagons at the mouth of the Lapwai at Reed's Ferry and at Kamai and as high water is navigable by steamboats to the Big Eddy 31 miles there is also a trail in the north side of the river, between Lewiston and Kamia. From Kamai to 4 miles above the forks of the Kooskooskai and Clearwater there is a trail that is available in low water without any additional work and for about 12 miles father to the lower cañon from Kamai, a trail can be made with very little expense.

The trail which Lewis & Clark passed over in 1805 must join the Nez Perce trail about 60 miles east of Reed's Ferry. I could not find it but the Indians use it every year going to the "Fishing place" for Salmon [the headwaters of the Lochsa], from that point, I think the river could be descended by a pack train or low water with very little cutting or grading to within say 30 miles of the lower cañon. For that distance supplies will either have to be carried on mens backs or brought down by horses from the trail. At the Nez Perce Agency, Indians can probably be found who have hunted through that country and would know of ridges on which it would be possible to descend to near the river. The services of Frank Tudor of the Ft Owens would be valuable here as I believe he & myself are the only white men who have followed the Kooskooskai.

From the fishing place to the mouth of the LouLou, there will be but little difficulty in supplying the party with provisions.

The Northern Nez Perce Trail was passed over in 1869 the 1st may without trouble from snow. I went over it between the 25th of June & 2nd of July this year and found snow in places for over 70 miles. A loaded train could not have got through. As it was we took 7 days of very hard work to get 81 miles the horses having their packs on form 7 to 10$\frac{1}{2}$ hours each day. Mr Moberly came over the trail between the 9th & 14th of October & found no snow.

As very few whites have passed over the trail except those who [illegible] the Government appropriation for opening it and as this must be used till a new trail is opened by the river I give an itinerary or description of it from Reed's Ferry to the mouth of the Lou-Lou.

From Reed's Ferry to Muscle Creek 33 miles. Good feed near ferry on the hills. Better at "the trough" 5 miles beyond. Good feed & wood but poor water is found at the "Kamas ground" from 11 to 15 miles from the ferry.

Figure 11. Rocky Ridge Lookout on the Lolo Trail, about 1920.

From within 6 miles of Muscle Creek to that creek, good camping anywhere.

From Muscle Creek for 86 miles, the trail [reconstructed by Bird and Truax, four years earlier] is marked by blazed trees and at each mile the distance is marked on a tree. At the 12th mile the trail has attained an elevation of about 7000 ft above the sea which is a fair average for it to the 79th mile where it commences to descend the Kooskooskai.

17th Mile - Grass to right of the trail. Marked on a tree.

19th miles – Bald mountains – good grass and water in basin to right of trail, note this grass was very good.

20th, 21, 22nd mile – Wet Creek – Grass along trail & to right of it, not very good.

36½ to 37½ miles – Squirrel creek. Very good feed

43rd mile – a little feed on ridge before reaching swamp & in the swamp.

60th mile – a spring crosses the trail here. Bunch grass [illegible] to the left of this

68th miles – good feed to the left of trail, towards lake, marked on a tree.

70 ½ miles – good grass down hill to right. Spring dries up in August but water between 71st & 72nd mile.

74 mile – "4th of July Camp" Feed & water to left of trail down gulch

81st mile – good camping for 2½ miles along this creek

At this point the blazing of trees ceases. Follow Indian trail

6 miles from leaving prairie cross Lou- Lou. Small prairies to right of trail at crossing

Good feed at and around Hot Springs.

8 miles below summit, also 3 miles below Hot Springs.

20 miles from Summit "Lou-Lou's Grave" Camp on small stream & turn horses up it. Good feed.

33 miles from summit reach the open bottoms and camp anywhere between here and the

Mouth of Lou-Lou 39 miles from summit and 12 miles from Missoula.

I have given to Mr Beebee a memorandum of the disposition I made of the Company's property entrusted to my care. Most of it having been left in stow at Missoula with Worden & Co. Of my barometers, I turned one over to Col. DeLacy intact. The other was broken on the morning of Oct 21st by the upsetting of a stage coach after I had carried it almost constantly since the 5th of may.

I am indebted to Frank Moberly my assistant for his efficiency and energy through many hard ships. Also to Col Summer and the other officers of Ft. Lapwai. Major Owens of Ft Owens, and Col Dunders of Helena for many kindnesses & valuable information

Sign

Edward P North

New York Dec 20th 1870

Account 15.4: Tudor's 1871 Winter Survey for the Northern Pacific Railroad. Source: Northern Pacific Railway Company. Engineering Department. Chief Engineers "Old Vault" files. Minnesota Historical Society. Published here with the permission of the Minnesota Historical Society.

Frank Tudor's Report of the snow at the Low-Low Pass.
Bitterroot Range
Feby & Mar. 1871

Fort Owen Montana
March [illegible] 1871

Sir

In accordance with order of Mr E. P. North C.E. N. P.R.R dated N.Y. Dec 2nd of 1870 I beg leave to respectfully submit the following report of my trip up the Low Low fork & over the divide on to the Clear Water.

On the first of last month [1 February 1871] I went to Missoula & bought my supplies necessary for the trip of Mes Nurdin & Co. & on my return went up the Lou-Lou fork & made a caché of provisions a short distance below Warm Spring Ronde. I then set to Fort Owen in order to get up my Snow Shoes & other things necessary for the arduous winter trip. I secured the services of one good reliable man. On the 15" Feby Maj. Owen drove me down as far as Lou- Lou fork where I remained all night preparing my packs for the trip. In the morning of the [Feb.] 16" Myself & man with our packs strap on our backs proceeded up the Lou-Lou fork.

The 16" & 17" had no snow. 18" & 19" no snow but heavy rains. The snow at Lou- Lous Grave near 9 in deep.

20"Weather clean & warm, snow soft.

21[st]Six miles below Warm Spring Snow 15 in deep in the bottom. Side hills bare. Had a terriffic snow storm wind blowing a perfect gale from the West. Timber falling in all directions.

22[nd]Weather clear & very cold. Snow 15 in deep in Warm Spring Ronde. No ice in the Creek for 4 miles below Warm Springs. No snow around the spring for some distance. Creek frozen over solid from Springs up.

23[rd]On the Prairie 3 miles above Warm Spring where the trail takes over the Mountain Snow 2 feet 3 in. deep

24"On the summit where the Nez Perce trail crosses the divide between the Lou-Lou fork & Clear Water I found the snow 7 foot 10 in deep. Two miles west on the head of Tudor Creek snow same depth. Another severe snow storm to day. Travelling hard the snow being soft & loose. There is no appearance of any thaw or rain here this winter. reached Clear Water this evening after dark at the mouth of Tudor Creek & Camped nearly tired out.

25"Snow 3 foot deep & snowing 1 1/2 miles below mouth of Tudor Creek where the trail crosses the Clear Water Snow 1 1/2 foot deep. River frosen over in places & difficult to get along. Camped some seven miles below the mouth of Tudor Creek on Clear Water in quite a rain storm. Snow on the decrease. It is only 14 in deep in the creek bottom. No snow on the south hill sides.

26"Having proceeded as far as my instructions deemed necessary I commenced my return to the mouth of Lou Lou fork & shall be heartily glad when I reach the Bitter root plain again. We have had a rainy ~~day~~ disagreable day. In fact we have not had a dry blanket to sleep under since we left the Warm Springs Camp. A night on Clear Water 1/2 mile below the crossing of the trail in snow storm.

Feby 27"Reached the summit again after a very severe days work in a raging storm of snow. Wind blowing a gale from the west & the snow drifting. It is impossible to see fifty feet ahead ~~of you~~. We are both nearly worn out. Our blankets are wet & heavy while our provisions are proving Exceedingly light.

28"Measured snow again on the summit & find it 18 in deeper than it was on our way over four days ago - & still snowing & drifting. Our provisions are out & we must make our Caché or turn into wet Blankets supperless. Passed the little prairie 3 miles above Warm Springs & find the snow 7 in deeper than when we passed some days ago & still snowing briskly. Succeeded in reaching Warm Springs after dark – raised our Caché made a pot of tea, baked a slice of bacon in the coals & turned into our wet Blankets for a nights sleep.

Mar 1st This morning find ourselves considerably refreshed after the nights rest. Breakfasted on Tea & boiled Bacon in a severe snow storm. Constructed a shelter of pine boughs & laid over for the day it being too stormy to move. Had a nice bath in the Warm Spring which entirely relived me of a cold I had been suffering with for some days.

2nd Still snowing. Not very cold. The snow in Warm Springs Ronde 6 in deeper than when I passed some days ago. Remained in Camp luxuriating on Tea and boiled Bacon. Killed a few Prairie chickens which were quite poor. Could have shot a large moose but declined killing an animal when we had no means of taking care of the meat.

3rd Cloudy snowing briskly & melting about as fast as it falls. Left Hot Spring & moved down the Lo Lo fork & camped some short distance below Lo Los grave. The snow here about the same as when passed up. We have had another severe day. Snow soft & giving way under our snow shoes.

Mar 4"Day fair with light breese. Made our way to Mouth of Lo Lo & find ourselves once more in the more congenial plain of the Bitter root valley.

5"Day fair with strong breese from the South. Proceeded up the Bitter root valley to Fort Owen – not a particle of snow on the Bitter root plain. The streams all open & free from ice. We are once more comfortably housed with a good square ration of Bitter root Beef and flour & a potent cup of coffee that reaches its centre of gravity without any difficulty & to this added the [illegible: ostentatious?] welcome of the inmates of Fort Owen makes me feel as though we had found an oasis in the desert.

E. F. Johnson Egr	Respt Yours
Engr in Chief	[illegible]
N.P.R.R	Frank Tudor
No 12 Broadway	
N.Y.	

Account 15.5: McCartney's 1879 Survey for the Northern Pacific Railroad. Source: Northern Pacific Railway Company. Engineering Department. Chief Engineer's "Old Vault" files. Minnesota Historical Society. Published here with the permission of the Minnesota Historical Society.

4th September 1879
H.M. McCartney
Report
on his Explorations
of the Clearwater or
Ska-Ka-ho Pass

Portland, Oregon, Sept. 4th 1879
J.W. Sprague
Gen. Supt N.P.R.R.
Dear Sir:

On July 8th I received orders from you to take charge of a barometer reconnoissance through the Bitter Root Mountains in Idaho. My instructions were to proceed to Lewiston where the citizens would furnish me with a party, and, outfit, as they had agreed with you. They claimed to have discovered a pass through the main range and I was to examine it, and report on its fitness for a railroad route into Montana. I left Portland on the 9th of July, and reached Lewiston on the evening of the 11th. I there met Mr. Vollmer [John P. Vollmer, a Lewiston merchant specializing in freight delivery. Both of the McBeth sisters, missionaries to the Nez Perce, used his services] one of the leading merchants of the place, and the agent of the O.L. M. Co. who informed me that it had been decided to outfit the party at Mt. Idaho – 65 miles further East and the last settlement this side of Montana – and I accordingly proceeded there the next day. At that place I met Mr. [Alonzo] Leland the editor, of the Lewiston paper, and one of the prime movers of the expedition, and after a talk with him and the man who had been selected as guide, John Eurich by name. I found their information on the subject, consisted of the following points.

In 1871 Moberly was conducting some examinations of the Bitter Root Range for the N.P.R.R. He came eastward, on the Lolo Trail, a short, distance beyond the summit, and established a supply camp there. In his explorations south of the trail he discovered a pass 2050 lower than the summit, crossed by the trail and attempted to follow the stream running westward form it. Arriving at a point where he considered it navigable, he built boats, and started down but was wrecked, and lost all his provisions which necessitated his return to the supply camp. He came over the Lolo Trail to Lewiston expecting to secure an outfit there, and go up this same stream but was ordered to join Eastwicks party then on the North Fork of the Clearwater and never returned.

The summit of the Lolo Trail was given to me by an officer who crossed with Howards command as 7000 ft which would make this supposed pass a little over 5000' above tide. After leaving Mt. Idaho I found I had a man in the party who knew something more about these old explorations in 1871 but his information was nothing to do with sending out the party.

The Clearwater, which empties in to the Snake at Lewiston has four principal branches. The first of these (going up stream) is the North Fork which comes in 40 miles above Lewiston, and heads far to the northward near Pot Mountain. It was examined by the Eastwick survey in 1871 – the champion piece of idiocy among all the foolish things done by the engineering administration of 1871–3.²

---

²See Philip G. Eastwick, *Report of the Northern Pacific Railroad's Survey of the North Fork of the Clearwater River in 1871* (Moscow: University of Idaho Library, 1999).

The next branch is the South Fork which comes in 75 miles above Lewiston runs through Elk City and heads with the Bitter Root in the main range about latitude 45°30'.

The third is the Lolo Fork coming in 104 miles above Lewiston and heading near the Lolo Trail crossing. The trail crosses one prong of it and we found the source of the other on our trip.

The last branch, the Middle Fork is really the main stream. It runs nearly due East from the mouth of the Lolo Fork and heads in the main range about opposite Doolittles ranch on the Bitter Root. It was this branch we examined. The guide Eurich had been up it last year 150 miles from Lewiston (to the place we named Elk Prairie) and claimed there was no serious obstacle for that distance and that from where he turned back he could see all the way to the summit. He estimated the distance to be 30 mi. and, asserted there was nothing in the way at all. He had published an article in the Lewiston paper calling attention to it as a railroad route and Mr. Leland had arrived at the conclusion, by some process of reasoning not clearly understood by me that this was the stream Moberly attempted to descend in boats and at whose head the low pass existed. We accordingly started out to trace the Middle Fork to its source. No directions or suggestions were given by any one connected with the organization of the party as to what to do in case that stream proved to be impracticable.

We were delayed two days in getting animals and finally left Mt. Idaho on the morning of July 16th.

The citizens were very enthusiastic about the matter, and offered me anything I wanted in the shape of men, horses or outfit.[3] I took five men and five pack animals and got some shelter tents from Camp Howard. I declined the offer of an escort as I believed we were too far north to meet the hostile Indians [probably referring to the Sheepeater campaign then underway in the Salmon River Valley] but had the whole party armed with rifles and fifty rounds of ammunition apiece. I sent the party to the ranch of the last white settlers on the Clearwater and myself and the guide went to Kamia (the site of the upper agency buildings on the Lapwai Reservation) to get our Indian guide. He had been engaged two days previously but could not be found at all when we got there. It turned out that the Indians had ascertained the proposed exploration was for a railroad, and as they are always hostile to such enterprises no one would go. We finally found one living just at the edge of the Reservation who volunteered and after waiting a day for him we left the last settlers on the 19th and started up stream. We followed the river bottom to the mouth of the Lolo Fork, 104 miles from Lewiston and 34 from Kamia. The river at Kamia was 550 ft wide and 5 ft deep (resembling the Cowlitz in appearance) and the report of the Engr. who examined it last year shows it can be made navigable for light draft boats from there to Lewiston 70 miles, at comparatively small expense. There was no formidable obstacle in the way between Kamia and the mouth of the Lolo. The basalt which exists all along the Columbia, runs up the Clearwater for 85 miles. There it stops, and nothing but pure granite occurs as far

---

[3]The Lewiston *Teller*, Leland's newspaper, reported this enthusiasm on July 18, 1879. Of the NPRR party: "They go with full confidence of success and if the condition of the country does not belie all representations of the route, which have been given by good and responsible men, the report of the engineer, Mr. McCartney will sustain all we have ever said of the route and the road instead of making the circuit via the Pen d'Orille lake will extend directly east from Lewiston, when contracted."

Figure 12. Sheep were a major ecological force along the Lolo Trail. Sheep grazing near Hemlock Butte about 1930.

as we went. Their were plenty of strips of bottom land along the river and the side hills were not bad.

The trail left the river at the mouth of the Lolo and ascended the ridge between the two streams, coming down to it again at Elk Prairie, 46 miles further up. We made this point to be 150 miles above Lewiston, rise in that distance 1700 - average less than 12 ft per mile. The prairie was a beautiful flat of some 500 acres and this was the highest point ever reached by either of our guides.

We could see up stream some ten miles from here and it was a broad flat covered with cedar. The prospect was favorable in the extreme. We had no trails above here and were often forced on to the side hills by the burns, and fallen timber. Our progress was very slow. Everything was favorable until the afternoon of Aug 1st when we suddenly came upon a rock bound cañon with high cliffs on either side. We made the mouth of the cañon 30 miles above Elk Prairie rise 1320' average grade 44' per mile. Half a days exploration satisfied us that it was impossible to get horses through this cañon and we climbed the hill to the northward, and took to the ridge again. It was one of the worst pulls we had, from the river to the summit was a rise of 2300 ft. The timber was thick and there was a dense under growth of thick birch brush and thorns. It took us over half a day to reach the top. We kept the ridge until the 5th when we struck a branch emptying into the river just at the head of the cañon and were unable to get down to either stream with our horses. We had been 4 days making 14 miles along the river. Progress [illegible] this was too exasperating to be borne. We climbed the highest part of the ridge, and took a look at the main range. From where we were we estimated the summit to be forty miles distant and concluded we could make the round trip in four days on foot. Two men were left to guard the train, the other five came down to shirt and pantaloons six cakes of bread and ten pounds of jerked elk meat and twenty cartridges a piece – no coats, or blankets allowed. We were gone three days & two nights, and had one of the roughest tramps I ever took part in. We found the head of the cañon to be 1300' higher than the mouth and taking its length at 14 miles an average grade of 93' [9.3%?] would be necessary to get through it. There must be some bad falls in it as there is not a fish anywhere in the stream above it. The stream at the head of the cañon was still 50' wide, and a foot deep and there were broad flats along it which continued for some eight miles. The stream rising about 65' per mile. It then came in to a gorge, and finally disappeared entirely under a tremendous rockslide which had come down from the overhanging mountain. Back of this slide was a lake some 600' in diameter and back of that were three miles of grassy flats from 300' to 1000' wide which did not rise more than 50' to the mile. We thought at first we had struck the summit but were speedily undeceived as the stream suddenly ran into the steep ridges near the summit range and began to come down in a succession of falls. We followed it until we reached a small flat surrounded by perpendicular cliffs. The elevation here was 6900' above tide and the stream had risen 1500' in the last six miles. On this flat it was not over three feet width and the small brooks which formed it came down from the snow above in every direction. We did not climb the cliff as it was inaccessible even at the bottom for a railroad, and too high to complete with the 2000' pass of the Pen. D'Oreille even if it had been. We estimated the lowest part of the cliff to be 600' high which would make the summit 7500' above tide. We came back to our camp and I resolved to start northward along the main range keeping as close to it as possible and endeavoring to find some low water course running from it which it would pay us to follow up. I expected to reach the Lolo Trail and return to Kamia on it as that was our quickest route. It is only five days drive from the summit of the Lolo Trail to Kamia while we had been 18 days coming from Kamia to this camp. From where we had been we could see southward to the Elk City trail and their was no show in that direction for a pass. During the trip I had discovered that our packer was a chum of Tutor, a rancher in the Bitter Root Valley who was a guide for North and Moberly during their exploration in the mountains there. Tutor had told about the trips made by him and this is the version which I received. North and Moberly came to the place where the Lolo Fork crosses the Lolo Trail (a little west of the summit) and established a supply camp there. They then built boats and attempted to descend the stream from their camp but were wrecked near the juncture of another branch of the Lolo which they named Boulder Fork. They saved a few provisions and it was decided that Moberly should take most of them and travel northwest until he struck the Lolo Trail then he was to follow it to Kamia. North was to return along the bank of the stream to the supply camp and bring it over also to Kamia whence they proposed to ascend the Lolo Fork on horse back as far as possible and complete the exploration on foot to the mouth of Boulder Fork. From where they had camped it was impossible to bring their horses down the stream. North reached Kamia first. Moberly having been lost several days and after they met Moberly for some reason was taken off the reconnoisance and sent to a survey party presumably Eastwicks. North returned as he had purposed – found himself obliged to abandon his horses a short distance above the mouth of the Lolo Fork and had a tramp of twelve days back to the site of his old supply camp on the Lolo Trail. The detailed reports of all these examinations should be in the New York office. At all events, they must have been communicated to Chief Engineer Roberts and I know he always held to the opinion that there was no practicable pass through the Bitter Root Range.

We started North on the morning of Aug. 9th and had been on the way but a few hours before we struck a goodsized stream running north. There were two forks which joined just where we struck it, the larger one came from a lake a mile and a half long by half a mile wide which lay a few miles North East of our camp. Our packer, who was a natural born guide, at once pronounced this to be Moberly's Boulder Fork and such it proved to be. We followed it to its intersection with the fork which crosses the Lolo Trail. It was a [missing?] …for anything but a goat in any direction except the one in which we had come in.

There was no feed and the pack train was on its last legs. Two of them were so badly injured by falls that they could barely walk without any load; and I was on foot as my saddle horse had to be abandoned. He went from bad to worse, and finally received a bad cut in the leg which severed an artery and we could not secure it. We had but a few days provision left, and if it had not been for the expense of paying for the horses and outfit I would have abandoned them, and come in over the Lolo trail on foot. It was useless to go back over the rough country we had passed through and we took as straight a course as possible for the mouth of the Lolo Fork. We started on the 11th and reached Mt Idaho on the 25th not striking our old trail until the 21st. It was a very rough trip. Fortunately we found plenty of elk as soon as we got away from the main range and did not go hungry. I [missing?]… Old Col. Craig, Maj. Owen, Fred Sherwood, and the old Nez Perce chief from Kamia have said and those living now say that the low pass exists not twenty five miles south of Lolo Trail crossing of the summit.

The first dispatch was rather incoherent. I answered the second one –
"Portland Sept 3rd
"Can not make agreement until Gen. Sprague returns. Country you mention explored by North and Moberly in Seventy One. Have telegraphed New York office for copy of their reports."

I sent your dispatch to New York asking for copies of these reports if they were on file.

I was told by several parties here before starting that I would find Mr. Leland rather unreliable. Everything connected with sending out our party however was done according to promise and the proposition about the new party is not unreasonable. The cloud of witnesses however who bear testimony as to this movable pass will not bear inspection.

Col. Craig died in 1871. Maj. Owen was in an insane asylum when I left this country in 1873 and I think he has since also been gathered to his fathers, while "the old Nez Perce chief from Kamia" went to the happy hunting grounds at a date to which the memory of Northern Pacific men runneth not back. "Fred Sherwood" is an utterly unreliable squaw man now living somewhere in the Colville country and the vague phrase "those now living" will hardly answer outside of a newspaper office. Mr Lelands assertion that my guides led me astray looks as though he was trying to hedge with his home constituency. The program was arranged by himself and the guide to examine the Middle Fork at whose head the pass said to have been described by Moberly was supposed to exist, and was faithfully carried out. Had any mention been made at the time of a "low pass not twenty five miles south of the Lolo Trail crossing of the summit" we would have gone to that summit which we could have reached in five days easy travel from Kamia over a splendid trail, and not chopped our way through an unexplored region. As I said before if Moberly discovered any such pass some record of it (and most likely Mr. Roberts objections to the route) should be on file among the old records of the Engineer department. Should no such record exist it might possibly pay to accept Lelands proposition, although I do not like the aspect of his dispatch in suddenly knowing the exact position of this pass and locating it at a point entirely different from the one mentioned in my conversation with him. The possibility of a direct line through this range is very tempting. Our summit was not thirty miles from the Bitter Root Valley and if that was accessible a line through the Big Hole to the junction of the three forks of the Missouri would save 125 to 150 miles of distance. I telegraphed you from Wallula that I would not recommend any further examination of the range. This was before I received Mr. Lelands dispatch or had telegraphed you about getting a copy of the old reports. If no such records exist and the survey can be made as suggested so as to be of no expense to the company in case of its failure it would be well to undertake it even on such a small stock of probabilities.

The Clearwater runs through the worst jumble of mountains I have seen this side of Peru. For 140 miles the whole country seems to have been lifted up to the height of 8000' and then cut to pieces by the water courses which run in every direction. There is no succession of ridges rising one above another until the summit range is reached – two days out from Kamia, our trail led us over snow covered ridges which were 1000' higher than the source of the stream we traced up. The main range is so called because it is solid and unbroken and controls the watershed. The highest peak of all – St Mary's – is on one of the side ridges running into the Bitter Root Valley. That such a country should be almost penetrated by a stream of so light a grade is a curiosity.

It is all a timbered country and were it not for the difficulty of getting in supplies most of the lumber for the first hundred miles of the Northern Pacific would come down the Clearwater. Bull pine, red and yellow fir and cedar are the principal varieties. The broad flats in the vicinity of Elk Prairie – 150 miles from Lewiston – contain millions of feet of the finest cedar I have seen on the coast. None of the trees are too large to saw and all told their size very uniformly from the ground up.

It was the best game country I ever travelled in. We had over 200 elk within gunshot and killed 18. We could have made the number 100 instead if we desired but could not use them.

The streams abound in trout and we caught some 3000 although most of our travelling was done on the high ridges. Those in the lower part of the Clearwater were 18 and 20 inches in length. A man with a pocket full of fishhooks and a belt full of cartridges can subsist anywhere in that region off of the snow ridges.

I took three barometers which registered very uniformly and checked well on my return to Lewiston. Trips of this kind will always demonstrate the impracticability of a route or in case it is considered doubtful or favorable will furnish the points to run by should a survey be deemed necessary afterward. They should have been generally used in the old explorations during 1871 – 73: and should be employed in the examinations which will have to be made to develop the pass through the Cascade.

It is a waste of time and money to put a transit party in a rough region not previously explored with a barometer. Nothing could have been more ridiculous than the Eastwick survey up the North Fork of the Clearwater. A large party was outfitted which slowly and laboriously ran 120 miles of careful transit line into a cul-de-sac from which there was no possible outlet. A barometer man with two Indians and a canoe would have gone to the head of the fork in two weeks and demonstrated that there was no earthly possibility of using it as a railroad route.

The manner in which that party was handled is still a standing joke in this region but even had it fallen into the hands of a competent man it would have been an inexcusable bill of expense.

The same mistake was made in the exploration of the west side of Skagit Pass and much of Wards mountain work done under the Morris regime.

I enclose a map showing the explorations we made and their relation to the location around Lake Pen d Oreille.

Thanking you most sincerely for entrusting me with this interesting examination which if successful would have change the entire location for four hundred miles and regretting that the saving in distance could not be effected.

I am

Very Resptfly Yours

sig. H. McCartney

Heights and distances Middle Fork		
Points	Dist from Lewiston	Height above tide
Lewiston	0	680
Kamia	70	1020
Mouth of South Fork	75	1110
Mouth of Lolo Fork	104	1300
Elk Prairie	150	2380
Lower End of Cañon	180	3700
Upper End of Cañon	194	5000
Moose Lake	203	5600
End of practicable route	206	5750
Summit	210	7550
Miscellaneous		
Forks of Lolo (end of survey)		4450
Mt. Idaho		3480
Cottonwood		3300

Craigs Mountain		4080 (average)
Spring Branch (stage station)		3170
Sweetwater crossing		1360
Lewiston		680

16

Richard Lansdale's Lolo Trail account of 1857

Richard Hyatt Lansdale, a physician, explorer, and Indian Agent whose Lolo Trail account follows, was born in Maryland in 1811. After service in the Mexican War, he migrated to California during the 1849 gold rush. In 1850, he traveled north to the Oregon Territory and eventually settled on Whidbey Island. He died there in 1898.

Late in 1854, he was appointed Indian Agent to the Flathead Indians of what is now western Montana. His charge also covered the Kalispel and Pend d'Oreille tribes, and his base of operations included both the Bitterroot and Flathead River Valleys. Lansdale assisted Governor Isaac Stevens with the arrangements for both the 1855 Walla Walla Treaty Council and the council held in the Walla Walla Valley the next year. During this time, he got to know many of the leaders of the Walla Walla, Cayuse, and Nez Perce tribes. He was also well acquainted with early pioneers like John Owen and William Craig, and worked well with the many Jesuit missionaries active in Montana and the Coeur d'Alene region of northern Idaho. He was generally regarded by his peers, by the Flatheads, and by the Jesuits as being an honest and thoughtful man. His two surviving diaries also show him to have been highly observant.

Lansdale was a tireless and enthusiastic traveler. He was in Lapwai in April of 1855 and returned there in August the next year. He passed through the Camas Ground (site of Moscow, Idaho) in both 1855 and 1856. In the summer of 1857, he was returning to Fort Owen in the Bitterroot Valley from a trip that had taken him to Vancouver and Portland. This trip appears to have been his first over the route of the Lolo Trail.

The records of the Oregon, Idaho, and Washington Indian Agencies contain a large amount of Lansdale correspondence, much of it of great value to historians and ethnographers. Lansdale was a close student not only of Flathead culture, but that of the Nez Perce as well. He was also a careful observer of Jesuit missionary work in the inland northwest. Lansdale's two diaries were given to Yale University by William R. Coe, and are Manuscript 292 at the Beinecke Rare Book and Manuscript Library. The account of the Lolo Trail published here comes from the second, or "official" diary, and is but a small part of that long and important document.

Further reading:

Dan L. Thrapp, "Richard Lansdale," In *Encyclopedia of Frontier Biography, Vol. 2* (Glendale: Arthur H. Clark, 1988), 812-13.

A brief but reliable account of Lansdale's life, with a fine bibliography.

Account 16: Excerpts from Lansdale's Lolo Trail diary. Source: Yale University. Beinecke Library. Mss. 292. Published here with the permission of the Beinecke Library.

June, 1857

Thurs. 4. Preparing for journey to Flathead Agency.

[Omitted: description of travel on route to Walla Walla]

Sat. 27th [Camping near "Craig's claim" in the Walla Walla Valley. William Craig was at this time the Nez Perce Indian Agent, with homes near Lapwai and at Walla Walla. The diary resumes in mid-entry] I shall remain here 2 or 3 days, resting, preparing beef, repairing arms, &c. I want also to get 2 or 3 Indians as spies & guides as far as Bitter Root valley. Thus far I have been undisturbed & have seen but very few Indians, & have not had a talk with any one. It was supposed all, or most, dangerous between this post & crossing of Snake river but fear seems to vanish as I advance.

Sun. 28th. Spent the Sabbath at rest, mostly, but had to commence "jerking" 212 lbs. Beef Col. Craig slaughtered today as it wouldn't keep in bulk. Every body is engaged in army employment in this valley, and all spend the Sabbath in riding about, talking, &c. The day hot and sultry.

Mon. 29. Deposited with Col. Craig for safe keeping till I return, 50 lbs. flour, 9_ lbs. bacon, 10 lbs. Sugar, 5 lbs. coffee, 1 lb. Tea. Got of Col. Craig 40 lbs. salt, 3_ lbs. soap, 10" lead, 5" [illegible], 250 Gun caps. As at Dalles, Col. [George] Wright assured me there was no danger in my travel to Walla Walla, so here also, as for W. Walla, Col. [E.J.] Steptoe assures me there is no danger in going through the Nez Perce country. He says (Col. S.) there is no trusting the Indians, as they are liable to break out in open hostilities any day, and yet says there is no danger—how this may be is not so clear to me. Col. Craig says there is no danger in going to the N.P. root ground. In the morning I shall leave en route for my destination. Had a long talk with Col. Steptoe. Gave Mr. Craig certified voucher for 212 lbs. Beef at 15c per lb. 31.80. Wrote to J.W. Nesmith, S. Ind. Affairs, W. & O. Trys. Sending dup. receipts for $228.80 $ receipted for at Olympia, June 2, 1857 & which, he writes, are lost; letter filed.

Gave W. Craig dup. receipts for pub. property got today, & took dup. invoices. Got two [unclear] certif. of 1 horse lost, Sept. 26, 1856. (Pri. [private] Wrote to Rev. I. Dillar, Olympia, W.T.)

Sent Sup. Ind. Affrs. certified schedule of certified vouchers issued up to this date. Sent 2 revolvers to be repaired by smith at Military post. Drying beef, cleaning arms, &c. Col. Craig gave me a few new potatoes. Engaged George, Nez Percé, to go as spy & guide to Lapwai.

Figure 13. A white pine forest near Musselshell Meadows.

June 18, 1857

Tues. 30. Find I cannot get off as I expected yesterday,-cause, beef not quite dried enough, pistols not repaired. Continued to dry beef, clean & repair arms, preparatory to leaving tomorrow.

Wed. July 1, Got up early, & got off early. Exchanged 1 red horse for 1 roan horse & 1 red mule bay or brown for 1 of same color, with Col. Craig, all I.D. property. Left 2 men, Hughes & José, to bring on mule & horse, the animals not being at home when I left camp on Touchet [the Touchet River, east of Walla Walla]; also, "George," a Nez Percé, living with Craig usually, joined me some place, to act as spy & guide to Lapwai. This has been a fine, cool, cloudy day, everything goes off well. Paid Mr. Dean for repairing 3 revolvers, $5.00; took voucher. Camped on Touchet at crossing, just on east side. Very little dust.

Thurs. 2d. Rained a little yesterday evening; recommenced early this morning, rained moderately till 8 a.m. Picked up, & started at 9 a.m. [in margin: "25 ms.]. Had a fine, cool day, without dust; came to halt on Pah ta hah where trail first strikes it, at 3.30 p.m. Animals & men in good condition.

Fri. 3d. Morning cloudy & cool. Started at 7 a.m.; had fine drive up Patahah and over divide to Alpowawee, & 3 miles down to camp. [in margin: "22 ms.] Day cool, with west wind, some dust. Animals a little fagged at time of camping 3 p.m. Had several visiters from village below, on Snake river: gave present of tobacco, & sent "George" down to buy salmon.

Sat. 4. Got an early start, passed Alpowawes village, & on to crossing of Snake river at mouth of Clearwater, ferried goods

July 1857

and men, swam horses, paid ferriage to Indians, $6.00, got 4th July dinner of fresh salmon roasted, apple dumplings with dip, & new potatoes, which Col. Craig presented to me at W. Walla; the apples I got at Alpowawes. [in margin: "Made 12 ms.] Treated many Indians to dinner, & got no thanks, as usual. In evening had to talk hard to my interpreter to keep him straight about the horse he rides. Day dark, (cloudy,) & cool.

Sun. 5. Contrary to my invariable rule, I concluded to travel a short journey today, because I had a very bad camp on the beach of Clearwater [in margin: "12 ms], & because of bad grazing; so at 7 a.m., packed up, & drove to Lapwai, & camped at m. [noon] on east side of valley, where road leaves it. Day cloudy, dark & cool; a few drops of rain, which thickens into quite a shower in the evening. I never imagined these hills could be so green in the Summer.

Mon. July 6. Rained a little in the morning: was delayed in starting by waiting for a guide [in margin: "12 ms."], having to send "George" back to Walla Walla. Paid "George" off, 10 days coming & going at $2 per day, $20—2 blankets & 2 shirts; took voucher. Bot 1 1/2 salmon, & 20 lbs new potatoes, paid for them, to be added to "Gs" voucher. Started at 9 a.m. having Teapohiucket N. Perce for guide: road led over rolling & hilly divide from Lapwai to Mahkah [snow, in Nez Perce] creek, where I camped at 1 p.m. in its deep valley. Hills green, plenty of springs in hills; day cool, rain at m., quite a shower; made 12 ms.

Tues. 7th. Left camp on Mahkah early; road led over rolling bare hills to a little brook where it enters rolling pine lands for a few miles, [unclear], it then comes out upon a high undulating plain through which runs the Clearwater

July, 1857

having Bitter Root mountains on North and East: route led eastward to Pee-poo-enim creek, now nearly dry, which runs in a very deep canon, having steep cliffs on either side. From the latter water, road leads over gentle hilly plains to Ahleah creek, also in a deep ravine. Here I camped; plenty of water, wood, & grass. Met a few N.P.'s returning from Camash ground. The country [in margin: "Made 25 ms."] passed over today is the most beautiful & fertile of all I have yet seen in Wash. & Or. Territories; it lies high, & must have a cool, healthy temperature, plenty of pine surrounds it on every side, but there are parts distant from any timber some few miles; springs of water are not so frequent, as desirable.

Wed. 8. Rearranged packages, equalizing the weight, & got a late start. Drove rapidly to Clearwater at what is called "Lawyer's Place," [Kamiah] & where that head chief & his people have their fields & head quarters. The river here runs in a very deep valley, enclosed by hills on the side about 1000 feet high. The valley is very beautiful, has plenty of the long leaved pine, a good loamy soil, nearly equal to the table, or plateau, lands to the west of this crossing. Here are a few field, the grain & vegetables look luxuriant. The river is deep [in margin: "15 ms."] at this time of year, & the Indians say navigable to its mouth; & I hope for steam boats; the current is strong. Swam animals over river, ferried men & goods in canoe, & camped just on banks east here. Paid ferriage $3.00, potatoes 51c, Beef 1.50, voucher No. 20—All the Nez Perces seen thus far are very friendly; even Joseph, a chief heretofore charged with hostile feelings, seems perfectly friendly. The day has been fair, but cool; had hard frost this morning, at camp on A-leah.

July, 1857

Thurs. 9. Got an early start: road ascends the high hills that bound river on the east side. Up-up, to level of country,—then down, down, down to quite a river, "Nahwa" [Nah wal, or Lolo Creek] flowing to north; then up a high hill to level& then a gentle sloping woodland to "O-i-up" [the Weippe Prairie] or N.P. "Camash Ground," where I found many people preparing camash, & many horses grazing tho' perhaps more than half save a few days since, have left [in margin: Made 13 ms.] , as I met great numbers. Here I found "Lawyer," "Looking-glass," & others; chiefs, gave them a smoke, & proposed a general talk at 4 p.m. I also proposed to buy & give them a beef for a feast in the name of the president, if one could be found. Soon a man drove up a two year old steer, estimated to weigh 400 lbs. I bought him for 4 blankets, and gave him to the chiefs, with 10 lbs. tobacco, for a feast & smoke tomorrow: they slaughtered him at once; he is fat &good; they gave me part of the liver & the kidneys. Talk postponed till tomorrow.

Fri. July 10, Took Richard Takhatooktis voucher for ox [in margin: "$40.00"], pay of guide from Lapwai to Oiup [in margin: "$16.00"] and got Lawyer's receipt for 400 lbs beef, & 10 lbs tobacco for feast & smoke to the N. Perces at "Oiup," estimated at 400 souls, & for 40 lbs. Camash at 12_c. [in margin: "$5.00"]

The "talk" was postponed till today at 10 a.m., that certain chiefs might come from Clearwater at Lawyer's Place; the feast, and smoke, & talk came off at that hour. I made a long, plain speech, in which I first deduced certain rules, from the nature of God & his works, & the Bible, for the guidance of men individually and in nations, in their conduct towards each other; spoke of the right of men to breathe

the free air, drink the moving water, & walk upon the solid ground, & sail upon the open seas, without hindrance, so long as they respect the rights of those amongst they reside.

July, 1857

The Americans claim those rights, and grant them to all others, so that anyone may not only live, but buy & hold property in U. States. Gave history of the treaties made at W. Walla in 1855. Told them the treaties were not yet confirmed, and that they would not be required to give up any part of their lands ceded in these treaties, nor could they expect the annuities & other pay promised, so long as the treaties were not approved. Told them the pres. Expected them to be at peace amongst themselves, & all other Indians, & to let white men pass through their country. Lastly, I spoke of the advantages they derived from their intercourse with white men,—the horse, the cow, fire arms, blankets, &c., of their own ignorance of all arts, & the utter dependence for nearly every good upon the whites. Several replied, thanking me for my speech, apparently highly gratified: Lawyer, Looking-glass, Timothy, Umaitselon , & others.

Fri. July 10. One mule strayed, or stolen, last night, had men looking for it till eve., not found, left interpreter, T.H., to have it found & packed up & started on my way at 3 p.m. Road led eastward through a chain of small wet prairies, full of camash, & now & then thru a wooded point [in margin: "8 ms."], to large field prairie at foot of mts; here I camped in the [pine?] grass, water, & wood, intending to wait for coming [in margin: "328 miles"] of Hughes, & lost mule. Weather—last night cold, heavy frost; day fair & clear & warm. Made 7 or 8 ms. Animals fresh.

Sat. 11ᵗʰ. Had another frost last night, but not heavy; these frosts seems to hurt neither flowers, nor fruits, nor anything, in fact. Animals in <u>clover</u>, emphatically. Six evening Hughes returned without mule; she had been seen, as supposed, returning to Clearwater & H. went thither, but could not find her: many Indians, of Lawyer's camp had

July, 1857

been looking for the mule at source their root-ground, & without success. The soil all about the camash ground, and as far as this last prairie is very good & fertile, but wet, generally,—a strong clay seems to hold the water.

Sun. 12ᵗʰ. At rest as usual, according to my rule; also, waiting & hoping some of the Nez Perces may bring the mare mule gone astray. The day very fair, clear, & warm, no wind. Two Flathead guests in camp, besides the two in my employment, one as guide, the other as a cultus tibicen [a musical entertainer], because I cannot well get rid of him. Forgot to say, in Friday's notes, that I had hired a Flathead Indian as guide, at $2 per day, for self & horse. I named him Jonathan;—the other is David,

Mon. 13ᵗʰ. The mare mule that went off at Ouip, not being found, I gave up all hope of recovering her, till I return at least. I made out a return of her loss, a certificate of her loss, signed by I.T. Turner, as pack-master, & also, certified by myself. Got early breakfast, got animals up, packed up, & got off at 5 min to 7, a.m. Road led down "Duplicate" creek, over wooded points, but mostly in grassy, wet bottom of creek to junction with "Triplicate" creek, then up the latter, say 2 ms., to "Last Prairie," or "First Prairie," [at or perhaps near Musselshell Meadows] as one may be traveling. Here my guide wants me to camp for the day, & take to the mts. early tomorrow. This I refused, as he had deceived as to the last place of camping, saying the prairie where I camped Friday was the last, &c. I resolved to go on, & took to the hills at last crossing of Triplicate creek. Held to one mountain ridge for some 6 ms., & then descended to where 2 streams meet, supposed to be second water crossed before reaching Ouip, and camped, the "Nahwa" waters [Lolo Creek]: this I am not positive of. Took high hill between the two, & kept it for 6 ms, then up & over several hills, with

July 1857

much snow, to pretty little snow brooklet, & fine green grass [in margin: "25 ms."], the first came to Called it "Quartz Camp," their being much dis integrated quartz, as also, granite all about. Camped at 4.30 p.m.

Tues. 14, Wed. 15, & Thurs. 16th, in the midst of the Bitter Root mountains, and difficult they are indeed. Nearly the whole path from the creek passed on Monday has over the highest & roughest hills, above snow, over & upon snow, rocky, rooty & boggy, the work has been slow & arduous for men & animals. Grass & water in juxposition scarce, making camping places far apart. [in margin: "30 & 30 ms."] Had good grass & water, 14th & 15th but no grass the 16th. Made 24 ms. 14th, 30 ms. 14th, & 30 ms. 16th—This route, so far, will not compete with the Coeur d'alene pass. Tues. eve it rained a little, at night copiously, and Wed. it rained, hailed, & snowed a little: Thurs. fine.

Fri. 17. Started at 5:30, drove abt. 6 ms. & came to good grass & staid all day to recruit the animals, as they have had a hard time in these mountains.

Sat. 18th. Made a very early start at 6. a.m, and drove on smartly, passed in a short distance a low divide [Lolo Pass] to Loh loh fork of the Bitter Root river, then along said water, over good ground a little way to high ascent, and then over hilly points to bottom of river, & followed river to B.R. valley, & camped at crossing of trail. [in margin: "35 ms."] Camped at 7.30 p.m. after a hard days drive, being some 12 1/2 hours in saddle. Country mostly rough—on L.Loh, some pretty places. Men out of humor & horses jaded: mosquitos very annoying. Made 35 miles.

Sun. 19th. Mosquitos very annoying to men, and animals, I directed Geog. Walker, F.H. interpreter, to move train to where none are, while I took a horse and rode to Fort Owen, where I arrived at 12 m.

July, 1857

Mon. 20. Spent yesterday pretty comfortably at Major Owen's in resting & conversation. Today saw Mr.Irvin, ex Lieut. U.S.A. for first time at Ft. Owen; also, Mr. T. Harris returned to Ft. O. from a trip he had just taken to Mormon settlement on Salmon river, O.T. He is full of reports of Indian stories, mountaineer movements, & Mormon news from Salt Lake, not one of which is worth recording.

17

The Indian Agency in the Clearwater Valley

The federal government has had a long and important presence in the Clearwater region. The Army maintained a small post at Fort Lapwai from 1862 until July of 1884. The Post Office began its first, somewhat irregular delivery of mail into the Clearwater Valley in 1862. In 1897, the Bitterroot Forest Reserve was established, managed at first by the General Land Office, and then by the newly established Forest Service. Important as the work of these federal agencies was, it was the Commissioner of Indian Affairs whose employees came first, had the greatest overall impact, and who remain influential in the valley even today.

In 1840, the Rev. Elijah White appeared in the nation's capitol. With the help of powerful friends, White convinced the War Department (which was responsible for Indian affairs until 1849) to name him "agent" to the American Indians living "west of the Rocky Mountains and north of California." White had been an early religious emigrant to the Oregon country, a vast region jointly controlled by the United States and Great Britain. He had been forced from the Willamette Valley mission of the Rev. Jason Lee when charged with financial and sexual irregularities. White's appointment to this new position meant that, for all practical purposes, he was actually agent to the Indians of Oregon, including most of the present states of Oregon, Washington, Idaho and Montana. Even though there *was* no American government in Oregon, White, carrying his new and somewhat dubious title, reached the Walla Walla Valley overland late in the summer of 1842 and continued on down the Columbia.

Word of unrest at Walla Walla reached White at his Willamette Valley home in November of the same year. Accompanied by Cornelius Rogers and Baptiste Dorion (both of whom spoke the Walla Walla and Nez Perce languages), Agent White returned to deal with these troubles, pausing briefly at Walla Walla and then continuing on to Lapwai. He arrived there on December 3, 1842, to hold a council with the Nez Perce people. The Rev. Henry Spalding played a major role in all aspects of this council, which was the first official meeting of the Nez Perce people with an employee of the United States since Lewis and Clark left the area.

At this council, Rev. White imposed on the Nez Perce people two notions wholly alien to their culture. First, he forced them to approve a written code of laws, which his written report called "the Laws of the Nez Perces." These "laws" applied only to the Nez Perce and not to the small number of white settlers resident in the area. They were probably written in large part by Spalding. In addition, White decreed that the Nez Perce people should now have a "head" chief. This, too, was a concept unknown to the Nez Perce. While we have an imperfect understanding of Nez Perce political culture ca. 1840, a contemporary and informed view is offered by the Rev. Asa Bowen Smith (elsewhere in this volume), who writes at length on the absence of a head chief. White also forced the council to name a band chief, Ellis (or Ellice), to this previously non-existent position. Ellis may have been picked because of his knowledge of English, obtained during the four years of formal education afforded him at Red River (the Selkirk settlement at Winnipeg) by the Hudson's Bay Company. Spalding, working with a printing press newly-arrived from Hawaii, printed a limited edition booklet of these "laws," some in English and a few in Nez Perce, with the name "Ellis" featured prominently.

Settlers around the Dalles detected turmoil in the Nez Perce country the next spring, and White returned. This time he was accompanied by another missionary, Gustavus Hines, who has left us an interesting account of Lapwai. Rev. White himself was viewed as a dishonest windbag by many Oregon citizens, who also came to characterize Hines as a poorly informed dupe. The presence of these "laws" seems to have had little long term impact on the Nez Perce people or upon anybody else. The written accounts of the two official visits do, however, contain many interesting details, as do the names and places attached to the Nez Perce language book printed by Spalding. Oregon officials arrived to visit the Nez Perce after the Whitman deaths in 1847, but it was not until 1855 that a serious and permanent Indian Agency presence began in Nez Perce country.

There is a vast and largely unpublished primary literature associated with the Indian Agency after 1855. Three treaties were negotiated with at least portions of the Nez Perce Tribe, and one war was fought. These primary accounts are too vast to describe or even summarize in this volume. Work has also begun on a separate series of books intended to collect the most important of these accounts for the time period before the 1877 war. In 2002, the University of Idaho Press published the first of what are expected to be several volumes on this subject: *The Nez Perce Nation Divided*, edited by Dennis Baird, Diane Mallickan, and William Swagerty. This book deals with the 1863 Treaty, often called the "steal treaty" by the Nez Perce people. Some of the primary sources associated with the 1855 Nez Perce Treaty appear on the University of Idaho Library's McBeth Sisters Web Site, www.lib.uidaho.edu/mcbeth.

Further reading:

Brad Asher, *Beyond the Reservation: Indians, Settlers, and the Law in Washington Territory, 1853-1889* (Norman: University of Oklahoma Press, 1999).

A good history of Indian policy, with an emphasis on legal status.

Robert E. Ficken, *Washington Territory* (Pullman: Washington State University Press, 2002).

A thorough and reliable history of early Washington, based on primary sources.

Terence O'Donnell, *An Arrow in the Earth: General Joel Palmer and the Indians of Oregon* (Portland: Oregon Historical Society Press, 1991).

A well-written and reliable account both of Joel Palmer's life, but also of Indian policy in Oregon. Especially useful for its account of the 1855 treaties.

Francis Paul Prucha, *The Great Father: The United States Government and the American Indians.* 2 Vols. (Lincoln: University of Nebraska Press, 1984).

The definitive and indispensable study of this subject. Includes a clear and totally reliable account Indian relations in Oregon on pages 392-413.

Kent D. Richards, *Isaac I. Stevens: Young Man in a Hurry* (Pullman: Washington State University Press, 1993). [Originally published in 1979]

The best biography of Stevens, based on thorough research and filled with controversial conclusions. A fine chapter on the 1855 treaties.

Erwin N. Thompson, *Historic Resource Study: Fort Lapwai, Nez Perce National Historical Park, Idaho* (Denver: National Park Service, 1973).

A thorough and superbly researched account of the post and the frontier Army's role in the region. Includes many rare maps and photos.

Clifford E. Trafzer, *Indians, Superintendents, and Councils: Northwestern Indian Policy, 1850-55* (Lanham, Md.: University Press of America, 1986).

A concise summary of the goals and methods of government Indian policy in the Pacific Northwest before 1860.

Account 17.1: Elijah White arrives in October of 1842 to impose the "Laws of the Nez Perce" upon the people. Source: Elijah White, *A Concise View of Oregon Territory, Its Colonial and Indian Relations* (Washington: T. Barnard, 1846), 6-17. Excerpts.

Oregon, April 1, 1843.
T. Hartley Crawford
Commissioner of Indian Affairs
Washington, D.C.
Sir:

On my arrival I had the honor and happiness of addressing you a brief communication, giving information of my safe arrival, and that of our numerous party, to these distant shores.

At that time it was confidently expected that a more direct, certain, and expeditious method would be presented to address you in a few weeks; but that failing, none has offered til now....

My arrival was in good time, and probably saved much evil. I had but a short season of rest after so long, tedious, and toilsome a journey, before information reached me of the very improper conduct of the upper country Indians toward the missionaries sent by the American board of commissioners, accompanied with a passport, and a desire for my interposition in their behalf at once.

I allude to the only three tribes from which much is to be hoped, or any thing to be feared, in this part of Oregon. These are the Wallawallas, Kayuse, and Nesperces, inhabiting a district of country on the Columbia and its tributaries, commencing two hundred and forty miles from its mouth, and stretching to four hundred and eighty in the interior....The Nesperces, still further in the interior, number something less than three thousand; they inhabit a beautiful grazing district, not surpassed by any I have seen for verdure, water privileges, climate, or health. This tribe form, to some extent, an honorable exception to the general Indian character, being more noble, industrious, sensible, and better disposed towards the whites, and their improvements in the arts and sciences; and, though as brave as Caesar, the whites have nothing to dread at their hands, in case of their dealing out to them what they conceive to be right and equitable. Of late, these three tribes have become strongly united by reason of much intermarriage. For the last twenty years they have been generally well disposed towards the whites; but at the time Captain Bonneville visited this district of country, he dealt more profusely in presents and paid a higher price for furs than Mr. Pambro [Chief Trader Pierre Pambrun], one of the traders of the Hudson Bay Company, established at Wallawalla [at Ft. Nez Perces near the mouth of the Walla Walla River], who had long dealt with them, and was previously a general favorite. On Mr. Bonneville's leaving, the chiefs assembled at the fort, and insisted on a change of the tariff in their favor. Pambro refusing, they seized him, stamped him violently upon his breast, beat him severely, and retained him prisoner, in rather unenviable circumstances, till they gained, to a considerable extent, their object. Since that time, they have been more consequential in feeling, and shown less deference and respect to the whites...

The Indians, having gained one and another victory, became more and more insolent, till at last, some time previously to my arrival, they were not only obtrusive and exceedingly annoying about and in the missionaries' houses, but seized one of the clergymen [Marcus Whitman] in his own house....

In addition to this, some of our own party [while traveling along the Columbia] were robbed openly of considerable property, and some twelve horses were stolen by night. All this information, coming near the same time, was embarrassing, especially as my instructions would not allow me to exceed, for office, interpreter, and every purpose, $1,250 per annum. On the other hand, their passport signed by the Secretary of War made it my imperative duty to protect them in their persons at least from outrage. I did not long hesitate, but called upon Thomas McKay, long in the employment of the Hudson Bay Company as explorer and leader of parties, who, from his frank, generous disposition, together with his universal success in Indian warfare, has obtained an extensive influence among the aborigines of this country, and placing the facts before him, he at once consented to accompany me to this scene of discord and contention.[1] We took but six men with us, armed in the best manner, a sufficient number to command

---

[1]This generosity by McKay got him into trouble with Dr. John McLoughlin, the Hudson's Bay Company's Chief Factor, at Vancouver. McKay was firmly told to never again accompany White on tribal visits.

respect and secure the object of our undertaking—McKay assuring me, from his familiar acquaintance with these Indians, and their thorough knowledge of the use of arms, that if hostile intentions were entertained, it would require a larger party than we could raise in this country to subdue them. Obtaining Cornelius Rogers [who had previously worked with Asa Bowen Smith at Kamiah] as interpreter, we set out on the 15th November [1842] (as McKay justly denominated it) on our voyage of misery, having a journey, by water and land, of not less than nine hundred and fifty miles, principally over open plains, covered with snow, and several times under the necessity of spending the night without wood or fire, other than what was made by a small growth of wild sage, hardly sufficient to boil the tea kettle....

[Reached the Spalding Mission on Lapwai Creek on December 3, 1842]. Seldom was a visit of an Indian agent more desired, nor could one be more necessary and proper. As they [the Nez Perce bands] were collecting, we had no meeting for eight-and-forty hours; in the mean time, through my able interpreter and McKay, I managed to secure confidence and prepare the way to a good understanding; visited and prescribed for their sick, made a short call at each of the chief's lodges, spent a season in school, hearing them read, spell, and sing; at the same time examined their printing and writing, and can hardly avoid here saying I was happily surprised and greatly interested at seeing such numbers so far advanced and so eagerly pursuing after knowledge. The next day I visited their little plantations, rude to be sure, but successfully carried on, so far as raising the necessities of life were concerned; and it was most gratifying to witness their fondness and care for their little herds, pigs, poultry, &c. The hour arriving for the public interview, I was ushered into the presence of the assembled chiefs, to the number of twenty-two, with some lesser dignitaries, and a large number of the common people. The gravity, fixed attention, and decorum, of these sons of the forest, was calculated to make for them a most favorable impression. I stated explicitly, but briefly as possible, the design of our great chief in sending me to this country, and the present object of my visit; assured them of the kind intentions of our Government, and of the sad consequences that would ensue to any white man, from this time, who should invade their rights, by stealing, murder, selling the damaged for good articles, or alcohol, of which they are not fond. Without threatening, I gave them to understand how highly Mr. and Mrs. Spalding were prized by the numerous whites, and with what pleasure the great chief gave them a paper to encourage them to come here to teach them what they were now so diligently employed in obtaining, in order that they and their children might become good, wise, and happy. After me, Mr. McKinley, the gentleman in charge of the Hudson Bay establishment at Wallawalla, spoke concisely, but very properly; alluded to his residence of some years, and of the good understanding that had generally existed between them, and of the happiness he felt that one of his brothers had come to stand and judge impartially between him, them, and whites and Indians in general; declared openly and frankly, that Boston, King George, and French, were all of one heart in this matter, as they, the Keyuse and Wallawallas, should be; flattered them delicately in view of their (to him) unexpected advancement in the arts and sciences, and resumed his seat, having made a most favorable impression. Next followed Mr. Rogers, the interpreter, who, years before, had been employed successfully as linguist in this section of the country by the American board of commissioners, and was ever a general favorite with this people.

He adverted sensibly and touchingly to past difficulties between whites and Indians east of the mountains, and the sad consequences to every tribe who had resisted honorable measures proposed by the more numerous whites; and having, as he hoped, secured their confidence in my favor, exhorted them feelingly to adopt such measures as should be thought proper for their benefit.

Next, and lastly, arose Mr. McKay, and remarked, with a manner peculiar to himself, and evidently with some emotion; I appear among you as one risen from the long sleep of death. You know of the violent death of my father on board the ship Tonquin [at the mouth of the Columbia], who was one of the partners of the Astor Company; I was but a youth; since which time, till the last five years, I have been a wanderer through these wilds; none of you, or any Indians of this country, having travelled so constantly or extensively as I have, and yet I saw you or your fathers once or more annually. I have mingled with you in bloody wars and profound peace; I have stood in your midst, surrounded by plenty, and suffered with you in seasons of scarcity; we have had our days of wild and joyous sports, and nights of watching and deep concern, till I vanished from among men, left the Hudson Bay Company, silently retired to my plantation, and there confined myself. There I was still, silent, and as one dead; the voice of my brother, at last, aroused me; I spoke and looked; I mounted my horse—am here. I am glad it is so. I come at the call of the great chief, the chief of all the whites in the country, as well as all the Indians, the son of the mighty chief whose children are more numerous than the stars in the heavens or the leaves in the forest. Will you hear, and be advised? You will. Your wonderful improvement in the arts and sciences prove you are not fools. Surely you will hear; but if disposed to close your ears and stop them, they will be torn wide open, and you will be made to hear. This speech from Mr. McKay, whose mother is part Indian, though the wife of Governor McLaughlin, had a singularly happy influence, and opened the way for expressions on the other side, from which there had not hitherto been a sentence uttered. First arose Five Crows [a well known figure with a Cayuse father], a wealthy chief of 45, neatly attired in English costume. He stepped gravely but modestly forward to the table, remarking: It does not become me to speak first; I am but a youth, as yet, when compared to many of these my fathers; but my feelings urge me to arise and say what I am about to utter in a very few words. I am glad the chief has come; I have listened to what has been said; have great hopes that brighter days are before us, because I see all the whites united in this matter; we have much, wanted some thing; hardly knew what; been groping and feeling for it in confusion and darkness. Here it is. Do we see it, and shall we accept it?

Soon the Bloody Chief[2] arose, (not less than 90 years old.) and said: I speak to-day, perhaps to-morrow I die. I am the oldest chief of the tribe; was the high chief when your great brothers, Lewis and Clark, visited this country; they visited me, and honored me with their friendship and counsel. I showed them my numerous wounds received in battle with the Snakes [he was sometimes called "Many Wounds"]; they told me it was not good, it was better to be at peace; gave

---

[2]This was Hohots Ilppilp, or Red Grizzly Bear. Lewis and Clark called him "Ho-hast-ill-pilp." Some scholars believe that Ellis (Ellice) was his grandson. This family came from lower White Bird Creek.

me a flag of truce; I held it up high; we met and talked, but never fought again. Clark pointed to this day, to you, and this occasion; we have long waited in expectation; sent three of our sons to Red river school to prepare for it; two of them sleep with their fathers; the other is here and can be ears, mouth, and pen, for us. I can say no more; I am quickly tired; my voice and limbs tremble. I am glad I live to see you and this day, but I shall soon be still and quiet in death.

That speech was affecting. Six more spoke, and the meeting adjourned three hours. Met at the hour appointed. All the chiefs and principal men being present, stated delicately that the embarrassed relation existing between whites and Indians in this upper country, by reason of a want of proper organization, or the chiefs' authority not being properly regarded; alluded to some cases of improprieties of young men, not sanctioned by the chiefs and old men; and where the chiefs had been in the wrong, hoped it had principally arisen from imperfectly understanding each other's language, or some other excusable cause, especially so far as they were concerned. Advised them, as they were now to some extent prepared, to choose one high chief of the tribe, and acknowledge him as such by universal consent; all the other subordinate chiefs being of equal power, and so many helps to carry out all his lawful requirements, which they were at once to have in writing, in their own language, to regulate their intercourse with whites, and in most cases with themselves. I advised that each chief have five men as a body guard, to execute all their lawful commands. They desired to hear the laws. I proposed them clause by clause, leaving them as free to reject as to accept. They were greatly pleased with all proposed, but wished a heavier penalty to some, and suggested the dog law, which was annexed.

We left them to choose the high chief, assuring them if they did this unanimously by the following day at ten, we would all dine together with the chief on a fat ox at three, himself and myself at the head of the table; this pleased them well, and they set about it in good cheer and high hopes; but this was a new and delicate task, and they soon saw and felt it; however, all agreed that I must make the selection, and so reported two hours after we left the council. Assuring them this would not answer; that they must select their own chief, they seemed somewhat puzzled, and wished to know if it would be proper to counsel with Messrs. McKay and Rogers. On telling them that it was not improper, they left a little relieved, and worked poor Rogers and McKay severely for many hours; but altogether at length figured it out, and in great good humor, so reported at ten, appointing Ellis high chief. He is the one alluded to by the Bloody Chief, a sensible man of thirty-two, reading, speaking, and writing the English language tolerably well; has a fine small plantation, a few sheep, some neat stock, and no less that eleven hundred head of horses. Then came on the feasting; our ox was fat, and cooked and served up in a manner reminding me of the days of yore; we ate beef, corn, and peas, to our fill, and in good cheer took the pipe, when Rev. Mr. Spalding, Messrs. McKinley, Rogers, and McKay, wished a song from our boatmen; it was no sooner given than returned by the Indians, and repeated again, again, and again, in high cheer. I thought it a good time, and required all having any claim to bring, or grievances to allege, against Mr. Spalding, to meet me and the high chief at evening in the council room, and requested Mr. Spalding to do the same on the part of the Indians. We met at six, and ended at eleven, having accomplished, in the happiest manner, much anxious business. Being too well fed to be irritable, or disposed to quarrel, both parties were frank and open, seeming anxious only to learn our opinion upon plain undisguised matters of fact, many of the difficulties having arisen from an honest difference of sentiment respecting certain measures.

Ellis, the chief, having conducted himself throughout in a manner creditable to his head and heart, was quite as correct in his conclusions and firm in his decisions as could have been expected. The next day we had our last meeting, and one full of interest, in which they proposed to me many grave and proper questions; and, as it was manifestly desired, I advised in many matters, especially in reference to begging or even receiving presents, without, in some way, returning an equivalent; pointed out in strong language who beggars are among the whites, and how regarded; and commended them for not troubling me, during my stay, with this disgusting practice; and as a token of respect, now, at the close of our long and happy meeting, they would please accept, in the name of my great chief, a present of fifty garden hoes, not for those in authority, or such as had no need of them, but for the chiefs and Mr. Spalding to distribute among their industrious poor. I likewise, as they were very needy, proposed and ordered them some medicines, to be distributed as they should from time to time be required. This being done, I exhorted them to be in obedience to their chiefs, highly approving the choice they had made, assuring them, as he and the other chiefs were responsible to me for their good behaviour, I should feel it my duty to see them sustained in all lawful measures to promote peace and order. I then turned, and with good effect desired all the chiefs to look upon the congregation as their own children, and the pointed to Mr. Spalding and lady, and told the chiefs, and all present, to look upon them as their father and mother, and treat them in all respects as such; and should they happen to differ in sentiment respecting any matter in my absence, be cautious not to differ in feeling, but leave it till I should again return, when the chief and myself would rectify it. Thus closed this mutually happy and interesting meeting, and, mounting our horses for home, Mr. Spalding and the chiefs accompanied me for some four or five miles, when we took leave of them in the pleasantest manner, not a single circumstance having occurred to mar our peace or shake each other's confidence.

I shall here introduce a note, previously prepared, giving some further information respecting this tribe, and appending a copy of their laws. The Nesperces have one governor or principal chief, twelve subordinate chiefs of equal power, being the heads of different villages or clans, with their five officers to execute all their lawful orders, which law they have printed in their own language, and read understandingly. The chiefs are held responsible to the whites for the good behaviour of the tribe. They are a happy and orderly people, forming an honorable exception to the general Indian character, being more industrious, cleanly, sensible, dignified, and virtuous.

This organization was effected last fall, and operates well, and with them, it is to be hoped, will succeed. A few days since Gov. McLaughlin favored me with a note addressed to him from the Rev. H.H. Spalding, missionary to this tribe, stating as follows:

"The Indians in this vicinity are remarkably quiet this winter, and are highly pleased with the laws recommended by Dr. White, which were unanimously adopted by the chiefs and people in council assembled. The visit of Dr. White and assistants to this upper country will evidently prove an incalculable blessing to this people.[3] The school now numbers two hundred and twenty-four in daily attendance, embracing most of the chiefs and principal men of the nation."

LAWS OF THE NESPERCES

Art. 1. Whoever willfully takes life shall be hung.

Art. 2.Whoever burns a dwelling shall be hung.

Art.3.Whoever burns an out building shall be imprisoned six months, receive fifty lashes, and pay all damages.

Art. 4.Whoever carelessly burns a house, or any property, shall pay damages.

Art. 5.If any one enter a dwelling, without permission of the occupant, the chiefs shall punish him as they think proper. Public rooms are excepted.

Art. 6.If any one steal he shall pay back two-fold; and if it be the value of a beaver skin or less, he shall receive twenty lashes; and if the value is over a beaver skin he shall pay back two-fold and receive fifty lashes.

Art. 7.If any one take a horse, and ride it, without permission, or take any articles, and use it, without liberty, he shall pay for the use of it, and receive from twenty to fifty lashes, as the chief shall direct.

Art. 8.If any one enter a field, and injure the crops, or throw down the fence, so that cattle or horses go in and do damage, he shall pay all damages, and receive twenty-five lashes for every offence.

Art. 9.Those only may keep dogs who travel or live among the game; if a dog kill a lamb, calf, or any domestic animal, the owner shall pay the damage, and kill the dog.

Art. 10. If any Indian raise a gun or other weapon against a white man, it shall be reported to the chiefs, and they shall punish him. If a white man do the same to an Indian, it shall be reported to Dr. White, and he shall punish or redress it.

Art. 11. If an Indian break these laws, he shall be punished by his chiefs; if a white man break them, he shall be reported to the agent, and punished at his instance.[4]

Account 17.2: The place and personal names portion of the Nez Perce language version of White's *Laws,* as published by Henry Spalding at Lapwai in December of 1842. Source: Papers of the ABCFM, Houghton Library, Harvard University. Published here with the permission of Wider Church Ministries of the United Church of Christ, the successor to the ABCFM. Published as: *Wilupupki, 1842 Lapwai* (Spalding Mission, 1842).

This is Spalding's version of what he felt the administrative organization of the Nez Perce people *should be*. The transcribed place names that follow appear in their original order, but the personal names have been moved to improve clarity. Brackets provide editorial clarification.

---

[3]For his part in this mutual admiration society, White stayed on a few days at Lapwai, writing several letters to missionary and political leaders. These letters praised and promoted Spalding, and proved vital to the retention of his mission.

[4]Oregon at this time was a condominium jointly administered by Great Britain and the United States. This system did not permit either nation to pass laws or regulations binding anybody in Oregon, Indian or white, to any standard of behavior.

ELLIS

Wiwatashpama Mimiohat [Chiefs of Different Lands]

KAMIAH.
Hiusinmelakin [Hiyúmm tamalákin, or Grizzly bear protection], Iutamalaikin

TISHAIAHPA [Middle Fork, near Syringa?].
Pakatash [Pa-Ka-Tas], Sisutlinkan

TSAINASHPA [up Lawyer Creek].[5]
Halhalthotsot [Lawyer],
Silupipaiu [Silúpe owyín, or Shot in the Eye]

PITA-LUAWI [S. Fk. Clearwater at Cottonwood Creek]
Aisak [Isaac]

LAMATA [White Bird Creek region]
Tamapsaiau-Haihai [White Hawk],
Hahasilpilp [Red Grizzly Bear], Autash

PIKUNAN [pikúnin, river, or Snake River]
Pakauialkalikt, Inintahshaukt

SHAKANMA [shady place, home of the Hells Canyon Band]
Toh-tamalwiun [Tuux Tamal'weun, one who carries the tobacco]

WAILUA [Wallowa Creek and the Grand Ronde River]
Josep [Old Joseph], Hahas-ilahni

HASHOTIN [place of eels, Asotin]
Apashwahaiakt [Looking Glass Sr.], Jeson

TAWA-IUAWI [Orofino]
Hahas-tamalwiat

IATOIN [mouth of the Grand Ronde R.]
Kuipelakin, Tahwaiash

IAHTOIN [Yahtoin, or Kendrick]
Lilhkimkan, Ilotin [Ilutín, Big Belly]

IAKA [Snake River at mouth of Yakawa Cr.]
Iumtamalukt

LAPWAI
Jems [Big Thunder, sometimes called "Old James," also Hinmatotqakeykt]

HATWAI
Noa

SOKOLAIKIN [North Lewiston]
Mitat-waptash [Three Feathers], Shakantain [adult Bald eagle]

ALAPAWAWI [Alpowa Creek]
Timoti [Timothy], Himim-ilpilp [Red Wolf]

WITKISHP [Snake River near Steptoe Canyon]
Luk [Luke], Ipilkin

---

[5]Can also be interpreted as a place to have a bowel movement.

TOKOHP [Burned place, Kooskia]
  Wawashtakan

Account 17.3: Gustavus Hines describes his 1843 visit to the Nez Perce. Source: Gustavus Hines, *Life on the Plains of the Pacific* (New York: C.M. Saxton, 1859), 170-185. Excerpts.

He was with a small party led by Rev. White designed to convince the Nez Perce people that whites were in Oregon "desirous of doing them good."

Friday, [May] 12th [1843].

As the Indians [the Cayuse and Walla Walla leaders living near the Whitman Mission] refused to come together until Ellis and his men came down to meet them, we informed them that we should go up and see Ellis in his own country, but being suspicious that we intended to prevent his coming down, they were much opposed to our going. Explaining to the chiefs the object of our visit, they seemed to be satisfied, and we went about preparing for the continuance of our journey.

At five, P.M., all were ready, and we started off on a round gallop in a northeasterly direction, and the sun went down beneath the waters of the Pacific. The light of the moon enabled us to keep along the winding trail as it led us over a beautifully undulating country, till eleven o'clock at night, when we camped on a small rivulet called the Toosha [the Touchet River, also known as the roasting place, or Tuuse], forty-five miles from where we started. Next morning at sunrise proceeded. At noon encamped on another little stream, having traveled thirty-five miles. Rested for an hour, and continued our course through an exceedingly romantic country. At five P.M., arrived at the Snake or Lewis river, where a portion of the Nez Perse tribe reside, headed by one whom they call "Red Wolf."

The village is situated on a small inclined plain [at the mouth of Alpowa Creek], quite fertile, but the country round about is very rocky and mountainous. The valleys, however, afford abundant grass to supply the numerous horses owned by the Indians. Red Wolf, in more than one instance, has proved himself a friend to the Americans. When Capt. Bonneville was in this country, many years ago, in his trade with the Indians, he met with violent opposition from the Hudson's Bay Company, and was compelled to leave that portion under the control of the company. But, in his attempt to do so, he lost his way, and wandered about until he and his men were reduced to a starving state. Fortunately, he struck a trail that led him to the lodge of Red Wolf, and he immediately told the chief of his great distress. Red Wolf was moved by the story, and ordered a horse to be butchered without delay. Bonneville and his men feasted themselves to their entire satisfaction; and when they were ready to leave, they were supplied with a guide, and provision for their journey.

From Dr. Whitman's to Red Wolf's place it is one hundred miles; and having traveled it in one day, our horses were leg weary. Consequently, we turned them loose among the hills to remain till we returned, and obtained fresh ones of Red Wolf, for the prosecution of our journey. It was twenty-five miles from Red Wolf's to the mission station among the Nez Perces, under the care of Rev. Mr. Spaulding and the sun was two hours high; the trail was difficult in some places but the horses were as light-footed as antelopes. Red Wolf had volunteered to accompany us, and crossing the river, swimming our horses in the rear of our canoe, we each mounted the animal designated by the chief, and himself taking the lead, we measured off the ground with wonderful rapidity. We passed a number of small villages, and found the vallies which were fertile, astonishingly filled with horses. From one eminence could be seen not less than one thousand. But Red Wolf led us on with such astonishing swiftness that we had scarcely time to cast a glance at the Indians, horses, rivers, mountains, &c., by which the scenery of our route was diversified, and which we left one after another in quick succession far in the rear. Just as the sun was setting we brought up on the Clear Water River, on the side opposite the house of Rev, Mr. Spaulding. We had traveled twenty-five miles in two hours, and sixty miles since we had dined at twelve o'clock. Hailing across the river, Mr. Spaulding came over in a small canoe, and took us and our baggage over, and, with his wife and Mr. and Mrs. Littlejohn, gave us a most cordial and hearty welcome to their isolated home.

Sunday, 14th [May 1843].

Some two hundred Indians, of all ages, met in the rear of Mr. Spaulding's house for religious worship. They behaved with great propriety, and some of them gave good evidence of genuine conversion. Mr. Spaulding had received three of them into church fellowship, two of them chiefs, by the name of [Old] Joseph and Timothy; and thirty others stood propounded for membership. According to the arrangements, these were to be received on the Sabbath after our arrival. Being examined according to the order of the Presbyterian church, and giving satisfaction as to their religious experience, they and their children received baptism, and they became members of Christ's visible church.

In the evening it fell to my lot to preach to the few Americans who providentially had been thus thrown together. This is evidently the most promising Indian mission to Oregon.

Monday, 15th.

Climbed to the top of a mountain, twenty-two hundred feet high, which overlooks the valley of Sapwai [Lapwai], and enables one to trace the windings of Clear Water, for several miles. We started a number of large rocks down the precipitous sides of the mountain towards the river, but on descending found that our sport was not gratuitous. Some Indians had just come up the trail on horseback, and a fragment of one of the rocks had struck a horse's leg and broken it. But the horse being not very valuable, the matter was easily adjusted.

When we arrived, Ellis, with some hundreds of his people, was fifty or sixty miles off [at Kamiah], and a letter was sent to him to come down and meet us.

Tuesday, 16th [May 1843].

Joseph, who is second to Ellis in the chieftainship, made a martial display of his band, in a little plain in the rear of the house, where he entertained us with a sham fight. We estimated the number under Joseph at seven hundred. Arrayed in their war dress, they made a very savage, not to say imposing, appearance.

Wednesday, 17th.

Joseph called out to his band and awaited the arrival of Ellis. We were requested to take our places in the front ranks of Joseph's band, in the centre, and soon appeared, coming over the mountain, behind which had been waiting, a cloud of Indians, that spread itself over its sides. The mountain seemed alive, as hundreds of Indians came moving towards the valley. They were all mounted on their best horses, and these were ornamented with scarlet belts and head dresses, while tassels dangled from their ears. They arrived on the borders of the plain, and the two bands were separated from each other about fifty rods, and now the scene that presented itself beggars description. A thousand savages rushed into all the manoevers of a deadly fight, while the road of musketry, the shrill sound of the war whistle, the horrible yelling, and the dashing too and fro upon their fiery steeds, which continued for half an hour, and approached us nearer and nearer until the froth from their horse's nostrils would fly into our faces as they passed—these, with the savage pomposity with which they were caparisoned, and the frightful manner in which they were daubed with paint, their fiery visages being striped with red, black, white, and yellow, were all calculated not only to inspire terror, but a dread of savage fury in the mind of every beholder. At the very height of the excitement, when it appeared that the next whirl of the savage cavalry would trample us all beneath their feet, Ellis stretched himself up to his utmost height upon the back of his splendid charger, and waving his hand over the dark mass, instantly all was quiet, and the terrifying yell of the savage was succeeded by profound silence. All dismounted, and the chiefs and principal men, shook hands with us, in token of friendship. All again mounted, ourselves joining the troop on horses provided by the Indians for our use, and they marched us back over the hill to a little plain beyond, for the purpose of entertaining us with a still farther exhibition of their customs.

Connected with Ellis's band were some braves whom the whole nation delight to honor. The Blackfeet Indians have always been the deadly enemies of the Nez Perces, and of all the braves, none are honored so much as those who have killed Blackfeet. One of them then present, has killed twelve with his own hands, taken their scalps and muskets, and brought them as trophies to his lodge. This he had done to revenge the death of an only brother, who, according to his story, was treacherously murdered by the Blackfeet. A large circle was formed around this brave, he occupying the centre of the

Circle, bearing on one arm the muskets he had captured from the enemy, and hanging on the other the scalps he had taken. He displayed these trophies before the multitude, and at the same time, gave a history of the manner in which each one was taken. Ellis said he was the greatest brave in the nation, and they always honor him in this way. A terrible battle had been recently fought by a party of the Nez Perces with a party of Blackfeet, in which the former were victorious. This battle was acted to the life, with the exception that no blood was shed. The scene then closed with a war dance, conducted by a chief whom the whites designate by the name of "Lawyer," and in whom is combined the cunning and shrewdness of the Indian, with the ability and penetration of the statesman.

Though this savage "training" was more exciting than any martial display I had ever witnessed, yet it closed up quietly and peacefully, and as it had been conducted upon strictly temperance principles, all retired from the scene perfectly sober. At dark, of the thousand Indians present during the day, scarcely one was to be seen outside of his lodge.

Ascertaining from Ellis that he designed to go down to meet the Kayuses when we returned, with some of his men, for the purpose of inducing them to accept of the laws which the Nez Perces had received, and with which they were well pleased, we waived our objections against his going, and on Thursday, the 18th, prepared to take our departure.

Here I would take occasion to observe, that the Rev. Mr. Spaulding and his worthy companion are laboring faithfully for both the spiritual and temporal good of this people, and in no place have I seen more visible fruits of labor thus bestowed. There are few missionaries in any part of the world more worthy of the confidence of the church that employs them, than these self-sacrificing servants of Jesus Christ. Far away from all civilized society, and depending for their safety from the fury of excited savages, alone in the protection of Heaven, they are entitled to the sympathies and prayers of the whole christian church. Bidding them farewell, we re-crossed the Clear-Water, where our horses were in waiting, rode back to Red Wolf's place, and slept.

Next morning [May 19, 1843] sent an Indian out among the hills to hunt for our horses, and as we were finishing our breakfast, which our boys had prepared for us, Red Wolf came out of his lodge and rung a large hand-bell, to call the Indians from the other lodges to their morning prayers. All assembled to the number of one hundred, an exhortation or harangue was given them by one of the chiefs, and then singing a hymn in the Indian tongue, two engaged in prayer. I was greatly surprised, in traveling through the Indian country, to find that these outward forms of christianity are observed in almost every lodge. The Indians generally are nominally christian, and about equally divided betwixt the Protestant and Catholic religion.

At eight o'clock, a hallooing upon the side of the mountain indicated that our horses were found, and would soon be at our camp. Packing, saddling, and bridling were done in short order, and, Mr. Spaulding joining our party. We soon left the valley of the Snake River behind us [headed toward Alpowa Summit]. Examining the country more critically on our return than when we went out, we found it to be indescribably beautiful and sublime, and generally well adapted to all pastoral purposes. No timber of any consequence appeared, except on the banks of the streams. Crossing the Tookanan, and Toosha, we stopped for supper on a beautiful brook, called Imaispa. We found we had barely provisions enough for this meal, and two of us resolved to proceed, rather than go hungry all the next day. Letting our horses crop the grass for an hour, we traveled on; Mr. Perkins and Mr. Spaulding preferring to remain where they were until morning. At daybreak we arrived at Dr. Whitman's, having set upon our horses all night.

During our absence the Kayuses had all collected within a few miles of Dr. Whitman's, and were preparing for the great meeting with the Nez Perces, on our return.

On Saturday, 20th, Ellis, with three hundred of his people, arrived, and camped within a short distance of the mission. Wearied out by excessive labor, we put off the meeting of the two tribes until the ensuing week....

During the day, Nez Perce Indians continued to arrive, until six hundred people, and a thousand horses, appeared on the plains. The Kayuse and Walla-Walla bands united, forming a troop of three hundred men, all mounted. These met the Nez Perces on the plain in front of Dr. Whitman's house, and then a scene similar to that at Lapwai, presented itself. The Indians worked themselves up into a high state of excitement, and Ellis said afterwards that he thought the Kayuses were determined to fight in good earnest. Tautau, the Catholic chief, as he approached us, appeared quite angry, and disposed to quarrel. Seeing the excitement increase, and fearing that it might end seriously, unless the attention of the Indians could be drawn to some other subject, Mr. Spaulding gave notice that all would repair to Dr. W's house, for the purpose of *Tallapoosa*, (worship). But Tauitau came forward in a very boisterous manner, and inquired what we had made all this disturbance for. We repaired to the house, followed by several hundred Indians, and after engaging in a season of prayer, found that the excitement had died away, and the Indians were scattering to their lodges for the night.

Tuesday, 23rd [May 1843].

The chiefs and principal men of both tribes came together at Dr. Whitman's to hear what we had to say. They were called to order by Tauitau, who by this time had got over his excitement, and then was placed before them the object of our visit. Among other things they were told that much had been said about war, and we had come to assure them that they had nothing to fear from that quarter; that the President of the United States had not sent the Doctor [White] to their country, to make war upon them, but to enter into arrangements with them to regulate their intercourse with white people. We were not there to catch them in a trap as a man would catch a beaver, but to do them good; and if they would lay aside their former practices and prejudices, stop their quarrels, cultivate their lands, and receive good laws, they might become a great and happy people; that in order to do this, they must all be united, for they were but few in comparison to the whites; and if they were not all of one heart, they would be able to accomplish nothing; that the chiefs should set the example and love each other, and not get proud and haughty, but consider the people as their brothers and children, and labor to do them good; that the people should be obedient, and in their morning and evening prayers they should remember their chiefs.

Liberty was then given for the chiefs to speak, and Ellis remarked that it would not be proper for the Nez Perce chiefs to speak until the Kayuse people should receive the laws. The Kayuse chiefs replied, "If you want us to receive the laws, bring them forward and let us see them, as we cannot take them unless we know what they are."

A speech was then delivered to the young men to impress them favorably with regard to the laws. They were told that they would soon take the places of the old men, and they should be willing to act for the good of the people; that they should not go here and there and spread false reports about war; and that this had been the cause of all the difficulty and excitement which had prevailed among them during the past winter.

The laws were then read, first in English, and then in the Nez Perce.

Yellow Serpent then rose and said: "I have a message to you. Where are these laws from? Are they from God or from the earth? I would think that you might say, they were from God. But I think they are from the earth, because, from what I know of white men they do not honor these laws.

In answer to this, the people were informed that the laws were recognized by God, and imposed on men in all civilized countries. Yellow Serpent was pleased with the explanation, and said that it was according to the instructions he had received from others, and he was very glad to learn that it was so, because many of his people had been angry with him when he had whipped them for crime, and had told him that God would send him to hell for it, and he was glad to know that it was pleasing to God."

Telaukaikt, a Kayuse chief, rose and said: "What do you read the laws for before we take them? We do not take the laws because Tauitau says so. He is a Catholic, and as a people we do not follow his worship." Dr. White replied that this did not make any difference about law; that the people in the States had different modes of worship, yet all had one law.

Then a chief, called the Prince, arose and said: "I understand you gave us liberty to examine every law—all the words and lines—and as questions are asked about it, we should get a better understanding of it. The people of this country have but one mind about it. I have something to say, but perhaps the people will dispute me. As a body, we have not had an opportunity to consult, therefore you come to us as in a wind, and speak to us as to the air, as we have no point, and we cannot speak because we have no point before us. The business before us is whole, like a body we have not dissected it. And perhaps you will say that it is out of place for me to speak, because I am not a great chief. Once I had influence, but now I have but little."

Here he was about to sit down, but was told to go on. He then said,—"When the whites first came among us, we had no cattle, they have given us none; what we have now got we have obtained by an exchange of property. A long time ago Lewis and Clark came to this country, and I want to know what they said about us. Did they say they found friends or enemies here?" Being told that they spoke well of the Indians, the prince said, "that is a reason why the whites should unite with us, and all become one people. Those who have been here before you, have left us no memorial of their kindness, by giving us presents. We speak by way of favor. If you have any benefit to bestow, we will then speak more freely. One thing that we cannot speak about is cattle, and the reason why we cannot speak out now is because we have not the thing before us. My people are poor and blind, and we must have something tangible. Other chiefs have bewildered me since they came; yet I am from an honorable stock. Promises which have been made to me and my fathers, have not been fulfilled, and I am made miserable; but it will not answer for me to speak out, for my people do not consider me as their chief. One thing more; you have reminded me of what was promised me sometime ago, and I am inclined to follow on and see; though I have been giving my beaver to the whites, and have received many promises, and have always been disappointed. I want to know what you are going to do."

Illutin, or Big Belly, then arose and said, that the old men were wearied with the wickedness of the young men. That if he was alone, he could say yes at once to the laws, and that the reason why the young men did not feel as he felt was because they had stolen property in their hands, and the laws condemned stealing. But he assured them that the laws were calculated to do them good, not evil.

But this did not satisfy the prince. He desired that the good which it was proposed to do them by adopting the laws, might be put in tangible form before them. He said that it had been a long time since the country had been discovered by whites, and that ever since that time, people had been coming along, and promising to do them good; but they had all passed by and left no blessing behind them. That the Hudson's Bay Company had persuaded them to continue with them, and not go after the Americans; that if the Americans designed to do them good why did they not bring goods with them to leave with the Indians? That they were fools to listen to what the Yankees had to say; that they would only talk, but the company would both talk and give them presents.

In reply to this the Doctor told them that he did not come to them as a missionary, nor as a trader....

In the evening Ellis and Lawyer came in to have a talk. They said they expected pay for being chiefs, and wished to know how much salary Dr. White was going to give them. Ellis said he had counted the months he had been in office, and thought that enough was due him to make him rich. They left at a late hour without receiving any satisfaction.

Wednesday, 24th [May 1843].

Some hundreds again assembled to resume the business relative to laws...

The Indians then continued to speak in reference to the laws, and their speeches were grave, energetic, mighty, and eloquent, and generally in favor of receiving the laws. After all had spoken it was signified that they were ready for the vote whether they would take the laws or not, and the vote was unanimous in the affirmative....

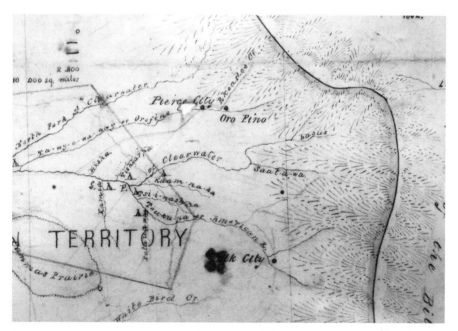

Figure 14. Detail from an 1863 Indian Agency map of Nez Perce country showing village locations and stream names.

18

Lolo Trail accounts from the
1877 Nez Perce War

Few events in the long history of the Columbia Valley are sadder than the 1877 war between the United States Army and a large portion of the Nez Perce people. Despite repeated promises to the contrary, in 1877 the Nez Perce people of the Wallowa Valley were ordered from their ancient and lovely homeland. Stung by killings, land grabs, insults, and broken promises, they refused, in the end, to comply. Pursued by soldiers of the frontier Army led by General O. O. Howard, the Joseph band of the Nez Perce conducted what is now seen as a heroic retreat during the late summer and early autumn of that year.

This war was covered in great detail by the regional and national press, and in the years subsequent, the events of 1877 have been the theme of dozens of fine books (see the attached bibliography for a list of the best of them). Readers interested in full accounts of the Nez Perce war will be rewarded by the high quality of writing on this subject. However, the story of this war will not be repeated here.

Most of the war was fought in places far removed from the path of Lewis and Clark. But in late July and early August, a large group of Nez Perce men and women, followed belatedly by Howard's soldiers, crossed over the Lolo Trail into the Bitterroot Valley. They were beginning a long trip that led them through Yellowstone Park and which, for most, ended on the plains of northern Montana. Others managed to reach the safety of nearby Canada. Several first-hand accounts exist to document this crossing of the Bitterroot Range, including some presenting the point of view of the Nez Perce. All of these accounts are well known to modern scholars, but many have been published only as excerpts. This chapter presents, some in their entirety, first-hand accounts from General Howard, his aide Charles E.S. Wood, and journalists on the trail with Howard, among them Thomas Sutherland of Portland, Oregon.

Based chiefly on the research of Ralph Space, most scholars of the Nez Perce War believe that the dates and locations of Howard's Lolo Trail camps are as follows: July 30, Weippe Prairie; July 31, Musselshell Meadows; August 1, Soldier Meadows; August 2, Weitas Meadows; August 3, Bald Mountain; August 4, Camp Howard;

August 5, ford at Crooked Fork Creek where the Lolo Trail crosses; August 6, Lolo Hot Springs; and August 7, the present site of the town of Lolo, Montana.

Further reading:

Mark H. Brown, *The Flight of the Nez Perce* (New York: G.P. Putnam's Sons, 1967).

> An important and well-documented history of the 1877 War.

Jerome A. Greene, *Nez Perce Summer 1877: The U.S. Army and the Nee-Me-Poo Crisis* (Helena: Montana Historical Society Press, 2000).

> The most thorough history of the war.

Duncan McDonald, "The Nez Perces: The History of Their Troubles and the Campaign Of 1877, " *Idaho Yesterdays* 21, no.1 (Spring 1977): 2-15, and 21, no.4 (Winter 1978): 2-10.

> A well-edited reprint of Duncan MacDonald's 1878 effort to compile first-hand oral history accounts of the war. MacDonald was related to Eagle from the Light, White Bird, and Looking Glass and spoke fluent Nez Perce.

Lucullus V. McWhorter, *Hear Me, My Chiefs! Nez Perce Legend and History* (Caldwell:Caxton, 1952). Reprinted 1983.

> A history of the Nez Perce people, including the 1877 War, written largely from the Nez Perce point of view, drawing on oral accounts and documentary sources.

Account 18.1: The Lolo Trail sections of Lieutenant Charles E.S. Wood's *Journal of Expedition against Hostile Nez Percé Indians.* Source: Huntington Library, C.E.S. Wood Papers, WD Box 26. Published here with the permission of the Huntington Library, San Marino, California.

30th [July 1877] Monday
Headquarters moves across Clearwater at 4 a.m. Command marched at 5.20 am Infantry at head of column. March to Wey-ipe about 16 miles over a narrow trail—General direction. Raining incessantly, soil a loam peculiar to fluvial deposit—Rain makes it slippery and slick. Abrupt descent at Lo-Lo fork, bad trail. Ascent somewhat better, trail runs through white pine forest, thick underbrush. Water & grazing at the Camass prairie, Wey-ipe. Snake scouts disaffected. Pioneer Company absent. Column pitches camp "Sanford" at the Wey-ipe at 1 p.m. Indian scouts come into camp seen afterwards 3 absent. Courier arrives from Kamiah about 4 p.m. Perry's applications, since Courier returned at about 5.30 Weather clear for the evening.

31st Tuesday
Leave Camp Sanford, Lo-Lo Trail at 8 a.m. Artillery at the head of column. Detailed Cav. Pioneer detachment in advance. Indian scouts some distance in advance. Weather clear, warmed, little wind—trail narrow & difficult from fallen timber, and mirey glades with deep bog holes at the crossing. Country level, slightly rolling. Timber—fir—spruce, & and arbor & pines, march 15 miles to Camp

R.H. Fletcher 3.30 p.m. in a series of glades on the Musselshell creek, excellent grass & water.

August 1st Wednesday
Leave Camp Fletcher at 6 a.m. Scouts in advance, Cavalry at head of Column. Trail much better, solid footing, broad, and not much fallen timber, runs along the ridges or backbone of a mountainous country, through dense evergreen forest, same kind of trees as yesterday, with dense undergrowth of [illegible], plenty of good water, no grazing. Several dead Indian animals found on the trail. Dispatches arrived this morning before we left Camp Fletcher. Indians said to be blocked at the mouth of this trail in Montana, & Courier from [illegible] who is one day behind us. Troops march 22 miles and arrive in Camp W.H. Winters at 3 oclock P.M. Train is very late getting in, four mules exhausted, Camp is [illegible] meadow, poor grazing, weather clear, rather cool, breezy, men not injured by long march but rather tired.

2 Thursday
Leave Camp W.H. Winters at 7 a.m. Artillery ahead of Column, day clear & pleasantly cool. Captain [William] Spurgin comes into camp at about 6 oclock with news from his pioneers, Is left at Camp Winters to bring them up. Trail through woods of same general character as before—rather slow trail owing to mountainous character of country & fallen timber; summits of hills are covered with a debris of granite bolders, making trail quite difficult, of no large extent however. Plenty of excellent springs on trail, men travel it well and are in good order. March 16 miles & camp on a slope of the mountain, poor grazing, only feed animals of wild [illegible] lupin & wire grass. Several mules exhausted, some packs of bacon abandoned. Captain Robbins reports loose Indian horses on the trail. Go into Camp Evan Miles at about 4 P.M. Spurgin arrived at about dark, his men later.

3 Friday
Heavy mist and cold in morning. Scouts leave camp, Engineers—Spurgin & Fletcher— 9 a.m. Troops 11 a.m. Infantry at head of column. Good trail, cold & foggy until late in afternoon. March about 7 miles go into Camp Spurgin at about 1 oclock P.M poor grazing—limited accomodation–Beef Cattle & remaining Engineers come up about 4 p.m. Scouts sent ahead to Missoula. Timber to day on higher part of mountains, has been rather scrubby—fine (long leaved) spruce & fir—boulders of white granite out cropping on top of mountains. Carlton brings letter from Grostein & Binnard [owners of a general store in Lewiston].

4th Saturday
Cold, clear morning. (Ice in basins) Leave Camp Spurgin at 7 a.m. Infantry at head of column, pass through same character of country as yesterday, rather better grazing—meet [James L.] Carley with dispatch from Rawn (about 1.30 P.M.) He returns with us. We march about 16 miles and camp on the warm ? side at Camp Robt. Pollock at about 4 p.m. Send out order detaching Cavalry for the forced march. Gen. Howard temporarily attached to [unclear: Engineers?].

5th Sunday
Send Carley to Kamiah with dispatches. Clear & cool weather—same character of country as past two or three days. Trail quite bad, column leaves camp about 8:30 Cavalry in advance as per circular order of date of 4th. Engineer

detachment and Co leave camp at 6 A.M. March 21 miles, little water, no grazing, mountainous country, very little level trail. Camp on the Clearwater [i.e., the upper Lochsa] about 4 P.M. Cavalry does not arrive till 7 P.M. Train arrives at 8.30 Sent dispatch to Gibbon per General. No grazing at camp.

6th Monday
March at 4 a.m. without breakfast, same character of trail & country as before. About 7 oclock reach summit prairie [the meadows near Lolo Pass] –graze the animals, leave at noon. Camp at Camp G.S. Hoyle—Warm Springs at about 4 P.M. 9 miles from Summit Prairie 16 from last camp. Fine camp at hot springs (Sulphur water) good grazing & ? brook. Pardee comes in with dispatch from Gibbon. Rumors of Crow outbreak. Sergt. Sutherland & Indian Scouts leave as Couriers to Gibbon.

7th Tuesday
Leave Camp G.S. Hoyle at 6.30 a.m. Fletcher & Pardee leave at 4 oclock. Engineer detachment at 5.30. rough mountainous trail. Forest thinning out, less underbrush, bunch grass begins to grow again march 22 miles to Camp General Sherman, arrive at about 3 oclock. Fine camp—good grazing & water, strike good road, timber runs out & grass comes in.

Account 18.2: The Lolo Trail letters of Major Edwin Mason, General Howard's Chief of Staff. These letters were published anonymously on September 28, 1877 in the St. Louis, Missouri *Republican*. The originals are in the Montana Historical Society, Mss. No. 80. Portions were also published in *Montana: The Magazine of Western History* 27, no. 4 (Autumn 1977).

Camp Evan Miles
August 3 1877 Friday

My dear Wife & Mother—
We left our camp at the "Wey-ipe" where my last letters were written Tuesday morning, arriving at Mussel-Shell river at about 3 p.m. Wednesday we marched to the foot of "Bald Mountain." Thursday we marched to this place, which is a bare place on the mountain side. This Friday morning is cold and disagreeable. It began raining during the night, and this morning it is almost cold enough to make ice, for we are up near the snow line, with the snow-peaks all around us. We are making a late start this morning, for our mules are almost played out with this trail. How can I describe this mountain trail? It runs through the thickest of forests and the most broken of mountains I have ever seen. The fallen timber covers the trail, so that every few feet there is a log to climb over or crawl around. We have to keep our pioneers at work with their axe all day. We start at 6 a.m. and work hard all day and make about sixteen miles by 6 p.m.

Our train and troops string out about five miles in length. As there is no danger of a flank attack in these forests—for no one can travel a foot off the trail— it makes no difference about the length of our line. The scenery is very grand from the tops of the mountains we cross, while all day long it has been very pleasant to travel through the dense woods, with the sunlight glinting through the trees. It looks a little lighter in the sky just now, and I think it will clear up. We will have only a short march to-day—about 8 miles—but that will take until late in the afternoon.

The grass is very scanty in these mountains and it is very poor feeding for the poor horses and mules, poor fellows. We are about 45 miles from the summit by the trail. It appears on the map as "Lou Lou" pass. From there it is about 30 miles to where the Indians were last heard of. We are all very anxious to strike them, for it is the shortest way home. If we can find them again we will be able to break them up and end the war. We have now an excellent band of Indian scouts under a Capt. Robbins from Boise. These Indians are just from the plains, having served with Crook and Miles against the Sioux. It is time to pack, so I will close for the present. My little tent in the first thing of this sort I have ever seen [some family news not transcribed here].

4:30 P.M.—"Camp Spurgeon," as this is named. We marched for eight miles through the mist, or rather clouds, for we are away up in the air on a high mountain—in fact we have been marching through and over the Bitter Root mountains for three days, and will be in them for three days more [some family matters not transcribed].

We hope to make a long march to-morrow, about twenty miles, and the same next day, which will bring us to the summit of Lou Lou pass. We would like to travel faster than we do, but it is useless to try to make more than we do. Yesterday and the three days before we were in the saddle eleven hours, which is long enough. It is always from two to three hours after we get in before the rear guard arrives. We have about six hundred animals. They string out over these rough trails at a great rate. It is a fortunate thing I did not bring my horses. They would have been ruined by these rough trips. We have Lt. Wood on the staff as A.D.C. I like Wood much better in camp than I did in garrison. He has plenty of pluck and energy and is doing his duty extraordinarily [family matter not transcribed].

It is very cold to-night, I am wrapped in my "ulster" and even with that find it difficult to keep warm. My fingers are very cold, so I will stop.

Camp Robert Pollock, Aug. 4.—Saturday evening, while marching to this point to-day, we met a courier coming from "Missoula" with dispatches from Capt. Rawn, who commands the new post at Missoula. He says that he talked with White Bird and Looking Glass, that the Indians are very short of ammunition and are offering as high as a dollar for cartridges. That they tell the people of the valley not to be afraid, as they will only fight the soldiers, but the volunteers on that agreement left him, he had only twenty-five regular soldiers and could not attack with that number. That the citizens are selling them goods and buying their horses. That they are going into the Sioux country. That they are only travelling about 5 or 6 miles per day in order to rest their stock. We hope to make the summit to-morrow night. We will then cut loose from the column and with the cavalry press on in pursuit. Gen. Gibbon, colonel of the Seventh infantry, is after them and will, we think, head them off. Gov. Potts of Montana is trying to raise volunteers and will join the pursuit. The hostiles have been routed repeatedly, and have only about 150 men with them. In their condition they cannot make a fight, and if we can only catch them, I feel confident we can end the war. A courier goes back from this camp, and will take this. We are camped again on a mountain side, which slopes as steep as the roof of our house. I have been obliged to dig out a place for my bed to lay level. This is the most difficult mountain trail I have ever seen. I shall be glad when we get into the open country. I am both hungry and tired so you will pardon my closing my letter. I have written just after getting into camp. It is now after sundown and growing cold. I am very anxious to overtake the Indians and hope we will not be disappointed. I am well, comfortable and dirty.

Camp Sherman, 20 miles from Missoula, Montana, Tuesday Evening, Aug.7.—We have named this camp after Gen. Sherman, who we are informed by our courier from Missoula is expected there this evening. My last letter was written on Friday, or rather closed and sent that morning. Saturday, Sunday and Monday we spent in working our way over this difficult mountain trail, climbing up one mountain for miles, only to plunge again into a deep gorge and do the same thing over again. Most tiresome work, and as we have had little else for the horses to feed on than leaves from the brush, they are in wretched condition, hardly able to move a leg. We are now on the range of the Bitterroots and well down the "Lolo-Lolo" canyon, and have good grass. Yesterday we camped at "Hot springs," a wonderful place, great basins of boiling hot water, flowing over the rocks in cascades—a grand sight and a fine place to wash clothes.

Account 18.3: A journalist's account from the trail. Source: Idaho Statesman (Boise), August 18, 1877.

WITH GENERAL HOWARD IN THE BITTERROOT MOUNTAINS
(from our War Correspondent)
Camp Spurgin, Square Mountain (in the Bitter-Root Mountains), August 3rd, 1877

This being the anniversary of the heathen Chinee, Ah Sin's dastardly attempt to ring in a cold hand on the virtuous Jim Nye, I propose to commemorate said anniversary by sending your readers the latest from the front.

As the Apostle Paul says things must be done "decently and in order," it may be as well to return to Kamai, where every prospect pleases and only man is vile. Previous to the command leaving that place the air was full of rumors as to the ultimate goal of the expedition under Gen. Howard. When I first ran with this expedition I was just verdant enough to place implicit confidence in what I was told; but having several times "slipped up on my calculation," I now take everything *cum grano salis.*

"'Tis a wicked world, my masters," and the sin your correspondent has encountered out here is beyond description. It will hardly by credited, but it is a solemn fact, that one night we had our coffee-pot stolen from off the fire just as we were going to eat our supper; but my partner being one of those fellows who glory in getting even, marched forth and shortly returned with a kettle of stew, which we enjoyed very much in the manner a school-boy would enjoy stolen apples. So much for camp life for the present.

Previous to leaving Kamai two wounded Indians were brought into camp. On of them was wounded by the Idaho volunteers in the fight at Clear creek, but our boys claim the other on the big fights of the 11th and 12th of July. One of them is the paternal progenitor of Indian Tom, who, throughout the troubles, has laid claim to be a "good Indian;" that his family has lots of fine stock may possibly account for the milk in that cocoa nut.

The whole command having crossed the river, started by dawn on Monday morning. The weather was terribly wet, and the roads thereby in very bad condition; yet in spite of all the General made one of his famous marches, and camped that night on the Weipe-Camas ground, where Levi was killed, and other scouts lately wounded. The route taken is the Lolo trail. It is in fearful condition, owing to the immense amount of fallen timber, blocking the way. We have had to cut our way through all of it. This is the fourth day out, yet we have made merely one hundred miles. Our engineer corps is now organized; composed of 50 men, under command of Capt. Spurgin; Jack Carleton, Lieutenant; and Ross, of Boise, 1st Sergeant. Their duties are to go ahead and clear the way for the main command. Rube Robbins and his scouts are in the lead. So far they have nothing to report. Joseph is evidently way ahead. We live in hopes that the Montana troops and the people will hold them level until we catch up. All hands are anxious for another fight. There is every indication that the Indians rushed through here in all haste, for they hardly left a sign to tell where they camped. They left one sign on a tree, which we interpret as of defiance. It is in the shape of a bow, at least ten feet in length, cut out with a perfect line of beauty, on the bark of a huge black pine tree.   •

We are now in the midst of a vast range of mountains, perfectly black with timber; of pine, fir and spruce. Grass is very scarce; the poor animals suffer very much. The very wildest cayuse in the outfit is now as gentle as a lamb. We hear that the Indians are in Montana, but the people and troops rather object to their passing through the country, and also that they may possibly have met and fought them.

As one days travel through the mountains is a fair sample of all of them, I will defer any further description, save that they are "grand, gloomy and peculiar," until we reach the enemy.

Account 18.4: An excerpt from Oregon journalist Thomas Sutherland's account. Source: New York *Herald,* September 1, 1877, Pg. 10.

GENERAL HOWARD'S CAMPAIGN. DESCRIPTION OF THE MARCH THROUGH THE LOLO TRAIL.
Camp James H. Bradley, Forty Miles from Bannock City, M.T., August 14, 1877.

As you can see from my despatches General Howard and command have been since the 30th of July in getting through the Lolo trail, the most notoriously bad pass in this entire country. The trip was made in excellent time, and to General Howard is due the full credit, as he alone appeared to be the man anxious to hurry through it, at all hazards to life and limb, and at all times. On leaving Kamiah we were accompanied by a severe rain which kept us company for the entire day, making the marching, which was single file on account of the narrowness of the path, one of the most slippery, sticky, mucky, and filthy of the trip. The first night we camped at the Wey-ipe (Nez Perce for a marshy place in the mountains), where camas was so plentiful that the path taken by our men was in places actually white with this favorite Indian bulb. I should like to carry you with me through the different camps, but as there was a great sameness in these I shall confine myself to presenting a few general outlines.

MILES AND MOUNTAINS
About twelve years ago several thousand dollars were appropriated by Congress to have the Lolo trail surveyed, and, judging by the great distances between the mile points, the engineers [Wellington Bird and Sewell Truax] were in league with some one who wanted to get a further appropriation for a wagon road. In connection with the extraordinary length of these miles they are nearly all

straight up and down mountains, which in height and in the language of the Oregon trapper, Joe Meek, make ordinary picnic mountains, as, for instance, the Adirondack's, appear as holes in the ground. For about three days and a half of our experience on the trail our horses were entirely without grass, the only semblance of it being a tough species of wire grass which mules and horses alike refused to eat. The rapid marches, without food and camping on the sides of mountains, which deprived the poor brutes of rest at night, made our last marches before reaching the mouth of the Lolo very precarious, not to say of the order in which a man "works his passage."

Account 18.5: Excerpts from the 1924 speech in Tacoma of volunteer soldier Eugene T. Wilson, in which he describes events of 1877 at the western end of the Lolo Trail. Source: This talk appeared in several newspapers in 1924, manuscript copies of the speech are in several archival collections, and an edited version was published in 1966: Eugene Tallmadge Wilson and Eugene Edward Wilson, *Hawks and Doves in the Nez Perce War of 1877* (Helena: Montana Historical Society).

The following day [July 16,1877] we [volunteer soldiers] retraced our steps, discouraged and angry [that Joseph had not surrendered or been captured], and when Kamia was reached most of the volunteers returned to their homes, our company, with a few straggling acquisitions from the others, remaining with General Howard. Soon after reaching Kamia orders were issued for the cavalry and remaining volunteers to proceed next morning on the trail of the hostiles, Colonel Mason in command, the volunteers to take the advance. The infantry having crossed the Clearwater before our arrival, it was short work swimming our horses over, a task accomplished without further incident than the arrest of a few packers who had offended the ears of the General by swearing at their animals, and that night we were encamped at the edge of the little fields of grain belonging to the Mission Indians. There was no grass for our horses and strict orders were issued forbidding us to cut the Indians' grain for forage. A hard march ahead of us for the morrow with a probable skirmish with the hostiles was not to be considered with famished horses and, despite the orders, as soon as it was dark dozens of crouching forms might have been seen bobbing around in the grain fields as the boys cut and gathered the coveted feed for their horses. A late supper of hard-tack and bacon of uncertain age was washed down with black coffee and we rolled in our single blankets for the night. At daylight [July 18,1877] the regular cavalry and volunteers were up and mounted after a hurried breakfast, and in less time than I can tell it the column was moving in the direction the enemy had taken the day before [along the ancient trail from Kamiah to Weippe, across the deep canyon of Lolo Creek].

The Lo Lo trail across the Bitter Root mountains is about 250 miles long and leads through magnificent fir and cedar timber of wonderful height, the trees growing closely together with a dense undergrowth of brush beneath them. Across divides and down deep canyons, twisting and turning among the timber as the topography of the country made it necessary, in many places the trail so narrow that two persons could not ride abreast, now entering a natural clearing or "camas" ground for a few rods or half a mile, to dive again into the dark depths of the primeval forest, Colonel Mason's command of 250 persons wended its way. The volunteers were given the advance, Colonel McConville riding at our head with Chapman, the interpreter, by his side. Shortly after leaving Kamia a dozen or more friendly Indians, under the leadership of old Captain John, had joined us, James Reubens, an educated Nez Perce, being among them. The latter had been somewhat under suspicion by the volunteers and settlers of Camas Prairie, but he had the confidence of General Howard and carried a better gun than was furnished us, all of which did not tend to decrease the haughtiness with which he looked upon the civilians.

For several hours before noon the Indian scouts reported plenty of Indian signs, and there were strong indications that a small party of hostiles was watching us closely, the fresh tracks of their saddle ponies being frequently seen where they had crossed and recrossed the trail. Shortly before noon we entered a large camas ground of several hundred acres and dismounted for a hasty lunch without unsaddling. Cinches were loosened and bridles slipped from the horses' heads, and the grateful animals were soon reveling in luxuriant bunchgrass from the ends of their riatas. The Indian scouts camped a few hundred yards beyond us and not knowing that our halt would be a short one, made a regular camps and prepared for cooking a warm dinner. They were, therefore, left temporarily behind when forward was sounded thirty minutes later. After leaving our noonday camp, we again plunged into the depths of the forest, the volunteers marching about 400 yards in advance. After traveling several miles among trees whose height made it literally necessary to look twice to see their tops, the trail led down the steep side of a canyon at the bottom of which the Lo Lo Creek rippled over its rocky bed, hidden in everlasting shade. Boots and shoes had long since become a curiosity among us, and moccasins, when obtainable, were substituted for them, but the sharp rocks and wiry grass wore them into strings and many of our boys were practically barefooted. In many places the trail was too precipitous for one to ride his horse, and there was more than one spot of blood left upon the rocks by torn and bleeding feet as we picked our way among them. The summit reached, our trail continued through the tall firs and cedars until about 3 o'clock in the afternoon, when we approached a small opening in the timber, probably 150 yards across, the friendly Indians under Captain John catching up with us just as we reached it. As the Indian signs had become numerous and fresh, Colonel McConville ordered the Indians to ride ahead and scout the trail.

They immediately obeyed and riding at a brisk trot across the opening, disappeared in the timber beyond. We had just reached the center of the clearing when three of our dusky allies were seen coming toward us, dismounted and without their guns, and motioning with their hands for us to go back. They were hardly in sight before three sharp volleys were heard from the trail ahead and the next moment the rest of them came out of the timber as fast as their ponies could run, each Indian yelling at the top of his voice: "Kalatwa! Klatawa! Hiyu Siwash! Hiyu Siwash!" At the sound of the firing, the regulars halted something like 400 yards in the rear, and when the scouts gave the alarm our interpreter put spurs to his horse and beat a hasty retreat to where Colonel Mason and his men were trying to dismount a howitzer from the back of a mule. The Indians were greatly excited and Captain John and one of his men were missing. Jim Reubens was nursing an arm through which a bullet has ploughed its way, and as no one in our company could understand them, they, too, went back to the regulars and we were left alone in the center of the narrow opening, with the woods, so far as we know and as we believed, full of hostiles upon every side. We did not fall back at once, and to some of us the seconds seemed hours, but in a few moments McConville gave the command to retire to the edge of the timber where we dismounted behind a big fallen tree with our horses strung out behind us at the ends of their lariats. Our cartridges were emptied on the ground in front of us and every preparation made for a fight to a finish, every man in the company prepared to sell his life as dearly as possible. One of the boys whose appetite was abnormal, remarked that he would " be d—d if he was going to die upon an empty stomach," and opened his cantinas and passed his hard-tack along the line.

As the moments glided by and no attack was made, the situation became ludicrous and we began to speculate upon the success Colonel Mason would have with a mountain howitzer in timber too thick to drag a cat through. Aside from our subdued voices not a sound could be heard but the soughing of the boughs overhead, and in the momentary expectation of attack, notwithstanding our suddenly aroused sense of humor at the thought of that deadly howitzer, the strain was becoming intense. This was soon relieved by a command from Mason that we deploy right and left through the timber, Captain Winter's company to take the right and Captain Trimble's the left, the volunteers to take the advance of the right. The order was gladly obeyed and it was not long before we discovered the ambuscade from which a small detachment of hostiles had fired upon our "friendlies" as they entered the timber. It was afterwards learned that the main body was heavily entrenched behind fallen timber seven miles beyond, their intention being to let the volunteers get beyond them so that they could be easily cut off from any assistance the regulars might give, and then destroy the entire command, but the sight of members of their own tribe friendly to and scouting for us was too much for the patience of the rear guard, and they could not resist the temptation to take a shot at them.

Few of the regulars went further than the edge of the timber, and as two of the "friendlies" were missing, we began a search for them, soon finding one, known as "Young Levi," lying in the grass with a forty-five bullet through his lungs. He was sent to the rear in charge of one of our men, but was hurt so badly that he could walk only a few steps without a hemorrhage. In the meantime, I took three men and went in search of Captain John, and when several hundred yards in the timber we heard seven or eight shots fired, apparently between us and the rest of our command. We immediately broke for the place where we had left the company and each developed sprinting qualities which would have made our fortunes on the tan bark under other circumstances. When we reached the volunteers we learned that the firing had been done by the soldiers who mistook Wishard and the wounded Indian for the enemy as they emerged from the tall rye grass in the edge of the timber. No one was hurt, as the bullets whistled harmlessly among the tree tops. Wishard relieved his mind with a few cuss-words and proceeded to the rear with his charge. My posse then returned to the search for Captain John. After hunting among the brush for some time we found the body of the old warrior with one bullet through the back of his head, another through his face just below the eye and another entering his throat and ranging downward into his lungs. It was now getting late and Colonel Mason ordered a retreat back to Kamia, the men to deploy in the timber, the volunteers covering the rear. No thought was given by the commander to the friendly Indians who had shed their blood in our service, and preparations were made to go off and leave them in a hostile country with their dead and wounded. But Colonel McConville would not hear of this and gave orders to the volunteers to let the soldiers go to Tophet or some equally undesirable country, while we remained with our faithful allies and helped them out of the scrape we had got them into. A couple of poles were cut, fashioned into a dray or travois and attached to the back of a pony upon which to carry Young Levi, the wounded Indian, and the body of Captain John was placed face downward across another pony, his feet and head hanging upon opposite sides and made fast with "riatas." It was nearly sunset when we were ready to start and the regulars were long out of sight.

I shall never forget that return march, the Indians silent and grieved over the death of their leader, escorted by the seventeen whites now composing our company, the momentary danger of attack under cover of the almost impenetrable forest surrounding us, the gradually increasing darkness, the accumulating difficulties of traveling over a trail almost impassable in daylight, and the utter unconcern for our safety by the soldiers who had gone ahead, secure in the knowledge that we were between them and the enemy. Silently we rode along the lonesome trail, the darkness partly dissipated by the moon now rising above the tree tops, until nearly midnight, when we reached the summit of the long hill leading down into the deep canyon of the Lo Lo. At the request of the Indians a temporary halt was made, and they were soon at work digging a grave for the body of Captain John in the rocky soil beneath a tall cedar, whose ghostly arms reaching out far above our heads seemed to pronounce a silent benediction for the soul of the brave old warrior about to be committed to its keeping. The only sound was the sighing of the boughs as the wind swept through them, and the white clouds flitting across the face of the moon cast grotesque shadows below. Around the now completed grave stood the solemn forms of a dozen or more dusky figures, while stretched upon a blanket at their feet lay all that was left of their leader. Off to one side in the shadow of the forest stood two or three other Indians who were not of the Presbyterian faith, their blankets gathered around their faces and their backs turned upon the ceremonies at the grave, the form of which they did not approve.

Those at the grave began a chant followed by a hymn sung in the Nez Perce tongue, and with a short prayer in the same language, the body was lowered into the grave. It was a shallow sepulcher and did not take long to fill, but a few rocks were piled upon the mound to keep the wolves from reaching the body, and in a few moments we were again upon the march, feeling our way down the sides of the canyon.

After overcoming the many difficulties of the trail, we finally reached the bottom and crawling into a thick grove of quaking asp[en], we tied our horses short, wrapped our blankets around us and with saddles for pillows, dropped off into slumber. Daylight [July 19] had not arrived when we were called by our Indian friends, a breakfast of hard-tack and water swallowed—it being inadvisable to build a fire for coffee—saddles thrown upon our horses and the march resumed. When the sun was well up in the heavens we reached the noon camp of the day before, where we found the regulars with their blankets airing upon the bushes, the smoldering embers of their campfires indicating that breakfast was long over, and, in fact, every evidence that they had passed a comfortable night, free from the worry of troublesome hostiles or pricking consciences. We passed them with the coolness of refrigerators but had not traveled many miles before they caught up with us and just before noon they arrived at Kamia, nearly an hour ahead of us. As we rode into the mission our attention was directed to the top of a hill behind us and down which the trail we had been following led, where a dozen or so of Joseph's young men were waiving their blankets in defiance of Uncle Sam and his army. This trip was all that was needed to make every man of the company decide upon an immediate return to the settlements, and the next morning we swam our horses across the river and started for Lewiston.

Account 18.6: Writing in 1881, General O.O. Howard recalls his days on the Lolo Trail. Source: Oliver O. Howard, *Nez Perce Joseph* (Boston: Lee and Shepard, 1881), 175-84. Excerpts.

On the 30th of July we were up before dawn; the headquarters were moved across the [Clearwater] river at four, a.m.; and the whole column was in motion by five. It rained heavily, the mud increased, and the path was narrow, steep, and slippery as we ascended the heights beyond Kamiah.

We found an abrupt descent at the Lolo fork; none but old frontiersmen and Indians could ride down, so we slipped and slid, fell, and scrambled up again. The pine trees were abundant, and, most of the way, filled in with a thick underbrush. We had, this day, our first trouble with the Bannock scouts. They had come from Boise; were tired, and did not mean to go any farther. Buffalo Horn, a young Indian, very handsomely decked off with skins and plumage, fortunately, for this time, took the side of their white chief, Robbins, and induced all but three to keep on with us for the present.

At the "We-ipe," the glade which we have before described, there was quite a lengthy opening in the forest, and plenty of water and grass. The hostile Indians had pastured this plat pretty well, and had dug over much of the land for camas roots, which are often used by the Nez Perces for food. They are shaped something like onions, but more elongated, and have a sweetish, clammy taste, which is quite palatable.

The weather cleared up before sundown, and we gladly put our weary soldiers into camp. They had marched sixteen miles up mountain-heights, by narrow, crooked horse-trails, where the mud was deep, and there could be no firmness to the tread, but is was slip, slip, all the day. Sixteen miles are equivalent to thirty on a good road, and in fair weather. Our trail ahead, we learned, was much obstructed by fallen trees. It is wonderful what vast numbers of trees, of all sizes and descriptions, were uprooted by the winds; and they had fallen in every possible troublesome way, so that, mated together, even when small, it was very perplexing to get them out of the path. Nothing but axes would do it. We were, therefore, looking anxiously for our "pioneers." Some forty or fifty of them, with axes, were coming from Lewiston. We named this glade-like opening in the almost endless forest for our commander of the cavalry battalion, "Camp Sanford." This was his first day with us. Miller continued in charge of the foot artillery, Otis of our howitzer battery, which is mounted on muleback, and Miles had command of the infantry battalion.

Every day's record of a march like this becomes monotonous; so that, for the benefit of patient readers, after giving a brief picture of one camp and headquarters, we will only add here and there a scrap from the journal.

The camp was generally rectangular in form. One battalion covered the front, usually, encamping in line, and sending guard and pickets well out. A second covered the sides or flanks, and a third the rear. The battery took its place at will, selecting as good a position as the nature of the ground afforded. For headquarters a place was sought of easy communication, and having a neat plat of ground, with wood and water convenient. On coming to the place selected for the night's halt, Colonel Mason distributed the troops, guards, and outposts.

The "big tent" was a common square tent. Mason had a similar one of special make, with joint and hinges in the uprights and in the ridge-pole. This arrangement enabled him to fold all in compact bundles for packing on the mules. His was put beside the big one, on one side; a tent-fly was pitched, with open front and back, on the other. These now were made to house Dr. Alexander, the army surgeon, Lieutenant Fletcher, aide-de-camp, and the news correspondent, Mr. Sutherland, who had joined us at Salmon River. I took Lieutenants C.E.S. Wood and Guy Howard, aides, into my tent. The quartermaster, Lieutenant Ebstein, pitched still another tent-fly for himself and his clerks. A small pack-train, under Louis, the Mexican, came up promptly after the night's halt was called.

The kitchen was placed some twenty paces off, to the left rear, near a stump, or clump of trees. The kitchen consisted of our mess-chest, and one or two canvas bags, one or two mule-loads, according to the state of the supplies. There were one man for cook and one for helper. Our cook had the suggestive name of "Kid." He had, in himself, a mine of practical helpfulness for tent life. At first we had no chair, none until Captain Pollock,—reluctant to admit the claims of age, insisted upon giving me his camp-stool. When the nights were damp or cold we always had a large fire made in front of the big tent. Our beds were common blankets or robes of skin, the buffalo, fox, squirrel skins, and the like, placed on the ground. Our table consisted of a square piece of canvas, spread near the "kitchen," in fair weather, and within the big tent when it was rainy. One soon learns, when his goods have to go on aparejos, fastened to mules' backs, that "man wants but little here below."

A more cheery, hearty, happy company than ours at headquarters is seldom found. Sometimes the officer is worn with anxiety, weary with long and tedious marches and loss of sleep, still he unbends at the mess-table, and tells lively stories to the circle around the camp-fire. There is no more intimate association among men than that, during a lengthy campaign, at a common mess. Generally we gave two hours in the morning, from the waking to the starting. Reveille at three or four, breakfast at four or five, and march at five or six.

On Thursday, the second day of August, the journal record was as follows: "the command left Camp Winters at seven, a.m. Artillery at head of column. Day clear and pleasantly cool. Captain Spurgin came into camp at six, a.m., bringing us news of his company of pioneers, still several miles behind. He was left, that morning, at Camp Winters, to bring them up. The trail led through woods of same general character as before; rather a 'slow trail,' owing to mountainous country and fallen timber. The summit of the hills was covered with rough granite boulders, making the path quite difficult. There was a plenty of excellent springs on trail; our men travel it well, and are in good order. We march sixteen miles, and encamp on a slope of the mountain. Poor grazing, indeed, here. The only feed consists of wild dwarf lupine, and wire-grass. Several mules were exhausted, and some packs of bacon were abandoned by the way. Robins, in charge of scouts, reports that 'loose Indian horses, broken down always, were seen along the trail.'"

We went into camp, named "Evan Miles," at about four, p.m. Spurgin, with pioneers, arrived at dark.

Such was the record of a day. If one could stand on Mount Washington, in New Hampshire, and look off northward toward Canada, he could see, in a clear day, much such a country as this through which we were wending our way. It does not appear far to the next peak. It is not so in a *straight* course, but such a course is impossible. "Keep to the hog-back!" That means there is usually a crooked connecting ridge between two neighboring mountain-heights, and you must keep on it. The necessity of doing so often made the distance three times greater than by straight lines; but the ground was too stony, too steep, the canyon too deep, to attempt the shorter course. Conceive this climbing ridge after ridge, in the wildest kind of wilderness, with the only possible pathway filled with timber, small and large, crossed and criss-crossed; and now, while the horses and mules are feeding on innutritious wire-grass, you will not wonder at "only sixteen miles a day."

"Didn't the hostile Indians go here?" the reader inquires. Yes; they jammed their ponies through, up the rocks, over, and under, and around the logs, and among the fallen trees, without attempting to cut a limb, leaving blood to mark their path; and abandoned animals, with broken legs, or "played out," or stretched dead by the wayside.

Our guide, Chapman, says, in frontier parlance, "No man living can get so much out of a horse like an Indian can." Had we, for three days, along the Lolo trail, followed closely the hostiles' unmerciful example, we would not then have had ten mules left on their feet fit to carry our sugar, coffee, and hard-bread.

[After learning from a courier that Joseph had escaped into the Bitterroot Valley, Howard's troops descended into the upper valley of the Crooked Fork, upstream from the current Powell Ranger Station] We had passed the last tine of the Clearwater, where at night, after twenty-one miles of the roughest country, with Spurgin's pioneers ahead, cutting out the trail, we came into camp in the twilight, where we had heard loud echoes of firing by the advanced scouts, and thought they had come upon Joseph's rear-guard. Then we spurred up the weary animals into a tired trot, and, along this narrow trail descended for miles through the almost impenetrable forest, till we came to the narrowest of valleys [Crooked Fork], to find not a mouthful of food for horse or mule, but the nicest of salmon for the men, in water about knee-deep,—water clear as crystal, rushing and [s]plashing over the rocks. The echoes which deceived us into thinking the enemy near, were from the scouts' carbines, shooting the bigger fish, as they were swimming up the Clearwater. Glad were we to get beyond that valley where the poor mule was obliged to fast all night, and tremble and sway himself back and forth as he undertook to take his load up the steep exit at four o'clock the next morning.

How strong and firm his step became seven miles ahead, when he came into a mountain glade [Packer Meadows], where there were little swampy lakes, and the greenest of grass in plenty. Here was the place where mule and man enjoyed a rest and a breakfast far more satisfying than in inhabited regions which are replete with abundance. Yes, we have passed this lovely oasis in the wild Lolo wilderness, and have come to an opening in the mountains, which makes us feel almost as if the tug of war was over. But one must not be sanguine, for appearances are deceptive. Our journal says: "Warm Springs, about four, P.M. Nine miles from Summit Prairie—(where the mule and man had the early breakfast); sixteen miles from our last camp. Fine camp here at [Lolo] Hot Springs, (sulphur water); good grazing, and mountain brook."

It requires but a little imagination for the reader to fill out the picture: Several beautiful pools of steaming water, at the foot of a gently-sloping, thinly-wooded hill. Down the hill, sweeping swiftly over ledges, and throwing up the spray, which sparkles in the sunshine, from fissures and crevices in the ledge, glides a broad, shallow stream. It was a charming place. The wilderness was speedily changed into a beautiful village....

Account 18.7: Excerpts from another journalist's Lolo Trail account. Source: Portland *Daily Standard*, 21 August 1877.

THROUGH LOLO TRAIL, Special Correspondent of the Standard
Missoula, M.T., Aug. 10, 1877.

On Monday, the 30th ult., Gen. Howard, with 700 troops, crossed the Clearwater, at Kamiah, in a drenching rain, at a most unreasonable hour for those indifferent to warm gathering, and began the passage of the famous Lolo trail. The ascent of the first mountain had the monotony—not to say fatigue—somewhat broken into by the inspection, we all felt in duty bound to make, of the breast-works thrown up by the Indians. By the time we had reached the summit of this hill (which, by the way, was only accomplished with the greatest amount of puffing and skipping, reminding one of the school boy and the monkey climbing the greased pole), we attempted the descent [down to Lolo Creek]. The rain, contrary to our most ardent prayers, and the wisest prognostications of a certain officer whom I dubbed "Young Probabilities," poured in sheets. The trail, "with scanty room for two abreast to pass"—as W. Tell expresses it on the English stage—was a stream of apparently inanimate mud....

Drenched to the skin, with boots like miniature wells, we went into camp in a rich grazing country, prolific with camas, called the wey-ipe. The exact derivation of this word is unknown to me, but judging from the mud upon our clothing it had some cousin-German connection to our good Anglo-Saxon wipe. This camp was named after Lieut. Fletcher, one of the most brilliant young officers, Ebstein excepted, in the command.

The next morning our trouble re-commenced, and as the fifty axmen— denominated "Engineer Corps"—for some unfathomable reason had not arrived, we were obliged to keep up a perpetual vaulting over fallen timber and wallowing in mud holes until our arrival at the next camp. Here we found a most delightful marsh, filled with mosquitoes and bog holes seemingly without depth. Our cavalry horses on being turned out fell into the holes, and it was only with a very evident stretching of neck and tail that they were extricated.

Along the road many Indian signs were noticeable on the trees, such as charcoal marks on places stripped of bark, stars, crosses, men, etc., cut in the trees, which, owing to my limited experience with savages I was unable to interpret.

The next camp was on Squirrel Mountain, so called on account of the entire absence of the bushy-tailed quadruped, and named in honor of the infantry hero of the Clearwater fight, Capt. Evan Miles. The tramp here was a repetition of our previous struggles up hills, that none but a mucilaginous-footed fly could climb, over fallen timber, and through sloughs of despond. The summits of the mountains were particularly noticeable for the weird appearance of the trees, which having braved the storms and lightnings of that altitude for years, were as gnarled and unshapely as the *coryphées* in an ordinary ballet troupe.

At the camp preceding this and until we arrived at Summit Prairie our horses got little or no grass, and the rapidity in which they wasted into shadows and became like unto "the harp of a thousand strings" was astonishing to one so ignorant as I of the celerity with which the good things of this earth waste away. (Those knowing my avoirdupois can understand this) I suppose I might at this juncture go into ecstacies over the thousand little valleys stretching out on either hand of the mountains we climbed, of the distant peaks "that wore their caps of snow in the very presence of the regal sun," of the crystal streams "that knew no sound save their own dashings," and all that sort of things, but I had to struggle up those mountains, and if that does not knock the romance and powers of description out of a feeble scribe, then it is because I have not arrived at that height, and would recommend the employment of Il Penseroso of the *Ara'anche*, the scout of the Chiahuahua and grand high sarrounder of caches.

This camp was on the side of a mountain, and so precipitous that at dinner (a good word that we don't particularize) General Howard had to rest his coffee cup on a stone, on one side, to keep it from going over the hill. According as the tents were pitched, or rather beds made in them, we slept almost erect or standing on our heads. At this place the Lewiston axemen, about fifty in number, under Jack Carleton, the great trout catcher, caught up to us and for the remainder of the trip did most excellent service.

On the 3d inst. Capt. Robbins, with Buffalo horn, the celebrated Indian of Crook's command, and several other Bannack scouts, started directly for Missoula Headquarters at the same time, wishing to reach the scene of trouble as rapidly as possible, pushed on with the cavalry.

On the 5th we crossed the line between Idaho and Montana, not far from Summit Prairie, and marked by a piece of bark being wound around a tree. After grazing our horses for a few hours at Summit Prairie we moved on to the Hot Springs. To say that I was enchanted with the place would fall far short of the delight I felt on arriving at such a beautiful spot. A lovely lawn of rich grass, looking almost like a half-mile long billiard table, rocks piled up in fantastical shapes, the steam arising from the Hot Springs, our bathing and washing in them, our trout fishing, the frosty morning, the ice in the mash puddles, the lost cavalry horses, and many other things I should like to describe, but as the lazy writers say, I have come to the end of my paper, or "space will not permit."

Gen. Howard deserves much credit for the rapidity with which he has hurried his men and jaded horses through this trail, and I feel confident that all those who have ever attempted the passage will do him similar justice. Reveille at 4 o'clock every morning and march to the farthest reachable camping ground, are about the style of his orders. We have unanimously agreed, that for an old gentleman, he has the most vigorous body in the service, and are beginning to suspect a plan on his part to kill us all by hard marches before we can provide a similar service for Joseph.

19

Celebrating the Centennial of Lewis and Clark's Visit

On June 1, 1905, a large crowd gathered at a site along the Willamette River, just north of downtown Portland, Oregon. They were there to help open "The Lewis and Clark Centennial and American Pacific Exposition and Oriental Fair." They were the first of over three million visitors to this event, which ran until mid-October and returned a profit to its investors of about $100,000.

In the tradition of similar fairs of the time, the Centennial Exposition in Portland was a commercial event. It was conceived by Portland business leaders as an event designed to boost business, promote American ties to the Pacific (hence the word "Oriental"), and to celebrate the victory of manifest destiny. The official seal of the exposition promoted the same theme, poorly drawn representations of Lewis and Clark shown being marched into the western sun by Columbia herself.

Portland civic leaders began to talk of a centennial exposition as early as 1899. In late 1900, the Oregon Historical Society began a successful effort to convince the Oregon Legislature to officially support the event. The commercial organizers of the fair incorporated in October of 1901, and by the end of 1903 they had talked sixteen states into exhibiting at the centennial. Some, including Idaho, agreed to construct official buildings. After a long struggle, a suspicious Congress officially endorsed the centennial as a "world fair" and appropriated $475,000 to build U.S. Government exhibits. President Theodore Roosevelt signed this legislation on April 8, 1905. He also agreed to send his Vice-President out to open the fair, and to use a telegraph key himself to signal the grand opening.

During the struggle to obtain federal money and recognition, the commercial aspects of the centennial quickly overwhelmed the earlier interest of the Oregon Historical Society in promoting history and culture. This was to be a fair by and about business, albeit with an attractive venue and plenty of good fun and entertainment. A large amusement park was constructed, and a range of other attractions was built along a special street called "The Trail." These included a large-scale dance and musical extravaganza with a Venetian theme. Nearby was one of the most popular of all the fair's shows, which featured a "thinking" horse and a large group of very nervous appearing elk that were trained to dive off a high platform into a pool. The elk survived their work in Portland, and in 1906 visited Lewiston, Idaho, where they also proved to be quite popular.

The U.S. Government's building was on a small island, and included educational exhibits from many agencies. Nearby was an "Indian Village," at which a small number of Nez Perce men and larger delegations from elsewhere appeared. An especially pretty Forestry Building was constructed from massive logs. The exposition also had an unusual fixation on lynx, and two very large and not-so-pretty statues were especially commissioned depicting lynx attacks and battles with cattle.

Most railroads established special fares and train schedules for the six month run of the fair. The event proved especially popular in the West. By every standard of the time, the Lewis and Clark Centennial Exposition was a popular, commercial success. About all that was missing was any effort to promote or understand history.

The fair attracted lots of attention in Idaho. The Legislature appropriated $10,000 to construct what turned out to be a rather attractive Idaho building, constructed as an oversize bungalow. Frugal as ever, the state's official fair commission moved portions of the state's 1903 St. Louis Fair exhibits to Portland. Organizing Idaho's commercial exhibits for the new building also provoked the usual north-south debates, with mining interests from north of the Salmon River complaining that they were being short-changed.

Figure 15. Trixie and the diving elk show at the Fair.

Figure 16. The Idaho Building at the Centennial Fair

Figure 17. Nez Perce Indians at the Fair

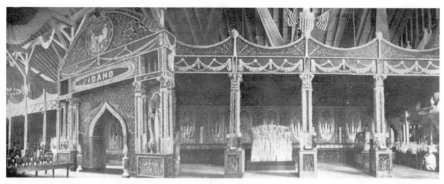

Figure 18. The interior of the Idaho Building at the Fair

In the end, the Portland fair featured an Idaho Day, which drew several thousand visitors from Idaho. There was also a special day to honor Lewiston, and the Northern Pacific Railroad arranged for cheap excursion rates from Lewiston to coincide with both dates. The exhibits in the Idaho building included art and literature developed by school children, but a long report in the *Lewiston Morning Tribune* on August 22, 1905, indicates that most of the exhibits were purely commercial. These included glass cases full of minerals and a display of Idaho wheat and potatoes. The grain exhibits offered an interesting historical touch, with both Twisted Hair and Sacajawea being portrayed on the wall in multicolored wheat and seeds.

The centennial fair seems to have provoked amazingly little interest or change in the Clearwater Valley. Efforts to obtain a legislative appropriation to construct a memorial at Lewiston honoring Lewis and Clark failed. No special events were held in the area, and the only historical research relating to Lewis and Clark did not occur until March of 1906. That's when a Nez Perce man, Charles Adams (described elsewhere in this book) and Frank Parkyn, of Lewiston, excavated the site of Canoe Camp. Their work was described in the *Lewiston Morning Tribune* on March 6, 1906. At the site, they found large tree remnants with partially completed canoes, plus several tree stumps which they asserted had been cut down by Lewis and Clark to make canoes.[1] Adams also described his family's connections to this site and to Lewis and Clark. According to the article, the two men also decided to try to rescue the partially cut log, but noted that it was heavily decayed. There is no evidence that they succeeded in this effort.

---

[1]Up until about 1940 a surprisingly large number of "Lewis and Clark canoes" were exhibited in various spots in the Clearwater Valley. The explorers took their canoes to their winter camp at the mouth of the Columbia, and returned with them in 1806, leaving them at the mouth of the Umatilla River. The Lewis journal of May 21st 1806 mentions that five men built a further canoe at Long Camp "for the purpose of fishing and passing the river. The Indians have already promised us a horse for this canoe when we have no longer any uce for her." The confusion about the large number of canoes that seem to have miraculously survived in the Clearwater region was only complicated by the work of Adams and Parkyn.

Lewiston had more important things on the table during the centennial years. In May of 1905, the Bitterroot Forest Reserve was enlarged, a controversial decision that angered many, and in the same month, construction began on the railroad link up the Snake River from Riparia. More interest, and plenty of unfounded optimism, was put in promoting a rail link from the east. Between 1904 and 1906, dozens of articles appeared in all of the region's newspapers, describing surveys, visits of rail executives, and discussions with bankers and promoters, all on the same theme: the certain construction of a direct rail route to Lewiston from Montana. The Northern Pacific and later the Milwaukee were picked as builders. Lolo Pass was usually portrayed as the certain route, but other boosters promoted Nez Perce Pass, the Salmon River Valley, and a host of mystery passes located at a fictional "low" spot in the Bitterroot Range. In the end, none of these routes were constructed. Only the checkerboard land ownership pattern easily seen near Lolo Pass survives to remind us of this railroad building era.

The Nez Perce people were similarly distracted, but for different reasons. One key concern was the issue of leadership after the death of Chief Joseph at Nespelem on September 21, 1904. The Colville Indian Agent, Captain John McA. Webster, moved quickly to obtain Joseph's personal possessions and relics for exhibit at the Centennial Exposition in Portland.[2] Joseph's relatives beat him to the punch, holding a large ceremony that distributed everything. Webster also attended the Joseph Monument dedication ceremony, held at Nespelem on June 20, 1905. Although friendly toward Albert Waters, who was elected as successor to Chief Joseph at a council held that same day, Webster worked tirelessly to weaken and reject the idea that there even *could be* a Chief of the Nez Perce people at Nespelem. Many elders from the Clearwater, including Peo-Peo-Talikt, attended this council. This meeting seems to have done much to reinforce the divisions among the Nez Perce people that arose from the 1863 Treaty. Proponents of Yellow Bull, an old friend and ally of Joseph, spoke in his support. Many of the visitors from the Clearwater promoted the leadership of "Sub-Chief Three Feathers," from Sweetwater. By December of 1905, even the press had picked up on these old divisions, with stories appearing with headlines such as "To Dethrone Chief," and "Dethrone Walter" (i.e., "Waters").[3] These issues were unresolved at the end of the centennial era.

Several councils held at Lapwai during the years of the centennial addressed broader questions of Nez Perce life. One concern was the seeming inability of the Indian Agency to stem the pernicious influence of liquor on the Nez Perce Reservation. A bigger issue was the paternalistic approach of the Indian Agency toward the control of both land and money. Deep resentment was expressed over this control, especially where allotment land sales and rents were concerned. One result of these councils was a decision to send James Stuart and George Moses as special delegates to Washington. They were "to present certain claims to the government and will also

---

[2]See the John McA. Webster Papers at the Washington State University Library, Cage 145, Box 1.

[3]*Lewiston Morning Tribune,* December 14 and 31, 1905.

endeavor, through the aid of the Idaho Congressional delegation, to place the matter of managing their own lands before the department of Indian affairs and ultimately before congress."[4]

A Lewiston fraternal lodge associated with the Improved Order of the Red Men worked throughout 1905 to send a small Nez Perce delegation to the Portland Fair.[5] In the end, a group from the Clearwater did attend the fair on a trip organized by the local agent of the Northern Pacific Railroad. While there, they met with a larger Yakama group whose visit had been arranged by Lucullus McWhorter.

The railroad also had another impact on Nez Perce life in 1905. In a rare bit of investigative journalism, the *Lewiston Morning Tribune* reported, on August 8, 1905, on the destruction of Nez Perce graves by railroad builders working along the Snake River below Lewiston. This long article also described the systematic looting of graves at Potlatch Junction (in 1899) and of Chief Jesse's grave at the mouth of Jim Ford Creek. The article was very sympathetic to the Nez Perce cause, noting that tribal elders "were much disappointed upon learning that the law would not permit them to shoot upon the spot any person or persons detected in this [grave looting] line of work."

The celebration of the Lewis and Clark Centennial boosted the economy of the Clearwater to some small extent, but had no lasting impact on the area. Public appreciation of the area's history was not advanced in any visible way. The Nez Perce people chose not to embrace the event and instead worked to deal with their own problems and divisions. Not much progress was made there either. Instead, in the summer of 1911, a remarkable Nez Perce lawyer named Starr J. Maxwell, began a new effort to improve Nez Perce life. He collected 128 notarized statements from Nez Perce men and women which are filled with details on the many problems plaguing the Reservation. In August of that year, with the help of Senator William Borah, the Congress published this important look at Nez Perce life. [6] This book testifies to the durability of the many problems facing the Nez Perce people at the time of the Lewis and Clark Centennial.

Account 19.1: Discoveries at Canoe Camp. Source: *Lewiston Morning Tribune,* March 6, 1906.

FROM CAMP OF EXPLORERS:
RELICS OF LEWIS AND CLARK EXPOSITION ARE FOUND NEAR AHSAKHA

Discoveries made Sunday by Frank E. Parkyn, of this city, assisted by Charles Adams, a Nez Perce Indian, of Ahsakha, point almost conclusively to the spot occupied by Lewis and Clark on their memorable journey down the

---

[4]*Lewiston Morning Tribune,* February 1, 1906.

[5]The Red Men, founded in Baltimore in 1834, did not allow American Indians membership.

[6]*Memorial of the Nez Perce Indians Residing in the State of Idaho to the Congress of the United States.* 62nd Congress, 1st Session. Senate Document 97. Serial 6108. (Washington: U.S. Government Printing Office, 1911). Reprinted in 2000 by the University of Idaho Library with a new introduction by Diane Mallickan.

Clearwater river 101 years ago. The subject of the Lewis and Clark stumps, which were known to exist in the vicinity of Ahsakha, has been many times before the public, but no one was ever able to locate the place. Mr. Parkyn yesterday brought to the city several pieces of wood from an old dugout canoe found at Ahsakha, and states that there is ample evidence that the explorers made the spot across the river from that town their winter quarters and that they felled trees and hollowed them out to make canoes. Charles Adams informed Mr. Parkyn that several years ago there were remains of dugouts where the members of the party lived, but these were later plowed up.

One tree about 50 rods from the river was cut down and parts of it still remain, though badly decayed. The first section of a tree was felled, about 20 feet in length is missing, and was presumably used by the party to make a canoe to transport a part of their equipment down the river. The next section, also about 20 feet in length, is shaped like a canoe and the stern is shaped into a seat. The section was hollowed out about half the length when the work was discontinued for some reason known only to the builders. The third section was faced up with an adz preparatory to digging out the interior but beyond that had not been touched. The stumps of two trees are about 100 yards distant from the camp before they were cut down several years ago. Adams said he had dug leaden slugs out of the trees, upon which the explorers had spent the winter in practice. Lead can still be found in the stumps.

Adams told Mr. Parkyn that his grandmother had many times taken him to the spot where the white men had camped, and told him the story. He said his grandfather told him that upon the appearance of the explorers, the Indians ran and hid in the brush and would not come out for a long time. The friendly attitude of Lewis and Clark however prevailed upon them and they soon had a conference at which presents were given the Indians. Adams said that the story that the explorers were guided to the Nez Perce country is untrue for the Bannocks and the Nez Perces fought on sight and had there been any of their enemies with the party they would have been killed.

Adams declares that his grandfather contracted to take care of the horses when they departed for the coast in boats the next spring and that upon their return the following year they were found in excellent condition by Lewis and Clark. In return for the services the captains gave the old Indian a small ax and an adz. The ax has since been lost but Adams declares that he can produce the adz, which is in the family of another Indian. Another thing to substantiate the fact that the camp of the explorers has been definitely located was the finding several years ago by Ed Bremer of an old cap and ball pistol, undoubtedly the property of one of the members of the party. Mr. Bremer's farm is near the site of the old camp.

It was especially desired by Idaho people that the stumps be exhibited at the Lewis and Clark exposition and although Adams then knew the exact spot where they could be found he would not divulge it because the parties who had the matter in charge were not his friends. Mr. Parkyn and Mr. Adams will make an effort to have the relics preserved and they may be exhibited at some of the fairs this fall. The old tree and the half finished canoe are greatly decayed, but it is thought by building a frame around them they might be transported.

Account 19.2: The Testimony of Charles Adams. Source: *Lewiston Morning Tribune,* March 7, 1906.

ADAMS MAKES STATEMENT RELATIVE TO LEWIS AND CLARK AHSAHKA CAMP

The discovery of the old Lewis and Clark stumps by Frank E. Parkyn, who was led to the place by Charles Adams, has aroused considerable interest among lovers of historical relics. Mr. Parkyn is confident that the finding of the remains of

Figure 19. Charles Adams with his wife and child.

a half constructed dugout, a section missing in the tree that was felled and the facing presumably through the means of an adz, of another section, is proof that the intrepid little band of explorers under the command of Captains Lewis and Clark, spent the winter across the river from Ahsahka.

In the diary kept by the commanders it is stated that they spent the winter among the Nez Perce Indians and that they constructed dugout canoes from trees near their camp in which they paddled down the river to their destination.

The tree was chopped down fifty rods from the stream and this is another fact to substantiate the theory that white men were the builders for an Indian was never known to leave the water edge for any distance when seeking a tree for a canoe. The tree that was cut down was about three feet in diameter and the base gives the evidence of having been cut with an ax. The marks on the half built canoe show that it was hollowed out with a small ax or an adz, tools the Indians had never seen. The stump filled with lead which served as a target for the explorers, is more mute evidence that Lewis and Clark made that point their winter quarters.

Mr. Parkyn, during his visit to Ahsahka Sunday, obtained the following signed statement from Mr. Adams:

Ahsahka, Idaho. March 4, 1906.—

This certifies that I, Charles Adams, am a member of the Nez Perce tribe of Indians. I wish to state that my grandfather met and became acquainted with Messrs. Lewis and Clark when they first crossed this country in 1805, when they wintered at the mouth of the north fork of the Clearwater river.

During the stay here from the month of September until the following month of April my grandfather assisted them in many ways, especially in caring for their horses, saddles, etc.

During the winter the explorers spent some of their time in making log canoes with which to continue their journey the following season. I have this day shown Frank E. Parkyn the very tree out of which these canoes was made, also trees shot at as targets during their stay here.

When they departed the next spring they left my grandfather in charge of their horses and packsaddles until their return about a year later. At the time of their return, finding their horses and saddles all safe and well cared for, they gave my grandfather a small foot adz and an ax as a present. I can produce the identical foot adz which was at that time given to him.

I was approached by certain parties prior to the Lewis and Clark fair at Portland to assist in making an exhibition of these relics, but did not do so at that time because not approached by the right parties.

I have this day promised to assist in preserving and exhibiting these relics in company with Frank E. Parkyn for one-half of whatever profit there may be in it.

(Signed) CHARLES ADAMS (His mark)

20

Visitors along the trail

In addition to the Nez Perce people, the Lolo Trail has had many other visitors. Some of their accounts appear in this book. Most left no written account at all. A handful of visitors went on to achieve great fame and influence, and others had ties to the trail extending far into the past. Two such accounts follow.

The first comes from pioneer conservationist Bob Marshall. Marshall arrived in Idaho in 1925 as a young scientist assigned to the Priest River Experiment Station. He worked for the Forest Service until 1929, but managed to spend a good part of his time away from Priest River and deep in what are now the Clearwater and Nez Perce National Forests. He fought fire on the North Fork of the Clearwater, examined white pine in Latah County, and hiked the area around Elk Summit, Nez Perce Pass, and much of the upper Selway. Two of his trips took him along the Lolo Trail near the Powell Ranger Station.

Marshall later was employed by the Bureau of Indian Affairs, and then returned to Forest Service employment as head of recreation. He was the key figure in the establishment of the Selway-Bitterroot Primitive Area and allied himself with Howard Flint and Elers Koch in their efforts to stop excessive truck trail construction. Marshall also played a major role in the enlargement of the Idaho Primitive Area and helped stop plans to build a road from Riggins to Salmon, along the main Salmon River.

The second account, a brief one, stems from a visit in 1938 by a party of twenty people who claimed to be descendents of Lewis, Clark, and even Sacajawea. Their guide west from Lolo Pass was Walter Sewell, of Orofino, who had helped relocate the Lolo Trail after 1905. This group's bus trip started in St. Louis, and was headed for Astoria. It is not known how they happened to hire Sewell, but in him they had a uniquely well qualified guide.

Account 20.1: Bob Marshall on the Lolo Trail, 1926 and 1927. Source: Robert Marshall Papers, Bancroft Library, University of California, Berkeley. Published here with the permission of the Bancroft Library. Excerpts.

Missoula, Montana   February 25, 1926
Washington's Birthday coming on a Monday this year, I determined to make

good use of the two day vacation...after due deliberation, I determined on Lolo Pass as my destination. This is the lowest gap in the Bitterroot range, being only a trifle over 5,000 ft. in elevation...The 17 miles up to Lolo Hot Springs were pleasant, but neither especially beautiful nor interesting...the fact that I was tramping over the exact ground of the first white man to cross the Continent, and tramped over a dozen decades before, should have added a great deal of interest, but as a matter of fact, the road, and the hills, most of which had been burned long after the days of Lewis and Clark, made it thoroughly impossible for me to image myself back in the thrilling days of 1805.

There was an old, red-ramshackle hotel at the Springs, probably erected in 1887, when the place was opened as a resort. In addition, there are about 50 cabins and shacks to house the summer guests. Among these may be found approximately 49 different architectural designs and about 15 different colors. I found Ed Mackaye, the ranger with whom I was going to spend the night....

After supper, we talked until 10 o'clock. Then I took a short stroll through the snowy woods, while the moonlight streamed through. It was certainly a great contrast to the city forty miles away.

The next morning I borrowed a pair of snowshoes and started for the divide seven and a half miles away. There were not steep places, yet the rise was continual. Up here, the same trees were still standing that had shaded Lewis and

Figure 20. Bob Marshall at the Priest River Experiment Station in 1927.

Clark on their journey. With the deep snow and practically no signs of civilization, it was now not hard to drift back in imagination 120 years. Indeed, I don't believe the adventure of this intrepid expedition ever seemed quite so vivid to me as it did when I stood in the center of Lolo Pass, with a young blizzard howling and snow-buried trail leading down into the greatest forest wilderness still left in this country. True, a hundred miles across the Selway, to the Snake River Settlements would have seemed very narrow to Lewis and Clark, but today, it is the last great core of the old wilderness they traversed. It forms the very heart of the 28,000 square miles of undissected wilderness by road, of which I have previously written. In a few years, the road from Lolo Hot Springs will push through this country and cut the last great wilderness in two. I am certainly glad I had the chance of standing at its edge in mid-winter, before this wilderness is ruined forever by a highway.

Three miles to Erickson's, were covered in moonlight. The road down here was free of snow. The stroll was really delightful. Ericksons, who had never seen or heard of me before, received me like a long lost brother. He talked a couple of hours…I slept down in a cabin with old Gus Erickson. He believed in sleeping warm, and after carefully considering all possible means of ventilation, with a roaring fire in the stove. It was so hot that, though mid-winter, I threw all the covers off. I had just gotten myself adjusted to the extremely rugged topography of my bed, when the bedbugs burst out in full strength…dosing was out of the question until after midnight and the fire died down and the vermin became more sluggish. I had just about fallen asleep about two a.m., when a cat crawled over me. I hurled him halfway across the room, but he was game and came back immediately. It was about three when I taught him proper manners. After a few minutes of further adjustment, with still noticeable attacks of my bed fellows, I entered the land of Nod once more, only to be almost instantly awakened by the loud sneeze of Gus's pet dog close by my ear. I drove him off, too, and wrapped myself around the miniature Mt. Marcy, which is located in the middle of my bed, fell asleep until about an hour later, the alarm went off.

I ate an excellent breakfast and almost had to beg to make the Ericksons accept anything for board and lodging.

Missoula, Montana   January 4, 1927

I shall now take you on a trip into the Upper Locksa River, three day's snowshoeing from the edge of civilization.

I left Missoula bright and early Christmas morning, with a heavy snow falling. I took the bus as far as Lolo and then commenced my long 29 miles walk along a road almost untraveled in winter, to Lolo Hot Springs.

On Sunday, I bade goodbye to civilization…at the Lolo Ranger Station, and headed for the Bitterroot Divide, seven miles away. I was accompanied by Carl and Andrew Erickson…leading trappers of the Locksa Country.

At the divide, which is also the state line, we separated. They started out on their nine-day trappers' line, while I dropped down the Idaho side of the Bitterroots, six miles to one of Erickson's cabins, near the junction of Crooked Fork of the Locksa and Brushy Creek. Here, 13 miles from my nearest neighbor, I made myself at home and spent a comfortable evening and night.…

Monday morning I was on the trail at nine o'clock and reached my destination, a deserted Pease cabin, by 2:40 that afternoon. Here, I was 26 miles from civilization, and only 10 miles from my trapper neighbors to the West.

Figure 21. The Powell Ranger Station in 1932.

Tuesday was the only bright day I had in the Locksa country. The scenery down the 10 miles of river to Winnis cabin was fine, especially for six to eight miles where the river rushed through a deep gorge. The snow here was not nearly as deep as at the divide where there were 48 inches on the level.

The Winnis cabin stands in a burned plot. Mr. Winnis was out on his trap line, but Mrs. Winnis, who had seen none but her husband in three weeks, greeted me like a long lost uncle from Siberia. In return, I gave her their mail, the pictorial section of the latest New York Times and two pounds of candy. Then after our conversation, I set out for a little jaunt down stream. I went as far as Colgate Licks, where 40 years before the cook of a party [the Carlin party] of Eastern sportsmen had died of starvation when early snow trapped the hunters.

Returned to the Winnises and found Mr. Winnis back. Then talked almost uninterruptedly until 11:40. They certainly seemed glad of this break in their three months' isolation and treated me with the hospitality characteristic of regions beyond the frontier.

It was very pleasant to reflect, sitting by the warm fire, that I was 36 miles and three days by the closest way from the most advanced outpost of civilization; that it was 65 miles to the nearest main highway; that it was 76 miles to the closest railroad, city, electric light, pavement or doctor. Also, it was nice to realize that, to the West, the nearest settlement was 54 miles, airline, across a trailless wilderness, while both north and south, it was 100 miles to civilization.

Next morning I bade a sorrowful farewell to my kind host and hostess, never seen before, and probably never to be seen again, but for one night, my most intimate friends. Once they were out of sight, I had an insatiable desire to get back to civilization. Seven years before, I had studied in Human Traits, "Man is a gregarious animal." Certainly, I realized it now, for I dreaded the thought of three long days alone. So I determined to push through all 23 miles to Erickson's cabin, where I had spent the first night. This was foolish; and violated the cardinal principle which I find that good woodsmen adopt in regard to wilderness snowshoe travel; never go farther in a day than you can make with ease well before dark...I made Erickson's all right, but without much to spare. The snow was soft and I had much trouble with the snowshoe harness breaking in four places. It taught me a good lesson....

The evening at Erickson's was largely spent writing letters. I retired late, but was away next morning at daylight...My makeshift harness worked fine and I crossed the divide and Lolo Pass (elevation 5,233 feet) at 10:00 o'clock. On the way up, I saw my first game of the trip, a large cow elk. It was shortly after noon that I reached the Lolo Ranger Station and ended my wilderness wandering....

This trip...satisfied an old craving to trip back beyond the edge of civilization where, for a few days, I would have to depend entirely upon myself. I think this is the most healthy experience for a person brought up under most dependent conditions of society. I think also that a few days alone like that in the wilderness gives a person a worthwhile perspective of his normal surroundings...Once one had had this experience, however, I have no great desire to repeat it. It is undeniably lonely, to be by one's self in the woods in winter. A single good companion would have improved things a lot.

Account 20.2: Walter Sewell guides family members, 1938.

RETRACE STEPS OF LEWIS-CLARK

Claiming descent from members of the Lewis-Clark expedition, a party of 20 is enroute to Astoria, Ore., at the mouth of the Columbia river, over the historic route taken by their ancestors, Walter Sewell and his son, Byron, reported yesterday after returning home after a weekend spent in the Weitas meadows country, near the Montana line. In the group is a 15 year old Indian boy, who claims he is a great grandson of Sacajawea, the Indian woman who guided the Lewis-Clark party over a portion of the treacherous journey. Unlike their ancestors, who struggled over the countless miles mostly on foot and by boat, the modern expedition is traveling by bus and automobile, with signs bearing the legend: "1938 Lewis-Clark Expedition," Mr. Sewell reported. He said members informed him they were from Fort Benton, Ind., and began their trip from St. Louis.

—*Lewiston Morning Tribune,* August 18, 1938

LEWIS-CLARK DESCENDENTS RETRACE OLD TRAIL

Walter Sewell, the Daniel Boone of Idaho and Major Bowe's radio fame, and Byron Sewell, spent Saturday and Sunday on a trip to the Montana line over the Lewis-Clark trail and report meeting the "1938 Lewis-Clark Expedition" of about 20 members, all descendents of Lewis and Clark and the great grandson of Sacajawea. The party came from Fort Benton, Indiana, Mr. Sewell said, and is retracing the Lewis-Clark route from St. Louis, Missouri, to Astoria, Oregon. Their mode of transportation was two buses and they were camped on Little Weitas Meadows. Members of the party seemed to be reticent and more detailed information could not be obtained, Mr. Sewell told the Tribune.

He also reported that travelers over the old trail have destroyed numerous historic signs at Indian Postoffice, Indian Grave and General Howard's camps.

Apparently they have been taken away as souvenirs. "It is a serious act of vandalism and action should be taken to prevent this, " Mr. Sewell said.

—Orofino *Clearwater Tribune*, August 19, 1938

21

Ancient trails in modern times

The Lolo and Southern Nez Perce Trails pass through the Clearwater, Nez Perce, and Bitterroot National Forests. These forest regions are places of great beauty, with fish, wildlife, and hiking resources that attract visitors from around the world, providing recreation, solace, and quiet. But these regions are, first of all, the ancient homeland of the Nez Perce people, and it is within the context of Nez Perce culture that they perhaps can be best understood. It's especially valuable to think of traditional Nez Perce use of the trail regions in both a horizontal and a vertical context.

The areas of the Lolo and Southern Nez Perce Trails served the Nez Perce people in many ways. These trails, and others used by the Nez Perce for centuries, were pathways to the buffalo country. They were part of a complex trading system that predated the arrival of the horse. In the 18th century, these trails unfortunately served as paths for the arrival of measles, smallpox, and other diseases.

The trails and the regions which they traversed were more than just places for routes and pathways. Pilot Knob, on the Nez Perce National Forest, was (and still is) a major religious site, as was Coolwater Ridge. Similar spiritual sites exist along much of the Lolo Trail, and also along the route of the Southern Trail. The importance and role of these places is rarely understood. In earlier times, when the Nez Perce population was greater, these mountain regions were also the permanent home for unknown numbers of people. Just as some people today live in the mountains, so too in ancient times there were those who did not leave the high country.

The lands along the trails also played a major role in the traditional food gathering systems of the Nez Perce people and are a key feature of the seasonal round of Nez Perce life. Young Albert (Parsons) Mallickan, who is buried along the Lolo Trail, was in the area hunting and gathering berries with his family when he died in 1895. This same family had long historical ties to the ancient Nez Perce villages that once existed far up the Selway River. Today many Nez Perce families still engage in the same activities.

None of these uses stopped after the 1863 Treaty was signed, and none stopped after Joseph and his people crossed the Lolo Trail in 1877. None stopped when the ancient trails were, in part, transformed into motorways after 1930. The trail areas are not only the aboriginal territory of the Nez Perce, but were retained, kept, and held on to regardless of each treaty. On horse, foot, and in cars, the Nez Perce people of today still use these remote regions of the Clearwater and Nez Perce National Forests as did their ancestors.

There is little statistical evidence to support this assertion, but many anecdotal accounts exist. Probably the best example is that of the family of Elizabeth Wilson, who gathered camas and other forest resources at Musselshell Meadows into the 1960s. The great Nez Perce historian, Allen Slickpoo, tells stories of his family's use of the Lolo Trail region and of Meadow Creek, near Selway Falls. Geologist John Leiberg photographed a Nez Perce family's camp at Nez Perce Pass in 1897 and called the remnant Southern Nez Perce Trail a "highway." On August 24, 1906, the Pierce City *Miner* newspaper noted the presence at the south end of town of a very large camp of Nez Perce families. Some Nez Perce families have closer ties to these places than others, and use is neither universal nor at the same scale as in the past. But neither trail was ever lost to the Nez Perce people, and neither place ever needed rediscovering by them. Instead, several key Nez Perce men and women, all with a remarkable knowledge of the past, were to play a major role in the mapping of the trails by the Forest Service, the Northern Pacific Railroad, and others working to understand the history of the Nez Perce country.

The government wagon road project led by Dr. Wellington Bird and Sewell Truax in 1865-67 had along as paid guides William Craig, a famous "mountain man" married into a prominent Nez Perce family, and a Nez Perce man, Ta-tu-tash (sometimes spelled Taha-tu-tash), about whom little is known.

Another Nez Perce man played a key role as a cultural and historical informant for anthropologist and allotment agent Alice Fletcher. His name was Jonathan Williams, also known as Billy Williams or Ku-ku-loo-ya (Kew-kew'-lu-yah). He was an ordained elder of the First Kamiah Church. He was probably born around 1815 at Te-sy'yak-poo, an important Nez Perce fishing village located east of Kamiah on the Clearwater. He was a respected and highly informed historian when Dr. Fletcher interviewed him over the course of several days in June of 1891. His work with Fletcher has left us with a detailed map, a rich oral history account, and detailed information on over 75 village sites.[1] It would be hard to overestimate the value of this collaboration between Williams and Fletcher.

In 1897, President Grover Cleveland proclaimed the establishment of the 4.1 million acre Bitterroot Forest Reserve, thus setting aside from most forms of settlement much of the mountainous home of the Nez Perce people. The most influential early leader of this forest was Major Frank Fenn. Fenn had come to Idaho in the 1862-63 mining rush, and fought in the 1877 Nez Perce War. Under his leadership, two Nez Perce men came to play an important role in the early

---

[1]For more information on this important man, see: Kate C. McBeth, *The Nez Perces Since Lewis and Clark* (New York: F.H. Revell, 1908), 234-43, and Robert Lee Sappington, "Alice Cunningham Fletcher's 'The Nez Perce Country'," *Northwest Anthropological Research Notes* 29, no. 2 (Fall 1995): 177-213.

management of this forest. They were James Stuart (occasionally spelled Stewart) and Charles Adams.

Stuart was the son of an influential Nez Perce woman, Susan Corbett, and had been educated at the Chimawe Indian School at Salem, Oregon. By 1889, he was employed by Alice Fletcher in her work on allotments, and served as driver and translator for her. He was present in this latter role during the 1891 interviews with Billy Williams. It's unclear just how much of the great value of these interviews can be attributed to Williams, and how much to Stuart. Stuart was later employed by Major Fenn in trail construction work, managing a large crew composed entirely of Nez Perce men. He also served the Forest Service as a surveyor and engineer. In 1906, the Nez Perce Tribe sent him to Washington to lobby on behalf of tribal issues.

In 1902, Stuart also served as a guide and key cultural resource for Olin D. Wheeler, an employee of the publicity branch of the Northern Pacific Railroad. Much of the information on Nez Perce life that appears in Wheeler's two volume study of Lewis and Clark's travels can be attributed to Stuart. It was also Stuart who took Wheeler down into Hungery Creek to examine the ancient trail system located there.

After 1905, federal money became available for trail work on the Bitterroot Reserve, and shortly thereafter, management was transferred to the newly-established Forest Service and the Clearwater, Selway, and Nez Perce National Forests were established. Major Fenn chose to spend some of this money clearing and remarking the Lolo Trail, and hired several men to do the work. Walter Sewell and Charles Adams were two of these employees.

Adams is generally believed to have been a grandson of Twisted Hair, the Nez Perce chief who played such an important a role in the visits of Lewis and Clark to the Clearwater.[2] He may also have been a scout for General Howard in the 1877 war (the roster of scouts includes a man named Charlie Tlitl kim). In any case, Adams possessed a great practical knowledge of the lands east of Lolo Creek, and of the Lolo Trail in particular. This knowledge proved valuable to Major Fenn, who hired him to work for the Forest Service. Fenn also hired Walter Sewell, who worked directly with Adams for many years. Only a few detailed stories of Adams' expertise survive. Ralph Space, in his book *The Clearwater Story*, tells us that "Charles Adams, grandson of Twistedhair, once told Walter Sewell that the Indians built the mounds [the cairns at Indian Post Office and elsewhere] to mark the place where the Lolo Trail turned off the divide. He also stated that the Indians had no means of conveying messages by stones other than pure directional."

Sewell, the self-styled "Daniel Boone of Idaho," was born about 1880 and came to the Clearwater region in 1903, working as a miner before joining the Forest Service. One of his first jobs was to mark out and clear the Lolo Trail route, which he did with the help and labor of Charlie Adams. Sewell quickly came to appreciate Adams'

---

[2]Members of the Lawyer family have always contended that they were descendents of Twisted Hair. For more information, see: J.F. Santee, "Lawyer of the Nez Perces," *Washington Historical Quarterly* 25 (January 1934), 37-48; Mylie Lawyer, "Chief Termed 'Noblest Man'," *Lewiston Morning Tribune*, June 12, 1955; and Mylie Lawyer, "How it Happened," *Lewiston Morning Tribune,* February 23, 2003.

Figure 22. Rev. William Wheeler with his second wife and child, April 1891.

cultural and geographic expertise, and acknowledged it in several advertising booklets that he later published. For his part, Adams was attracted by the amazing skills that Sewell had in talking to and luring in animals of all types. Taught by his mother, Sewell regularly demonstrated his skills at communicating with animals, a power greatly appreciated by Adams and other Forest Service employees. Sewell also brought this skill to several nationally broadcast radio programs.

Sewell chose to pass on the knowledge of the Lolo Trail region obtained from Adams, and from about 1935 onwards, worked with Clearwater Valley historian Zoa Swayne to locate old trails and camps in the region. In 1945, for instance, the two spent several days after gas rationing ended exploring the high country east of Musselshell. Sewell also ran a camp at Warm Lake for eastern youth, and guided many prominent visitors around the Clearwater region. For many years, Sewell also ran a barbershop in Orofino.

Swayne also had a second, and more direct, source of information with which to work: her close friendship with the leading Nez Perce elders and historians of the pre-World War II generation. These included David J. Miles and his wife Beatrice, as well as Rev. Harry Wheeler and his wife Ida. Wheeler, born in 1884, was the son of another Presbyterian minister, the Rev. William Wheeler. The Wheeler family came from Ahsakha, and William Wheeler was probably the son of one of the young men who watched over the horses of Lewis and Clark while they went down the Columbia. Harry Wheeler was on the tribal council in the 1930s and 1940s. These and other families were good friends of Swayne and regular visitors to her home. She regularly corresponded with them and with other Nez Perce families, and recorded several lengthy historical interviews with them after World War II. There were also frequent field trips to examine sites, and Wheeler shared his family's knowledge of various Lolo Trail stories. Among them was the important tale of the young Nez Perce boy who was carried along the trail by a grizzly bear, which shared with the child all its knowledge of the area. Swayne worked with these wonderful sources of traditional knowledge of the Clearwater and her personal knowledge of the Lolo Trail to produce her 1990 book, *Do Them*

Figure 23. Mr. and Mrs. Harry Wheeler in May, 1957.

Figure 24.Waldemar Lindgren's 1902 drawing from Rocky Ridge.

No Harm. This is a fictionalized history of the encounters between the Nez Perce people and Lewis and Clark. Swayne acknowledges her debt to Nez Perce elders in this book, but chose a citation method that credits these sources incompletely.

For her part, Swayne chose to be a bridge to later investigators of the history of the Clearwater region. She spent much time in the field with Ralph Space. Space was Supervisor of the Clearwater National Forest and came from a pioneer Weippe Prairie family. He later wrote an important history of the Lolo Trail, as well as the standard history of the Clearwater National Forest. Both books are still in print, and include photos taken by Zoa Swayne.

The General Land Office began formal surveys of the reduced Nez Perce Reservation not long after the 1863 Treaty was ratified. These manuscript survey maps provide a rich and little used source of information about trail locations and cultural sites, but do not cover areas east of Weippe. The first serious survey of the Lolo Trail region was conducted for the United States Geological Survey by botanist John B. Leiberg in 1897. His report on the Idaho portion of the Bitterroot Forest Reserve was published in part five of the U.S. Geological Survey's *Twentieth Annual Report,* printed by the Government Printing Office in 1900.

Leiberg was a remarkably observant scientist and possessed the skills to analyze fire ecology patterns far in advance of most scholars of the time. His maps of the Bitterroot contain useful trail information and remain valuable to historical ecologists even today. They also provide key base information about fire and vegetation patterns in the Bitterroots.

Figure 25. Lindgren's 1898 photo of Packer Meadow near Lolo Pass.

Two years later, a second U.S.G.S. employee, Waldemar Lindgren, spent a summer exploring the Clearwater Mountains. His report, *A Geological Reconnaissance Across the Bitterroot Range and Clearwater Mountains in Montana and Idaho* was published by the Geological Survey in 1904 as *Professional Paper 27.*

The Lindgren report contains an especially clear map of the routes of the Lolo and Southern Trails, and some fine photographs. Other photos were taken for this book, but not used; many are still in the Survey's collections. The report also includes an attractive drawing of the view north of Rocky Ridge Lake, and a large amount of geologic data and descriptions. The research for this report is the basis of the earliest topographic maps produced for the Clearwater region. Lindgren was a highly respected geologist and wrote many other studies for the Geological Survey.

Another powerful force was also at work in the Clearwater during this same time period—the Northern Pacific Railroad. Some of their early exploration accounts appear elsewhere in this book, but after 1900, the railroad's public relations department began to take an interest in the Clearwater. The firm's magazine, *Wonderland*, was edited by a Minnesota resident named Olin D. Wheeler. This magazine had always promoted tourism in the West, including historical tourism. Its editor also had broad experience in the region, having worked as a topographer with John Wesley Powell. With the Lewis and Clark centennial approaching, Wheeler spent the summer of 1902 on a long visit to the Clearwater after two earlier trips at either end of the Lolo Trail. He was aided by James Stuart and guided by William H. Wright, a famed bear hunter and packer. Artist and photographer Ralph E. DeCamp was also along on this trip.

Wheeler's two volume set of books on the route of Lewis and Clark was published by Putnam in 1904. It is rich in cultural and historical insights on the Clearwater, and contains some important photos of the Weippe Prairie, the site of Long Camp, and Weitas Meadows. The volumes are the foundation and starting point for all the later efforts at relocating and marking the Lolo Trail.

At the end of the First World War, two other men took up the task of research on Lewis and Clark's route. The first of them was Clearwater County Assessor John P. Harlan, who worked with Weippe packer Chub Wilson.

By the early 1920's, large parts of Clearwater County had been transferred from the public domain into private ownership, often by fraudulent means. Most of this land ended up in the hands of firms linked to the Weyerhaeuser family, which had moved to the Pacific Northwest after stripping the timber from the cutover lands of Michigan, Wisconsin, and Minnesota. One of Harlan's jobs was to evaluate this land for tax purposes, but an early date, he chose to incorporate historical research into his assessment pack trips. He carried with him the 1904 edition of the journals of Lewis and Clark, and was one of the first researchers to try to seriously link the journal accounts to the land.

In the autumn of 1921, after an especially long and productive summer field season, Harlan published the results of his exploration. These appeared in two weekly newspapers, the *Clearwater Republican* (Orofino) and the *Press-Times* (Wallace). These accounts are full of insights and important observations about the trails and the inhabitants of the region. They remain today an essential resource for understanding the history of the Clearwater region, and they also provided a starting point for later researchers such as Zoa Swayne, Ralph Space, Andy Arvish, and Gene and Mollie Eastman.

The other researcher to enter the field after the end of World War I was Elers Koch. Koch was born in Bozeman, Montana in 1880. As a young graduate of Montana State College, he met famed forester Gifford Pinchot. This meeting led Koch to Yale University, where he earned an M.S. in forestry in 1903. He immediately joined the Bureau of Forestry (later the Forest Service) and in 1906 was named Supervisor of the combined Lolo, Bitterroot, and Missoula National Forests. In 1921, he became Assistant Regional Forester for the Northern Region, based in Missoula. He held this position until his retirement in 1944.

Koch had a rich career as a forest manager. He was an expert in white pine silviculture and a pioneer of Forest Service tree nursery work. He played an important role in fighting the great forest fires of 1910 and wrote the first serious history of those fires. He also helped formulate fire management policies after 1930.

The Koch home also played host to an amazing number of friends and visitors. These included historian Elliot Coues, conservationist and forester Bob Marshall, pioneer aviator Howard Flint, and the official photographer for the Northern Region, K.D. Swan. Writers Norman Maclean and Bernard DeVoto were also his good friends. Koch was, in addition, a famed hiker and mountaineer, and expert with snow shoes as well. Those interests, plus his work in fire management, frequently took him to the Lolo Trail country. Like many well-educated men of his time, he took a personal interest in history. He often gave historical talks to Missoula civic clubs, and as early as 1925, the theme was the Lolo Trail. In all, he spent a quarter century researching the history of this region.

Koch published three articles about the Lolo Trail. All have lasting value and offer useful insights even today. Excerpts from two of them appear in this book. The first of these, "The Passing of the Lolo Trail," appeared in the *Journal of Forestry* in February of 1935. Writing about the Lolo Trail region rather broadly interpreted, Koch asked, and answered, two important questions. Were the permanent roads being built by the Civilian Conservation Corps into the back country a good idea? Were forest fires in such steep, remote, and dry places as the Lochsa and Selway country even worth fighting? In Koch's mind, the answer was no. Instead, Koch argued, these places should be left wild. Fighting fires here was not cost effective. Koch felt that the Lolo Trail had been turned into a road with no real gain for society.

This kind of thinking was not popular in the Forest Service of the 1930's, and publication of these ideas did nothing to advance Koch's career. But two causes *were* advanced with help from this article. Just one year later, Regional Forester Evan Kelley caved into relentless pressure from Bob Marshall and allowed the 1.8 million acre Selway-Bitterroot Primitive Area to be established. Soon after, Marshall's other Idaho goal, the enlargement of the Idaho Primitive Area, was achieved.

The *Oregon Historical Quarterly* published the other important Koch article in June of 1940. It was called "Lewis and Clark Route Retraced Across the Bitterroots." In this article, Koch summarized a lifetime of field work and research on the history of the Lolo Trail. This article is a detailed look at camps and routes, and includes a valuable map. Koch also had available Olin Wheeler's study and the Coues edition of the Lewis and Clark journals. An excerpt from this article appears in this chapter. The research used to develop this article was also used in the signing and trail marking effort that began in 1933.

Serious efforts to map, mark, and manage the trails didn't resume again until the decade of the 1960s. Two men led these efforts along the Lolo Trail: John Peebles, an engineering professor at the University of Idaho, and Ralph Space, who was a Weippe native who served as Supervisor of the Clearwater National Forest from 1954 to 1963.

The exact details of Peebles' field work have been lost, but it's clear that he spent a considerable amount of time on the Lolo Trail. The results of his work appeared in two long articles that were published (accompanied by a detailed map) in *Idaho Yesterdays* (Summer 1964 and Summer 1966). Peebles was especially precise in explaining where he felt his data was clear, and where it was not.

Ralph Space began serious research along the Lolo Trail shortly after his retirement. He published a small book on Lewis and Clark in 1963, compiled his detailed notes on this topic in 1965, and in 1970 published his fine history of the Lolo Trail. This book, *The Lolo Trail: A History of Events Connected with the Lolo Trail Since Lewis and Clark,* was reprinted several times between 1970 and 1988, and as an edited version in 2001. While it contains some errors, it still remains to be a valuable guide to the history of the Lolo Trail region.

Space was given important assistance in his work by many individuals. Nez Perce elder Corbett Lawyer provided him with a valuable map showing historic sites and trails on the Weippe Prairie. Zoa Swayne helped with photographic work and shared her vast knowledge of the area's culture. Two employees of the Clearwater National Forest, Robert Schloss and Andy Arvish, were also especially helpful. Both men spent a considerable amount of time in the field. Schloss helped name some new sites related to Lewis and Clark, and Arvish produced an extremely detailed set of maps locating historic trails.[3] Arvish was also the author of a very useful brochure and map guide published by the Forest Service in 1971 called *Following Lewis and Clark Across the Clearwater National Forest,* which served as the core research in establishing the Lolo Trail National Historic Landmark.

The region east of Elk City is known as the Magruder Corridor and much of it was set aside as Wilderness due to the efforts of conservationists Doris Milner and Morton Brigham. The Southern Nez Perce Trail passes through this high and remote region, which is more wild and much less modified by man than the Lolo Trail region. As can be seen from reading other parts of this book, the Southern Trail region has a rich history of human use over a very long period of time. Beginning in the 1960s, some efforts have been made to understand the general history of this beautiful region, and also to locate the original Southern Nez Perce Trail.

Two histories of this part of Nez Perce country exist. The first is William Cunningham's thoroughly researched 1968 University of Montana M.S. Thesis, *The Magruder Corridor Controversy: A Case History.* Cunningham, who went on to become a leader in Montana conservation and wilderness efforts, chiefly addresses land allocation questions. By using important primary sources, this thesis also looks at the broader history of the corridor, including trails and the construction of the Darby-Red River road.

A more anecdotal approach was taken by two Forest Service employees, O. Frank Schumaker and James E. Dewey, who worked, respectively, for the Bitterroot and Nez Perce National Forests. Their small 1970 study, *A History of the Salmon River Breaks Primitive Area*, is a valuable look at the people of the corridor and their impact on the land.

The pioneering work in trying to map the ancient Southern Trail was done in the early 1960s by two Montana men. One was Hamilton photographer Ernst Peterson. The other was the Supervisor of the Bitterroot National Forest, Harold E. Andersen. The two worked with many early written descriptions of the Southern Trail, especially Samuel Parker's 1835 journal (reprinted elsewhere in this book). They also spent many days in the field trying to match these journal accounts to the land. The result was their thorough 1966 article in *Montana: the Magazine of Western History*, cited below.

The Southern Trail was also the subject of another University of Montana thesis, the 1996 M.A. Thesis of Michael H. Koeppen. Koeppen's research, done chiefly in

---

[3]Reprinted in Gene and Mollie Eastman, *Bitterroot Crossing,* Pp. 21-26.

Figure 26. Ralph Space on the trail to the Sinque Hole, about 1960.

the field, focused on the eastern portion of the trail, from the valley of the Little Clearwater River east to Nez Perce Pass. Koeppen located extensive trail tread remnants, dozens of culturally modified trees, and some ancient camp spots.

Improved technology has come into play in the past decade, with most of the serious field and archival research being focused on the Lolo Trail corridor. One of the leading researchers has been Steve Russell, an Idaho native and professor of electrical engineering at Iowa State University. Russell has coupled extensive field work with the use of modern GPS technology. Only partial results of his work have been published.

Similar technology has been used by Gene and Mollie Eastman, longtime residents of Weippe, where Gene Eastman also served many years as Conservation Officer. The Eastmans have also invested several thousand hours of field time, and have been especially adept at incorporating rare written resources, as well as air photo and cartographic sources into their research. *Bitterroot Crossing*, the first of three planned volumes of Lolo Trail history, was published in 2002. Their findings sometimes diverge from the tentative conclusions reported to date by Russell.

Despite all of these substantial efforts at mapping and location, our knowledge of the ancient trail system of the Nez Perce people remains incomplete and fragmentary. Because of that, many students of these trails have argued for special care and caution in the management of the public lands along the trails. Preservation, rather than mitigation, has become a concern.

Further reading:

Robert G. Bailey, *The River of No Return* (Lewiston: R.G. Bailey Printing, 1935-47).

A version of the important 1940 article by Elers Koch appears at 73-88.

William P. Cunningham, *The Magruder Corridor Controversy: A Case History.* (M.S. Thesis, University of Montana, 1968).

A thorough history of the corridor based on key primary sources.

Gene and Mollie Eastman, *Bitterroot Crossing: Lewis & Clark Across the Lolo Trail* (Moscow: University of Idaho Library, 2002).

A reliable history of the mapping, modification, and rediscovery of the trail.

Michael Howard Koeppen, *An Examination and Mapping of the Southern Nez Perce Trail in the Selway-Bitterroot Wilderness, Bitterroot National Forest, Idaho Using the Global Positioning System* (M.A. Thesis, University of Montana,1996).

A thorough look at the eastern half of the South Nez Perce Trail.

Kirby Lambert, "Through the Artist's Eye: The Paintings and Photographs of R.E.DeCamp," *Montana: The Magazine of Western History* 49, no. 2 (Summer 1999): 38-49.

A biography of an early (1902) photographer of the Lolo Trail.

Ernst Peterson, "Retracing the Southern Nez Perce Trail With Rev. Samuel Parker," *Montana: The Magazine of Western History* 16, no. 4 (Autumn 1966): 12-27.

Describes the first serious effort to relocate the old Nez Perce trail.

Steve F. Russell, "The Riddle of Hungery Creek, September 18-20, 1805, and June 16,18, 25, 1806," *Idaho Yesterdays* 44 (Spring 2000): 25-31.

Presents the author's version of the confusing route in Fish and Hungery Creek.

Sage Notes, 21, no. 4 (Fall 1999).

A special issue of the magazine of the Idaho Native Plant Society devoted entirely to the life and work of John B. Leiberg. A great job of research.

O. Frank Schumaker and Jim Dewey, *A History of the Salmon River Breaks Primitive Area* (Hamilton: Bitterroot National Forest, 1970)

An anecdotal history of an area later incorporated into the Frank Church-River of No Return Wilderness Area.

Ralph S. Space, *The Lolo Trail: A History of Events Connected with the Lolo Trail Since Lewis and Clark* (Lewiston: Printcraft, 1970).

Summarizes the work of a lifetime of research on the Lolo Trail.

Zoa Swayne, *Do them no harm!: an Interpretation of the Lewis and Clark Expedition Among the Nez Perce Indians* (Caldwell: Caxton, 2003).

Olin D. Wheeler, "One Hundred and Fifty Miles with a Pack Train," *Wonderland 1903*:71-86.

A detailed and fully illustrated (DeCamp photos) account of Wheeler's important 1902 Lolo Trail trip to Weitas Meadows and Rocky Ridge.

Account 21.1: Excerpts from the report of John B. Leiberg in 1897. Source: *The Bitterroot Forest Reserve,* In U.S. Geological Survey, *Twentieth Annual Report, 1898-99.* Pt. 5. (Washington: U.S. Government Printing Office, 1900), 317-409.

The forest fires which have ravaged the Clearwater and Salmon river basins fall naturally, as to time, into two periods, namely, those that occurred during the Indian occupancy of the country and those that have originated since the coming of the white man. The extent of the former can best be learned by examining the stands of second-growth forest. The tracts covered by these comprise in the aggregate 1,110,000 acres and are of all ages from 75 to 175 years. It is certain that this much, at least, represents one complete cycle of burns during 200 years of Indian occupancy [and examining other forest types] there is to be charged to the last two hundred years of Indian occupancy a total of 2,270,000 acres burned forest, assuming that fires due to Indians ceased thirty-five years ago.

The white man came in force into the region thirty-five or forty years ago. Destructive conflagrations have invariably followed in his wake. There are no large portions of either the Clearwater or the Salmon river basins but show some evidence of fires of recent date....

If an average is struck, based upon the number of years included in above estimates, it will be found that during the Indian occupancy there were fire losses of 11,350 acres per annum, while during the time that the white man has been in possession 35,000 acres per annum have been destroyed, or a yearly average 300 per cent greater....

From time immemorial the Indians had three trails from west to east across the region now embraced within the limits of the Bitterroot Reserve. Two of these trails were used for through travel between the Rocky Mountain regions and the Plains of the Columbia. These trails were what are now known as the Lolo and the Nez Perces trails. The former was a northern route, the latter a southern. The third trail extended eastward to the summit of the Bitterroot Mountains and was used principally as a hunting trail. Its course was along the crest of the Lochsa-Selway divide [Coolwater Ridge], and as it ran through the heart of the game region in the Clearwater basins must have been very largely traveled. Most of the fires that can be traced to Indian occupancy appear to have originated along the lines of these trails. Almost the entire forest adjoining is second growth, and the areas known as "Bald Mountains," grassy southern slopes long since deforested by fires, are also confined to the tracts traversed by these routes.

It is difficult to state with absolute certainty the reason why the Indians burned the forest. An educated Nez Percé, with whom I conversed regarding the matter, stated that forest fires were never started through design, but might have accidentally spread from signal fires kindled by different bands or individuals while on the hunt, that they might know the whereabouts of one another. The probability is that many fires spread from their camps and others were set purposely to destroy the forest and encourage the grass growth. This latter seems to have been the case in the alpine-fir type of forest along their trails, where now occur so many of the bald or grassy mountain slopes. It is a well-known fact that deer and elk exhibit a special liking for tracts freshly burned, due to the profuse growth of various kinds of weeds springing up there, which constitute a favorite browse for them. Large tracts of forest doubtless were burned with intent of thus, causing the game to congregate in considerable numbers in some particular localities.

Account 21.2: Excerpts from Olin D. Wheeler's study of the route of Lewis and Clark. Source: Olin D. Wheeler, *The Trail of Lewis and Clark, 1804-1904, Vol. 2* (New York: Putnam, 1904), 278-80.

Wheeler and his party are following Lewis and Clark's route eastward from Camp Chopunnish (Long Camp), located across the river from Kamiah.

It was with great interest that, with Messrs. DeCamp and Wright, I followed this old trail in the summer of 1902. After reaching the divide we travelled for a mile across a pine and tamarack tree country, which is being gradually cleared by settlers, and then began the descent to the crossing of Lolo—Collins—Creek. The old trail and a modern wagon road had been more or less commingled, but now the road disappeared and we followed the fine old Indian trail, wide, plain, and deep, three feet or more at places, winding down through the forest and along the mountain side in the usual sharp, zigzag fashion.[4] At last we reached the creek, a clear, rushing stream thirty feet wide and knee-deep, in a wild, secluded pocket in the mountains and forming a beautiful camping spot. Other visitors had just arrived. A fine-looking Nez Percé Indian; his comely squaw and her mother, perhaps; a black-headed, black-eyed youngster, five or six years old and stark naked, and a tiny miss clad in a very dirty calico shift, were there. About a little fire the women were preparing a noon-day meal. To the young squaw's credit be it told, she carefully washed her hands and face at the border of the stream before beginning her culinary duties.

After some bantering conversation back and forth, we climbed slowly out of the canon, over a hard, tiresome trail, and then, down a gentle grade through the deep, cool forest, made our way to the eastern edge of Weippe Prairie, where we bivouacked for the night under a pine tree in a forty acre pasture.

Like the Three Forks of the Missouri, Weippe Prairie was a converging point for trails from all directions. Here at the western extremity of the big trail across the mountains the Indian roads centered, and here to-day traces of them may yet be seen.

---

[4]Crossing Lolo Creek near Incendiary Creek. This trail is still visible on the Kamiah side.

The Weippe Prairie is a wide, level stretch of country watered by the Jim Ford Creek, a very sluggish one, which flows to the north and into the main Kooskooskee River. Grain, including winter wheat, and the hardier vegetables, grow luxuriantly, but melons, cucumbers, etc. have not yet been successfully cultivated.

The settling up and fencing in of the prairie have resulted in the obliteration, to a great extent, of the old trails. Two of them I learned upon inquiry came together near our camp and continued eastward along the edge of the timber. One of these was the trail followed by Lewis and Clark and by us also.

Up on the succeeding day, early in the morning. As we were proceeding mountainward [toward Musselshell and then on to Rocky Ridge and Weitas Meadow], we saw "a point of woods" that exactly fitted the description of the place where Lewis and Clark had camped, and which I doubt not was the spot.

Lewis and Clark remained at their Weippe camp from June 10th to 15th [1806]. In the meantime they sent one of the Fields brothers and Willard forward "eight miles to a prairie on this side of Collins [Lolo] Creek, with orders to hunt till our arrival." Dr. Coues [the editor of the best version of Lewis and Clark's journals then available] mistakenly supposed that this was Weippe Prairie. It may have been a prairie on either Brown Creek or Musselshell Creek. These streams are not far apart and there is a beautiful clearing on each stream, either of which meets the meager description given by the explorers.

Figure 27. Olin Wheeler's 1902 camp at Weitas Meadow.

Figure 28. A possible Lewis and Clark campsite on the Weippe Prairie in 1902.

Account 21.3: Clearwater County Assessor John Harlan's description of the Weippe Prairie. Source: Orofino *Clearwater Republican*, 11 November 1921.

Weippe has always been a beautiful situation with sublime scenic surroundings. It had long been a gathering place for the Nez Perces before the advent of the Lewis and Clark expedition, and even long before the coming of the horse among them, when the women were mostly the burden bearers.

It was the most prolific kamas field in all their habitat. The Nez Perces tell me the fields in the regions of Moscow were the first to be frequented, for Kamas was ready to gather here earlier in the season than elsewhere, but Weippe and vicinity was where they made their last and greatest harvest.[5] Some of the older Nez Perce women tell me they have dug kamas in many places. They say it was a hard days task to dig two fair sized baskets full in the regions of Moscow, but at Weippe they could easily fill four and five of the same baskets in a day.

The old fashioned kamas digger used by them was a flattened stick of the thorn, and a piece of elk horn with a rectangular hole mortised in the center of it which fit over one end of the thorn stick. This handle devise was carried with them from place to place, the stick could be procured at the field.

---

[5]The camas grounds at Moscow were located just south of town, along the South Fork of the Palouse River, a stream that early cartographers called Smokodol. This is the Salish word, S'maqw'l. Some Coeur d'Alene linguists believe that this word is the origin of the modern name of the town. Moscow also has a very pretty Nez Perce name. It is Tuxtinmapa, the place of the spotted fawn.

In later years this prairie also became a favorite play ground for them, where much pony racing was indulged in and gambling and betting ran wild. At these big gatherings it was no uncommon thing for an Indian to bet everything he possessed from his cayuse to his clothes. Among other tribes of the Northwest I have seen Indian men lose their clothes by betting on their favorite horse, and mingle with the crowd wearing nothing but a breechclout and a grim smile. And they would get some hard calling down from their women.

Today Weippe prairie is still the same beautiful location it always was, with many prosperous farm homes, where much hay, grain, and stock is raised. The immediate meadow has about 3000 acres under cultivation. The elevation is 3000 feet. The climate is good and the change of seasons about properly balanced. At the northern end of the prairie, close to where Lewis and Clark camped, is the village of Weippe with a store, post office and meat market, pool hall and blacksmith shop, and a fine Rural High School. It is fifteen miles from the railroad on a State Highway running from Greer on the railroad, through Pierce to the Bungalow on the North Fork river. There are numerous good roads about the locality.

This prairie was even larger at the time of Lewis and Clark than now; owing to the fact that the Indians kept the surrounding land well burned off, and much of the timber, particularly the jack pine, now seen growing, was not growing then. There were numerous long narrow meadows then branching off from the main meadow, and open grass land has been almost closed over by more recent timber growth. Adjacent to this to the north and east was a fine stand and thrifty growth of white pine, cedar, tamarack, and red and white fir. Immediately, after the advent of Lewis and Clark, a forest fire got into this fine timber belt to the northeast of Weippe, and destroyed a large body of it. A large part of this stand of timber in still growing in the regions of Brown's, Musselshell, and the Lolo creek basins. Lewis and Clark spoke of this timber. It is now some of the best in the state.[6]

Many have asked me the meaning of the word Weippe. I have asked many others both Indian and whites. All the Indians have said the same thing, "it has no meaning." It is a name only, just as we had names for other places and for the streams and the animals. Many of the whites versed in the Nez Perce language say the same thing. But some of the whites tell me it has a meaning. They say Weippe means a low beautiful valley. This does not belie the facts, but it might be fitting the facts to the name. The Indians used the name for the place long before any whites came among them. They tell of a mythological White Bear that named some of the places, streams and mountains. Miss Kate McBeth relates many of their myths in her book "The Nez Perces after Lewis and Clark." But she did not relate the myth of the Grizzly Bear.

Our Nez Perce friends are a people full of folk-lore and have many old traditions. They told their children fireside tales just as all other races have done. At one time they believed in myths. They would relate their many different myths of the animals and birds who held dominion over the Earth before the real people (the Nim-e-poo) came. These tales were passed on from generation to generation. I will relate their myth of the Grizzly Bear.

---

[6]It was clearcut in the 1950's.

Long, long ago in the period of transition of the dominions of the Earth from the animals to the Nim-e-poo, when these first people pushed their canoes up the Kooskooskee (Clearwater) and made settlement at Kamiah and other places along its course, a boy became lost from his people and in his wanderings met Ha-ha-ats, the grizzly bear. Now the grizzly knew of the coming of the people to supplant the animals. Itsi-ya-yai, the coyote, who was the ruler and wisest of the animals, had told him; for the animals of this time had the gift of speech. This information made Ha-ha-ats very wroth, for he loved the domain over which he roamed, and his great strength and fierce disposition and ill temper made it hard for him to pass it over. When he met this boy for the first time, who was one of the progeny of the Nim-e-poo he flew into a towering rage. He raised on his hind feet to a crouching position, his neck stretched out, his ears laid back, his nose turned up by a snarling lip, his teeth gleaming, his mouth driveling foam, his eyes glowering with intense hate, his powerful arms with long protruding claws were raised to strike and with hoarse guttural growls and short gasping pants which shook his sides and chest, causing the mountains to quake in sympathetic vibrations he advanced upon this boy with the intent of sudden destruction.

"So you are of the people who would rob me of my domains. I can crush you with a single blow. I shall devour you," roared Ha-ha-ats. But this Indian boy never flinched nor quavered as he replied "I can but die—death is only the last change in the phase of life. I have no fear."

When Ha-ha-ats heard these indifferent words and saw the brave attitude of this boy, his rage subsided and he relented from his purpose of destruction. He viewed the boy in calm surprise mingled with admiration. "Surely," he said, "you are of a different type of being than the animals, for they would have cowered in abject terror. You have the daring courage of my tribe, the shrewd wisdom of Itsi-ya-yai, the coyote; the proud bearing of He-yume, the Eagle. Now do I know our sun is set. You are of a race worthy to succeed to these dominions. [Gladly will I show you over my domains."

So saying he tossed the boy upon his broad furry back and hied him away to the mountains, where he cared for him and feasted him on many different foods from nature's store house, and showed him where and how to find them.

Showed he him the home of Tsu-schrlim, the buffalo, over and across the mountains, then returning, named he many of the rivers and creeks. Sol-weh (the Selway), Ah-sah-ka (the North Fork), Naw-weh (Lolo creek), Taw-weh (Orofino creek), You-sha (Elk creek), Mish-ah (Ford's creek), Loch-sa and Kami-ah, names not changed, and many others.

Then showed he him the dark pools and purling rapids, and pebbly riffles of these crystal waters, where sported and splashed Naw-tsoh, the salmon, then went they through the favorite haunts of Woo-ke-eh, the elk, Sarch-lochsa, the moose, and Im-mish, the deer.

Then showed he him where in greatest abundance grew the sweetest berries, Tsa-mith, the huckleberry, Ki-ke-yai, the service berry, Shesh-nim, the thorn berry and Timpa, the chokeberry, growing through all these regions.

When they passed through Weippe on their return to Kamiah, they feasted on the kamas, and the boy pronounced all things good of which he had partaken. The Ha-ha-ats took him to the breaks overlooking the site of Kamiah. "This," said he, "is where your people have settled. Go and tell them of the many bounties of nature I have shown you and the wonderful domain bequeathed them."][7] Then silently he vanished. This is the myth of the Grizzly Bear.

The old Indians used to believe in their myths, but no more. No matter what may be the meaning of Weippe, it is an old historic spot to the Nez Perces, and it was Weippe to them when Lewis and Clark first saw it. Meeting first these white men here has made it more historic to them as well as to us.

Sept. 23rd 1805. Lewis and Clark conferred with the chiefs today and told them of their mission. Great crowds of Indians are about them, but all is harmony. The men trade a few of the old empty canisters they have carried for a few elk skins and proceed to make themselves shirts. Towards evening they break camp and go on two miles to the second village near the present town of Weippe. Here they make camp again. All night the Indians are with them. It is a gala time for them. The whites have missed nothing but a knife taken from their effects. This speaks well for the integrity of the red men they are now among. The village they speak of is made mostly of brush covered with bark.

Tuesday, Sept. 24th. They pack up and "hit the trail" for the Clearwater. Before leaving they send Colter back into the mountains for [the lost horses, then they proceed. The old Indian trail at that time was the same as the old miners found it to the mouth of Ford's creek. Many of the whites still living in that vicinity know where it was. The old wagon road followed it from Weippe to McCullough's, then it passed the Fraser saw-mill, then across Dennis Keane's to in front of the parsonage, then to the Schroeder place, now Kingen's, then across the old McElvoy place, down across the Arth's, White's, and Nat Keum places to the mouth of Ford's creek.

Capt. Lewis and many of the men were taken very sick while traveling today; they over indulged in the new diets. Many laid down along the trail. The country they pass through is all an open plain with scattering pines. Today there are some fine ranches on this route. On reaching the island bar on the Koos Kooskee, they pick up the five hunters left here by Clark who have killed only two deer as the most of them are sick with the same complaint as the others. They now all go down the river a little farther to what is now known as China Island.][8]

Account 21.4: Harlan marks the Lolo Trail in 1935. Source: *Clearwater Tribune* (Orofino), September 6, 1935.

LEWIS AND CLARK TRAIL MARKED

Three bronze tablets were placed at important historic points along the trail through the Clearwater taken by the Lewis and Clark expedition 130 years ago by John P. Harlan, local historian. The Forest Service furnished a car and driver (Tommy Thompson of Pierce) to Mr. Harlan and the expedition required Friday, Saturday and Sunday. Gas pipes holding the markers were cemented in the ground to make a permanent and lasting job.

---

[7]All surviving copies of the *Clearwater Republican* for November 11, 1921, lack the portion of Harlan's article that appears here in brackets. The transcribed portion in brackets comes from the Wallace *Press-Times* of January 15, 1922.

[8]Ibid.

The markers were furnished by Alice Whitman chapter of the Daughters of the American Revolution, Lewiston, and were on display several months in the local Washington Water Power company windows. They are the first permanent markers to be put along the Lewis and Clark route in the Clearwater country, although the D.A.R. in Montana has marked many of the important camp sites of the Lewis and Clark expedition, and Idaho chapters have done some marking at Spalding Mission and along the Old Oregon Trail.

Mr. Harlan placed a marker at Indian Grave where Lewis and Clark camped September 17, 1805. At this point the journals of the expedition speak of the men as being "dispirited" and hungry. They killed a colt and ate it for their supper when camped there one hundred and thirty years ago. The party divided at this point, six men going ahead to hunt for game. Indian Grave is about 1000 feet from the forest development road along Lolo divide.

Another one was put at Howard Camp which is right on the forest road. Lewis and Clark reached this place September 16, 1805, and state in their journals that it "snowed all day." Chief Broken Arm camped there on his way to St. Louis after the "White man's book" in 1831. General Howard, from whom this camp got its modern name, camped there in 1877 when he went over the Lolo trail in pursuit of Chief Joseph.

The other marker was placed at the site of Lewis and Clark's first camp on the Lolo trail at a place called by the explorers "Squamash Glade," now called Packers Meadow.[9] This is near the Montana line and marks the camp of September 13, 1805, when the famous expedition was enroute to the Pacific. The marker was placed on the edge of the meadows which are three quarters of a mile from the new forest road. The actual camp site was about 1000 feet from the marker. A side road leads to the meadows, but there is none going to the camp site, Mr. Harlan stated.

Signs were left at each marker by Mr. Harlan asking each passerby to add a stone around the base in order the keep up interest in the historical spots and to let future generations know of previous visitors. The Forest Service, Mr. Harlan said, has agreed to take care of the markers.

Account 21.5: Excerpts from Assistant Regional Forester Elers Koch's history of the Lolo Trail. Source: Elers Koch, "Lewis and Clark Route Retraced Across the Bitterroots," *Oregon Historical Quarterly* 41, no. 2 (June 1940): 160-74. ©Oregon Historical Society. Reprinted with permission.

Most of the route of Lewis and Clark from St. Louis to the mouth of the Columbia River, in 1804 to 1806, has been retraced by historians, and fully correlated with modern maps and present cultural features. This, however, is not true of one section, which until a very few years ago remained in its almost primitive wilderness condition—the passage of the Bitterroot Mountains from the Bitterroot Valley in western Montana to the foot of the ranges on the Clearwater River in Idaho, a distance of about 150 miles....

Excellent government maps for this rugged and forbidding section of mountain country, now included in the Lolo and Clearwater National Forests, are available;

---

[9]This tablet was recovered by the Forest Service in 1999.

and the writer, during the past 25 years, has traversed nearly every foot of the Lewis and Clark route across the mountains afoot or horseback. It has been possible to locate nearly every camp on both the west-bound and return courses....

The Lolo Trail, in common with most Indian trails, followed the tops of the major divides as much as possible. From Lolo Springs in Montana it crossed the summit of the Bitterroot Range at Lolo Pass, descended to a crossing of the Crooked Fork of the Lochsa River, thence up a spur ridge to the main divide between the Lochsa River and the North Fork of the Clearwater, which it followed over summits and through saddles to Rocky Ridge. From there it descended into the drainage of Lolo Creek at the Musselshell meadows. The trail was much used by the early-day rangers in the Forest Service, to whom its familiarity is attested by the naming of all the common campgrounds and other reference points—Snowy Summit, Bald Mountain, Indian Grave, Soldier Camp, Howard Camp, Sherman Saddle, Indian Post Office.

Except for a few improvements in grade and the cutting out of down timber by the Army and the Forest Service, the trail remained in almost its primitive condition until 1934. Its well-worn tread looped over the high points and down into the saddles, with little change in appearance from the early track of the Nez Perce Indians.

In 1927, the Forest Service constructed a road through Lolo Pass and down the Lochsa River to the Powell Ranger Station. In 1934 this road was extended the entire length of the Lolo Trail, coming out at Pierce, Idaho. The old trail can still be seen in many places, but the automobile has replaced the saddle horse and the pack mule in the crossing of the mountains....

[Following Lewis and Clark westward in 1805]

September 17. A late start due to hunting lost horses. They made only 10 miles along the divide, and camped squarely on top of the ridge at what Whitehouse describes as "near a round, deep sinque hole full of water." A small pond on the ridge one-quarter east of the Indian Grave Lookout exactly fits this description. The third colt went for supper. The party was dispirited, and there seemed no end to the barren mountains which enveloped them. It was decided that Captain Clark should go ahead with six hunters and endeavor to kill some game.

Wheeler places this camp at Bald Mountain, 9 miles farther west, which, interpreted on the basis of the next day's journey, is manifestly impossible. The camp of the 17th is further located by references on the return journey, which will be discussed later.

September 18. Clark, proceeding ahead, at 20 miles was rejoiced at sighting from a high point the open grass country west of the mountains. He continued beyond this point 12$\frac{1}{2}$ miles to a large stream, on which he camped, and which, having nothing to eat, he called "Hungry Creek."

The main party under Lewis followed behind him more slowly and at 18 miles made a dry camp on the ridge, where they had to procure water with difficulty in deep ravine at a distance of half a mile. This camp is placed on the ridge about two miles west of Bald Mountain.

This day's journey, with discrepancies in distances and bearings, has caused more difficulty than any other part of the route. By checking back on the records of the return journey and on the country itself, the route seems unmistakable. Clark continued on the main divide, past Bald Mountain to Sherman Peak, where he got his view of the open prairie. He then continued down through Sherman Saddle, up to the top of the next mountain, and at this point left the Lolo Trail and plunged down the mountain southwesterly into Hungry Creek. Lewis, following him the next day, took the same course. "At a distance of six miles from camp the ridge terminated, and to our inexpressible joy discovered a large tract of prairie country." Six miles beyond this point he reached Hungry Creek.

22

The Story of the Lolo Trail Motorway
(Road 500)

This book began with David Thompson standing atop Mount Jumbo looking down the Bitterroot Valley and examining the primitive and hardly visible start of the Lolo Trail route off in the distance. Appropriately, perhaps, the book ends with the transformation of portions of the Lolo Trail into a road.

The Lolo Trail Motorway was constructed by the Forest Service between 1930 and 1934.[1] It was located chiefly on the Selway National Forest, which ceased to exist the same month that the motorway was completed. A narrow, steep, and winding road, built at low cost, the motorway ran between Musselshell Meadows on the west and a spot on what would be called the Lewis and Clark Highway (US 12), near the Powell Ranger Station. Parts of the Pioneer Mine road were incorporated in the project. Construction was started using regular road building funds and crews, and was administered initially by the Clearwater National Forest. The work force was later augmented with "emergency" funds coming from the Roosevelt Administration's efforts to reduce the impact of the Depression. These funds paid for work by Civilian Conservation Corps (CCC) and National Industrial Recovery Administration (NIRA) crews. The driving force behind this project was Major Evan Kelly, the powerful and respected Regional Forester, based at Missoula. For many of his key employees, Kelly's dream was a destructive waste of money.

To understand the construction of Road 500 and dozens of similar mountain roads built at the same time, one must turn to the large forest fires of 1910, a year of severe drought in the Northern Rockies. These fires burned over five million acres and employed nearly 10,000 men in the largely futile efforts at control. In the big scheme of fire ecology in the West, neither the size nor the impact was unprecedented. But these large fires did manage to humble and humiliate the newly-established Forest Service. By 1928, when Congress finally got around to making serious

---

[1] It was originally called the Lolo "truck trail" and later a "forest development road." Its route, especially on the western end, has varied over the years. The designation as Road 500 came into use in 1972.

appropriations for fire control efforts, the men who had fought the 1910 fires were now in charge of the Forest Service. Most of them had no intention of repeating what they viewed as their failure in 1910. With money and then substantial emergency work manpower in hand, these men (in 1935) wrote the new Forest Service policy of extinguishing *all* fires by 10 a.m. the next morning.

Beginning in 1928, Major Kelly committed his Region to an energetic effort at building "truck trails" into what was then called the back country. Although Kelly recognized that these low standard roads might provide access for recreation and some logging, his chief purpose in supporting their construction was fire control. If crews couldn't reach a fire, he wondered, how could they possibly stop it? Kelly visited Kooskia in the summer of 1930, and the *Kooskia Mountaineer* published a thorough report on the rationale of the Northern Region's road building efforts (see Account 1, below).

There was a surprisingly vigorous debate within the Northern Region about the wisdom of Major Kelly's plans. Howard Flint, a Forest Service pioneer in the use of aircraft for photography, fire detection, and fire transport, was a participant in this debate. Flint argued that a network of small backcountry airstrips would be a useful tool in fire fighting. Bob Marshall, then a researcher at Priest Lake in northern Idaho, expressed concern that the road system avoid the Selway River country. Marshall's fears were shared by the great photographer of the Northern Region, K.D. Swan.

But it was Elers Koch who offered the most sustained and informed criticism. Koch was by this time Assistant Regional Forester, and had been in the Region since 1907. He was a great historian of the back country, and of the Lolo Trail in particular (see previous chapter). Koch doubted that all forest fires were even harmful, and felt deeply that it was simply a waste of money to fight fires in the steep, dry, and remote backcountry areas of the Northern Region. Koch opposed the road building plans quietly and strictly in-house. He lost two key battles—the road over the southern (Nez Perce Trail) route and the Lolo Trail Motorway. He won several others, helping to stop plans for roads into the heart of the Selway and into the Great Burn country located north of the Lolo Trail. In 1935, Koch published in the *Journal of Forestry* a remarkable and poetic reflection on what had been lost in the rush to build forest truck trails. A part of this article appears in this chapter.

In the autumn of 1929, R.P. Hilleary, the Northern Region's Reconnaissance Engineer, published his plan for the first phase of the Lolo Trail Motorway.[2] This plan proposed a 41.5 mile construction project at the west end of the Lolo Trail region, to be managed by the Clearwater National Forest using construction funds provided by the Bureau of Public Roads. The route from Musselshell Ranger Station followed the existing sheep driveway toward Hemlock Butte and Beaver Saddle, and then followed the ridge east via Pete Forks Junction, Rocky Ridge, Sherman Saddle and Bald Mountain to Indian Grave. Cost was estimated at $1040 per mile

---

[2]R.P. Hilleary, *Report of Reconnaissance and Estimate of Low Standard Ridge Road from Musselshell Ranger Station to Indian Grave Peak.* Missoula: USFS Northern Region, 1929.

with a maximum 20% gradient in the road. Appended to this report was a draft map showing a vastly greater fire protection road system for the Lolo Trail region. This included over fifty miles of possible roads to be built north of Liz Butte. Planning for this truck route did not address the historical values of the trails that were located on the same ridge top.

Figure 29. Northern Region Forester Maj. Evan Kelly.

Construction on the sheep driveway portion of the route began in the summer of 1930. By the end of the 1932 construction season, road construction had passed east of Rocky Ridge Lake, and crews from the Selway National Forest were now doing the work. In the summer of 1933, the first CCC crews arrived to work on the project. The workers came mostly from eastern states by direct trains to Orofino. A second camp was established near Powell to work west along the divide. About sixty men were employed on the project that year.

In 1934, the work force for the road project shifted to the National Industrial Recovery Administration, a short-lived agency that tried to provide employment at good wages for unemployed-but-skilled workers. A few NIRA workers had been employed near Bungalow the previous year. Completion of the motorway was delayed a bit by the huge forest fires burning on the Selway, the Pete King fire in particular.

About sixty men employed by NIRA worked from two camps during the summer of 1934 to complete the road. The crews met near Indian Grave in September, and on the 24th celebrated the completion of the Lolo Trail Motorway with a chicken dinner. Several Forest Service officials were scheduled to be on hand, but failed to appear. The workers spent the rest of the day "in a leisurely way."[3] The first party to cover the new route in a car came through the same week, just ahead of a big snow storm. This was the family of a Lolo National Forest employee named Will Samsel. They found the route a tough one, and returned to Montana via Spokane.

The surviving records for this project reflect no concern at all for the ancient Nez Perce trail that occupied the general route of the motorway. Even so, an examination of the surviving 1932 and 1934 air photos that cover portions of the motorway reveals that road construction failed to obliterate large segments of the ancient route. The new road was not very wide, and unlike the Nez Perce trail, the road went around knolls and high points, rather than over them in a straight line.

In the end, Major Kelly got his fire protection truck trail, and Koch, his assistant, was provoked to make public his doubts about the whole idea.

Further reading:

Elers Koch, *Forty Years a Forester, 1903-1943* (Missoula: Mountain Press, 1998).

An edited collection of writing by Koch, plus some biographical information.

Bud Moore, *The Lochsa Story: Land Ethics in the Bitterroot Mountains* (Missoula:Mountain Press, 1996).

A remarkable and insightful history of the Lochsa by a Forest Service employee with over fifty years of experience in the region.

Stephen J. Pyne, *Fire in America* (Princeton: Princeton University Press, 1982).

The definitive history of public land and rural fire in America. A pioneering work.

---

[3]Kamiah *Progress,* October 4, 1934.

Figure 30. A road building crew working on the Lolo Motorway in 1934.

Figure 31. Dedication of the Lolo Trail road at Indian Grave in 1934.

Stephen J. Pyne, *Year of the Fires* (New York: Viking, 2001).

A reliable and nicely written history of the 1910 fires, and their impact.

Account 22.1: The editor of the *Kooskia Mountaineer*, after a visit by the Regional Forester, summarizes the logic behind the forest truck trail building effort. Source: *Kooskia Mountaineer*, June 25, 1930.

Motor Route Fire Control: Forest Service Protection Plans Call for More Rapid Transportation

Modern methods of forest protection call for a constant revision of tactics on the part of forest officers if they hope to avail themselves of the numerous advancements in modes of travel communication. This is especially true of the men engaged in protection work of forests where the areas are largely undeveloped and without ready access, such as the Selway [with its headquarters in Kooskia], Clearwater, and Nezperce National Forests.

Recently congress provided a fund of a million and a half dollars in addition to the usual appropriation for the construction of roads, trails, and telephone lines within the national forests and the units within district one [i.e., Region One, the Northern Region] of the service will receive approximately three hundred and twenty thousand dollars of this sum for expenditure this year.

An outstanding necessity in fire prevention and control is that of transportation. Consideration of figures obtained from the disastrous fire in the Bald Mt. Area of the Selway last year furnishes a very striking example of the decided inadequacy of the present method of transporting men and supplies. Answering a call for help from the Kooskia office, officials at the Missoula office loaded men, horses, equipment and supplies on trucks and in three hours travel time these items were landed at Powell, a distance of nearly sixty miles [on the recently completed Lolo Pass road]. At this point a change was made to the present method of pack train and foot travel—the fire about fifty miles away was not reached until the third day thereby occasioning a loss of approximately sixty hours in addition to the serious distress of the firefighters who were virtually exhausted and in no condition to meet the trying demands of the fire line.

Relief from such vexing situations is now the aim of the national forests and in keeping with this view Major Kelly, regional forester with headquarters at Missoula, is making a personal tour of the forests under his jurisdiction in company with Fred Theme, regional engineer, for the purpose of preparing an extensive program of motor routes traversing the ridges and topographic points of ready accessibility. Such a program has been initiated in California forests and construction started last year with most gratifying results. Major Kelly while in California the past winter took occasion to study the methods of construction and personally investigated some of the building operations to the end that his office might be thoroughly informed concerning the type of roads and necessary machinery for construction.

Experience has demonstrated that a serviceable type of motor road may be constructed for approximately a thousand dollars per mile. These roads are not highways but are merely means of providing motor truck driveway sufficient to permit an average speed of fifteen miles an hour under normal loading. Grades of twenty percent are allowable for short distances and not to exceed fifteen per cent on extended inclines. Construction is carried on largely by means of tractor and push grader of heavy proportions. Combined weight of the two pieces of machinery is more than five tons and hillside slopes of not to exceed forty percent may be graded readily.

Upon completion of the so-called truck drive ways it will be found expedient and practically costless to extend by-way down ridges to the breaks in the hills. Some construction will over-run the cost of a thousand dollars a mile but compensation will be had on many miles of practically costless road. These routes will serve a like purpose relative to the highways that the present foot trails serve

Figure 32. Assistant Regional Forester Elers Koch

to the trunk trails on the forests—just a means of increasing the use of trucks for protection and fire purposes.

Recently the writer in company with Supervisor Wolfe of the Selway and Supervisor Wohlen of the Clearwater forests joined the two district officials in a trip along Lolo Trail from Bald Mt. to Rocky Ridge where data was secured for roadway purposes. Major Kelly is very enthusiastic about the possibility of the proposed means of transportation and stated that $220,000 would be used this year within District No. 1 [the Northern Region] and that a portion of the funds would be used on a roadway leading from the Musselshell ranger district towards Hemlock Butte on the Clearwater forest. It will require an initial expenditure of approximately $100,000 for equipment to inaugurate the work.

While these roads will be constructed primarily for protection purposes there will be no restriction placed upon the traveling public as to their use, however, motorists should remember that these by-ways are to be constructed, solely, as a cheap and rapid means of transportation in case of fire; users must consider them in this light when availing themselves of the privilege of use since they are not highways in any sense of the word.

Account 22.2: A lament on the loss of the Lolo Trail to road construction. Excerpts. Source: Elers Koch, "The Passing of the Lolo Trail," *Journal of Forestry* 33, no. 2 (February 1935): 98-104.

The Lolo Trail is no more.

The bulldozer blade has ripped out the hoof tracks of Chief Joseph's ponies. The trail was worn deep by centuries of Nezperce and Blackfeet Indians, by Lewis and Clark, by companies of Northwest Company fur traders, by General Howard's cavalry horses, by Captain Mullan, the engineer, and by the early-day forest ranger. It is gone, and in its place there is only the print of the automobile tire in the dust.

What of the camps of fragrant memory—Camp Martin, Rocky Ridge, No Seeum Meadows, Bald Mountain, Indian Grave, Howard Camp, Indian Post Office, Spring Mountain, Cayuse Junction, Packers Meadows? No more will the traveler unsaddle his ponies to roll and graze on the bunch grass of the mountain tops. No more the "mule train coughing in the dust." The trucks roll by on the new Forest Service road, and the old camps are no more than a place to store spare barrels of gasoline....

It is now but three hours' drive from the streets of Missoula to the peak where Captain Lewis smoked his pipe...Only ten years ago it was just as Lewis and Clark saw it.

So it is everywhere.

The hammer rings in the CCC camp on the remotest waters of the Selway. The bulldozer snorts on Running Creek, that once limit of the back of the beyond [two references to the construction of the Southern Nez Perce Trail—Magruder—Road over Nez Perce Pass]. The moose at Elk Summit lift their heads from the lily pads to gaze at the passing motor truck. Major Fenn's beloved Coolwater Divide has become a motor road.

No more can one slip up to the big lick at Powell for a frosty October morning and see the elk in droves. The hunters swarm in motor cars in the public campgrounds.

And all to what end?....

Has all this effort and expenditure of millions of dollars added anything to the human good? Is it possible that it was all a ghastly mistake like plowing up the good buffalo grass sod of the dry prairies? Has the country as it stands now as much human value as it had in the nineties when Major Fenn's forest rangers first rode into it?...

Figure 33. The Lolo Trail Motorway in 1936 at Indian Post Office.

Figure 34. Along the Lolo Motorway near Saddle Camp, August 1938.

Appendix

Campsites of Historical Travelers
Across the Lolo Trail, 1800s,
researched and located by Gene and Mollie Eastman

John Work's campsites Sept 30 – Oct 8, 1831

Date	Location
Sept 16	Mouth of Clearwater River, north side
Sept 17-18	Hatwai Creek
Sept 19	Mouth of Potlatch Creek
Sept 20-21	Hubbard Gulch
Sept 22	Agatha or Lenore
Sept 23	Bench, north side 3 miles west of Ahsahka
Sept 24	Ahsahka, north side or on south side (Canoe Camp)
Sept 25	Mouth of Jim Ford Creek
Sept 26	Weippe Prairie
Sept 28	Musselshell Meadows
Sept 30	Camp Martin and head of Hemlock (Zoe) Creek
Sept 30 (duplicated)	Beaver Dam Saddle
Oct 1	Sherman Saddle
Oct 3	Bald Mountain
Oct 5	Howard Creek Meadows
Oct 6	Spring Mountain

Oct 7	Camp 70 (Bird-Traux milepost 70+, head of Papoose Creek)
Oct 8	Crooked Fork Crossing of the Lolo Trail
Oct 9	Glade Creek or Packer Meadows

John Mullan's campsites Sept 23-30, 1854

Date	Location
Sept 19	Bitterroot River 20 miles north of Fort Owen
Sept 21	near Howard Creek, tributary of Lolo Creek, Montana
Sept 23	Packer Meadows or Glade Creek
Sept 24	Mullan Spring (Bird-Traux est. milepost 71 north of Papoose Saddle)
Sept 25	Camp 70 (Bird-Traux milepost 70+, head of Papoose Creek)
Sept 26	Howard Creek Meadows
Sept 27	Noseeum Meadows
Sept 28	Weitas Meadows
Sept 29	Musselshell Meadows
Sept 30	Lawyers Creek near Kamiah, Idaho

General Howard's campsites July 30-Aug 6, 1877

Date	Location
July 30	Weippe Prairie (Camp Sanford)
July 31	Musselshell Meadows (Camp R.H. Fletcher)
Aug 1	Weitas Meadows (Camp W. H. Winters)
Aug 2	Bald Mountain (Camp Evan Miles)
Aug 3	Indian Grave Meadows (Camp Spurgin)
Aug 4	Spring Mountain (Camp Robt. Pollock)
Aug 5	Crooked Fork Crossing of the Lolo Trail
Aug 6	Lolo Hot Springs (Camp G.S. Hoyle)

Bird-Truax camping Places from Muscle Creek to Takon Creek, *With Bird and Truax on the Lolo Trail,* 1866, page 27 with the geographic locations from research and study by Gene and Mollie Eastman.[1]

Mile Marker	Bird-Traux name	Geographic Location
0	Muscle Creek	Musselshell Meadows
11+	The Neck, down gulch to the north	camp at Camp Martin, grass at head of Hemlock (Zoe) Cr.
12+	Horse Gulch, to the north	Soldier Meadows
15	Pond Saddle, gulch to north	Beaver Dam Saddle & Creek
16+	Shepherder's Gulch on east	Meadows head of Gass Creek
18+	Excellent Grass and plenty of it	Meadows head of Obia Creek
20+	Huston Creek	head of Little Weitas Creek or Rocky Ridge Creek
21	Swamp Prairie	Weitas Meadows
33	Prairie Saddle, down gulch to south	Noseeum Meadows
37	Meadow Mt. best grass & plenty	Bald Mountain
43+	Swampy Saddle, 100 yards to north	Indian Grave Meadows
47	At head of Snow Bridge Gulch, 100 yards down gulch to S.	Saddle Camp
50	Duck Creek, 100 yards to N. & down creek.	Howard Creek Meadows
52	Leaning Tree Camp, grass on hill side – camp on saddle	Moon Saddle
55	An inferior kind of grass on high dry ridge in this neighborhood	4/5 mile west of intersection of Doe Cr. Road 566
60	Swan Springs; + mile up ridge to N. Good grass & plenty	Spring Mountain
62	Moose Lake, 100 yards north, A little	Moose Lake - Trail 72 intersection with Lolo Trail
63+	Lake Templin Saddle; down gulch to north; abundance	Cayuse Saddle
68+	"Hole in the Ground" 200 yards to south, under hill; tree blazed.	Lost Lakes Trailhead

[1]Dennis Baird, ed., *With Bird and Truax on the Lolo Trail,* Moscow, University of Idaho Library, 1999, 27. (note: Bird-Traux located good camps with grass for travelers. They may or may not have camped at these locations when constructing their trail.)

70+	Good grass and plenty Papoose Creek.	Head of West fork of
73+	Independence Camp, down gulch to north.	Junction of old Powell Trail with Lolo Trail
85	Takon Creek; good grass in abundance on prairies	Glade Cr. Meadow & Packer Meadows

Campsites (without grass) used by Bird-Traux when improving and reconstructing the Lolo Trail.[2]

Mile Marker	Bird-Truax name	Geographic location
Est. 9	Ridge Camp South of Camp Martin	Camp Mildred 2 miles
Est. 23	Butte Camp	Green Saddle

---

[2]Baird, *With Bird and Truax*, 13.

Index

Index prepared by Cher Paul
Indexing & Editing Services
8558 N. Allegheny Ave.
Portland, OR 97203

Page numbers of illustrations are in **bold**. Refeences to footnotes are indicated with "n" and the note number. *Passim* indicates numerous mentions over the given range of pages.